G000141120

ENGLIS

FOOTBALL LEAGUE

AND

F.A. PREMIER LEAGUE TABLES

1888-2016

EDITOR
Michael Robinson

British Library Cataloguing in Publication Data

A catalogue record for this book is available from the British Library

ISBN: 978-1-86223-334-8

Copyright © 2016, Soccer Books Limited, 72 St. Peters Avenue, Cleethorpes, DN35 8HU (01472) 696226

E-mail – info@soccer-books.co.uk

Web site – www.soccer-books.co.uk

All rights are reserved. No part of this publication may be reproduced, stored into a retrieval system or transmitted, in any form or by any means, electronic, mechanical, photocopying, recording, or otherwise, without the prior written permission of Soccer Books Limited.

Manufactured in the UK by Ashford Colour Press Ltd.

THE FORMATION OF THE FOOTBALL LEAGUE

By 1888, there were around 1,000 clubs in England playing football according to the laws and rules of the Football Association. These clubs would arrange a set of fixtures that began in early September and ended in mid-April with the vast majority of games being played on Saturday afternoons. Most fixtures were kept but there was no guarantee that they would be. Sometimes, visiting teams would not turn up at all, or they might turn up with a reserve side because they had arranged another, more attractive game elsewhere, or they might arrive late, or with less than 11 players.

In the early, 'free and easy' days of football, this did not matter too much but after the legalisation of professionalism in 1885, things were very different. The leading clubs, most of whom were based in the North and the Midlands, as well as their normal running costs, also now had to pay their players. While supporters knew that games in the F.A. Cup and other major cup competitions would generally mean that both clubs would field their strongest teams, they could not be so sure about the ordinary 'friendly' games that filled most of the fixture calendar. It was by no means uncommon for supporters to turn up at the ground to find that one of the clubs 'could not raise a team' or 'had missed their (railway) connection'.

Unsurprisingly then, crowds for 'friendly' games were usually very much smaller than those for cup games, a worrying fact for clubs now facing a weekly wage bill. Furthermore, with the random nature of cup draws, even the best clubs could find themselves making an early exit from the most attractive competitions, a situation that could prove to be absolutely disastrous as the 'friendlies' that had been already arranged were liable to be cancelled if the opponents were still making progress in the cup competitions and the dates clashed.

This was the background that on 2nd March 1888 caused Mr. William McGregor, an Aston Villa official, to write to 5 leading clubs – Aston Villa, Blackburn Rovers, Bolton Wanderers, Preston North End and West Bromwich Albion. His letter read:

> "Every year it is becoming more and more difficult for football clubs of any standing to meet their friendly engagements and even arrange friendly matches. The consequence is that at the last moment, through cup-tie interference, clubs are compelled to take on teams who will not attract the public.
>
> I beg to tender the following suggestion as a means of getting over the difficulty – that ten or twelve of the most prominent clubs in England combine to arrange home and away fixtures each season, the said fixtures to be arranged at a friendly conference about the same time as the International Conference. This Combination might be known as the Association Football Union, and could be managed by a representative from each club.
>
> Of course, this is in no way to interfere with the National Association. Even the suggested matches might be played under Cup-tie rules. However, this is a detail. My object in writing at present is merely to draw your attention to the subject, and to suggest a friendly conference to discuss the matter more fully. I would take it as a favour if you would kindly think the matter over, and make whatever suggestion you may deem necessary."

The initial response was not encouraging. McGregor received only 2 replies, 1 of which was from Bolton Wanderers who suggested the inclusion of 8 more clubs: Accrington, Burnley, Halliwell (a Lancashire club), Notts County, Mitchell St. George's (from Birmingham), Old Carthusians (a prominent amateur club), Stoke and Wolverhampton Wanderers.

When the idea was more widely discussed, it was received with doubt, or even suspicion, in some quarters. In Sheffield for example, it was feared that the proposed organisation would be antagonistic to the F.A. and would be too costly for clubs. It was because of this that Sheffield Wednesday were excluded from the list of clubs invited to take part.

However, in Derby, Stoke, West Bromwich and Wolverhampton, the idea was warmly received and in Nottingham, where Forest were at the time still an amateur club, County readily agreed to join the nascent organisation. It should be noted that Mr. McGregor originally intended that there should be only one club from each town or city. With support growing, a meeting was organised at Anderton's Hotel, London on 22nd March. Those represented were: Aston Villa, Blackburn Rovers, Burnley, Notts County, Stoke, West Bromwich Albion and Wolverhampton Wanderers. Preston and Bolton each decided not to send a delegate while Derby County's delegate attended, but only as an observer.

The meeting decided "To form a League or Union of twelve of the most prominent clubs, the twelve selected being Accrington, Aston Villa, Blackburn Rovers, Bolton Wanderers, Burnley, Derby County, Everton, Notts County, Preston North End, Stoke, West Bromwich Albion and Wolverhampton Wanderers". Note that Accrington and Everton had been added to raise the number from 10 to 12. Note also that the only club south of Birmingham who had even been suggested were Old Carthusians but they, along with all clubs in the South-East, were strictly amateur and the playing standards of the top professional clubs were by 1888 so far ahead of the rest that it is highly unlikely that any amateurs could have competed effectively.

It was agreed that all league games would be played under the Cup rules of the F.A. and that clubs would play full strength teams in all matches. There were also rules regarding players' eligibility, admission prices (to be set at the discretion of the home club) and how gate money would be divided.

The 'average' that would determine the finishing order in the league was to be calculated from wins, draws and losses and not from goals scored but how that 'average' was to be calculated was not yet decided. It was, however, decided that the four clubs having the lowest 'average' would retire at the end of the season but be eligible for re-election.

Another meeting took place, at the Royal Hotel in Manchester on 17th April, attended by all 12 clubs and it was then that it was definitely decided to proceed with the idea. Thus, 17th April 1888 is the generally accepted date for the league's formation.

It was thought though that the proposed title of the 'Association Football Union' might be confused with the Rugby Football Union and so instead, it was decided to call it the Football League, a title about which Mr. McGregor had some misgivings as the word 'League' was often used by political and other organisations.

Three other clubs – Nottingham Forest, Sheffield Wednesday and Halliwell – also attended the meeting in the hope of gaining admittance but they were unsuccessful as it was felt that no more than 22 league fixtures could be fitted in.

McGregor also had the idea that there should be a subsidiary competition for the members' reserve teams and although that was not taken forward then, it eventually happened when the Central League was formed in 1911, followed by the London Combination a few years later.

There were a multitude of details to be agreed which were settled during the summer months but one, extremely important, area took a while longer. That was the means by which the order of clubs in the final table would be decided, what Mr. McGregor originally referred to as the 'average'.

While the principle of 2 points for a win and 1 for a draw was proposed at an early stage, there was a school of thought led by West Bromwich Albion that preferred that only wins would count, draws and defeats both being ignored. Eventually, the 2 points for a win and 1 for a draw system was adopted but only by 6 votes to 4 and not until 21st November 1888, when the season was already well under way.

There was one further point of particular interest in the League's first set of rules, that being the rule that there would be 'two classes of League clubs – First and Second – each to consist of twelve clubs'. The rules went on to state: 'There shall be first and second-class championships, and last four in each class to retire, but be eligible for re-election. The League shall have power to order any of the retiring clubs or the first four of the second class, to compete in order to decide the question of superiority'.

The second 'class' or 'division' eventually came into existence in 1892 but for 1888-89, there was just the 12-club 'first class', the world's first ever football league. The first games were played on Saturday 8th September 1888 and the results were as follows:

Bolton Wanderers	3	Derby County	6
Everton	2	Accrington	1
Preston North End	5	Burnley	2
Stoke	0	West Bromwich Albion	2
Wolverhampton Wanderers	1	Aston Villa	1

Blackburn Rovers' first ever league game was on 15th September, a 5-5 home draw with Accrington and Notts County's first game was on the same day, a 2-1 defeat at Everton.

	1885-86	1886-87	1887-88
F.A. Cup			
Winners	**Blackburn Rovers**	**Aston Villa**	**West Bromwich Albion**
Finalists	**West Brom. Albion**	**West Brom. Albion**	**Preston North End**
Semi-Finalists	*Small Heath Alliance*	**Preston North End**	*Crewe Alexandra*
	Swifts	*Rangers (Glasgow)*	*Derby Junction*
Birmingham Senior Cup			
Winners	**West Brom. Albion**	*Long Eaton Rangers*	**Aston Villa**
Finalists	*Walsall Swifts*	**West Brom. Albion**	**West Bromwich Albion**
Semi-Finalists	**Wolverhampton W.**	*Burslem Port Vale*	**Stoke**
	Burslem Port Vale	*Small Heath Alliance*	**Wolverhampton Wands.**
Lancashire Cup			
Winners	**Bolton Wanderers**	**Preston North End**	**Accrington**
Finalists	**Blackburn Rovers**	**Bolton Wanderers**	**Preston North End**
Semi-Finalists	**Preston North End**	*Padiham*	*Witton*
	Darwen	*Witton*	*Darwen Old Wanderers*
Staffordshire Senior Cup			
Winners	**West Brom. Albion**	**West Brom. Albion**	**Wolverhampton Wands.**
Finalists	**Stoke**	*Walsall Swifts*	**West Bromwich Albion**
Semi-Finalists	*Burton Wanderers*	**Wolverhampton W.**	**Stoke**
	Walsall Town	*Burslem Port Vale*	*Walsall Town*
Lord Mayor of Birmingham's Charity Cup			
Winners	**Aston Villa**	**Wolverhampton W.**	**Aston Villa**
Finalists	*Wednesbury Old Ath.*	**Aston Villa**	*Mitchell St. George's*
	1885-86	**1886-87**	**1887-88**
Liverpool Senior Cup			
Winners	**Everton**	**Everton**	*Bootle*
Sheffield Challenge Cup			
Winners	*Mexborough*	Sheffield Wednesday	Sheffield Wednesday
Wharncliffe Charity Cup			
Winners	Sheffield Wednesday	*Staveley*	Sheffield Wednesday
Nottinghamshire Senior Cup			
Winners	Nottingham Forest	Nottingham Forest	*Notts Rangers*

How the league expanded

The table below shows the number of clubs in each division of the Football League.

	F.L.				Total
1888-1891	12				12
1891-1892	14				14
	Div. 1	**Div. 2**			
1892-1893	16	12			28
1893-1894	16	15*			31
1894-1898	16	16			32
1898-1905	18	18			36
1905-1915	20	20			40
1919-1920	22	22			44
	Div. 1	**Div. 2**	**Div. 3(S)**	**Div. 3(N)**	
1920-1921	22	22	22	0	66
1921-1923	22	22	22	20	86
1923-1950	22	22	22	22	88
1950-1958	22	22	24	24	92
	Div. 1	**Div. 2**	**Div. 3**	**Div. 4**	
1958-1987	22	22	24	24	92
1987-1988	21	23	24	24	92
1988-1991	20	24	24	24	92
1991-1992	22	24	24	23	93
	P.L.	**Div. 1**	**Div. 2**	**Div. 3**	
1992-1993	22	24	24	22†	92
1993-1995	22	24	24	22	92
1995-2004	20	24	24	24	92
	P.L.	**Champsh.**	**Lge. 1**	**Lge. 2**	
2004-2012	20	24	24	24	92

* Excluding Bootle who resigned just before the start of the season.

† Excluding Maidstone United who resigned before playing a game.

Changes to League membership

When the league was formed, the last 4 clubs in the table had to seek re-election. In 1889, at the end of the first season, all of the bottom 4 were re-elected. All subsequent changes are listed below. Years when there were no changes in membership are omitted.

1890   Sunderland were elected in place of Stoke. Sunderland had previously played only cup-ties and friendlies. Stoke joined the Football Alliance for the 1890-91 season.

1891   The League expanded from 12 to 14 members. The clubs elected to fill the 2 vacancies were Stoke (Football Alliance champions) and Darwen, who had finished 6th in the Football Alliance.

1892   The League expanded from 14 to 16 members. Darwen were not re-elected and so 3 new members were elected. They were: Nottingham Forest (Football Alliance champions), Newton Heath (runners-up in the Football Alliance) and Sheffield Wednesday (4th in the Football Alliance).

It was also decided to form a Second Division of 12 clubs with the original Football League becoming known as the First Division.

The 12 clubs elected to the new Second Division were: Darwen (following their failure to win re-election to the First Division) and 8 of the 9 remaining members of the Football Alliance. They were: Small Heath (who had finished 3rd), Burton Swifts (5th), Crewe Alexandra (6th), Ardwick (7th), Bootle (8th), Lincoln City (9th), Grimsby Town (10th) and Walsall Town Swifts (11th). The Football Alliance club who were not elected were Birmingham St. George, who had disbanded. The clubs elected to fill the final 3 places were Burslem Port Vale who had finished 3rd in the Midland League, Northwich Victoria (2nd in The Combination) and Sheffield United (3rd in the Northern League).

The League had invited 2 clubs to join from the Northern League but both declined. The 2 clubs invited were Newcastle East End who had finished 4th, and a proposed club to be formed by a merger of Middlesbrough Ironopolis (champions) and Middlesbrough (runners-up). The merger was abandoned and the 2 clubs continued separately.

1893   Division Two expanded from 12 to 16 clubs. The 4 clubs elected to the vacancies were: Liverpool (Lancashire League champions), Newcastle United (2nd in the Northern League), Rotherham Town (Midland League champions) and Woolwich Arsenal who had never played in a league. Later, when Accrington decided to join the Lancashire League rather than accept relegation to the Second Division, Middlesbrough Ironopolis (Northern League champions) accepted an invitation to take their place. Shortly before the start of the new season, Bootle resigned and disbanded, leaving 15 clubs in Division Two.

1894   Ardwick were declared bankrupt and, on 16th April 1894, they were wound up. A new club called Manchester City was formed to replace them and they were elected to take Ardwick's place in the League. Northwich Victoria chose not to seek re-election to the League and joined The Combination instead. Rotherham Town were not re-elected but, soon afterwards, Middlesbrough Ironopolis resigned and disbanded. Rotherham Town subsequently accepted an invitation to replace them. Bootle had resigned the previous August and so there were 3 vacancies. The clubs elected to fill these were Burton Wanderers (Midland League champions), Leicester Fosse (Midland League runners-up) and Bury (Lancashire League runners-up).

1895   Walsall Town Swifts were not re-elected and joined the Midland League, changing their name to Walsall. Loughborough Town (Midland League champions) were elected to replace them.

1896   The number of clubs required to seek re-election was reduced from 4 to 3. Rotherham Town did not seek re-election and disbanded soon afterwards. Burslem Port Vale and Crewe Alexandra were not re-elected. Burslem Port Vale joined the Midland League and Crewe Alexandra joined The Combination. The 3 clubs elected to fill the vacancies were Gainsborough Trinity (Midland League runners-up), Walsall (3rd in the Midland League) and Blackpool (13th in the Lancashire League).

1897   Burton Wanderers were not re-elected and joined the Midland League. Luton Town (United League runners-up) were elected to replace them.

1898   Both divisions were expanded to 18 clubs. The 4 clubs elected to fill the vacancies created in the Second Division were Burslem Port Vale (5th in the Midland League), Barnsley (Midland League runners-up), Glossop North End (9th in the Midland League) and New Brighton Tower (Lancashire League champions).

1899   Glossop North End changed their name to Glossop. Darwen did not seek re-election and disbanded soon afterwards. However, they were quickly reformed and, after taking over a local junior club called Darwen Woodfold, joined the Lancashire League. Blackpool were not re-elected and joined the Lancashire League. The 2 clubs elected to fill the vacancies were Chesterfield (4th in the Midland League) and Middlesbrough (3rd in the Northern League, Division One).

1900   Luton Town did not seek re-election and joined the Southern League, Division One instead. Loughborough Town were not re-elected and applied to join the Midland League but disbanded before the start of the new season. The 2 clubs elected to fill the vacancies were Stockport County (Lancashire League champions) and Blackpool (3rd in the Lancashire League).

1901   Burton Swifts merged with Burton Wanderers of the Midland League and were re-elected under their merged name of Burton United. Walsall were not re-elected and moved to the Midland League. Bristol City (runners-up in the Southern League, Division One) were elected in their place. Shortly before the start of the new season, New Brighton Tower resigned and disbanded and Doncaster Rovers (Midland League runners-up) accepted an invitation to replace them.

1902   Newton Heath changed their name to Manchester United.

1903   Doncaster Rovers were not re-elected and joined the Midland League instead. Newly formed Bradford City, who had not played a single game, were elected in their place.

1904   Stockport County were not re-elected and joined the Lancashire Combination, Division One instead. Doncaster Rovers (11th in the Midland League) were elected in their place. Chesterfield changed their name to Chesterfield Town.

1905   Small Heath changed their name to Birmingham. Burton United and Doncaster Rovers were not re-elected. Leeds City (11th in the West Yorkshire League) and Chelsea (a newly formed club who had not played a single game) were elected in their places.

However, it was then decided to extend both divisions to 20 clubs, creating 4 more Second Division places. The clubs elected to take these were Burton United, who were thus re-elected, Hull City, who had previously played only friendlies, Clapton Orient (8th in the Southern League, Division Two and 7th in the London League, Premier Division) and Stockport County (Lancashire Combination, First Division champions). Doncaster Rovers then moved to the Midland League.

1907   Burton United were not re-elected and joined the Birmingham League. Fulham (Southern League First Division champions) were elected in their place. Subsequently, Burslem Port Vale resigned and disbanded, creating a further vacancy. Oldham Athletic (Lancashire Combination, First Division champions) accepted an invitation to fill it. A new club called Port Vale were quickly formed and joined the North Staffordshire Federation.

1908   Lincoln City were not re-elected and joined the Midland League. Bradford Park Avenue (13th in the Southern League, First Division) were elected in their place. Later, Stoke resigned and disbanded. They quickly reformed and asked to withdraw their resignation but were refused and Tottenham Hotspur (7th in the Southern League First Division) were elected in their place. Stoke joined the Birmingham League.

1909   The number of clubs required to seek re-election was reduced from 3 to 2. Chesterfield Town were not re-elected and moved to the Midland League. Lincoln City (Midland League champions) were elected in their place.

1910   Grimsby Town were not re-elected and moved to the Midland League. Huddersfield Town (5th in the Midland League) were elected in their place.

1911   Lincoln City were not re-elected and became a founder member of the Central League. Grimsby Town (Midland League champions) were elected in their place.

1912   Gainsborough Trinity were not re-elected and moved to the Midland League. Lincoln City (Central League champions) were elected in their place.

1913   Woolwich Arsenal changed their name to The Arsenal.

1915   Glossop were not re-elected and joined the Lancashire Combination for 1915-16. In 1916, they closed down until 1919 when they rejoined the Lancashire Combination. Stoke (Southern League, Second Division champions) were elected in their place. However, it was later decided that the league should close down until the war ended.

1919   It was decided to extend both divisions to 22 clubs, creating 4 Second Division vacancies. The clubs elected into these vacancies (with their 1914-15 positions in brackets) were: Coventry City (5th in the Southern League, Division Two), Rotherham County (Midland League champions), South Shields (North-Eastern League champions) and West Ham United (4th in the Southern League, Division One). Leicester Fosse changed their name to Leicester City.

1919   On 19th October 1919, Leeds City refused to submit their books to a committee investigating illegal war-time payments to players. As a result, the club were expelled from the League and disbanded by order of the F.A.

Their record at the time of expulsion was: P8 W4 D2 L2 F17 A10 P10. Port Vale, who were playing in the Central League where they had finished 3rd in 1914-15, accepted an invitation to take over Leeds' fixtures and completed the season in their place.

The Arsenal changed their name simply to 'Arsenal'.

1920   Grimsby Town and Lincoln City were not re-elected. The clubs elected in their places were Cardiff City (4th in the Southern League, First Division) and Leeds United, who were formed immediately after the demise of Leeds City and had gained entry to the Midland League for the rest of the 1919-20 season, finishing 12th.

It was then decided to form a Third Division which would consist of two sections, South and North. Only the champions of each section would be promoted to Division Two from where the bottom 2 would be relegated as replacements. The bottom 2 clubs in each of the Third Division sections would be required to seek re-election.

The Southern section was to start in 1920-21 by the absorption en masse of all clubs in the Southern League, Division One. These were, (their 1919-20 finishing positions in brackets):

Brentford (15th), Brighton & Hove Albion (16th), Bristol Rovers (17th), Crystal Palace (3rd), Exeter City (10th), Gillingham (22nd), Luton Town (20th), Merthyr Town (21st), Millwall (14th), Newport County (18th), Northampton Town (19th), Norwich City (12th), Plymouth Argyle (5th), Portsmouth (1st), Queens Park Rangers (6th), Reading (7th), Southampton (8th), Southend United (11th), Swansea Town (9th), Swindon Town (13th), Watford (2nd).

The other club who had been in the Southern League, First Division were Cardiff City, who had already been elected to Division Two and so one vacancy remained. Grimsby Town, who had not been re-elected to Division Two, accepted an invitation to fill it. Lincoln City, the other club not to have been re-elected, moved to the Midland League

The Northern section of the Third Division would start in 1921-22, as long as enough clubs of the desired strength could be found.

1921   It was agreed that Division Three (North) would be formed with 20 clubs, which would include the bottom club in Division Two (Stockport County) and Grimsby Town, who were transferred from Division Three (South). 14 of the remaining 18 vacancies were accepted on the recommendation of the Management Committee. Those 14, with their 1920-21 finishing position in brackets, consisted of 4 clubs from the Central League: Crewe Alexandra (2nd), Tranmere Rovers (7th), Rochdale (10th) and Nelson (17th); 4 clubs from the North-Eastern League: Darlington (champions), Hartlepools United (8th), Ashington (9th) and Durham City (11th); 2 clubs from the Lancashire Combination, Division One: Barrow (champions) and Accrington Stanley (6th); 2 clubs from the Midland League: Lincoln City (champions) and Chesterfield (3rd); and 2 clubs from the Birmingham League: Wrexham (3rd) and Walsall (5th).

The clubs elected to the remaining 4 places were Wigan Borough (11th in the Lancashire Combination, Division One), Halifax Town (11th in the Midland League), Stalybridge Celtic (13th in the Central League) and Southport (18th in the Central League).

Third Division (South) champions (Crystal Palace) had been promoted and Grimsby Town had been transferred to Division Three (North) so, with no club being relegated from Division Two, there were 2 vacancies in Division Three (South). The clubs elected to fill these vacancies were Aberdare Athletic (Welsh League champions and runners-up in the Southern League, Welsh Section) and Charlton Athletic (8th in the Southern League, English Section and 6th in the South-Eastern League).

1923   It was decided to expand Division Three (North) from 20 to 22 clubs while Stalybridge Celtic resigned and moved to the Cheshire League, creating a total of 3 vacancies. Two clubs were relegated from Division Two to Division Three (North) and none to Division Three (South) which thus had 1 vacancy. Bournemouth & Boscombe Athletic (runners-up in the Southern League, English Section) were elected to fill it. The 2 clubs elected to fill the vacancies in Division Three (North) were Doncaster Rovers (Midland League runners-up and New Brighton (4th in the Lancashire Combination).

1925   Stoke changed their name to Stoke City and Rotherham County merged with Rotherham Town (12th in the Midland League) to form Rotherham United.

1926   Aberdare Athletic merged with Aberaman Athletic (15th in the Welsh League) but continued in Division Three (South) as Aberdare Athletic. Coventry City transferred from Division Three (North) to Division Three (South).

1927   Walsall transferred from Division Three (North) to Division Three (South). Aberdare Athletic were not re-elected and moved to the Southern League, Western Section as Aberdare & Aberaman and to the Welsh League as Aberdare. Torquay United (champions of the Southern League, Western Section and runners-up in the Western League, Division One) were elected to Division Three (South) in their place.

1928   Durham City were not re-elected and moved to the North-Eastern League, Division One. Carlisle United (runners-up in the North-Eastern League, Division One) were elected to Division Three (North) in their place.

1929   Ashington were not re-elected and moved to the North-Eastern League, Division Two. York City (9th in the Midland League) were elected to Division Three (North) in their place. The Wednesday officially changed their name to Sheffield Wednesday.

1930   Merthyr Town were not re-elected and moved to the Southern League, Western Section and Welsh League, Division One. Thames Association (3rd in the Southern League, Eastern Section) were elected to Division Three (South) in their place. South Shields moved from South Shields to a new ground in Gateshead and changed their name to Gateshead.

1931   Walsall transferred from Division Three (South) to Division Three (North). Newport County were not re-elected and moved to the Southern League, Western Section and Welsh League, Division One. Mansfield Town (10th in the Midland League) were elected to Division Three (South) in their place. Nelson were not re-elected and moved to the Lancashire Combination. Chester (runners-up in the Cheshire League) were elected to Division Three (North) in their place.

1931   One 26th October 1931, Wigan Borough resigned and disbanded. Their record was P12 W3 D1 L8 F12 A33 P7. Merthyr Town offered to take over their fixtures but the offer was refused.

1932   Mansfield Town transferred from Division Three (South) to Division Three (North) where they replaced Wigan Borough. Thames Association resigned and disbanded. The clubs elected to fill the 2 vacancies in Division Three (South) were Newport County (6th in the Southern League, Western Section and runners-up in the Welsh League, Division One) and Aldershot (9th in the Southern League, Eastern Section and 7th in the London Combination, Division Two).

1936   Walsall transferred from Division Three (North) to Division Three (South).

1937   Mansfield Town transferred from Division Three (North) to Division Three (South).

1938   Port Vale transferred from Division Three (North) to Division Three (South). Gillingham were not re-elected and moved to the Southern League. Ipswich Town (3rd in the Southern League) were elected to Division Three (South) in their place.

1945   Birmingham changed their name to Birmingham City.

1946   Clapton Orient changed their name to Leyton Orient.

1947   Mansfield Town transferred from Division Three (South) to Division Three (North).

1950   It was decided to extend both sections of the Third Division from 22 to 24 clubs. The 2 clubs elected to the vacancies in the Southern Section were Colchester United (runners-up in the Southern League) and Gillingham (5th in the Southern League). The 2 clubs elected to the vacancies in the Northern Section were Scunthorpe & Lindsey United (3rd in the Midland League) and Shrewsbury Town (10th in the Midland League).

1951   Shrewsbury Town transferred from Division Three (North) to Division Three (South). New Brighton were not re-elected and moved to the Lancashire Combination, Division One. Workington (5th in the North-Eastern League) were elected to Division Three (North) in their place.

1952   Port Vale transferred from Division Three (South) to Division Three (North).

1958   Scunthorpe & Lindsey United changed their name to Scunthorpe United.

It was decided to restructure the two regional sections of the Third Division into two national divisions, Division Three and Division Four. The 1957-58 champions of each of the two regional sections were promoted to Division Two as usual, while the new Division Three was made up of the clubs finishing from 2nd to 12th in each of the two regional sections plus the 2 clubs relegated from Division Two. Division Four was made up of the clubs finishing 13th to 24th in each of the two regional sections. The bottom four clubs in Division Four would be required to seek re-election.

1960   Gateshead were not re-elected and moved to the Northern Counties League. Peterborough United (Midland League champions) were elected in their place.

1962   On 6th March 1962, Accrington Stanley resigned from the League. Their record at the time was P33 W5 D8 L20 F19 A60 P18. They joined the Lancashire Combination, Division Two in 1962-63. At the 1962 A.G.M., Oxford United (champions of the Southern League, Premier Division) were elected to replace them.

1967   Leyton Orient changed their name to Orient.

1968   Hartlepools United changed their name to Hartlepool.

1970   Swansea Town changed their name to Swansea City. Bradford Park Avenue were not re-elected and moved to the Northern Premier League. Cambridge United (champions of the Southern League, Premier Division) were elected in their place.

1971   Bournemouth & Boscombe Athletic changed their name to A.F.C. Bournemouth.

1972   Barrow were not re-elected and moved to the Northern Premier League. Hereford United (runners-up in the Southern League, Premier Division) were elected in their place.

1977   Hartlepool changed their name to Hartlepool United. Workington were not re-elected and moved to the Northern Premier League. Wimbledon (champions of the Southern League, Premier Division) were elected in their place.

1978   Southport were not re-elected and moved to the Northern Premier League. Wigan Athletic (runners-up in the Northern Premier League) were elected in their place.

1983   Chester changed their name to Chester City.

1987   Orient changed their name to Leyton Orient.

Re-election was scrapped and instead, automatic promotion and relegation was introduced between Division Four and the Football Conference, the champions of the latter replacing the bottom club in Division Four. The first club promoted under this system were Scarborough who replaced Lincoln City.

1988   Newport County were relegated to the Football Conference from where Lincoln City were promoted.

1989   Darlington were relegated to the Football Conference from where Maidstone United were promoted.

1990   Colchester United were relegated to the Football Conference from where Darlington were promoted.

1991   The League was expanded to 93 clubs. No club was relegated and Barnet were promoted from the Football Conference.

1992   On 25th March 1992, Aldershot resigned from the League and disbanded. Their record at the time was P36 W3 D8 L25 F21 A63 P17. A new club called Aldershot Town was quickly formed and joined the Isthmian League, Division Three in 1992-93.

1992   The clubs who were members of Division One all joined the new F.A. Premier League, an organisation outside of the control of the Football League. The rules for promotion and relegation between the new Premier League and Football League remained unchanged. The remaining Divisions of the Football League were all renamed, Division Two becoming Division One, Division Three becoming Division Two and Division Four becoming Division Three.

No clubs were relegated from the Football League but Colchester United were promoted from the Football Conference. Shortly before the start of the 1992-93 season, Maidstone United resigned and disbanded. A club called Maidstone Invicta was formed as a replacement in 1992 and joined the Kent County League, Division Four (West) in 1993-94.

1993   Halifax Town were relegated to the Football Conference from where Wycombe Wanderers were promoted.

1997   Hereford United were relegated to the Football Conference from where Macclesfield Town were promoted.

1998   Doncaster Rovers were relegated to the Football Conference from where Halifax Town were promoted.

1999   Scarborough were relegated to the Football Conference from where Cheltenham Town were promoted.

2000   Chester City were relegated to the Football Conference from where Kidderminster Harriers were promoted.

2001   Barnet were relegated to the Football Conference from where Rushden & Diamonds were promoted.

2002   Halifax Town were relegated to the Football Conference from where Boston United were promoted.

2003   The number of clubs to be promoted and relegated to the Football Conference increased from 1 to 2. Shrewsbury Town and Exeter City were relegated and Doncaster Rovers and Yeovil Town were promoted.

2004   Wimbledon moved to a new ground in Milton Keynes and changed their name to Milton Keynes Dons. Carlisle United and York City were relegated to the Football Conference from where Chester City and Shrewsbury Town were promoted. Division One of the Football League was renamed The Championship, Division Two was renamed League One and Division Three was renamed League Two.

2005   Kidderminster Harriers and Cambridge United were relegated to the Football Conference from where Carlisle United and Barnet were promoted.

2006   Oxford United and Rushden & Diamonds were relegated to the Football Conference from where Hereford United and Accrington Stanley were promoted.

2007   Boston United were relegated to the Football Conference (North) and Torquay United were relegated to the Football Conference from where Dagenham & Redbridge and Morecambe were promoted.

2008   Mansfield Town and Wrexham were relegated to the Football Conference from where Aldershot Town and Exeter City were promoted.

2009   Chester City and Luton Town were relegated to the Football Conference from where Burton Albion and Torquay United were promoted.

2010   Grimsby Town and Darlington were relegated to the Football Conference from where Stevenage Borough and Oxford United were promoted.

2011   Lincoln City and Stockport County were relegated to the Football Conference from where Crawley Town and A.F.C. Wimbledon were promoted.

2012   Macclesfield Town and Hereford United were relegated to the Football Conference from where Fleetwood Town and York City were promoted.

2013   Barnet and Aldershot Town were relegated to the Football Conference from where Mansfield Town and Newport County were promoted.

2014   Bristol Rovers and Torquay United were relegated to the Football Conference from where Luton Town and Cambridge United were promoted.

2015   Cheltenham Town and Tranmere Rovers were relegated to the Football Conference from where Barnet and Bristol Rovers were promoted.

2016   Dagenham and Redbridge and York City were relegated to the Football Conference from where Cheltenham Town and Grimsby Town were promoted.

Test Matches and Play-offs

It was anticipated when the League was first formed that there would be two 'classes' of clubs and that promotion and relegation between the two would be decided by 'Test Matches' (see under 'The Formation of the Football League', on page 3).

The Second Division was formed in 1892 and initially, there were 3 one-off games between the top Second Division clubs and the bottom First Division clubs. This, though, produced the occasional anomaly such as at the end of the very first season in which they were used when Second Division champions Small Heath lost their Test Match and so were not promoted whereas Sheffield United and Darwen, who had finished 2nd and 3rd, won their games and so leapfrogged Small Heath into the First Division.

In 1895-96, the system was refined into a mini-league for 2 places but Test Matches were scrapped altogether in 1898 after Stoke and Burnley drew their final mini-league game 0-0 when both clubs needed a point to ensure a top flight place.

The idea of extra games to decide promotion was revived in 1986 with the introduction of the play-offs. Initially, the club finishing just above the relegation zone competed for one place in the higher division with the 3 clubs who had finished just out of the promotion places in the division below. This was changed in 1988 to the present system whereby the 4 clubs finishing just below the automatic promotion places compete for one promotion place. The results of all Test Matches are listed below and results of the the play-offs are included alongside the tables for each season they have been held.

1892-93

Darwen vs Notts County	3-2

(played at Hyde Road, Ardwick)

Sheffield United vs Accrington	1-0

(played at the Town Ground, Nottingham)

Small Heath vs Newton Heath	1-1

(played at the Victoria Ground, Stoke)

Replay

Newton Heath vs Small Heath	5-2

(played at the Olive Grove, Sheffield)

Promoted: Darwen, Sheffield United
Relegated: Notts County, *Accrington

*Accrington resigned rather than accept relegation.

1893-94

Liverpool vs Newton Heath	2-0

(played at Ewood Park, Blackburn)

Preston North End vs Notts County	4-0

(played at the Olive Grove, Sheffield)

Small Heath vs Darwen	3-1

(played at the Victoria Ground, Stoke)

Promoted: Liverpool, Small Heath
Relegated: Newton Heath, Darwen

1894-95

Bury vs Liverpool   1-0
(at Ewood Park, Blackburn)

Derby County vs Notts County   2-1
(at Walnut Street, Leicester)

Stoke vs Newton Heath   3-0
(at the Athletic Ground, Cobridge, Burslem)

Promoted: Bury
Relegated: Liverpool

1895-96

The Test Match format changed into a mini-league in which each of the bottom two in Division One played home and away against each of the top two in Division Two. The top two in the table were promoted to, or remained in, Division One.

	P	W	D	L	F	A	Pts
Liverpool	4	2	1	1	6	2	5
West Bromwich Albion	4	2	1	1	9	4	5
Small Heath	4	1	1	2	8	7	3
Manchester City	4	1	1	2	5	15	3

Promoted: Liverpool
Relegated: Small Heath

1896-97

	P	W	D	L	F	A	Pts
Notts County	4	2	2	0	3	1	6
Sunderland	4	1	2	1	3	2	4
Burnley	4	1	1	2	3	4	3
Newton Heath	4	1	1	2	3	5	3

Promoted: Notts County
Relegated: Burnley

1897-98

	P	W	D	L	F	A	Pts
Stoke	4	2	1	1	4	2	5
Burnley	4	2	1	1	5	3	5
Newcastle United	4	2	0	2	9	6	4
Blackburn Rovers	4	1	0	3	5	12	2

Stoke and Burnley both needed 1 point from their last game to secure a place in Division One and they subsequently drew 0-0. Both divisions were later extended to 18 clubs with the above 4 teams all being placed in Division One.

Test matches were then replaced by automatic promotion and relegation for the following season.

1872 F.A. Cup

Semi-finals

Wanderers vs Queen's Park   0-0
Royal Engineers vs Crystal Palace   3-0

Final

Kennington Oval, 16 March 1872

Wanderers 1   (Betts)
Royal Engineers 0

Attendance 2,000

1873 F.A. Cup

Semi-finals

Queen's Park vs Oxford University   †
(Wanderers received a bye)
† After playing Oxford, Queen's Park scratched from the final because they could not afford to travel to London.

Final

Lillie Bridge, 29th March 1873

Wanderers 2   (Kinnaird, Wollaston)
Oxford University 0

Attendance 3,000

1874 F.A. Cup

Semi-finals

Oxford University vs Clapham Rovers   1-0
Royal Engineers vs Swifts   2-0

Final

Kennington Oval, 14th March 1874

Oxford University 2   (Mackarness, Patton)
Royal Engineers 0

Attendance 2,500

1875 F.A. Cup

Semi-finals

Royal Engineers vs Oxford University   1-0
Old Etonians vs Shropshire Wanderers   1-0

Final

Kennington Oval, 13th March 1875

Royal Engineers 1   (Scorer Not Known)
Old Etonians 1 (aet.)   (Bonsor)

Attendance 3,000

Replay

Kennington Oval, 16th March 1875

Royal Engineers 2   (Renny-Tailyour, Stafford)
Old Etonians 0

Attendance 3,000

1876 F.A. Cup

Semi-finals

Wanderers vs Swifts   2-1
Oxford University vs Old Etonians   0-1

Final

Kennington Oval, 11th March 1876

Wanderers 1   (Edwards)
Old Etonians 1   (Bonsor)

Attendance 3,500

Replay

Kennington Oval, 18th March 1876

Wanderers 3   (Hughes 2, Wollaston)
Old Etonians 0

Attendance 3,200

1877 F.A. Cup

Semi-finals

Wanderers vs Cambridge University   1-0
(Oxford University received a bye)

Final

Kennington Oval, 24th March 1877

Wanderers 2   (Heron, Kenrick)
Oxford University 1   (Kinnaird (og))

Attendance 3,000

1878 F.A. Cup

Semi-finals

Royal Engineers vs Old Harrovians   2-1
(Wanderers received a bye)

Final

Kennington Oval, 23rd March 1878

Wanderers 3   (Kenrick 2, Kinnaird)
Royal Engineers 1   (Scorer Not Known)

Attendance 4,500

1879 F.A. Cup

Semi-finals

Old Etonians vs Nottingham Forest   2-1
(Clapham Rovers received a bye)

Final

Kennington Oval, 29th March 1879

Old Etonians 1   (Clerke)
Clapham Rovers 0

Attendance 5,000

1880 F.A. Cup

Semi-finals

Oxford University vs Nottingham Forest   1-0
(Clapham Rovers received a bye)

Final

Kennington Oval, 10th April 1880

Clapham Rovers 1   (Lloyd-Jones)
Oxford University 0

Attendance 6,000

1881 F.A. Cup

Semi-finals

Old Carthusians vs Clapham Rovers   4-1
(Old Etonians received a bye)

Final

Kennington Oval, 9th April 1881

Old Carthusians 3   (Page, Wynyard, Parry)
Old Etonians 0

Attendance 4,500

1882 F.A. Cup

Semi-finals

Old Etonians vs Great Marlow   5-0
Blackburn Rovers vs The Wednesday   0-0, 5-1

Final

Kennington Oval, 25th March 1882

Old Etonians 1   (Anderson)
Blackburn Rovers 0

Attendance 6,500

1883 F.A. Cup

Semi-finals
Blackburn Olympic vs Old Carthusians   4-0
Old Etonians vs Notts County   2-1

Final
Kennington Oval, 31st March 1883
Blackburn Olympic 2   (Matthews, Costley)
Old Etonians 1 (aet.)   (Goodhart)

Attendance 8,000

1884 F.A. Cup

Semi-finals
Blackburn Rovers vs Notts County   1-0
Queen's Park vs Blackburn Olympic   4-1

Final
Kennington Oval, 29th March 1884
Blackburn Rovers 2   (Brown, Forrest)
Queen's Park 1   (Christie)

Attendance 4,000

1885 F.A. Cup

Semi-finals
Blackburn Rovers vs Old Carthusians   5-0
Queen's Park vs Nottingham Forest   1-1, 3-0

Final
Kennington Oval, 4th April 1885
Blackburn Rovers 2   (Forrest, Brown)
Queen's Park 0

Attendance 12,500

1886 F.A. Cup

Semi-finals
Blackburn Rovers vs Swifts   2-1
West Bromwich vs Small Heath Alliance   4-0

Final
Kennington Oval, 3rd April 1886
Blackburn Rovers 0
West Bromwich Albion 0

Attendance 15,000

Replay
Racecourse Ground, Derby, 10th April 1886
Blackburn Rovers 2   (Brown, Sowerbutts)
West Bromwich Albion 0

Attendance 12,000

1887 F.A. Cup

Semi-finals
Aston Villa vs Glasgow Rangers   3-1
West Bromwich Albion vs Preston North End   3-1

Final
Kennington Oval, 2nd April 1887
Aston Villa 2   (Hunter, Hodgetts)
West Bromwich Albion 0

Attendance 15,500

1888 F.A. Cup

Semi-finals
West Bromwich Albion vs Derby Junction   3-0
Preston North End vs Crewe Alexandra   4-0

Final
Kennington Oval 24th March 1888
West Bromwich Albion 2   (Woodhall, Bayliss)
Preston North End 1   (Dewhurst)

Attendance 19,000

FOOTBALL LEAGUE 1888-89

PRESTON NORTH END	22	18	4	0	74	15	40
Aston Villa	22	12	5	5	61	43	29
Wolverhampton Wanderers	22	12	4	6	50	37	28
Blackburn Rovers	22	10	6	6	66	45	26
Bolton Wanderers	22	10	2	10	63	59	22
West Bromwich Albion	22	10	2	10	40	46	22
Accrington	22	6	8	8	48	48	20
Everton	22	9	2	11	35	46	20
Burnley	22	7	3	12	42	62	17
Derby County	22	7	2	13	41	61	16
Notts County	22	5	2	15	40	73	12
Stoke	22	4	4	14	26	51	12

1889 F.A. Cup

Semi-finals
Preston North End vs West Bromwich Albion   1-0
Wolverhampton Wands. vs Blackburn Rovers   1-1, 3-1

Final
Kennington Oval, 30th March 1889
Preston North End 3   (Dewhurst, J. Ross, Thompson)
Wolverhampton Wanderers 0

Attendance 22,000

FOOTBALL LEAGUE 1889-90

PRESTON NORTH END	22	15	3	4	71	30	33
Everton	22	14	3	5	65	40	31
Blackburn Rovers	22	12	3	7	78	41	27
Wolverhampton Wanderers	22	10	5	7	51	38	25
West Bromwich Albion	22	11	3	8	47	50	25
Accrington	22	9	6	7	53	56	24
Derby County	22	9	3	10	43	55	21
Aston Villa	22	7	5	10	43	51	19
Bolton Wanderers	22	9	1	12	54	65	19
Notts County	22	6	5	11	43	51	17
Burnley	22	4	5	13	36	65	13
Stoke	*22*	*3*	*4*	*15*	*27*	*69*	*10*

1890 F.A. Cup

Semi-finals
Blackburn Rovers vs Wolverhampton Wanderers   1-0
Bolton Wanderers vs The Wednesday   1-2

Final
Kennington Oval, 29th March 1890
Blackburn Rovers 6   (Townley 3, Lofthouse, John
Southworth, Walton)
The Wednesday 1   (Bennett)

Attendance 20,000

FOOTBALL LEAGUE 1890-91

EVERTON	22	14	1	7	63	29	29
Preston North End	22	12	3	7	44	23	27
Notts County	22	11	4	7	52	35	26
Wolverhampton Wanderers	22	12	2	8	39	50	26
Bolton Wanderers	22	12	1	9	47	34	25
Blackburn Rovers	22	11	2	9	52	43	24
Sunderland	22	10	5	7	51	31	23
Burnley	22	9	3	10	52	63	21
Aston Villa	22	7	4	11	45	58	18
Accrington	22	6	4	12	28	50	16
Derby County	22	7	1	14	47	81	15
West Bromwich Albion	22	5	2	15	34	57	12

Sunderland had two points deducted

1891 F.A. Cup

Semi-finals
Blackburn Rovers vs West Bromwich Albion   3-2
Sunderland vs Notts County   3-3, 0-2

Final
Kennington Oval, 21st March 1891
Blackburn Rovers 3   (Southworth, Dewar, Townley)
Notts County 1   (Oswald)

Attendance 23,000

FOOTBALL LEAGUE 1891-92

SUNDERLAND	26	21	0	5	93	36	42
Preston North End	26	18	1	7	61	31	37
Bolton Wanderers	26	17	2	7	51	37	36
Aston Villa	26	15	0	11	89	56	30
Everton	26	12	4	10	49	49	28
Wolverhampton Wanderers	26	11	4	11	59	46	26
Burnley	26	11	4	11	49	45	26
Notts County	26	11	4	11	55	51	26
Blackburn Rovers	26	10	6	10	58	65	26
Derby County	26	10	4	12	46	52	24
Accrington	26	8	4	14	40	78	20
West Bromwich Albion	26	6	6	14	51	58	18
Stoke	26	5	4	17	38	61	14
Darwen	*26*	*4*	*3*	*19*	*38*	*112*	*11*

1892 F.A. Cup

Semi-finals

West Brom. Albion vs Nottingham Forest   1-1, 1-1, 6-2
Aston Villa vs Sunderland   4-1

Final

Kennington Oval, 12th March 1892

West Bromwich Albion 3   (Nicholls, Geddes, Reynolds)

Aston Villa 0

Attendance 25,000

DIVISION ONE 1892-93

SUNDERLAND	30	22	4	4	100	36	48
Preston North End	30	17	3	10	57	39	37
Everton	30	16	4	10	74	51	36
Aston Villa	30	16	3	11	73	62	35
Bolton Wanderers	30	13	6	11	56	55	32
Burnley	30	13	4	13	51	44	30
Stoke	30	12	5	13	58	48	29
West Bromwich Albion	30	12	5	13	58	69	29
Blackburn Rovers	30	8	13	9	47	56	29
Nottingham Forest	30	10	8	12	48	52	28
Wolverhampton Wanderers	30	12	4	14	47	68	28
The Wednesday	30	12	3	15	55	65	27
Derby County	30	9	9	12	52	64	27
Notts County	*30*	*10*	*4*	*16*	*53*	*61*	*24*
Accrington	*30*	*6*	*11*	*13*	*57*	*81*	*23*
Newton Heath	30	6	6	18	50	85	18

DIVISION TWO 1892-93

Small Heath	22	17	2	3	90	35	36
Sheffield United	22	16	3	3	62	19	35
Darwen	22	14	2	6	60	36	30
Grimsby Town	22	11	1	10	42	41	23
Ardwick	22	9	3	10	45	40	21
Burton Swifts	22	9	2	11	47	47	20
Northwich Victoria	22	9	2	11	42	58	20
Bootle	*22*	*8*	*3*	*11*	*49*	*63*	*19*
Lincoln City	22	7	3	12	45	51	17
Crewe Alexandra	22	6	3	13	42	69	15
Burslem Port Vale	22	6	3	13	30	57	15
Walsall Town Swifts	22	5	3	14	37	75	13

1893 F.A. Cup

Semi-finals

Wolverhampton Wanderers vs Blackburn Rovers   2-1
Everton vs Preston North End   2-2, 0-0, 2-1

Final

Fallowfield, Manchester, 25th March 1893

Wolverhampton Wanderers 1   (Allen)

Everton 0

Attendance 45,000

DIVISION ONE 1893-94

ASTON VILLA	30	19	6	5	84	42	44
Sunderland	30	17	4	9	72	44	38
Derby County	30	16	4	10	73	62	36
Blackburn Rovers	30	16	2	12	69	53	34
Burnley	30	15	4	11	61	51	34
Everton	30	15	3	12	90	57	33
Nottingham Forest	30	14	4	12	57	48	32
West Bromwich Albion	30	14	4	12	66	59	32
Wolverhampton Wanderers	30	14	3	13	52	63	31
Sheffield United	30	13	5	12	47	61	31
Stoke	30	13	3	14	65	79	29
The Wednesday	30	9	8	13	48	57	26
Bolton Wanderers	30	10	4	16	38	52	24
Preston North End	30	10	3	17	44	56	23
Darwen	*30*	*7*	*5*	*18*	*37*	*83*	*19*
Newton Heath	*30*	*6*	*2*	*22*	*36*	*72*	*14*

DIVISION TWO 1893-94

Liverpool	28	22	6	0	77	18	50
Small Heath	28	21	0	7	103	44	42
Notts County	28	18	3	7	70	31	39
Newcastle United	28	15	6	7	66	39	36
Grimsby Town	28	15	2	11	71	58	32
Burton Swifts	28	14	3	11	79	61	31
Burslem Port Vale	28	13	4	11	66	64	30
Lincoln City	28	11	6	11	59	58	28
Woolwich Arsenal	28	12	4	12	52	55	28
Walsall Town Swifts	28	10	3	15	51	61	23
Middlesbrough Ironopolis	*28*	*8*	*4*	*16*	*37*	*72*	*20*
Crewe Alexandra	28	6	7	15	42	73	19
Ardwick	28	8	2	18	47	71	18
Rotherham Town	28	6	3	19	44	91	15
Northwich Victoria	*28*	*3*	*3*	*22*	*30*	*98*	*9*

1894 F.A. Cup

Semi-finals

Notts County vs Blackburn Rovers   1-0
Bolton Wanderers vs The Wednesday   2-1

Final

Goodison Park, 31st March 1894

Notts County 4   (Logan 3, Watson)

Bolton Wanderers 1   (Cassidy)

Attendance 37,000

DIVISION ONE 1894-95

SUNDERLAND	30	21	5	4	80	37	47
Everton	30	18	6	6	82	50	42
Aston Villa	30	17	5	8	82	43	39
Preston North End	30	15	5	10	62	46	35
Blackburn Rovers	30	11	10	9	59	49	32
Sheffield United	30	14	4	12	57	55	32
Nottingham Forest	30	13	5	12	50	56	31
The Wednesday	30	12	4	14	50	55	28
Burnley	30	11	4	15	44	56	26
Bolton Wanderers	30	9	7	14	61	62	25
Wolverhampton Wanderers	30	9	7	14	43	63	25
Small Heath	30	9	7	14	50	74	25
West Bromwich Albion	30	10	4	16	51	66	24
Stoke	30	9	6	15	50	67	24
Derby County	30	7	9	14	45	68	23
Liverpool	*30*	*7*	*8*	*15*	*51*	*70*	*22*

DIVISION TWO 1894-95

Bury	30	23	2	5	78	33	48
Notts County	30	17	5	8	75	45	39
Newton Heath	30	15	8	7	78	44	38
Leicester Fosse	30	15	8	7	72	53	38
Grimsby Town	30	18	1	11	79	52	37
Darwen	30	16	4	10	74	43	36
Burton Wanderers	30	14	7	9	67	39	35
Woolwich Arsenal	30	14	6	10	75	58	34
Manchester City	30	14	3	13	82	72	31
Newcastle United	30	12	3	15	72	84	27
Burton Swifts	30	11	3	16	52	74	25
Rotherham Town	30	11	2	17	55	62	24
Lincoln City	30	10	0	20	52	92	20
Walsall Town Swifts	*30*	*10*	*0*	*20*	*47*	*92*	*20*
Burslem Port Vale	30	7	4	19	39	77	18
Crewe Alexandra	30	3	4	23	26	103	10

1895 F.A. Cup

Semi-finals

Aston Villa vs Sunderland	2-1
West Bromwich Albion vs The Wednesday	2-0

Final

Crystal Palace, 20th April 1895

Aston Villa 1 (Chatt)

West Bromwich Albion 0

Attendance 42,560

DIVISION ONE 1895-96

ASTON VILLA	30	20	5	5	78	45	45
Derby County	30	17	7	6	68	35	41
Everton	30	16	7	7	66	43	39
Bolton Wanderers	30	16	5	9	49	37	37
Sunderland	30	15	7	8	52	41	37
Stoke	30	15	0	15	56	47	30
The Wednesday	30	12	5	13	44	53	29
Blackburn Rovers	30	12	5	13	40	50	29
Preston North End	30	11	6	13	44	48	28
Burnley	30	10	7	13	48	44	27
Bury	30	12	3	15	50	54	27
Sheffield United	30	10	6	14	40	50	26
Nottingham Forest	30	11	3	16	42	57	25
Wolverhampton Wanderers	30	10	1	19	61	65	21
Small Heath	*30*	*8*	*4*	*18*	*39*	*79*	*20*
West Bromwich Albion	30	6	7	17	30	59	19

DIVISION TWO 1895-96

Liverpool	30	22	2	6	106	32	46
Manchester City	30	21	4	5	63	38	46
Grimsby Town	30	20	2	8	82	38	42
Burton Wanderers	30	19	4	7	69	40	42
Newcastle United	30	16	2	12	73	50	34
Newton Heath	30	15	3	12	66	57	33
Woolwich Arsenal	30	14	4	12	59	42	32
Leicester Fosse	30	14	4	12	57	44	32
Darwen	30	12	6	12	72	67	30
Notts County	30	12	2	16	57	54	26
Burton Swifts	30	10	4	16	39	69	24
Loughborough	30	9	5	16	40	67	23
Lincoln City	30	9	4	17	53	75	22
Burslem Port Vale	*30*	*7*	*4*	*19*	*43*	*78*	*18*
Rotherham Town	*30*	*7*	*3*	*20*	*34*	*97*	*17*
Crewe Alexandra	*30*	*5*	*3*	*22*	*30*	*95*	*13*

1896 F.A. Cup

Semi-finals

The Wednesday vs Bolton Wanderers	1-1, 3-1
Wolverhampton Wanderers vs Derby County	2-1

Final

Crystal Palace, 18th April 1896

The Wednesday 2 (Spiksley 2)

Wolverhampton Wanderers 1 (Black)

Attendance 48,836

DIVISION ONE 1896-97

ASTON VILLA	30	21	5	4	73	38	47
Sheffield United	30	13	10	7	42	29	36
Derby County	30	16	4	10	70	50	36
Preston North End	30	11	12	7	55	40	34
Liverpool	30	12	9	9	46	38	33
The Wednesday	30	10	11	9	42	37	31
Everton	30	14	3	13	62	57	31
Bolton Wanderers	30	12	6	12	40	43	30
Bury	30	10	10	10	39	44	30
Wolverhampton Wanderers	30	11	6	13	45	41	28
Nottingham Forest	30	9	8	13	44	49	26
West Bromwich Albion	30	10	6	14	33	56	26
Stoke	30	11	3	16	48	59	25
Blackburn Rovers	30	11	3	16	35	62	25
Sunderland	30	7	9	14	34	47	23
Burnley	*30*	*6*	*7*	*17*	*43*	*61*	*19*

DIVISION TWO 1896-97

Notts County	30	19	4	7	92	43	42
Newton Heath	30	17	5	8	56	34	39
Grimsby Town	30	17	4	9	66	45	38
Small Heath	30	16	5	9	69	47	37
Newcastle United	30	17	1	12	56	52	35
Manchester City	30	12	8	10	58	50	32
Gainsborough Trinity	30	12	7	11	50	47	31
Blackpool	30	13	5	12	59	56	31
Leicester Fosse	30	13	4	13	59	56	30
Woolwich Arsenal	30	13	4	13	68	70	30
Darwen	30	14	0	16	67	61	28
Walsall	30	11	4	15	53	69	26
Loughborough	30	12	1	17	50	64	25
Burton Swifts	30	9	6	15	46	61	24
Burton Wanderers	*30*	*9*	*2*	*19*	*31*	*67*	*20*
Lincoln City	30	5	2	23	27	85	12

1897 F.A. Cup

Semi-finals

Aston Villa vs Liverpool	3-0
Everton vs Derby County	3-2

Final

Crystal Palace, 10th April 1897

Aston Villa 3 (Campbell, Wheldon, Crabtree)

Everton 2 (Bell, Boyle)

Attendance 62,017

DIVISION ONE 1897-98

SHEFFIELD UNITED	30	17	8	5	56	31	42
Sunderland	30	16	5	9	43	30	37
Wolverhampton Wanderers	30	14	7	9	57	41	35
Everton	30	13	9	8	48	39	35
The Wednesday	30	15	3	12	51	42	33
Aston Villa	30	14	5	11	61	51	33
West Bromwich Albion	30	11	10	9	44	45	32
Nottingham Forest	30	11	9	10	47	49	31
Liverpool	30	11	6	13	48	45	28
Derby County	30	11	6	13	57	61	28
Bolton Wanderers	30	11	4	15	28	41	26
Preston North End	30	8	8	14	35	43	24
Notts County	30	8	8	14	36	46	24
Bury	30	8	8	14	39	51	24
Blackburn Rovers	30	7	10	13	39	54	24
Stoke	30	8	8	14	35	55	24

DIVISION TWO 1897-98

Burnley	30	20	8	2	80	24	48
Newcastle United	30	21	3	6	64	32	45
Manchester City	30	15	9	6	66	36	39
Newton Heath	30	16	6	8	64	35	38
Woolwich Arsenal	30	16	5	9	69	49	37
Small Heath	30	16	4	10	58	50	36
Leicester Fosse	30	13	7	10	46	35	33
Luton Town	30	13	4	13	68	50	30
Gainsborough Trinity	30	12	6	12	50	54	30
Walsall	30	12	5	13	58	58	29
Blackpool	30	10	5	15	49	61	25
Grimsby Town	30	10	4	16	52	62	24
Burton Swifts	30	8	5	17	38	69	21
Lincoln City	30	6	5	19	43	82	17
Darwen	30	6	2	22	31	76	14
Loughborough	30	6	2	22	24	87	14

1898 F.A. Cup

Semi-finals

Southampton vs Nottingham Forest	1-1, 0-2
Derby County vs Everton	3-1

Final

Crystal Palace, 16th April 1898

Nottingham Forest 3   (Capes 2, McPherson)
Derby County 1   (Bloomer)

Attendance 62,017

DIVISION ONE 1898-99

ASTON VILLA	34	19	7	8	76	40	45
Liverpool	34	19	5	10	49	33	43
Burnley	34	15	9	10	45	47	39
Everton	34	15	8	11	48	41	38
Notts County	34	12	13	9	47	51	37
Blackburn Rovers	34	14	8	12	60	52	36
Sunderland	34	15	6	13	41	41	36
Wolverhampton Wanderers	34	14	7	13	54	48	35
Derby County	34	12	11	11	62	57	35
Bury	34	14	7	13	48	49	35
Nottingham Forest	34	11	11	12	42	42	33
Stoke	34	13	7	14	47	52	33
Newcastle United	34	11	8	15	49	48	30
West Bromwich Albion	34	12	6	16	42	57	30
Preston North End	34	10	9	15	44	47	29
Sheffield United	34	9	11	14	45	51	29
Bolton Wanderers	34	9	7	18	37	51	25
The Wednesday	34	8	8	18	32	61	24

DIVISION TWO 1898-99

Manchester City	34	23	6	5	92	35	52
Glossop North End	34	20	6	8	76	38	46
Leicester Fosse	34	18	9	7	64	42	45
Newton Heath	34	19	5	10	67	43	43
New Brighton Tower	34	18	7	9	71	52	43
Walsall	34	15	12	7	79	36	42
Woolwich Arsenal	34	18	5	11	72	41	41
Small Heath	34	17	7	10	85	50	41
Burslem Port Vale	34	17	5	12	56	34	39
Grimsby Town	34	15	5	14	71	60	35
Barnsley	34	12	7	15	52	56	31
Lincoln City	34	12	7	15	51	56	31
Burton Swifts	34	10	8	16	51	70	28
Gainsborough Trinity	34	10	5	19	56	72	25
Luton Town	34	10	3	21	51	95	23
Blackpool	34	8	4	22	49	90	20
Loughborough	34	6	6	22	38	92	18
Darwen	34	2	5	27	22	141	9

1899 F.A. Cup

Semi-finals

Sheffield United vs Liverpool	2-2, 4-4, 0-1*, 1-0
Derby County vs Stoke	3-1
* match abandoned	

Final

Crystal Palace, 15th April 1899

Sheffield United 4   (Bennett, Priest, Beers, Almond)
Derby County 1   (Boag)

Attendance 73,833

DIVISION ONE 1899-1900

ASTON VILLA	34	22	6	6	77	35	50
Sheffield United	34	18	12	4	63	33	48
Sunderland	34	19	3	12	50	35	41
Wolverhampton Wanderers	34	15	9	10	48	37	39
Newcastle United	34	13	10	11	53	43	36
Derby County	34	14	8	12	45	43	36
Manchester City	34	13	8	13	50	44	34
Nottingham Forest	34	13	8	13	56	55	34
Stoke	34	13	8	13	37	45	34
Liverpool	34	14	5	15	49	45	33
Everton	34	13	7	14	47	49	33
Bury	34	13	6	15	40	44	32
West Bromwich Albion	34	11	8	15	43	51	30
Blackburn Rovers	34	13	4	17	49	61	30
Notts County	34	9	11	14	46	60	29
Preston North End	34	12	4	18	38	48	28
Burnley	34	11	5	18	34	54	27
Glossop	34	4	10	20	31	74	18

DIVISION TWO 1899-1900

The Wednesday	34	25	4	5	84	22	54
Bolton Wanderers	34	22	8	4	79	25	52
Small Heath	34	20	6	8	78	38	46
Newton Heath	34	20	4	10	63	27	44
Leicester Fosse	34	17	9	8	53	36	43
Grimsby Town	34	17	6	11	67	46	40
Chesterfield	34	16	6	12	65	60	38
Woolwich Arsenal	34	16	4	14	61	43	36
Lincoln City	34	14	8	12	46	43	36
New Brighton Tower	34	13	9	12	66	58	35
Burslem Port Vale	34	14	6	14	39	49	34
Walsall	34	12	8	14	50	55	32
Gainsborough Trinity	34	9	7	18	47	75	25
Middlesbrough	34	8	8	18	39	69	24
Burton Swifts	34	9	6	19	43	84	24
Barnsley	34	8	7	19	46	79	23
Luton Town	34	5	8	21	40	75	18
Loughborough	34	1	6	27	18	100	8

1900 F.A. Cup

Semi-finals

Nottingham Forest vs Bury	1-1, 2-3
Southampton vs Millwall Athletic	0-0, 3-0

Final

Crystal Palace, 21st April 1900

Bury 4   (McLuckie 2, Wood, Plant)
Southampton 0

Attendance 68,945

DIVISION ONE 1900-01

LIVERPOOL	34	19	7	8	59	35	45
Sunderland	34	15	13	6	57	26	43
Notts County	34	18	4	12	54	46	40
Nottingham Forest	34	16	7	11	53	36	39
Bury	34	16	7	11	53	37	39
Newcastle United	34	14	10	10	42	37	38
Everton	34	16	5	13	55	42	37
The Wednesday	34	13	10	11	52	42	36
Blackburn Rovers	34	12	9	13	39	47	33
Bolton Wanderers	34	13	7	14	39	55	33
Manchester City	34	13	6	15	48	58	32
Derby County	34	12	7	15	55	42	31
Wolverhampton Wanderers	34	9	13	12	39	55	31
Sheffield United	34	12	7	15	35	52	31
Aston Villa	34	10	10	14	45	51	30
Stoke	34	11	5	18	46	57	27
Preston North End	*34*	*9*	*7*	*18*	*49*	*75*	*25*
West Bromwich Albion	*34*	*7*	*8*	*19*	*35*	*62*	*22*

DIVISION TWO 1900-01

Grimsby Town	34	20	9	5	60	33	49
Small Heath	34	19	10	5	57	24	48
Burnley	34	20	4	10	53	29	44
New Brighton Tower	*34*	*17*	*8*	*9*	*57*	*38*	*42*
Glossop	34	15	8	11	51	33	38
Middlesbrough	34	15	7	12	50	40	37
Woolwich Arsenal	34	15	6	13	39	35	36
Lincoln City	34	13	7	14	43	39	33
Burslem Port Vale	34	11	11	12	45	47	33
Newton Heath	34	14	4	16	42	38	32
Leicester Fosse	34	11	10	13	39	37	32
Blackpool	34	12	7	15	33	58	31
Gainsborough Trinity	34	10	10	14	45	60	30
Chesterfield	34	9	10	15	46	58	28
Barnsley	34	11	5	18	47	60	27
Walsall	*34*	*7*	*13*	*14*	*40*	*56*	*27*
Stockport County	34	11	3	20	38	68	25
Burton Swifts	34	8	4	22	34	66	20

1901 F.A. Cup

Semi-finals

Tottenham Hotspur vs West Bromwich Albion	4-0
Sheffield United vs Aston Villa	2-2, 3-0

Final

Crystal Palace, 20th April 1901

Tottenham Hotspur 2   (Brown 2)
Sheffield United 2   (Bennett, Priest)

Attendance 114, 815

Replay

Burnden Park, Bolton, 27th April 1901

Tottenham Hotspur 3   (Cameron, Smith, Brown)
Sheffield United 1   (Priest)

Attendance 20,740

DIVISION ONE 1901-02

SUNDERLAND	34	19	6	9	50	35	44
Everton	34	17	7	10	53	35	41
Newcastle United	34	14	9	11	48	34	37
Blackburn Rovers	34	15	6	13	52	48	36
Nottingham Forest	34	13	9	12	43	43	35
Derby County	34	13	9	12	39	41	35
Bury	34	13	8	13	44	38	34
Aston Villa	34	13	8	13	42	40	34
The Wednesday	34	13	8	13	48	52	34
Sheffield United	34	13	7	14	53	48	33
Liverpool	34	10	12	12	42	38	32
Bolton Wanderers	34	12	8	14	51	56	32
Notts County	34	14	4	16	51	57	32
Wolverhampton Wanderers	34	13	6	15	46	57	32
Grimsby Town	34	13	6	15	44	60	32
Stoke	34	11	9	14	45	55	31
Small Heath	*34*	*11*	*8*	*15*	*47*	*45*	*30*
Manchester City	*34*	*11*	*6*	*17*	*42*	*58*	*28*

DIVISION TWO 1901-02

West Bromwich Albion	34	25	5	4	82	29	55
Middlesbrough	34	23	5	6	90	24	51
Preston North End	34	18	6	10	71	32	42
Woolwich Arsenal	34	18	6	10	50	26	42
Lincoln City	34	14	13	7	45	35	41
Bristol City	34	17	6	11	52	35	40
Doncaster Rovers	34	13	8	13	49	58	34
Glossop	34	10	12	12	36	40	32
Burnley	34	10	10	14	41	45	30
Burton United	34	11	8	15	46	54	30
Barnsley	34	12	6	16	51	63	30
Burslem Port Vale	34	10	9	15	43	59	29
Blackpool	34	11	7	16	40	56	29
Leicester Fosse	34	12	5	17	38	56	29
Newton Heath	34	11	6	17	38	53	28
Chesterfield	34	11	6	17	47	68	28
Stockport County	34	8	7	19	36	72	23
Gainsborough Trinity	34	4	11	19	30	80	19

1902 F.A. Cup

Semi-finals

Sheffield United vs Derby County	1-1, 1-1, 1-0
Southampton vs Nottingham Forest	3-1

Final

Crystal Palace, 19th April 1902

Sheffield United 1   (Common)
Southampton 1   (Wood)

Attendance 76,914

Replay

Crystal Palace, 26th April 1902

Sheffield United 2   (Hedley, Barnes)
Southampton 1   (Brown)

Attendance 33,068

DIVISION ONE 1902-03

THE WEDNESDAY	34	19	4	11	54	36	42
Aston Villa	34	19	3	12	61	40	41
Sunderland	34	16	9	9	51	36	41
Sheffield United	34	17	5	12	58	44	39
Liverpool	34	17	4	13	68	49	38
Stoke	34	15	7	12	46	38	37
West Bromwich Albion	34	16	4	14	54	53	36
Bury	34	16	3	15	54	43	35
Derby County	34	16	3	15	50	47	35
Nottingham Forest	34	14	7	13	49	47	35
Wolverhampton Wanderers	34	14	5	15	48	57	33
Everton	34	13	6	15	45	47	32
Middlesbrough	34	14	4	16	41	50	32
Newcastle United	34	14	4	16	41	51	32
Notts County	34	12	7	15	41	49	31
Blackburn Rovers	34	12	5	17	44	63	29
Grimsby Town	*34*	*8*	*9*	*17*	*43*	*62*	*25*
Bolton Wanderers	*34*	*8*	*3*	*23*	*37*	*73*	*19*

DIVISION TWO 1902-03

Manchester City	34	25	4	5	95	29	54
Small Heath	34	24	3	7	74	36	51
Woolwich Arsenal	34	20	8	6	66	30	48
Bristol City	34	17	8	9	59	38	42
Manchester United	34	15	8	11	53	38	38
Chesterfield	34	14	9	11	67	40	37
Preston North End	34	13	10	11	56	40	36
Barnsley	34	13	8	13	55	51	34
Burslem Port Vale	34	13	8	13	57	62	34
Lincoln City	34	12	6	16	46	53	30
Glossop	34	11	7	16	43	58	29
Gainsborough Trinity	34	11	7	16	41	59	29
Burton United	34	11	7	16	39	59	29
Blackpool	34	9	10	15	44	59	28
Leicester Fosse	34	10	8	16	41	65	28
Doncaster Rovers	*34*	*9*	*7*	*18*	*35*	*72*	*25*
Stockport County	34	7	6	21	39	74	20
Burnley	34	6	8	20	30	77	20

1903 F.A. Cup

Semi-finals

Aston Villa vs Bury	0-3
Derby County vs Millwall Athletic	3-0

Final

Crystal Palace, 18th April 1903

Bury 6   (Leeming 2, Ross, Sagar, Plant, Wood)

Derby County 0

Attendance 63,102

DIVISION ONE 1903-04

THE WEDNESDAY	34	20	7	7	48	28	47
Manchester City	34	19	6	9	71	45	44
Everton	34	19	5	10	59	32	43
Newcastle United	34	18	6	10	58	45	42
Aston Villa	34	17	7	10	70	48	41
Sunderland	34	17	5	12	63	49	39
Sheffield United	34	15	8	11	62	57	38
Wolverhampton Wanderers	34	14	8	12	44	66	36
Nottingham Forest	34	11	9	14	57	57	31
Middlesbrough	34	9	12	13	46	47	30
Small Heath	34	11	8	15	39	52	30
Bury	34	7	15	12	40	53	29
Notts County	34	12	5	17	37	61	29
Derby County	34	9	10	15	58	60	28
Blackburn Rovers	34	11	6	17	48	60	28
Stoke	34	10	7	17	54	57	27
Liverpool	*34*	*9*	*8*	*17*	*49*	*62*	*26*
West Bromwich Albion	*34*	*7*	*10*	*17*	*36*	*60*	*24*

DIVISION TWO 1903-04

Preston North End	34	20	10	4	62	24	50
Woolwich Arsenal	34	21	7	6	91	22	49
Manchester United	34	20	8	6	65	33	48
Bristol City	34	18	6	10	73	41	42
Burnley	34	15	9	10	50	55	39
Grimsby Town	34	14	8	12	50	49	36
Bolton Wanderers	34	12	10	12	59	41	34
Barnsley	34	11	10	13	38	57	32
Gainsborough Trinity	34	14	3	17	53	60	31
Bradford City	34	12	7	15	45	59	31
Chesterfield	34	11	8	15	37	45	30
Lincoln City	34	11	8	15	41	58	30
Burslem Port Vale	34	10	9	15	54	52	29
Burton United	34	11	7	16	45	61	29
Blackpool	34	11	5	18	40	67	27
Stockport County	*34*	*8*	*11*	*15*	*40*	*72*	*27*
Glossop	34	10	6	18	57	64	26
Leicester Fosse	34	6	10	18	42	82	22

1904 F.A. Cup

Semi-finals

Manchester City vs The Wednesday	3-0
Bolton Wanderers vs Derby County	1-0

Final

Crystal Palace, 23rd April 1904

Manchester City 1   (Meredith)

Bolton Wanderers 0

Attendance 61,374

DIVISION ONE 1904-05

NEWCASTLE UNITED	34	23	2	9	72	33	48
Everton	34	21	5	8	63	36	47
Manchester City	34	20	6	8	66	37	46
Aston Villa	34	19	4	11	63	43	42
Sunderland	34	16	8	10	60	44	40
Sheffield United	34	19	2	13	64	56	40
Small Heath	34	17	5	12	54	38	39
Preston North End	34	13	10	11	42	37	36
The Wednesday	34	14	5	15	61	57	33
Woolwich Arsenal	34	12	9	13	36	40	33
Derby County	34	12	8	14	37	48	32
Stoke	34	13	4	17	40	58	30
Blackburn Rovers	34	11	5	18	40	51	27
Wolverhampton Wanderers	34	11	4	19	47	73	26
Middlesbrough	34	9	8	17	36	56	26
Nottingham Forest	34	9	7	18	40	61	25
Bury	34	10	4	20	47	67	24
Notts County	34	5	8	21	36	69	18

DIVISION TWO 1904-05

Liverpool	34	27	4	3	93	25	58
Bolton Wanderers	34	27	2	5	87	32	56
Manchester United	34	24	5	5	81	30	53
Bristol City	34	19	4	11	66	45	42
Chesterfield Town	34	14	11	9	44	35	39
Gainsborough Trinity	34	14	8	12	61	58	36
Barnsley	34	14	5	15	38	56	33
Bradford City	34	12	8	14	45	49	32
Lincoln City	34	12	7	15	42	40	31
West Bromwich Albion	34	13	4	17	56	48	30
Burnley	34	12	6	16	43	52	30
Glossop	34	10	10	14	37	46	30
Grimsby Town	34	11	8	15	33	46	30
Leicester Fosse	34	11	7	16	40	55	29
Blackpool	34	9	10	15	36	48	28
Burslem Port Vale	34	10	7	17	47	72	27
Burton United	34	8	4	22	30	84	20
Doncaster Rovers	*34*	*3*	*2*	*29*	*23*	*81*	*8*

1905 F.A. Cup

Semi-finals

Everton vs Aston Villa	1-1, 1-2
Newcastle United vs The Wednesday	1-0

Final

Crystal Palace, 15th April 1905

Aston Villa 2   (Hampton 2)

Newcastle United 0

Attendance 101,117

DIVISION ONE 1905-06

LIVERPOOL	38	23	5	10	79	46	51
Preston North End	38	17	13	8	54	39	47
The Wednesday	38	18	8	12	63	52	44
Newcastle United	38	18	7	13	74	48	43
Manchester City	38	19	5	14	73	54	43
Bolton Wanderers	38	17	7	14	81	67	41
Birmingham	38	17	7	14	65	59	41
Aston Villa	38	17	6	15	72	56	40
Blackburn Rovers	38	16	8	14	54	52	40
Stoke	38	16	7	15	54	55	39
Everton	38	15	7	16	70	66	37
Woolwich Arsenal	38	15	7	16	62	64	37
Sheffield United	38	15	6	17	57	62	36
Sunderland	38	15	5	18	61	70	35
Derby County	38	14	7	17	39	58	35
Notts County	38	11	12	15	55	71	34
Bury	38	11	10	17	57	74	32
Middlesbrough	38	10	11	17	56	71	31
Nottingham Forest	*38*	*13*	*5*	*20*	*58*	*79*	*31*
Wolverhampton Wanderers	*38*	*8*	*7*	*23*	*58*	*99*	*23*

DIVISION TWO 1905-06

Bristol City	38	30	6	2	83	28	66
Manchester United	38	28	6	4	90	28	62
Chelsea	38	22	9	7	90	37	53
West Bromwich Albion	38	22	8	8	79	36	52
Hull City	38	19	6	13	67	54	44
Leeds City	38	17	9	12	59	47	43
Leicester Fosse	38	15	12	11	53	48	42
Grimsby Town	38	15	10	13	46	46	40
Burnley	38	15	8	15	42	53	38
Stockport County	38	13	9	16	44	56	35
Bradford City	38	13	8	17	46	60	34
Barnsley	38	12	9	17	60	62	33
Lincoln City	38	12	6	20	69	72	30
Blackpool	38	10	9	19	37	62	29
Gainsborough Trinity	38	12	4	22	44	57	28
Glossop	38	10	8	20	49	71	28
Burslem Port Vale	38	12	4	22	49	82	28
Chesterfield Town	38	10	8	20	40	72	28
Burton United	38	10	6	22	34	67	26
Clapton Orient	38	7	7	24	35	78	21

1906 F.A. Cup

Semi-finals

Everton vs Liverpool   2-0
Woolwich Arsenal vs Newcastle United   0-2

Final

Crystal Palace, 21st April 1906

Everton 1   (Young)
Newcastle United 0

Attendance 75,609

DIVISION ONE 1906-07

NEWCASTLE UNITED	38	22	7	9	74	46	51
Bristol City	38	20	8	10	66	47	48
Everton	38	20	5	13	70	46	45
Sheffield United	38	17	11	10	57	55	45
Aston Villa	38	19	6	13	78	52	44
Bolton Wanderers	38	18	8	12	59	47	44
Woolwich Arsenal	38	20	4	14	66	59	44
Manchester United	38	17	8	13	53	56	42
Birmingham	38	15	8	15	52	52	38
Sunderland	38	14	9	15	65	66	37
Middlesbrough	38	15	6	17	56	63	36
Blackburn Rovers	38	14	7	17	56	59	35
The Wednesday	38	12	11	15	49	60	35
Preston North End	38	14	7	17	44	57	35
Liverpool	38	13	7	18	64	65	33
Bury	38	13	6	19	58	68	32
Manchester City	38	10	12	16	53	77	32
Notts County	38	8	15	15	46	50	31
Derby County	38	9	9	20	41	59	27
Stoke	38	8	10	20	41	64	26

DIVISION TWO 1906-07

Nottingham Forest	38	28	4	6	74	36	60
Chelsea	38	26	5	7	80	34	57
Leicester Fosse	38	20	8	10	62	39	48
West Bromwich Albion	38	21	5	12	83	45	47
Bradford City	38	21	5	12	70	53	47
Wolverhampton Wanderers	38	17	7	14	66	53	41
Burnley	38	17	6	15	62	47	40
Barnsley	38	15	8	15	73	55	38
Hull City	38	15	7	16	65	57	37
Leeds City	38	13	10	15	55	63	36
Grimsby Town	38	16	3	19	57	62	35
Stockport County	38	12	11	15	42	52	35
Blackpool	38	11	11	16	33	51	33
Gainsborough Trinity	38	14	5	19	45	72	33
Glossop	38	13	6	19	53	79	32
Burslem Port Vale	38	12	7	19	60	83	31
Clapton Orient	38	11	8	19	45	67	30
Chesterfield Town	38	11	7	20	50	66	29
Lincoln City	38	12	4	22	46	73	28
Burton United	38	8	7	23	34	68	23

1907 F.A. Cup

Semi-finals

Woolwich Arsenal vs The Wednesday   1-3
West Bromwich Albion vs Everton   1-2

Final

Crystal Palace, 20th April 1907

The Wednesday 2   (Stewart, Simpson)
Everton 1   (Sharp)

Attendance 84,584

DIVISION ONE 1907-08

MANCHESTER UNITED	38	23	6	9	81	48	52
Aston Villa	38	17	9	12	77	59	43
Manchester City	38	16	11	11	62	54	43
Newcastle United	38	15	12	11	65	54	42
The Wednesday	38	19	4	15	73	64	42
Middlesbrough	38	17	7	14	54	45	41
Bury	38	14	11	13	58	61	39
Liverpool	38	16	6	16	68	61	38
Nottingham Forest	38	13	11	14	59	62	37
Bristol City	38	12	12	14	58	61	36
Everton	38	15	6	17	58	64	36
Preston North End	38	12	12	14	47	53	36
Chelsea	38	14	8	16	53	62	36
Blackburn Rovers	38	12	12	14	51	63	36
Woolwich Arsenal	38	12	12	14	51	63	36
Sunderland	38	16	3	19	78	75	35
Sheffield United	38	12	11	15	52	58	35
Notts County	38	13	8	17	39	51	34
Bolton Wanderers	38	14	5	19	52	58	33
Birmingham	38	9	12	17	40	60	30

DIVISION TWO 1907-08

Bradford City	38	24	6	8	90	42	54
Leicester Fosse	38	21	10	7	72	47	52
Oldham Athletic	38	22	6	10	76	42	50
Fulham	38	22	5	11	82	49	49
West Bromwich Albion	38	19	9	10	61	39	47
Derby County	38	21	4	13	77	45	46
Burnley	38	20	6	12	67	50	46
Hull City	38	21	4	13	73	62	46
Wolverhampton Wanderers	38	15	7	16	50	45	37
Stoke	38	16	5	17	57	52	37
Gainsborough Trinity	38	14	7	17	47	71	35
Leeds City	38	12	8	18	53	65	32
Stockport County	38	12	8	18	48	67	32
Clapton Orient	38	11	10	17	40	65	32
Blackpool	38	11	9	18	51	58	31
Barnsley	38	12	6	20	54	68	30
Glossop	38	11	8	19	54	74	30
Grimsby Town	38	11	8	19	43	71	30
Chesterfield Town	38	6	11	21	46	92	23
Lincoln City	38	9	3	26	46	83	21

1908 F.A. Cup

Semi-finals

Wolverhampton Wanderers vs Southampton   2-0
Newcastle United vs Fulham   6-0

Final

Crystal Palace, 25th April 1908

Wolverhampton Wanderers 3   (Hunt, Hedley, Harrison)
Newcastle United 1   (Howie)

Attendance 74,967

DIVISION ONE 1908-09

NEWCASTLE UNITED	38	24	5	9	65	41	53
Everton	38	18	10	10	82	57	46
Sunderland	38	21	2	15	78	63	44
Blackburn Rovers	38	14	13	11	61	50	41
The Wednesday	38	17	6	15	67	61	40
Woolwich Arsenal	38	14	10	14	52	49	38
Aston Villa	38	14	10	14	58	56	38
Bristol City	38	13	12	13	45	58	38
Middlesbrough	38	14	9	15	59	53	37
Preston North End	38	13	11	14	48	44	37
Chelsea	38	14	9	15	56	61	37
Sheffield United	38	14	9	15	51	59	37
Manchester United	38	15	7	16	58	68	37
Nottingham Forest	38	14	8	16	66	57	36
Notts County	38	14	8	16	51	48	36
Liverpool	38	15	6	17	57	65	36
Bury	38	14	8	16	63	77	36
Bradford City	38	12	10	16	47	47	34
Manchester City	*38*	*15*	*4*	*19*	*67*	*69*	*34*
Leicester Fosse	*38*	*8*	*9*	*21*	*54*	*102*	*25*

DIVISION TWO 1908-09

Bolton Wanderers	38	24	4	10	59	28	52
Tottenham Hotspur	38	20	11	7	67	32	51
West Bromwich Albion	38	19	13	6	56	27	51
Hull City	38	19	6	13	63	39	44
Derby County	38	16	11	11	55	41	43
Oldham Athletic	38	17	6	15	55	43	40
Wolverhampton Wanderers	38	14	11	13	56	48	39
Glossop	38	15	8	15	57	53	38
Gainsborough Trinity	38	15	8	15	49	70	38
Fulham	38	13	11	14	58	48	37
Birmingham	38	14	9	15	58	61	37
Leeds City	38	14	7	17	43	53	35
Grimsby Town	38	14	7	17	41	54	35
Burnley	38	13	7	18	51	58	33
Clapton Orient	38	12	9	17	37	49	33
Bradford Park Avenue	38	13	6	19	51	59	32
Barnsley	38	11	10	17	48	57	32
Stockport County	38	14	3	21	39	71	31
Chesterfield Town	*38*	*11*	*8*	*19*	*37*	*67*	*30*
Blackpool	38	9	11	18	46	68	29

1909 F.A. Cup

Semi-finals

Manchester United vs Newcastle United	1-0
Bristol City vs Derby County	1-1, 2-1

Final

Crystal Palace, 24th March 1909

Manchester United 1 (A. Turnbull)

Bristol City 0

Attendance 71,401

DIVISION ONE 1909-10

ASTON VILLA	38	23	7	8	84	42	53
Liverpool	38	21	6	11	78	57	48
Blackburn Rovers	38	18	9	11	73	55	45
Newcastle United	38	19	7	12	70	56	45
Manchester United	38	19	7	12	69	61	45
Sheffield United	38	16	10	12	62	41	42
Bradford City	38	17	8	13	64	47	42
Sunderland	38	18	5	15	66	51	41
Notts County	38	15	10	13	67	59	40
Everton	38	16	8	14	51	56	40
The Wednesday	38	15	9	14	60	63	39
Preston North End	38	15	5	18	52	58	35
Bury	38	12	9	17	62	66	33
Nottingham Forest	38	11	11	16	54	72	33
Tottenham Hotspur	38	11	10	17	53	69	32
Bristol City	38	12	8	18	45	60	32
Middlesbrough	38	11	9	18	56	73	31
Woolwich Arsenal	38	11	9	18	37	67	31
Chelsea	*38*	*11*	*7*	*20*	*47*	*70*	*29*
Bolton Wanderers	*38*	*9*	*6*	*23*	*44*	*71*	*24*

DIVISION TWO 1909-10

Manchester City	38	23	8	7	81	40	54
Oldham Athletic	38	23	7	8	79	39	53
Hull City	38	23	7	8	80	46	53
Derby County	38	22	9	7	72	47	53
Leicester Fosse	38	20	4	14	79	58	44
Glossop	38	18	7	13	64	57	43
Fulham	38	14	13	11	51	43	41
Wolverhampton Wanderers	38	17	6	15	64	63	40
Barnsley	38	16	7	15	62	59	39
Bradford Park Avenue	38	17	4	17	64	59	38
West Bromwich Albion	38	16	5	17	58	56	37
Blackpool	38	14	8	16	50	52	36
Stockport County	38	13	8	17	50	47	34
Burnley	38	14	6	18	62	61	34
Lincoln City	38	10	11	17	42	69	31
Clapton Orient	38	12	6	20	37	60	30
Leeds City	38	10	7	21	46	80	27
Gainsborough Trinity	38	10	6	22	33	75	26
Grimsby Town	*38*	*9*	*6*	*23*	*50*	*77*	*24*
Birmingham	38	8	7	23	42	78	23

1910 F.A. Cup

Semi-finals

Newcastle United vs Swindon Town	2-0
Barnsley vs Everton	0-0, 3-0

Final

Crystal Palace, 23rd April 1910

Newcastle United 1 (Rutherford)

Barnsley 1 (Tufnell)

Attendance 77,747

Replay

Goodison Park, 28th April 1910

Newcastle United 2 (Shepherd 2 (1 pen))

Barnsley 0

Attendance 69,000

DIVISION ONE 1910-11

MANCHESTER UNITED	38	22	8	8	72	40	52
Aston Villa	38	22	7	9	69	41	51
Sunderland	38	15	15	8	67	48	45
Everton	38	19	7	12	50	36	45
Bradford City	38	20	5	13	51	42	45
The Wednesday	38	17	8	13	47	48	42
Oldham Athletic	38	16	9	13	44	41	41
Newcastle United	38	15	10	13	61	43	40
Sheffield United	38	15	8	15	49	43	38
Woolwich Arsenal	38	13	12	13	41	49	38
Notts County	38	14	10	14	37	45	38
Blackburn Rovers	38	13	11	14	62	54	37
Liverpool	38	15	7	16	53	53	37
Preston North End	38	12	11	15	40	49	35
Tottenham Hotspur	38	13	6	19	52	63	32
Middlesbrough	38	11	10	17	49	63	32
Manchester City	38	9	13	16	43	58	31
Bury	38	9	11	18	43	71	29
Bristol City	*38*	*11*	*5*	*22*	*43*	*66*	*27*
Nottingham Forest	*38*	*9*	*7*	*22*	*55*	*75*	*25*

DIVISION TWO 1910-11

West Bromwich Albion	38	22	9	7	67	41	53
Bolton Wanderers	38	21	9	8	69	40	51
Chelsea	38	20	9	9	71	35	49
Clapton Orient	38	19	7	12	44	35	45
Hull City	38	14	16	8	55	39	44
Derby County	38	17	8	13	73	52	42
Blackpool	38	16	10	12	49	38	42
Burnley	38	13	15	10	45	45	41
Wolverhampton Wanderers	38	15	8	15	51	52	38
Fulham	38	15	7	16	52	48	37
Leeds City	38	15	7	16	58	56	37
Bradford Park Avenue	38	14	9	15	53	55	37
Huddersfield Town	38	13	8	17	57	58	34
Glossop	38	13	8	17	48	62	34
Leicester Fosse	38	14	5	19	52	62	33
Birmingham	38	12	8	18	42	64	32
Stockport County	38	11	8	19	47	79	30
Gainsborough Trinity	38	9	11	18	37	55	29
Barnsley	38	7	14	17	52	62	28
Lincoln City	*38*	*7*	*10*	*21*	*28*	*72*	*24*

DIVISION TWO 1911-12

Derby County	38	23	8	7	74	28	54
Chelsea	38	24	6	8	64	34	54
Burnley	38	22	8	8	77	41	52
Clapton Orient	38	21	3	14	61	44	45
Wolverhampton Wanderers	38	16	10	12	57	33	42
Barnsley	38	15	12	11	45	42	42
Hull City	38	17	8	13	54	51	42
Fulham	38	16	7	15	66	58	39
Grimsby Town	38	15	9	14	48	55	39
Leicester Fosse	38	15	7	16	49	66	37
Bradford Park Avenue	38	13	9	16	44	45	35
Birmingham	38	14	6	18	55	59	34
Bristol City	38	14	6	18	41	60	34
Blackpool	38	13	8	17	32	52	34
Nottingham Forest	38	13	7	18	46	48	33
Stockport County	38	11	11	16	47	54	33
Huddersfield Town	38	13	6	19	50	64	32
Glossop	38	8	12	18	42	56	28
Leeds City	38	10	8	20	50	78	28
Gainsborough Trinity	*38*	*5*	*13*	*20*	*30*	*64*	*23*

1911 F.A. Cup

Semi-finals

Bradford City vs Blackburn Rovers	3-0
Newcastle United vs Chelsea	3-0

Final

Crystal Palace, 22nd April 1911

Bradford City 0
Newcastle United 0

Attendance 69,098

Replay

Old Trafford, 26th April 1911

Bradford City 1 (Spiers)
Newcastle United 0

Attendance 58,000

1912 F.A. Cup

Semi-finals

Swindon Town vs Barnsley	0-0, 0-1
Blackburn Rovers vs West Bromwich Albion	0-0, 0-1

Final

Crystal Palace, 20th April 1912

Barnsley 0
West Bromwich Albion 0

Attendance 54,556

Replay

Bramall Lane, 24th April 1912

Barnsley 1 (Tufnell)
West Bromwich Albion 0 (aet.)

Attendance 38,555

DIVISION ONE 1911-12

BLACKBURN ROVERS	38	20	9	9	60	43	49
Everton	38	20	6	12	46	42	46
Newcastle United	38	18	8	12	64	50	44
Bolton Wanderers	38	20	3	15	54	43	43
The Wednesday	38	16	9	13	69	49	41
Aston Villa	38	17	7	14	76	63	41
Middlesbrough	38	16	8	14	56	45	40
Sunderland	38	14	11	13	58	51	39
West Bromwich Albion	38	15	9	14	43	47	39
Woolwich Arsenal	38	15	8	15	55	59	38
Bradford City	38	15	8	15	46	50	38
Tottenham Hotspur	38	14	9	15	53	53	37
Manchester United	38	13	11	14	45	60	37
Sheffield United	38	13	10	15	63	56	36
Manchester City	38	13	9	16	56	58	35
Notts County	38	14	7	17	46	63	35
Liverpool	38	12	10	16	49	55	34
Oldham Athletic	38	12	10	16	46	54	34
Preston North End	*38*	*13*	*7*	*18*	*40*	*57*	*33*
Bury	*38*	*6*	*9*	*23*	*32*	*59*	*21*

DIVISION ONE 1912-13

SUNDERLAND	38	25	4	9	86	43	54
Aston Villa	38	19	12	7	86	52	50
The Wednesday	38	21	7	10	75	55	49
Manchester United	38	19	8	11	69	43	46
Blackburn Rovers	38	16	13	9	79	43	45
Manchester City	38	18	8	12	53	37	44
Derby County	38	17	8	13	69	66	42
Bolton Wanderers	38	16	10	12	62	63	42
Oldham Athletic	38	14	14	10	50	55	42
West Bromwich Albion	38	13	12	13	57	50	38
Everton	38	15	7	16	48	54	37
Liverpool	38	16	5	17	61	71	37
Bradford City	38	12	11	15	50	60	35
Newcastle United	38	13	8	17	47	47	34
Sheffield United	38	14	6	18	56	70	34
Middlesbrough	38	11	10	17	55	69	32
Tottenham Hotspur	38	12	6	20	45	72	30
Chelsea	38	11	6	21	51	73	28
Notts County	*38*	*7*	*9*	*22*	*28*	*56*	*23*
Woolwich Arsenal	*38*	*3*	*12*	*23*	*26*	*74*	*18*

DIVISION TWO 1912-13

Preston North End	38	19	15	4	56	33	53
Burnley	38	21	8	9	88	53	50
Birmingham	38	18	10	10	59	44	46
Barnsley	38	19	7	12	57	47	45
Huddersfield Town	38	17	9	12	66	40	43
Leeds City	38	15	10	13	70	64	40
Grimsby Town	38	15	10	13	51	50	40
Lincoln City	38	15	10	13	50	52	40
Fulham	38	17	5	16	65	55	39
Wolverhampton Wanderers	38	14	10	14	56	54	38
Bury	38	15	8	15	53	57	38
Hull City	38	15	6	17	60	56	36
Bradford Park Avenue	38	14	8	16	60	60	36
Clapton Orient	38	10	14	14	34	47	34
Leicester Fosse	38	13	7	18	50	65	33
Bristol City	38	9	15	14	46	72	33
Nottingham Forest	38	12	8	18	58	59	32
Glossop	38	12	8	18	49	68	32
Stockport County	38	8	10	20	56	78	26
Blackpool	38	9	8	21	39	69	26

1913 F.A. Cup

Semi-finals
Aston Villa vs Oldham Athletic   1-0
Sunderland vs Burnley   0-0, 3-2

Final
Crystal Palace, 19th April 1913

Aston Villa 1 (Barber)
Sunderland 0

Attendance 120,081

DIVISION ONE 1913-14

BLACKBURN ROVERS	38	20	11	7	78	42	51
Aston Villa	38	19	6	13	65	50	44
Middlesbrough	38	19	5	14	77	60	43
Oldham Athletic	38	17	9	12	55	45	43
West Bromwich Albion	38	15	13	10	46	42	43
Bolton Wanderers	38	16	10	12	65	52	42
Sunderland	38	17	6	15	63	52	40
Chelsea	38	16	7	15	46	55	39
Bradford City	38	12	14	12	40	40	38
Sheffield United	38	16	5	17	63	60	37
Newcastle United	38	13	11	14	39	48	37
Burnley	38	12	12	14	61	53	36
Manchester City	38	14	8	16	51	53	36
Manchester United	38	15	6	17	52	62	36
Everton	38	12	11	15	46	55	35
Liverpool	38	14	7	17	46	62	35
Tottenham Hotspur	38	12	10	16	50	62	34
The Wednesday	38	13	8	17	53	70	34
Preston North End	38	12	6	20	52	69	30
Derby County	38	8	11	19	55	71	27

DIVISION TWO 1913-14

Notts County	38	23	7	8	77	36	53
Bradford Park Avenue	38	23	3	12	71	47	49
The Arsenal	38	20	9	9	54	38	49
Leeds City	38	20	7	11	76	46	47
Barnsley	38	19	7	12	51	45	45
Clapton Orient	38	16	11	11	47	35	43
Hull City	38	16	9	13	53	37	41
Bristol City	38	16	9	13	52	50	41
Wolverhampton Wanderers	38	18	5	15	51	52	41
Bury	38	15	10	13	39	40	40
Fulham	38	16	6	16	46	43	38
Stockport County	38	13	10	15	55	57	36
Huddersfield Town	38	13	8	17	47	53	34
Birmingham	38	12	10	16	48	60	34
Grimsby Town	38	13	8	17	42	58	34
Blackpool	38	9	14	15	33	44	32
Glossop	38	11	6	21	51	67	28
Leicester Fosse	38	11	4	23	45	61	26
Lincoln City	38	10	6	22	36	66	26
Nottingham Forest	38	7	9	22	37	76	23

1914 F.A. Cup

Semi-finals
Sheffield United vs Burnley   0-0, 0-1
Aston Villa vs Liverpool   0-2

Final
Crystal Palace, 25th April 1914

Burnley 1 (Freeman)
Liverpool 0

Attendance 72,778

DIVISION ONE 1914-15

EVERTON	38	19	8	11	76	47	46
Oldham Athletic	38	17	11	10	70	56	45
Blackburn Rovers	38	18	7	13	83	61	43
Burnley	38	18	7	13	61	47	43
Manchester City	38	15	13	10	49	39	43
Sheffield United	38	15	13	10	49	41	43
The Wednesday	38	15	13	10	61	54	43
Sunderland	38	18	5	15	81	72	41
Bradford Park Avenue	38	17	7	14	69	65	41
West Bromwich Albion	38	15	10	13	49	43	40
Bradford City	38	13	14	11	55	49	40
Middlesbrough	38	13	12	13	62	74	38
Liverpool	38	14	9	15	65	75	37
Aston Villa	38	13	11	14	62	72	37
Newcastle United	38	11	10	17	46	48	32
Notts County	38	9	13	16	41	57	31
Bolton Wanderers	38	11	8	19	68	84	30
Manchester United	38	9	12	17	46	62	30
Chelsea	38	8	13	17	51	65	29
Tottenham Hotspur	38	8	12	18	57	90	28

DIVISION TWO 1914-15

Derby County	38	23	7	8	71	33	53
Preston North End	38	20	10	8	61	42	50
Barnsley	38	22	3	13	51	51	47
Wolverhampton Wanderers	38	19	7	12	77	52	45
The Arsenal	38	19	5	14	69	41	43
Birmingham	38	17	9	12	62	39	43
Hull City	38	19	5	14	65	54	43
Huddersfield Town	38	17	8	13	61	42	42
Clapton Orient	38	16	9	13	50	48	41
Blackpool	38	17	5	16	58	57	39
Bury	38	15	8	15	61	56	38
Fulham	38	15	7	16	53	47	37
Bristol City	38	15	7	16	62	56	37
Stockport County	38	15	7	16	54	60	37
Leeds City	38	14	4	20	65	64	32
Lincoln City	38	11	9	18	46	65	31
Grimsby Town	38	11	9	18	48	76	31
Nottingham Forest	38	10	9	19	43	77	29
Leicester Fosse	38	10	4	24	47	88	24
Glossop	38	6	6	26	31	87	18

1915 F.A. Cup

Semi-finals
Sheffield United vs Bolton Wanderers   2-1
Chelsea vs Everton   2-0

Final
Old Trafford, 24th April 1915

Sheffield United 3 (Simmons, Kitchen, Fazackerley)
Chelsea 0

Attendance 49,557

DIVISION ONE 1919-20

WEST BROMWICH ALBION	42	28	4	10	104	47	60
Burnley	42	21	9	12	65	59	51
Chelsea	42	22	5	15	56	51	49
Liverpool	42	19	10	13	59	44	48
Sunderland	42	22	4	16	72	59	48
Bolton Wanderers	42	19	9	14	72	65	47
Manchester City	42	18	9	15	71	62	45
Newcastle United	42	17	9	16	44	39	43
Aston Villa	42	18	6	18	75	73	42
Arsenal	42	15	12	15	56	58	42
Bradford Park Avenue	42	15	12	15	60	63	42
Manchester United	42	13	14	15	54	50	40
Middlesbrough	42	15	10	17	61	65	40
Sheffield United	42	16	8	18	59	69	40
Bradford City	42	14	11	17	54	63	39
Everton	42	12	14	16	69	68	38
Oldham Athletic	42	15	8	19	49	52	38
Derby County	42	13	12	17	47	57	38
Preston North End	42	14	10	18	57	73	38
Blackburn Rovers	42	13	11	18	64	77	37
Notts County	*42*	*12*	*12*	*18*	*56*	*74*	*36*
The Wednesday	*42*	*7*	*9*	*26*	*28*	*64*	*23*

DIVISION ONE 1920-21

BURNLEY	42	23	13	6	79	36	59
Manchester City	42	24	6	12	70	50	54
Bolton Wanderers	42	19	14	9	77	53	52
Liverpool	42	18	15	9	63	35	51
Newcastle United	42	20	10	12	66	45	50
Tottenham Hotspur	42	19	9	14	70	48	47
Everton	42	17	13	12	66	55	47
Middlesbrough	42	17	12	13	53	53	46
Arsenal	42	15	14	13	59	63	44
Aston Villa	42	18	7	17	63	70	43
Blackburn Rovers	42	13	15	14	57	59	41
Sunderland	42	14	13	15	57	60	41
Manchester United	42	15	10	17	64	68	40
West Bromwich Albion	42	13	14	15	54	58	40
Bradford City	42	12	15	15	61	63	39
Preston North End	42	15	9	18	61	65	39
Huddersfield Town	42	15	9	18	42	49	39
Chelsea	42	13	13	16	48	58	39
Oldham Athletic	42	9	15	18	49	86	33
Sheffield United	42	6	18	18	42	68	30
Derby County	*42*	*5*	*16*	*21*	*32*	*58*	*26*
Bradford Park Avenue	*42*	*8*	*8*	*26*	*43*	*76*	*24*

DIVISION TWO 1919-20

Tottenham Hotspur	42	32	6	4	102	32	70
Huddersfield Town	42	28	8	6	97	38	64
Birmingham	42	24	8	10	85	34	56
Blackpool	42	21	10	11	65	47	52
Bury	42	20	8	14	60	44	48
Fulham	42	19	9	14	61	50	47
West Ham United	42	19	9	14	47	40	47
Bristol City	42	13	17	12	46	43	43
South Shields	42	15	12	15	58	48	42
Stoke City	42	18	6	18	60	54	42
Hull City	42	18	6	18	78	72	42
Barnsley	42	15	10	17	61	55	40
Port Vale	42	16	8	18	59	62	40
Leicester City	42	15	10	17	41	61	40
Clapton Orient	42	16	6	20	51	59	38
Stockport County	42	14	9	19	52	61	37
Rotherham County	42	13	8	21	51	83	34
Nottingham Forest	42	11	9	22	43	73	31
Wolverhampton Wanderers	42	10	10	22	55	80	30
Coventry City	42	9	11	22	35	73	29
Lincoln City	*42*	*9*	*9*	*24*	*44*	*101*	*27*
Grimsby Town	*42*	*10*	*5*	*27*	*34*	*75*	*25*

Leeds City were expelled from the League after 8 matches of the season due to financial irregularities. Port Vale took over their fixtures and their final figures include the following statistics from Leeds City   8   4   2   2   17   10   10

DIVISION TWO 1920-21

Birmingham	42	24	10	8	79	38	58
Cardiff City	42	24	10	8	59	32	58
Bristol City	42	19	13	10	49	29	51
Blackpool	42	20	10	12	54	42	50
West Ham United	42	19	10	13	51	30	48
Notts County	42	18	11	13	55	40	47
Clapton Orient	42	16	13	13	43	42	45
South Shields	42	17	10	15	61	46	44
Fulham	42	16	10	16	43	47	42
The Wednesday	42	15	11	16	48	48	41
Bury	42	15	10	17	45	49	40
Leicester City	42	12	16	14	39	46	40
Hull City	42	10	20	12	43	53	40
Leeds United	42	14	10	18	40	45	38
Wolverhampton Wanderers	42	16	6	20	49	66	38
Barnsley	42	10	16	16	48	50	36
Port Vale	42	11	14	17	43	49	36
Nottingham Forest	42	12	12	18	48	55	36
Rotherham County	42	12	12	18	37	53	36
Stoke City	42	12	11	19	46	56	35
Coventry City	42	12	11	19	39	70	35
Stockport County	*42*	*9*	*12*	*21*	*42*	*75*	*30*

DIVISION THREE 1920-21

Crystal Palace	42	24	11	7	70	34	59
Southampton	42	19	16	7	64	28	54
Queen's Park Rangers	42	22	9	11	61	32	53
Swindon Town	42	21	10	11	73	49	52
Swansea Town	42	18	15	9	56	45	51
Watford	42	20	8	14	59	44	48
Millwall Athletic	42	18	11	13	42	30	47
Merthyr Town	42	15	15	12	60	49	45
Luton Town	42	16	12	14	61	56	44
Bristol Rovers	42	18	7	17	68	57	43
Plymouth Argyle	42	11	21	10	35	34	43
Portsmouth	42	12	15	15	46	48	39
Grimsby Town	42	15	9	18	49	59	39
Northampton Town	42	15	8	19	59	75	38
Newport County	42	14	9	19	43	64	37
Norwich City	42	10	16	16	44	53	36
Southend United	42	14	8	20	44	61	36
Brighton & Hove Albion	42	14	8	20	42	61	36
Exeter City	42	10	15	17	39	54	35
Reading	42	12	7	23	42	59	31
Brentford	42	9	12	21	42	67	30
Gillingham	42	8	12	22	34	74	28

1920 F.A. Cup

Semi-finals

Aston Villa vs Chelsea	3-1
Huddersfield Town vs Bristol City	2-1

Final

Stamford Bridge, 24th April 1920

Aston Villa 1 (Kirton)
Huddersfield Town 0 (aet.)

Attendance 50,018

1921 F.A. Cup

Semi-finals

Tottenham Hotspur vs Preston North End	2-1
Wolverhampton Wanderers vs Cardiff City	0-0, 3-1

Final

Stamford Bridge, 23rd April 1921

Tottenham Hotspur 1 (Dimmock)
Wolverhampton Wanderers 0

Attendance 72,805

DIVISION ONE 1921-22

LIVERPOOL	42	22	13	7	63	36	57
Tottenham Hotspur	42	21	9	12	65	39	51
Burnley	42	22	5	15	72	54	49
Cardiff City	42	19	10	13	61	53	48
Aston Villa	42	22	3	17	74	55	47
Bolton Wanderers	42	20	7	15	68	59	47
Newcastle United	42	18	10	14	59	45	46
Middlesbrough	42	16	14	12	79	69	46
Chelsea	42	17	12	13	40	43	46
Manchester City	42	18	9	15	65	70	45
Sheffield United	42	15	10	17	59	54	40
Sunderland	42	16	8	18	60	62	40
West Bromwich Albion	42	15	10	17	51	63	40
Huddersfield Town	42	15	9	18	53	54	39
Blackburn Rovers	42	13	12	17	54	57	38
Preston North End	42	13	12	17	42	65	38
Arsenal	42	15	7	20	47	56	37
Birmingham	42	15	7	20	48	60	37
Oldham Athletic	42	13	11	18	38	50	37
Everton	42	12	12	18	57	55	36
Bradford City	*42*	*11*	*10*	*21*	*48*	*72*	*32*
Manchester United	*42*	*8*	*12*	*22*	*41*	*73*	*28*

DIVISION TWO 1921-22

Nottingham Forest	42	22	12	8	51	30	56
Stoke City	42	18	16	8	60	44	52
Barnsley	42	22	8	12	67	52	52
West Ham United	42	20	8	14	52	39	48
Hull City	42	19	10	13	51	41	48
South Shields	42	17	12	13	43	38	46
Fulham	42	18	9	15	57	38	45
Leeds United	42	16	13	13	48	38	45
Leicester City	42	14	17	11	39	34	45
The Wednesday	42	15	14	13	47	50	44
Bury	42	15	10	17	54	55	40
Derby County	42	15	9	18	60	64	39
Notts County	42	12	15	15	47	51	39
Crystal Palace	42	13	13	16	45	51	39
Clapton Orient	42	15	9	18	43	50	39
Rotherham County	42	14	11	17	32	43	39
Wolverhampton Wanderers	42	13	11	18	44	49	37
Port Vale	42	14	8	20	43	57	36
Blackpool	42	15	5	22	44	57	35
Coventry City	42	12	10	20	51	60	34
Bradford Park Avenue	*42*	*12*	*9*	*21*	*46*	*62*	*33*
Bristol City	*42*	*12*	*9*	*21*	*37*	*58*	*33*

DIVISION THREE (N) 1921-22

Stockport County	38	24	8	6	60	21	56
Darlington	38	22	6	10	81	37	50
Grimsby Town	38	21	8	9	72	47	50
Hartlepools United	38	17	8	13	52	39	42
Accrington Stanley	38	19	3	16	73	57	41
Crewe Alexandra	38	18	5	15	60	56	41
Stalybridge Celtic	38	18	5	15	62	63	41
Walsall	38	18	3	17	66	65	39
Southport	38	14	10	14	55	44	38
Ashington	38	17	4	17	59	66	38
Durham City	38	17	3	18	68	67	37
Wrexham	38	14	9	15	51	56	37
Chesterfield	38	16	3	19	48	67	35
Lincoln City	38	14	6	18	48	59	34
Barrow	38	14	5	19	42	54	33
Nelson	38	13	7	18	48	66	33
Wigan Borough	38	11	9	18	46	72	31
Tranmere Rovers	38	9	11	18	51	61	29
Halifax Town	38	10	9	19	56	76	29
Rochdale	38	11	4	23	52	77	26

DIVISION THREE (S) 1921-22

Southampton	42	23	15	4	68	21	61
Plymouth Argyle	42	25	11	6	63	24	61
Portsmouth	42	18	17	7	62	39	53
Luton Town	42	22	8	12	64	35	52
Queen's Park Rangers	42	18	13	11	53	44	49
Swindon Town	42	16	13	13	72	60	45
Watford	42	13	18	11	54	48	44
Aberdare Athletic	42	17	10	15	57	51	44
Brentford	42	16	11	15	52	43	43
Swansea Town	42	13	15	14	50	47	41
Merthyr Town	42	17	6	19	45	56	40
Millwall Athletic	42	10	18	14	38	42	38
Reading	42	14	10	18	40	47	38
Bristol Rovers	42	14	10	18	52	67	38
Norwich City	42	12	13	17	50	62	37
Charlton Athletic	42	13	11	18	43	56	37
Northampton Town	42	13	11	18	47	71	37
Gillingham	42	14	8	20	47	60	36
Brighton & Hove Albion	42	13	9	20	45	51	35
Newport County	42	11	12	19	44	61	34
Exeter City	42	11	12	19	38	59	34
Southend United	42	8	11	23	34	74	27

1922 F.A. Cup

Semi-finals

Huddersfield Town vs Notts County	3-1
Preston North End vs Tottenham Hotspur	2-1

Final

Stamford Bridge, 29th April 1922

Huddersfield Town 1 (Smith (pen))
Preston North End 0

Attendance 53,000

DIVISION ONE 1922-23

LIVERPOOL	42	26	8	8	70	31	60
Sunderland	42	22	10	10	72	54	54
Huddersfield Town	42	21	11	10	60	32	53
Newcastle United	42	18	12	12	45	37	48
Everton	42	20	7	15	63	59	47
Aston Villa	42	18	10	14	64	51	46
West Bromwich Albion	42	17	11	14	58	49	45
Manchester City	42	17	11	14	50	49	45
Cardiff City	42	18	7	17	73	59	43
Sheffield United	42	16	10	16	68	64	42
Arsenal	42	16	10	16	61	62	42
Tottenham Hotspur	42	17	7	18	50	50	41
Bolton Wanderers	42	14	12	16	50	58	40
Blackburn Rovers	42	14	12	16	47	62	40
Burnley	42	16	6	20	58	59	38
Preston North End	42	13	11	18	60	64	37
Birmingham	42	13	11	18	41	57	37
Middlesbrough	42	13	10	19	57	63	36
Chelsea	42	9	18	15	45	53	36
Nottingham Forest	42	13	8	21	41	70	34
Stoke City	*42*	*10*	*10*	*22*	*47*	*67*	*30*
Oldham Athletic	*42*	*10*	*10*	*22*	*35*	*65*	*30*

DIVISION THREE (N) 1922-23

Nelson	38	24	3	11	61	41	51
Bradford Park Avenue	38	19	9	10	67	38	47
Walsall	38	19	8	11	51	44	46
Chesterfield	38	19	7	12	68	52	45
Wigan Borough	38	18	8	12	64	39	44
Crewe Alexandra	38	17	9	12	48	38	43
Halifax Town	38	17	7	14	53	46	41
Accrington Stanley	38	17	7	14	59	65	41
Darlington	38	15	10	13	59	46	40
Wrexham	38	14	10	14	38	48	38
Stalybridge Celtic	*38*	*15*	*6*	*17*	*42*	*47*	*36*
Rochdale	38	13	10	15	42	53	36
Lincoln City	38	13	10	15	39	55	36
Grimsby Town	38	14	5	19	55	52	33
Hartlepools United	38	10	12	16	48	54	32
Tranmere Rovers	38	12	8	18	49	59	32
Southport	38	12	7	19	32	46	31
Barrow	38	13	4	21	50	60	30
Ashington	38	11	8	19	51	77	30
Durham City	38	9	10	19	43	59	28

DIVISION TWO 1922-23

Notts County	42	23	7	12	46	34	53
West Ham United	42	20	11	11	63	38	51
Leicester City	42	21	9	12	65	44	51
Manchester United	42	17	14	11	51	36	48
Blackpool	42	18	11	13	60	43	47
Bury	42	18	11	13	55	46	47
Leeds United	42	18	11	13	43	36	47
The Wednesday	42	17	12	13	54	47	46
Barnsley	42	17	11	14	62	51	45
Fulham	42	16	12	14	43	32	44
Southampton	42	14	14	14	40	40	42
Hull City	42	14	14	14	43	45	42
South Shields	42	15	10	17	35	44	40
Derby County	42	14	11	17	46	50	39
Bradford City	42	12	13	17	41	45	37
Crystal Palace	42	13	11	18	54	62	37
Port Vale	42	14	9	19	39	51	37
Coventry City	42	15	7	20	46	63	37
Clapton Orient	42	12	12	18	40	50	36
Stockport County	42	14	8	20	43	58	36
Rotherham County	*42*	*13*	*9*	*20*	*44*	*63*	*35*
Wolverhampton Wanderers	*42*	*9*	*9*	*24*	*42*	*77*	*27*

DIVISION THREE (S) 1922-23

Bristol City	42	24	11	7	66	40	59
Plymouth Argyle	42	23	7	12	61	29	53
Swansea Town	42	22	9	11	78	45	53
Brighton & Hove Albion	42	20	11	11	52	34	51
Luton Town	42	21	7	14	68	49	49
Millwall Athletic	42	14	18	10	45	40	46
Portsmouth	42	19	8	15	58	52	46
Northampton Town	42	17	11	14	54	44	45
Swindon Town	42	17	11	14	62	56	45
Watford	42	17	10	15	57	54	44
Queen's Park Rangers	42	16	10	16	54	49	42
Charlton Athletic	42	14	14	14	55	51	42
Bristol Rovers	42	13	16	13	35	36	42
Brentford	42	13	12	17	41	51	38
Southend United	42	12	13	17	49	54	37
Gillingham	42	15	7	20	51	59	37
Merthyr Town	42	11	14	17	39	48	36
Norwich City	42	13	10	19	51	71	36
Reading	42	10	14	18	36	55	34
Exeter City	42	13	7	22	47	84	33
Aberdare Athletic	42	9	11	22	42	70	29
Newport County	42	8	11	23	40	70	27

1923 F.A. Cup

Semi-finals

Bolton Wanderers vs Sheffield United	1-0
West Ham United vs Derby County	5-2

Final

Wembley, 28th April 1923

Bolton Wanderers 2 (Jack, J.R. Smith)

West Ham United 0

Official Attendance 126,047 (the actual attendance could have been as high as 200,000)

DIVISION ONE 1923-24

HUDDERSFIELD TOWN	42	23	11	8	60	33	57
Cardiff City	42	22	13	7	61	34	57
Sunderland	42	22	9	11	71	54	53
Bolton Wanderers	42	18	14	10	68	34	50
Sheffield United	42	19	12	11	69	49	50
Aston Villa	42	18	13	11	52	37	49
Everton	42	18	13	11	62	53	49
Blackburn Rovers	42	17	11	14	54	50	45
Newcastle United	42	17	10	15	60	54	44
Notts County	42	14	14	14	44	49	42
Manchester City	42	15	12	15	54	71	42
Liverpool	42	15	11	16	49	48	41
West Ham United	42	13	15	14	40	43	41
Birmingham	42	13	13	16	41	49	39
Tottenham Hotspur	42	12	14	16	50	56	38
West Bromwich Albion	42	12	14	16	51	62	38
Burnley	42	12	12	18	55	60	36
Preston North End	42	12	10	20	52	67	34
Arsenal	42	12	9	21	40	63	33
Nottingham Forest	42	10	12	20	42	64	32
Chelsea	*42*	*9*	*14*	*19*	*31*	*53*	*32*
Middlesbrough	*42*	*7*	*8*	*27*	*37*	*60*	*22*

DIVISION THREE (N) 1923-24

Wolverhampton Wanderers	42	24	15	3	76	27	63
Rochdale	42	25	12	5	60	26	62
Chesterfield	42	22	10	10	70	39	54
Rotherham County	42	23	6	13	70	43	52
Bradford Park Avenue	42	21	10	11	69	43	52
Darlington	42	20	8	14	70	53	48
Southport	42	16	14	12	44	42	46
Ashington	42	18	8	16	59	61	44
Doncaster Rovers	42	15	12	15	59	53	42
Wigan Borough	42	14	14	14	55	53	42
Grimsby Town	42	14	13	15	49	47	41
Tranmere Rovers	42	13	15	14	51	60	41
Accrington Stanley	42	16	8	18	48	61	40
Halifax Town	42	15	10	17	42	59	40
Durham City	42	15	9	18	59	60	39
Wrexham	42	10	18	14	37	44	38
Walsall	42	14	8	20	44	59	36
New Brighton	42	11	13	18	40	53	35
Lincoln City	42	10	12	20	48	59	32
Crewe Alexandra	42	7	13	22	32	58	27
Hartlepools United	42	7	11	24	33	70	25
Barrow	42	8	9	25	35	80	25

DIVISION TWO 1923-24

Leeds United	42	21	12	9	61	35	54
Bury	42	21	9	12	63	35	51
Derby County	42	21	9	12	75	42	51
Blackpool	42	18	13	11	72	47	49
Southampton	42	17	14	11	52	31	48
Stoke City	42	14	18	10	44	42	46
Oldham Athletic	42	14	17	11	45	52	45
The Wednesday	42	16	12	14	54	51	44
South Shields	42	17	10	15	49	50	44
Clapton Orient	42	14	15	13	40	36	43
Barnsley	42	16	11	15	57	61	43
Leicester City	42	17	8	17	64	54	42
Stockport County	42	13	16	13	44	52	42
Manchester United	42	13	14	15	52	44	40
Crystal Palace	42	13	13	16	53	65	39
Port Vale	42	13	12	17	50	66	38
Hull City	42	10	17	15	46	51	37
Bradford City	42	11	15	16	35	48	37
Coventry City	42	11	13	18	52	68	35
Fulham	42	10	14	18	45	56	34
Nelson	*42*	*10*	*13*	*19*	*40*	*74*	*33*
Bristol City	*42*	*7*	*15*	*20*	*32*	*65*	*29*

DIVISION THREE (S) 1923-24

Portsmouth	42	24	11	7	87	30	59
Plymouth Argyle	42	23	9	10	70	34	55
Millwall Athletic	42	22	10	10	64	38	54
Swansea Town	42	22	8	12	60	48	52
Brighton & Hove Albion	42	21	9	12	68	37	51
Swindon Town	42	17	13	12	58	44	47
Luton Town	42	16	14	12	50	44	46
Northampton Town	42	17	11	14	64	47	45
Bristol Rovers	42	15	13	14	52	46	43
Newport County	42	17	9	16	56	64	43
Norwich City	42	16	8	18	60	59	40
Aberdare Athletic	42	12	14	16	45	58	38
Merthyr Town	42	11	16	15	45	65	38
Charlton Athletic	42	11	15	16	38	45	37
Gillingham	42	12	13	17	43	58	37
Exeter City	42	15	7	20	37	52	37
Brentford	42	14	8	20	54	71	36
Reading	42	13	9	20	51	57	35
Southend United	42	12	10	20	53	84	34
Watford	42	9	15	18	45	54	33
Bournemouth	42	11	11	20	40	65	33
Queen's Park Rangers	42	11	9	22	37	77	31

1924 F.A. Cup

Semi-finals

Newcastle United vs Manchester City	2-0
Aston Villa vs Burnley	3-0

Final

Wembley, 26th April 1924

Newcastle United 2 (Harris, Seymour)

Aston Villa 0

Attendance 91,695

DIVISION ONE 1924-25

HUDDERSFIELD TOWN	42	21	16	5	69	28	58
West Bromwich Albion	42	23	10	9	58	34	56
Bolton Wanderers	42	22	11	9	76	34	55
Liverpool	42	20	10	12	63	55	50
Bury	42	17	15	10	54	51	49
Newcastle United	42	16	16	10	61	42	48
Sunderland	42	19	10	13	64	51	48
Birmingham	42	17	12	13	49	53	46
Notts County	42	16	13	13	42	31	45
Manchester City	42	17	9	16	76	68	43
Cardiff City	42	16	11	15	56	51	43
Tottenham Hotspur	42	15	12	15	52	43	42
West Ham United	42	15	12	15	62	60	42
Sheffield United	42	13	13	16	55	63	39
Aston Villa	42	13	13	16	58	71	39
Blackburn Rovers	42	11	13	18	53	66	35
Everton	42	12	11	19	40	60	35
Leeds United	42	11	12	19	46	59	34
Burnley	42	11	12	19	46	75	34
Arsenal	42	14	5	23	46	58	33
Preston North End	*42*	*10*	*6*	*26*	*37*	*74*	*26*
Nottingham Forest	*42*	*6*	*12*	*24*	*29*	*65*	*24*

DIVISION TWO 1924-25

Leicester City	42	24	11	7	90	32	59
Manchester United	42	23	11	8	57	23	57
Derby County	42	22	11	9	71	36	55
Portsmouth	42	15	18	9	58	50	48
Chelsea	42	16	15	11	51	37	47
Wolverhampton Wanderers	42	20	6	16	55	51	46
Southampton	42	13	18	11	40	36	44
Port Vale	42	17	8	17	48	56	42
South Shields	42	12	17	13	42	38	41
Hull City	42	15	11	16	50	49	41
Clapton Orient	42	14	12	16	42	42	40
Fulham	42	15	10	17	41	56	40
Middlesbrough	42	10	19	13	36	44	39
The Wednesday	42	15	8	19	50	56	38
Barnsley	42	13	12	17	46	59	38
Bradford City	42	13	12	17	37	50	38
Blackpool	42	14	9	19	65	61	37
Oldham Athletic	42	13	11	18	35	51	37
Stockport County	42	13	11	18	37	57	37
Stoke City	42	12	11	19	34	46	35
Crystal Palace	*42*	*12*	*10*	*20*	*38*	*54*	*34*
Coventry City	*42*	*11*	*9*	*22*	*45*	*84*	*31*

DIVISION THREE (N) 1924-25

Darlington	42	24	10	8	78	33	58
Nelson	42	23	7	12	79	50	53
New Brighton	42	23	7	12	75	50	53
Southport	42	22	7	13	59	37	51
Bradford Park Avenue	42	19	12	11	84	42	50
Rochdale	42	21	7	14	75	53	49
Chesterfield	42	17	11	14	60	44	45
Lincoln City	42	18	8	16	53	58	44
Halifax Town	42	16	11	15	56	52	43
Ashington	42	16	10	16	68	76	42
Wigan Borough	42	15	11	16	62	65	41
Grimsby Town	42	15	9	18	60	60	39
Durham City	42	13	13	16	50	68	39
Barrow	42	16	7	19	51	74	39
Crewe Alexandra	42	13	13	16	53	78	39
Wrexham	42	15	8	19	53	61	38
Accrington Stanley	42	15	5	19	60	72	38
Doncaster Rovers	42	14	10	18	54	65	38
Walsall	42	13	11	18	44	53	37
Hartlepools United	42	12	11	19	45	63	35
Tranmere Rovers	42	14	4	24	59	78	32
Rotherham County	42	7	7	28	42	88	21

DIVISION THREE (S) 1924-25

Swansea Town	42	23	11	8	68	35	57
Plymouth Argyle	42	23	10	9	77	38	56
Bristol City	42	22	9	11	60	41	53
Swindon Town	42	20	11	11	66	38	51
Millwall Athletic	42	18	13	11	58	38	49
Newport County	42	20	9	13	62	42	49
Exeter City	42	19	9	14	59	48	47
Brighton & Hove Albion	42	19	8	15	59	45	46
Northampton Town	42	20	6	16	51	44	46
Southend United	42	19	5	18	51	61	43
Watford	42	17	9	16	38	47	43
Norwich City	42	14	13	15	53	51	41
Gillingham	42	13	14	15	35	44	40
Reading	42	14	10	18	37	38	38
Charlton Athletic	42	13	12	17	46	48	38
Luton Town	42	10	17	15	49	57	37
Bristol Rovers	42	12	13	17	42	49	37
Aberdare Athletic	42	14	9	19	54	67	37
Queen's Park Rangers	42	14	8	20	42	63	36
Bournemouth & Boscombe Ath.	42	13	8	21	40	58	34
Brentford	42	9	7	26	38	91	25
Merthyr Town	42	8	5	29	35	77	21

1925 F.A. Cup

Semi-finals

Sheffield United vs Southampton	2-0
Cardiff City vs Blackburn Rovers	3-1

Final

Wembley, 25th April 1925

Sheffield United 1   (Tunstall)

Cardiff City 0

Attendance 91,763

DIVISION ONE 1925-26

HUDDERSFIELD TOWN	42	23	11	8	92	60	57
Arsenal	42	22	8	12	87	63	52
Sunderland	42	21	6	15	96	80	48
Bury	42	20	7	15	85	77	47
Sheffield United	42	19	8	15	102	82	46
Aston Villa	42	16	12	14	86	76	44
Liverpool	42	14	16	12	70	63	44
Bolton Wanderers	42	17	10	15	75	76	44
Manchester United	42	19	6	17	66	73	44
Newcastle United	42	16	10	16	84	75	42
Everton	42	12	18	12	72	70	42
Blackburn Rovers	42	15	11	16	91	80	41
West Bromwich Albion	42	16	8	18	79	78	40
Birmingham	42	16	8	18	66	81	40
Tottenham Hotspur	42	15	9	18	66	79	39
Cardiff City	42	16	7	19	61	76	39
Leicester City	42	14	10	18	70	80	38
West Ham United	42	15	7	20	63	76	37
Leeds United	42	14	8	20	64	76	36
Burnley	42	13	10	19	85	108	36
Manchester City	*42*	*12*	*11*	*19*	*89*	*100*	*35*
Notts County	*42*	*13*	*7*	*22*	*54*	*74*	*33*

DIVISION THREE (N) 1925-26

Grimsby Town	42	26	9	7	91	40	61
Bradford Park Avenue	42	26	8	8	101	43	60
Rochdale	42	27	5	10	104	58	59
Chesterfield	42	25	5	12	100	54	55
Halifax Town	42	17	11	14	53	50	45
Hartlepools United	42	18	8	16	82	73	44
Tranmere Rovers	42	19	6	17	73	83	44
Nelson	42	16	11	15	89	71	43
Ashington	42	16	11	15	70	62	43
Doncaster Rovers	42	16	11	15	80	72	43
Crewe Alexandra	42	17	9	16	63	61	43
New Brighton	42	17	8	17	69	67	42
Durham City	42	18	6	18	63	70	42
Rotherham United	42	17	7	18	69	92	41
Lincoln City	42	17	5	20	66	82	39
Coventry City	42	16	6	20	73	82	38
Wigan Borough	42	13	11	18	68	74	37
Accrington Stanley	42	17	3	22	81	105	37
Wrexham	42	11	10	21	63	92	32
Southport	42	11	10	21	62	92	32
Walsall	42	10	6	26	58	107	26
Barrow	42	7	4	31	50	98	18

DIVISION TWO 1925-26

The Wednesday	42	27	6	9	88	48	60
Derby County	42	25	7	10	77	42	57
Chelsea	42	19	14	9	76	49	52
Wolverhampton Wanderers	42	21	7	14	84	60	49
Swansea Town	42	19	11	12	77	57	49
Blackpool	42	17	11	14	76	69	45
Oldham Athletic	42	18	8	16	74	62	44
Port Vale	42	19	6	17	79	69	44
South Shields	42	18	8	16	74	65	44
Middlesbrough	42	21	2	19	77	68	44
Portsmouth	42	17	10	15	79	74	44
Preston North End	42	18	7	17	71	84	43
Hull City	42	16	9	17	63	61	41
Southampton	42	15	8	19	63	63	38
Darlington	42	14	10	18	72	77	38
Bradford City	42	13	10	19	47	66	36
Nottingham Forest	42	14	8	20	51	73	36
Barnsley	42	12	12	18	58	84	36
Fulham	42	11	12	19	46	77	34
Clapton Orient	42	12	9	21	50	65	33
Stoke City	*42*	*12*	*8*	*22*	*54*	*77*	*32*
Stockport County	*42*	*8*	*9*	*25*	*51*	*97*	*25*

DIVISION THREE (S) 1925-26

Reading	42	23	11	8	77	52	57
Plymouth Argyle	42	24	8	10	107	67	56
Millwall	42	21	11	10	73	39	53
Bristol City	42	21	9	12	72	51	51
Brighton & Hove Albion	42	19	9	14	84	73	47
Swindon Town	42	20	6	16	69	64	46
Luton Town	42	18	7	17	80	75	43
Bournemouth & Boscombe Ath.	42	17	9	16	75	91	43
Aberdare Athletic	42	17	8	17	74	66	42
Gillingham	42	17	8	17	53	49	42
Southend United	42	19	4	19	78	73	42
Northampton Town	42	17	7	18	82	80	41
Crystal Palace	42	19	3	20	75	79	41
Merthyr Town	42	14	11	17	69	75	39
Watford	42	15	9	18	73	89	39
Norwich City	42	15	9	18	58	73	39
Newport County	42	14	10	18	64	74	38
Brentford	42	16	6	20	69	94	38
Bristol Rovers	42	15	6	21	66	69	36
Exeter City	42	15	5	22	72	70	35
Charlton Athletic	42	11	13	18	48	68	35
Queen's Park Rangers	42	6	9	27	37	84	21

1926 F.A. Cup

Semi-finals

Bolton Wanderers vs Swansea Town	3-0
Manchester City vs Manchester United	3-0

Final

Wembley, 24th April 1926

Bolton Wanderers 1   (Jack)

Manchester City 0

Attendance 91,447

DIVISION ONE 1926-27

NEWCASTLE UNITED	42	25	6	11	96	58	56
Huddersfield Town	42	17	17	8	76	60	51
Sunderland	42	21	7	14	98	70	49
Bolton Wanderers	42	19	10	13	84	62	48
Burnley	42	19	9	14	91	80	47
West Ham United	42	19	8	15	86	70	46
Leicester City	42	17	12	13	85	70	46
Sheffield United	42	17	10	15	74	86	44
Liverpool	42	18	7	17	69	61	43
Aston Villa	42	18	7	17	81	83	43
Arsenal	42	17	9	16	77	86	43
Derby County	42	17	7	18	86	73	41
Tottenham Hotspur	42	16	9	17	76	78	41
Cardiff City	42	16	9	17	55	65	41
Manchester United	42	13	14	15	52	64	40
The Wednesday	42	15	9	18	75	92	39
Birmingham	42	17	4	21	64	73	38
Blackburn Rovers	42	15	8	19	77	96	38
Bury	42	12	12	18	68	77	36
Everton	42	12	10	20	64	90	34
Leeds United	*42*	*11*	*8*	*23*	*69*	*88*	*30*
West Bromwich Albion	*42*	*11*	*8*	*23*	*65*	*86*	*30*

DIVISION THREE (N) 1926-27

Stoke City	42	27	9	6	92	40	63
Rochdale	42	26	6	10	105	65	58
Bradford Park Avenue	42	24	7	11	101	59	55
Halifax Town	42	21	11	10	70	53	53
Nelson	42	22	7	13	104	75	51
Stockport County	42	22	7	13	93	69	49
Chesterfield	42	21	5	16	92	68	47
Doncaster Rovers	42	18	11	13	81	65	47
Tranmere Rovers	42	19	8	15	85	67	46
New Brighton	42	18	10	14	79	67	46
Lincoln City	42	15	12	15	90	78	42
Southport	42	15	9	18	80	85	39
Wrexham	42	14	10	18	65	73	38
Walsall	42	14	10	18	68	81	38
Crewe Alexandra	42	14	9	19	71	81	37
Ashington	42	12	12	18	60	90	36
Hartlepools United	42	14	6	22	66	81	34
Wigan Borough	42	11	10	21	66	83	32
Rotherham United	42	10	12	20	70	92	32
Durham City	42	12	6	24	58	105	30
Accrington Stanley	42	10	7	25	62	98	27
Barrow	42	7	8	27	34	117	22

Stockport County had two points deducted

DIVISION TWO 1926-27

Middlesbrough	42	27	8	7	122	60	62
Portsmouth	42	23	8	11	87	49	54
Manchester City	42	22	10	10	108	61	54
Chelsea	42	20	12	10	62	52	52
Nottingham Forest	42	18	14	10	80	55	50
Preston North End	42	20	9	13	74	72	49
Hull City	42	20	7	15	63	52	47
Port Vale	42	16	13	13	88	78	45
Blackpool	42	18	8	16	95	80	44
Oldham Athletic	42	19	6	17	74	84	44
Barnsley	42	17	9	16	88	87	43
Swansea Town	42	16	11	15	68	72	43
Southampton	42	15	12	15	60	62	42
Reading	42	16	8	18	64	72	40
Wolverhampton Wanderers	42	14	7	21	73	75	35
Notts County	42	15	5	22	70	96	35
Grimsby Town	42	11	12	19	74	91	34
Fulham	42	13	8	21	58	92	34
South Shields	42	11	11	20	71	96	33
Clapton Orient	42	12	7	23	60	96	31
Darlington	*42*	*12*	*6*	*24*	*79*	*98*	*30*
Bradford City	*42*	*7*	*9*	*26*	*50*	*88*	*23*

DIVISION THREE (S) 1926-27

Bristol City	42	27	8	7	104	54	62
Plymouth Argyle	42	25	10	7	95	61	60
Millwall	42	23	10	9	89	51	56
Brighton & Hove Albion	42	21	11	10	79	50	53
Swindon Town	42	21	9	12	100	85	51
Crystal Palace	42	18	9	15	84	81	45
Bournemouth & Boscombe Ath.	42	18	8	16	78	66	44
Luton Town	42	15	14	13	68	66	44
Newport County	42	19	6	17	57	71	44
Bristol Rovers	42	16	9	17	78	80	41
Brentford	42	13	14	15	70	61	40
Exeter City	42	15	10	17	76	73	40
Charlton Athletic	42	16	8	18	60	61	40
Queen's Park Rangers	42	15	9	18	65	71	39
Coventry City	42	15	7	20	71	86	37
Norwich City	42	12	11	19	59	71	35
Methyr Town	42	13	9	20	63	80	35
Northampton Town	42	15	5	22	59	87	35
Southend United	42	14	6	22	64	77	34
Gillingham	42	11	10	21	54	72	32
Watford	42	12	8	22	57	87	32
Aberdare Athletic	*42*	*9*	*7*	*26*	*62*	*101*	*25*

1927 F.A. Cup

Semi-finals

Cardiff City vs Reading	3-0
Arsenal vs Southampton	2-1

Final

Wembley, 23rd April 1927

Cardiff City 1 (Ferguson)

Arsenal 0

Attendance 91,206

DIVISION ONE 1927-28

EVERTON	42	20	13	9	102	66	53
Huddersfield Town	42	22	7	13	91	68	51
Leicester City	42	18	12	12	96	72	48
Derby County	42	17	10	15	96	83	44
Bury	42	20	4	18	80	80	44
Cardiff City	42	17	10	15	70	80	44
Bolton Wanderers	42	16	11	15	81	66	43
Aston Villa	42	17	9	16	78	73	43
Newcastle United	42	15	13	14	79	81	43
Arsenal	42	13	15	14	82	86	41
Birmingham	42	13	15	14	70	75	41
Blackburn Rovers	42	16	9	17	66	78	41
Sheffield United	42	15	10	17	79	86	40
The Wednesday	42	13	13	16	81	78	39
Sunderland	42	15	9	18	74	76	39
Liverpool	42	13	13	16	84	87	39
West Ham United	42	14	11	17	81	88	39
Manchester United	42	16	7	19	72	80	39
Burnley	42	16	7	19	82	98	39
Portsmouth	42	16	7	19	66	90	39
Tottenham Hotspur	*42*	*15*	*8*	*19*	*74*	*86*	*38*
Middlesbrough	*42*	*11*	*15*	*16*	*81*	*88*	*37*

DIVISION TWO 1927-28

Manchester City	42	25	9	8	100	59	59
Leeds United	42	25	7	10	98	49	57
Chelsea	42	23	8	11	75	45	54
Preston North End	42	22	9	11	100	66	53
Stoke City	42	22	8	12	78	59	52
Swansea Town	42	18	12	12	75	63	48
Oldham Athletic	42	19	8	15	75	51	46
West Bromwich Albion	42	17	12	13	90	70	46
Port Vale	42	18	8	16	68	57	44
Nottingham Forest	42	15	10	17	83	84	40
Grimsby Town	42	14	12	16	69	83	40
Bristol City	42	15	9	18	76	79	39
Barnsley	42	14	11	17	65	85	39
Hull City	42	12	15	15	41	54	39
Notts County	42	13	12	17	68	74	38
Wolverhampton Wanderers	42	13	10	19	63	91	36
Southampton	42	14	7	21	68	77	35
Reading	42	11	13	18	53	75	35
Blackpool	42	13	8	21	83	101	34
Clapton Orient	42	11	12	19	55	85	34
Fulham	*42*	*13*	*7*	*22*	*68*	*89*	*33*
South Shields	*42*	*7*	*9*	*26*	*56*	*111*	*23*

DIVISION THREE (N) 1927-28

Bradford Park Avenue	42	27	9	6	101	45	63
Lincoln City	42	24	7	11	91	64	55
Stockport County	42	23	8	11	89	51	54
Doncaster Rovers	42	23	7	12	80	44	53
Tranmere Rovers	42	22	9	11	105	72	53
Bradford City	42	18	12	12	85	60	48
Darlington	42	21	5	16	89	74	47
Southport	42	20	5	17	79	70	45
Accrington Stanley	42	18	8	16	76	67	44
New Brighton	42	14	14	14	72	62	42
Wrexham	42	18	6	18	64	67	42
Halifax Town	42	13	15	14	73	71	41
Rochdale	42	17	7	18	74	77	41
Rotherham United	42	14	11	17	65	69	39
Hartlepools United	42	16	6	20	69	81	38
Chesterfield	42	13	10	19	71	78	36
Crewe Alexandra	42	12	10	20	77	86	34
Ashington	42	11	11	20	77	103	33
Barrow	42	10	11	21	54	102	31
Wigan Borough	42	10	10	22	56	97	30
Durham City	*42*	*11*	*7*	*24*	*53*	*100*	*29*
Nelson	42	10	6	26	76	136	26

DIVISION THREE (S) 1927-28

Millwall	42	30	5	7	127	50	65
Northampton Town	42	23	9	10	102	64	55
Plymouth Argyle	42	23	7	12	85	54	53
Brighton & Hove Albion	42	19	10	13	81	69	48
Crystal Palace	42	18	12	12	79	72	48
Swindon Town	42	19	9	14	90	69	47
Southend United	42	20	6	16	80	64	46
Exeter City	42	17	12	13	70	60	46
Newport County	42	18	9	15	81	84	45
Queen's Park Rangers	42	17	9	16	72	71	43
Charlton Athletic	42	15	13	14	60	70	43
Brentford	42	16	8	18	76	74	40
Luton Town	42	16	7	19	94	87	39
Bournemouth & Boscombe Ath.	42	13	12	17	72	79	38
Watford	42	14	10	18	68	78	38
Gillingham	42	13	11	18	62	81	37
Norwich City	42	10	16	16	66	70	36
Walsall	42	12	9	21	75	101	33
Bristol Rovers	42	14	4	24	67	93	32
Coventry City	42	11	9	22	67	96	31
Merthyr Town	42	9	13	20	53	91	31
Torquay United	42	8	14	20	53	103	30

1928 F.A. Cup

Semi-finals

Blackburn Rovers vs Arsenal	1-0
Huddersfield Town vs Sheffield United	2-2, 0-0, 1-0

Final

Wembley, 21st April 1928

Blackburn Rovers 3 (Roscamp 2, McLean)

Huddersfield Town 1 (Jackson)

Attendance 92,041

DIVISION ONE 1928-29

THE WEDNESDAY	42	21	10	11	86	62	52
Leicester City	42	21	9	12	96	67	51
Aston Villa	42	23	4	15	98	81	50
Sunderland	42	20	7	15	93	75	47
Liverpool	42	17	12	13	90	64	46
Derby County	42	18	10	14	86	71	46
Blackburn Rovers	42	17	11	14	72	63	45
Manchester City	42	18	9	15	95	86	45
Arsenal	42	16	13	13	77	72	45
Newcastle United	42	19	6	17	70	72	44
Sheffield United	42	15	11	16	86	85	41
Manchester United	42	14	13	15	66	76	41
Leeds United	42	16	9	17	71	84	41
Bolton Wanderers	42	14	12	16	73	80	40
Birmingham	42	15	10	17	68	77	40
Huddersfield Town	42	14	11	17	70	61	39
West Ham United	42	15	9	18	86	96	39
Everton	42	17	4	21	63	75	38
Burnley	42	15	8	19	81	103	38
Portsmouth	42	15	6	21	56	80	36
Bury	*42*	*12*	*7*	*23*	*62*	*99*	*31*
Cardiff City	*42*	*8*	*13*	*21*	*43*	*59*	*29*

DIVISION TWO 1928-29

Middlesbrough	42	22	11	9	92	57	55
Grimsby Town	42	24	5	13	82	61	53
Bradford Park Avenue	42	22	4	16	88	70	48
Southampton	42	17	14	11	74	60	48
Notts County	42	19	9	14	78	65	47
Stoke City	42	17	12	13	74	51	46
West Bromwich Albion	42	19	8	15	80	79	46
Blackpool	42	19	7	16	92	76	45
Chelsea	42	17	10	15	64	65	44
Tottenham Hotspur	42	17	9	16	75	81	43
Nottingham Forest	42	15	12	15	71	70	42
Hull City	42	13	14	15	58	63	40
Preston North End	42	15	9	18	78	79	39
Millwall	42	16	7	19	71	86	39
Reading	42	15	9	18	63	86	39
Barnsley	42	16	6	20	69	66	38
Wolverhampton Wanderers	42	15	7	20	77	81	37
Oldham Athletic	42	16	5	21	54	75	37
Swansea Town	42	13	10	19	62	75	36
Bristol City	42	13	10	19	58	72	36
Port Vale	*42*	*15*	*4*	*23*	*71*	*86*	*34*
Clapton Orient	*42*	*12*	*8*	*22*	*45*	*72*	*32*

DIVISION THREE (N) 1928-29

Bradford City	42	27	9	6	128	43	63
Stockport County	42	28	6	8	111	58	62
Wrexham	42	21	10	11	91	69	52
Wigan Borough	42	21	9	12	82	49	51
Doncaster Rovers	42	20	10	12	76	66	50
Lincoln City	42	21	6	15	91	67	48
Tranmere Rovers	42	22	3	17	79	77	47
Carlisle United	42	19	8	15	86	77	46
Crewe Alexandra	42	18	8	16	80	68	44
South Shields	42	18	8	16	83	74	44
Chesterfield	42	18	5	19	71	77	41
Southport	42	16	8	18	75	85	40
Halifax Town	42	13	13	16	63	62	39
New Brighton	42	15	9	18	64	71	39
Nelson	42	17	5	20	77	90	39
Rotherham United	42	15	9	18	60	77	39
Rochdale	42	13	10	19	79	96	36
Accrington Stanley	42	13	8	21	68	82	34
Darlington	42	13	7	22	64	88	33
Barrow	42	10	8	24	64	93	28
Hartlepools United	42	10	6	26	59	112	26
Ashington	*42*	*8*	*7*	*27*	*45*	*115*	*23*

DIVISION THREE (S) 1928-29

Charlton Athletic	42	23	8	11	86	60	54
Crystal Palace	42	23	8	11	81	67	54
Northampton Town	42	20	12	10	96	57	52
Plymouth Argyle	42	20	12	10	83	51	52
Fulham	42	21	10	11	101	71	52
Queen's Park Rangers	42	19	14	9	82	61	52
Luton Town	42	19	11	12	89	73	49
Watford	42	19	10	13	79	74	48
Bournemouth & Boscombe Ath.	42	19	9	14	84	77	47
Swindon Town	42	15	13	14	75	72	43
Coventry City	42	14	14	14	62	57	42
Southend United	42	15	11	16	80	75	41
Brentford	42	14	10	18	56	60	38
Walsall	42	13	12	17	73	79	38
Brighton & Hove Albion	42	16	6	20	58	76	38
Newport County	42	13	9	20	69	86	35
Norwich City	42	14	6	22	69	81	34
Torquay United	42	14	6	22	66	84	34
Bristol Rovers	42	13	7	22	60	79	33
Merthyr Town	42	11	8	23	55	103	30
Exeter City	42	9	11	22	67	88	29
Gillingham	42	10	9	23	43	83	29

1929 F.A. Cup

Semi-finals

Bolton Wanderers vs Huddersfield Town	3-1
Portsmouth vs Aston Villa	1-0

Final

Wembley, 27th April 1929

Bolton Wanderers 2 (Butler, Blackmore)

Portsmouth 0

Attendance 92,576

DIVISION ONE 1929-30

SHEFFIELD WEDNESDAY	42	26	8	8	105	57	60
Derby County	42	21	8	13	90	82	50
Manchester City	42	19	9	14	91	81	47
Aston Villa	42	21	5	16	92	83	47
Leeds United	42	20	6	16	79	63	46
Blackburn Rovers	42	19	7	16	99	93	45
West Ham United	42	19	5	18	86	79	43
Leicester City	42	17	9	16	86	90	43
Sunderland	42	18	7	17	76	80	43
Huddersfield Town	42	17	9	16	63	69	43
Birmingham	42	16	9	17	67	62	41
Liverpool	42	16	9	17	63	79	41
Portsmouth	42	15	10	17	66	62	40
Arsenal	42	14	11	17	78	66	39
Bolton Wanderers	42	15	9	18	74	74	39
Middlesbrough	42	16	6	20	82	84	38
Manchester United	42	15	8	19	67	88	38
Grimsby Town	42	15	7	20	73	89	37
Newcastle United	42	15	7	20	71	92	37
Sheffield United	42	15	6	21	91	96	36
Burnley	*42*	*14*	*8*	*20*	*79*	*97*	*36*
Everton	*42*	*12*	*11*	*19*	*80*	*92*	*35*

DIVISION TWO 1929-30

Blackpool	42	27	4	11	98	67	58
Chelsea	42	22	11	9	74	46	55
Oldham Athletic	42	21	11	10	90	51	53
Bradford Park Avenue	42	19	12	11	91	70	50
Bury	42	22	5	15	78	67	49
West Bromwich Albion	42	21	5	16	105	73	47
Southampton	42	17	11	14	77	76	45
Cardiff City	42	18	8	16	61	59	44
Wolverhampton Wanderers	42	16	9	17	77	79	41
Nottingham Forest	42	13	15	14	55	69	41
Stoke City	42	16	8	18	74	72	40
Tottenham Hotspur	42	15	9	18	59	61	39
Charlton Athletic	42	14	11	17	59	63	39
Millwall	42	12	15	15	57	73	39
Swansea Town	42	14	9	19	57	61	37
Preston North End	42	13	11	18	65	80	37
Barnsley	42	14	8	20	56	71	36
Bradford City	42	12	12	18	60	77	36
Reading	42	12	11	19	54	67	35
Bristol City	42	13	9	20	61	83	35
Hull City	*42*	*14*	*7*	*21*	*51*	*78*	*35*
Notts County	*42*	*9*	*15*	*18*	*54*	*70*	*33*

DIVISION THREE (N) 1929-30

Port Vale	42	30	7	5	103	37	67
Stockport County	42	28	7	7	106	44	63
Darlington	42	22	6	14	108	73	50
Chesterfield	42	22	6	14	76	56	50
Lincoln City	42	17	14	11	83	61	48
York City	42	15	16	11	77	64	46
South Shields	42	18	10	14	77	74	46
Hartlepools United	42	17	11	14	81	74	45
Southport	42	15	13	14	81	74	43
Rochdale	42	18	7	17	89	91	43
Crewe Alexandra	42	17	8	17	82	71	42
Tranmere Rovers	42	16	9	17	83	86	41
New Brighton	42	16	8	18	69	79	40
Doncaster Rovers	42	15	9	18	62	69	39
Carlisle United	42	16	7	19	90	101	39
Accrington Stanley	42	14	9	19	84	81	37
Wrexham	42	13	8	21	67	88	34
Wigan Borough	42	13	7	22	60	88	33
Nelson	42	13	7	22	51	80	33
Rotherham United	42	11	8	23	67	113	30
Halifax Town	42	10	8	24	44	79	28
Barrow	42	11	5	26	41	98	27

DIVISION THREE (S) 1929-30

Plymouth Argyle	42	30	8	4	98	38	68
Brentford	42	28	5	9	94	44	61
Queen's Park Rangers	42	21	9	12	80	68	51
Northampton Town	42	21	8	13	82	58	50
Brighton & Hove Albion	42	21	8	13	87	63	50
Coventry City	42	19	9	14	88	73	47
Fulham	42	18	11	13	87	83	47
Norwich City	42	18	10	14	88	77	46
Crystal Palace	42	17	12	13	81	74	46
Bournemouth & Boscombe Ath.	42	15	13	14	72	61	43
Southend United	42	15	13	14	69	59	43
Clapton Orient	42	14	13	15	55	62	41
Luton Town	42	14	12	16	64	78	40
Swindon Town	42	13	12	17	73	83	38
Watford	42	15	8	19	60	73	38
Exeter City	42	12	11	19	67	73	35
Walsall	42	13	8	21	71	78	34
Newport County	42	12	10	20	74	85	34
Torquay United	42	10	11	21	64	94	31
Bristol Rovers	42	11	8	23	67	93	30
Gillingham	42	11	8	23	51	80	30
Merthyr Town	*42*	*6*	*9*	*27*	*60*	*135*	*21*

1930 F.A. Cup

Semi-finals

Arsenal vs Hull City	2-2, 1-0
Huddersfield Town vs Sheffield Wednesday	2-1

Final

Wembley, 26th April 1930

Arsenal 2 (James, Lambert)

Huddersfield Town 0

Attendance 92,448

DIVISION ONE 1930-31

ARSENAL	42	28	10	4	127	59	66
Aston Villa	42	25	9	8	128	78	59
Sheffield Wednesday	42	22	8	12	102	75	52
Portsmouth	42	18	13	11	84	67	49
Huddersfield Town	42	18	12	12	81	65	48
Derby County	42	18	10	14	94	79	46
Middlesbrough	42	19	8	15	98	90	46
Manchester City	42	18	10	14	75	70	46
Liverpool	42	15	12	15	86	85	42
Blackburn Rovers	42	17	8	17	83	84	42
Sunderland	42	16	9	17	89	85	41
Chelsea	42	15	10	17	64	67	40
Grimsby Town	42	17	5	20	82	87	39
Bolton Wanderers	42	15	9	18	68	81	39
Sheffield United	42	14	10	18	78	84	38
Leicester City	42	16	6	20	80	95	38
Newcastle United	42	15	6	21	78	87	36
West Ham United	42	14	8	20	79	94	36
Birmingham	42	13	10	19	55	70	36
Blackpool	42	11	10	21	71	125	32
Leeds United	*42*	*12*	*7*	*23*	*68*	*81*	*31*
Manchester United	*42*	*7*	*8*	*27*	*53*	*115*	*22*

DIVISION THREE (N) 1930-31

Chesterfield	42	26	6	10	102	57	58
Lincoln City	42	25	7	10	102	59	57
Wrexham	42	21	12	9	94	62	54
Tranmere Rovers	42	24	6	12	111	74	54
Southport	42	22	9	11	88	56	53
Hull City	42	20	10	12	99	55	50
Stockport County	42	20	9	13	77	61	49
Carlisle United	42	20	5	17	98	81	45
Gateshead	42	16	13	13	71	73	45
Wigan Borough	42	19	5	18	76	86	43
Darlington	42	16	10	16	71	59	42
York City	42	18	6	18	85	82	42
Accrington Stanley	42	15	9	18	84	108	39
Rotherham United	42	13	12	17	81	83	38
Doncaster Rovers	42	13	11	18	65	65	37
Barrow	42	15	7	20	68	89	37
Halifax Town	42	13	9	20	55	89	35
Crewe Alexandra	42	14	6	22	66	93	34
New Brighton	42	13	7	22	49	76	33
Hartlepools United	42	12	6	24	67	86	30
Rochdale	42	12	6	24	62	107	30
Nelson	*42*	*6*	*7*	*29*	*43*	*113*	*19*

DIVISION TWO 1930-31

Everton	42	28	5	9	121	66	61
West Bromwich Albion	42	22	10	10	83	49	54
Tottenham Hotspur	42	22	7	13	88	55	51
Wolverhampton Wanderers	42	21	5	16	84	67	47
Port Vale	42	21	5	16	67	61	47
Bradford Park Avenue	42	18	10	14	97	66	46
Preston North End	42	17	11	14	83	64	45
Burnley	42	17	11	14	81	77	45
Southampton	42	19	6	17	74	62	44
Bradford City	42	17	10	15	61	63	44
Stoke City	42	17	10	15	64	71	44
Oldham Athletic	42	16	10	16	61	72	42
Bury	42	19	3	20	75	82	41
Millwall	42	16	7	19	71	80	39
Charlton Athletic	42	15	9	18	59	86	39
Bristol City	42	15	8	19	54	82	38
Nottingham Forest	42	14	9	19	80	85	37
Plymouth Argyle	42	14	8	20	76	84	36
Barnsley	42	13	9	20	59	79	35
Swansea Town	42	12	10	20	51	74	34
Reading	*42*	*12*	*6*	*24*	*72*	*96*	*30*
Cardiff City	*42*	*8*	*9*	*25*	*47*	*87*	*25*

DIVISION THREE (S) 1930-31

Notts County	42	24	11	7	97	46	59
Crystal Palace	42	22	7	13	107	71	51
Brentford	42	22	6	14	90	64	50
Brighton & Hove Albion	42	17	15	10	68	53	49
Southend United	42	22	5	15	76	60	49
Northampton Town	42	18	12	12	77	59	48
Luton Town	42	19	8	15	76	51	46
Queen's Park Rangers	42	20	3	19	82	75	43
Fulham	42	18	7	17	77	75	43
Bournemouth & Boscombe Ath.	42	15	13	14	72	73	43
Torquay United	42	17	9	16	80	84	43
Swindon Town	42	18	6	18	89	94	42
Exeter City	42	17	8	17	84	90	42
Coventry City	42	16	9	17	75	65	41
Bristol Rovers	42	16	8	18	75	92	40
Gillingham	42	14	10	18	61	76	38
Walsall	42	14	9	19	78	95	37
Watford	42	14	7	21	72	75	35
Clapton Orient	42	14	7	21	63	91	35
Thames Association	42	13	8	21	54	93	34
Newport County	*42*	*11*	*6*	*25*	*69*	*111*	*28*
Norwich City	42	10	8	24	47	76	28

1931 F.A. Cup

Semi-finals

Everton vs West Bromwich Albion	0-1
Birmingham vs Sunderland	2-0

Final

Wembley, 25th April 1931

West Bromwich Albion 2 (W.G. Richardson 2)

Birmingham 1 (Bradford)

Attendance 92,406

DIVISION ONE 1931-32

EVERTON	42	26	4	12	116	64	56
Arsenal	42	22	10	10	90	48	54
Sheffield Wednesday	42	22	6	14	96	82	50
Huddersfield Town	42	19	10	13	80	63	48
Aston Villa	42	19	8	15	104	72	46
West Bromwich Albion	42	20	6	16	77	55	46
Sheffield United	42	20	6	16	80	75	46
Portsmouth	42	19	7	16	62	62	45
Birmingham	42	18	8	16	78	67	44
Liverpool	42	19	6	17	81	93	44
Newcastle United	42	18	6	18	80	87	42
Chelsea	42	16	8	18	69	73	40
Sunderland	42	15	10	17	67	73	40
Manchester City	42	13	12	17	83	73	38
Derby County	42	14	10	18	71	75	38
Blackburn Rovers	42	16	6	20	89	95	38
Bolton Wanderers	42	17	4	21	72	80	38
Middlesbrough	42	15	8	19	64	89	38
Leicester City	42	15	7	20	74	94	37
Blackpool	42	12	9	21	65	102	33
Grimsby Town	*42*	*13*	*6*	*23*	*67*	*98*	*32*
West Ham United	*42*	*12*	*7*	*23*	*62*	*107*	*31*

DIVISION TWO 1931-32

Wolverhampton Wanderers	42	24	8	10	115	49	56
Leeds United	42	22	10	10	78	54	54
Stoke City	42	19	14	9	69	48	52
Plymouth Argyle	42	20	9	13	100	66	49
Bury	42	21	7	14	70	58	49
Bradford Park Avenue	42	21	7	14	72	63	49
Bradford City	42	16	13	13	80	61	45
Tottenham Hotspur	42	16	11	15	87	78	43
Millwall	42	17	9	16	61	61	43
Charlton Athletic	42	17	9	16	61	66	43
Nottingham Forest	42	16	10	16	77	72	42
Manchester United	42	17	8	17	71	72	42
Preston North End	42	16	10	16	75	77	42
Southampton	42	17	7	18	66	77	41
Swansea Town	42	16	7	19	73	75	39
Notts County	42	13	12	17	75	75	38
Chesterfield	42	13	11	18	64	86	37
Oldham Athletic	42	13	10	19	62	84	36
Burnley	42	13	9	20	59	87	35
Port Vale	42	13	7	22	58	89	33
Barnsley	*42*	*12*	*9*	*21*	*55*	*91*	*33*
Bristol City	*42*	*6*	*11*	*25*	*39*	*78*	*23*

DIVISION THREE (N) 1931-32

Lincoln City	40	26	5	9	106	47	57
Gateshead	40	25	7	8	94	48	57
Chester	40	21	8	11	78	60	50
Tranmere Rovers	40	19	11	10	107	58	49
Barrow	40	24	1	15	86	59	49
Crewe Alexandra	40	21	6	13	95	66	48
Southport	40	18	10	12	58	53	46
Hull City	40	20	5	15	82	53	45
York City	40	18	7	15	76	81	43
Wrexham	40	18	7	15	64	69	43
Darlington	40	17	4	19	66	69	38
Stockport County	40	13	11	16	55	53	37
Hartlepools United	40	16	5	19	78	100	37
Accrington Stanley	40	15	6	19	75	80	36
Doncaster Rovers	40	16	4	20	59	80	36
Walsall	40	16	3	21	57	85	35
Halifax Town	40	13	8	19	61	87	34
Carlisle United	40	11	11	18	64	79	33
Rotherham United	40	14	4	22	63	72	32
New Brighton	40	8	8	24	38	76	24
Rochdale	40	4	3	33	48	135	11

Wigan Borough resigned from the League during the season and their record was expunged

DIVISION THREE (S) 1931-32

Fulham	42	24	9	9	111	62	57
Reading	42	23	9	10	97	67	55
Southend United	42	21	11	10	77	53	53
Crystal Palace	42	20	11	11	74	63	51
Brentford	42	19	10	13	68	52	48
Luton Town	42	20	7	15	95	70	47
Exeter City	42	20	7	15	77	62	47
Brighton & Hove Albion	42	17	12	13	73	58	46
Cardiff City	42	19	8	15	87	73	46
Norwich City	42	17	12	13	76	67	46
Watford	42	19	8	15	81	79	46
Coventry City	42	18	8	16	108	97	44
Queen's Park Rangers	42	15	12	15	79	73	42
Northampton Town	42	16	7	19	69	69	39
Bournemouth & Boscombe Ath.	42	13	12	17	70	78	38
Clapton Orient	42	12	11	19	77	90	35
Swindon Town	42	14	6	22	70	84	34
Bristol Rovers	42	13	8	21	65	92	34
Torquay United	42	12	9	21	72	106	33
Mansfield Town	42	11	10	21	75	108	32
Gillingham	42	10	8	24	40	82	28
Thames Association	*42*	*7*	*9*	*26*	*53*	*109*	*23*

1932 F.A. Cup

Semi-finals

Chelsea vs Newcastle United	1-2
Arsenal vs Manchester City	1-0

Final

Wembley, 23rd April 1932

Newcastle United 2 (Allen 2)

Arsenal 1 (John)

Attendance 92,298

DIVISION ONE 1932-33

ARSENAL	42	25	8	9	118	61	58
Aston Villa	42	23	8	11	92	67	54
Sheffield Wednesday	42	21	9	12	80	68	51
West Bromwich Albion	42	20	9	13	83	70	49
Newcastle United	42	22	5	15	71	63	49
Huddersfield Town	42	18	11	13	66	53	47
Derby County	42	15	14	13	76	69	44
Leeds United	42	15	14	13	59	62	44
Portsmouth	42	18	7	17	74	76	43
Sheffield United	42	17	9	16	74	80	43
Everton	42	16	9	17	81	74	41
Sunderland	42	15	10	17	63	80	40
Birmingham	42	14	11	17	57	57	39
Liverpool	42	14	11	17	79	84	39
Blackburn Rovers	42	14	10	18	76	102	38
Manchester City	42	16	5	21	68	71	37
Middlesbrough	42	14	9	19	63	73	37
Chelsea	42	14	7	21	63	73	35
Leicester City	42	11	13	18	75	89	35
Wolverhampton Wanderers	42	14	7	21	80	96	35
Bolton Wanderers	*42*	*12*	*9*	*21*	*78*	*92*	*33*
Blackpool	*42*	*14*	*5*	*23*	*69*	*85*	*33*

DIVISION TWO 1932-33

Stoke City	42	25	6	11	78	39	56
Tottenham Hotspur	42	20	15	7	96	51	55
Fulham	42	20	10	12	78	65	50
Bury	42	20	9	13	84	59	49
Nottingham Forest	42	17	15	10	67	59	49
Manchester United	42	15	13	14	71	68	43
Millwall	42	16	11	15	59	57	43
Bradford Park Avenue	42	17	8	17	77	71	42
Preston North End	42	16	10	16	74	70	42
Swansea Town	42	19	4	19	50	54	42
Bradford City	42	14	13	15	65	61	41
Southampton	42	18	5	19	66	66	41
Grimsby Town	42	14	13	15	79	84	41
Plymouth Argyle	42	16	9	17	63	67	41
Notts County	42	15	10	17	67	78	40
Oldham Athletic	42	15	8	19	67	80	38
Port Vale	42	14	10	18	66	79	38
Lincoln City	42	12	13	17	72	87	37
Burnley	42	11	14	17	67	79	36
West Ham United	42	13	9	20	75	93	35
Chesterfield	*42*	*12*	*10*	*20*	*61*	*84*	*34*
Charlton Athletic	*42*	*12*	*7*	*23*	*60*	*91*	*31*

DIVISION THREE (N) 1932-33

Hull City	42	26	7	9	100	45	59
Wrexham	42	24	9	9	106	51	57
Stockport County	42	21	12	9	99	58	54
Chester	42	22	8	12	94	66	52
Walsall	42	19	10	13	75	58	48
Doncaster Rovers	42	17	14	11	77	79	48
Gateshead	42	19	9	14	78	67	47
Barnsley	42	19	8	15	92	80	46
Barrow	42	18	7	17	60	60	43
Crewe Alexandra	42	20	3	19	80	84	43
Tranmere Rovers	42	17	8	17	70	66	42
Southport	42	17	7	18	70	67	41
Accrington Stanley	42	15	10	17	78	76	40
Hartlepools United	42	16	7	19	87	116	39
Halifax Town	42	15	8	19	71	90	38
Mansfield Town	42	14	7	21	84	100	35
Rotherham United	42	14	6	22	60	84	34
Rochdale	42	13	7	22	58	80	33
Carlisle United	42	13	7	22	51	75	33
York City	42	13	6	23	72	92	32
New Brighton	42	11	10	21	63	88	32
Darlington	42	10	8	24	66	109	28

DIVISION THREE (S) 1932-33

Brentford	42	26	10	6	90	49	62
Exeter City	42	24	10	8	88	48	58
Norwich City	42	22	13	7	88	55	57
Reading	42	19	13	10	103	71	51
Crystal Palace	42	19	8	15	78	64	46
Coventry City	42	19	6	17	106	77	44
Gillingham	42	18	8	16	72	61	44
Northampton Town	42	18	8	16	76	66	44
Bristol Rovers	42	15	14	13	61	56	44
Torquay United	42	16	12	14	72	67	44
Watford	42	16	12	14	66	63	44
Brighton & Hove Albion	42	17	8	17	66	65	42
Southend United	42	15	11	16	65	82	41
Luton Town	42	13	13	16	78	78	39
Bristol City	42	12	13	17	83	90	37
Queen's Park Rangers	42	13	11	18	72	87	37
Aldershot	42	13	10	19	61	72	36
Bournemouth & Boscombe Ath.	42	12	12	18	60	81	36
Cardiff City	42	12	7	23	69	99	31
Clapton Orient	42	8	13	21	59	93	29
Newport County	42	11	7	24	61	105	29
Swindon Town	42	9	11	22	60	105	29

1933 F.A. Cup

Semi-finals

Everton vs West Ham United	2-1
Manchester City vs Derby County	3-2

Final

Wembley, 29th April 1933

Everton 3 (Stein, Dean, Dunn)

Manchester City 0

Attendance 92,950

DIVISION ONE 1933-34

ARSENAL	42	25	9	8	75	47	59
Huddersfield Town	42	23	10	9	90	61	56
Tottenham Hotspur	42	21	7	14	79	56	49
Derby County	42	17	11	14	68	54	45
Manchester City	42	17	11	14	65	72	45
Sunderland	42	16	12	14	81	56	44
West Bromwich Albion	42	17	10	15	78	70	44
Blackburn Rovers	42	18	7	17	74	81	43
Leeds United	42	17	8	17	75	66	42
Portsmouth	42	15	12	15	52	55	42
Sheffield Wednesday	42	16	9	17	62	67	41
Stoke City	42	15	11	16	58	71	41
Aston Villa	42	14	12	16	78	75	40
Everton	42	12	16	14	62	63	40
Wolverhampton Wanderers	42	14	12	16	74	86	40
Middlesbrough	42	16	7	19	68	80	39
Leicester City	42	14	11	17	59	74	39
Liverpool	42	14	10	18	79	87	38
Chelsea	42	14	8	20	67	69	36
Birmingham	42	12	12	18	54	56	36
Newcastle United	42	10	14	18	68	77	34
Sheffield United	42	12	7	23	58	101	31

DIVISION TWO 1933-34

Grimsby Town	42	27	5	10	103	59	59
Preston North End	42	23	6	13	71	52	52
Bolton Wanderers	42	21	9	12	79	55	51
Brentford	42	22	7	13	85	60	51
Bradford Park Avenue	42	23	3	16	86	67	49
Bradford City	42	20	6	16	73	67	46
West Ham United	42	17	11	14	78	70	45
Port Vale	42	19	7	16	60	55	45
Oldham Athletic	42	17	10	15	72	60	44
Plymouth Argyle	42	15	13	14	69	70	43
Blackpool	42	15	13	14	62	64	43
Bury	42	17	9	16	70	73	43
Burnley	42	18	6	18	60	72	42
Southampton	42	15	8	19	54	58	38
Hull City	42	13	12	17	52	68	38
Fulham	42	15	7	20	48	67	37
Nottingham Forest	42	13	9	20	73	74	35
Notts County	42	12	11	19	53	62	35
Swansea Town	42	10	15	17	51	60	35
Manchester United	42	14	6	22	59	85	34
Millwall	42	11	11	20	39	68	33
Lincoln City	42	9	8	25	44	75	26

DIVISION THREE (N) 1933-34

Barnsley	42	27	8	7	118	61	62
Chesterfield	42	27	7	8	86	43	61
Stockport County	42	24	11	7	115	52	59
Walsall	42	23	7	12	97	60	53
Doncaster Rovers	42	22	9	11	83	61	53
Wrexham	42	23	5	14	102	73	51
Tranmere Rovers	42	20	7	15	84	63	47
Barrow	42	19	9	14	116	94	47
Halifax Town	42	20	4	18	80	91	44
Chester	42	17	6	19	89	86	40
Hartlepools United	42	16	7	19	89	93	39
York City	42	15	8	19	71	74	38
Carlisle United	42	15	8	19	66	81	38
Crewe Alexandra	42	15	6	21	81	97	36
New Brighton	42	14	8	20	62	87	36
Darlington	42	13	9	20	70	101	35
Mansfield Town	42	11	12	19	81	88	34
Southport	42	8	17	17	63	90	33
Gateshead	42	12	9	21	76	110	33
Accrington Stanley	42	13	7	22	65	101	33
Rotherham United	42	10	8	24	53	91	28
Rochdale	42	9	6	27	53	103	24

DIVISION THREE (S) 1933-34

Norwich City	42	25	11	6	88	49	61
Coventry City	42	21	12	9	100	54	54
Reading	42	21	12	9	82	50	54
Queen's Park Rangers	42	24	6	12	70	51	54
Charlton Athletic	42	22	8	12	83	56	52
Luton Town	42	21	10	11	83	61	52
Bristol Rovers	42	20	11	11	77	47	51
Swindon Town	42	17	11	14	64	68	45
Exeter City	42	16	11	15	68	57	43
Brighton & Hove Albion	42	15	13	14	68	60	43
Clapton Orient	42	16	10	16	75	69	42
Crystal Palace	42	16	9	17	71	67	41
Northampton Town	42	14	12	16	71	78	40
Aldershot	42	13	12	17	52	71	38
Watford	42	15	7	20	71	63	37
Southend United	42	12	10	20	51	74	34
Gillingham	42	11	11	20	75	96	33
Newport County	42	8	17	17	49	70	33
Bristol City	42	10	13	19	58	85	33
Torquay United	42	13	7	22	53	93	33
Bournemouth & Boscombe Ath.	42	9	9	24	60	102	27
Cardiff City	42	9	6	27	57	105	24

1934 F.A. Cup

Semi-finals

Manchester City vs Aston Villa	6-1
Portsmouth vs Leicester City	4-1

Final

Wembley, 28th April 1934

Manchester City 2 (Tilson 2)

Portsmouth 1 (Rutherford)

Attendance 93,258

DIVISION ONE 1934-35

ARSENAL	42	23	12	7	115	46	58
Sunderland	42	19	16	7	90	51	54
Sheffield Wednesday	42	18	13	11	70	64	49
Manchester City	42	20	8	14	82	67	48
Grimsby Town	42	17	11	14	78	60	45
Derby County	42	18	9	15	81	66	45
Liverpool	42	19	7	16	85	88	45
Everton	42	16	12	14	89	88	44
West Bromwich Albion	42	17	10	15	83	83	44
Stoke City	42	18	6	18	71	70	42
Preston North End	42	15	12	15	62	67	42
Chelsea	42	16	9	17	73	82	41
Aston Villa	42	14	13	15	74	88	41
Portsmouth	42	15	10	17	71	72	40
Blackburn Rovers	42	14	11	17	66	78	39
Huddersfield Town	42	14	10	18	76	71	38
Wolverhampton Wanderers	42	15	8	19	88	94	38
Leeds United	42	13	12	17	75	92	38
Birmingham	42	13	10	19	63	81	36
Middlesbrough	42	10	14	18	70	90	34
Leicester City	*42*	*12*	*9*	*21*	*61*	*86*	*33*
Tottenham Hotspur	*42*	*10*	*10*	*22*	*54*	*93*	*30*

DIVISION TWO 1934-35

Brentford	42	26	9	7	93	48	61
Bolton Wanderers	42	26	4	12	96	48	56
West Ham United	42	26	4	12	80	63	56
Blackpool	42	21	11	10	79	57	53
Manchester United	42	23	4	15	76	55	50
Newcastle United	42	22	4	16	89	68	48
Fulham	42	17	12	13	76	56	46
Plymouth Argyle	42	19	8	15	75	64	46
Nottingham Forest	42	17	8	17	76	70	42
Bury	42	19	4	19	62	73	42
Sheffield United	42	16	9	17	79	70	41
Burnley	42	16	9	17	63	73	41
Hull City	42	16	8	18	63	74	40
Norwich City	42	14	11	17	71	61	39
Bradford Park Avenue	42	11	16	15	55	63	38
Barnsley	42	13	12	17	60	83	38
Swansea Town	42	14	8	20	56	67	36
Port Vale	42	11	12	19	55	74	34
Southampton	42	11	12	19	46	75	34
Bradford City	42	12	8	22	50	68	32
Oldham Athletic	*42*	*10*	*6*	*26*	*56*	*95*	*26*
Notts County	*42*	*9*	*7*	*26*	*46*	*97*	*25*

DIVISION THREE (N) 1934-35

Doncaster Rovers	42	26	5	11	87	44	57
Halifax Town	42	25	5	12	76	67	55
Chester	42	20	14	8	91	58	54
Lincoln City	42	22	7	13	87	58	51
Darlington	42	21	9	12	80	59	51
Tranmere Rovers	42	20	11	11	74	55	51
Stockport County	42	22	3	17	90	72	47
Mansfield Town	42	19	9	14	75	62	47
Rotherham United	42	19	7	16	86	73	45
Chesterfield	42	17	10	15	71	52	44
Wrexham	42	16	11	15	76	69	43
Hartlepools United	42	17	7	18	80	78	41
Crewe Alexandra	42	14	11	17	66	86	39
Walsall	42	13	10	19	81	72	36
York City	42	15	6	21	76	82	36
New Brighton	42	14	8	20	59	76	36
Barrow	42	13	9	20	58	87	35
Accrington Stanley	42	12	10	20	63	89	34
Gateshead	42	13	8	21	58	96	34
Rochdale	42	11	11	20	53	71	33
Southport	42	10	12	20	55	85	32
Carlisle United	42	8	7	27	51	102	23

DIVISION THREE (S) 1934-35

Charlton Athletic	42	27	7	8	103	52	61
Reading	42	21	11	10	89	65	53
Coventry City	42	21	9	12	86	50	51
Luton Town	42	19	12	11	92	60	50
Crystal Palace	42	19	10	13	86	64	48
Watford	42	19	9	14	76	49	47
Northampton Town	42	19	8	15	65	67	46
Bristol Rovers	42	17	10	15	73	77	44
Brighton & Hove Albion	42	17	9	16	69	62	43
Torquay United	42	18	6	18	81	75	42
Exeter City	42	16	9	17	70	75	41
Millwall	42	17	7	18	57	62	41
Queen's Park Rangers	42	16	9	17	63	72	41
Clapton Orient	42	15	10	17	65	65	40
Bristol City	42	15	9	18	52	68	39
Swindon Town	42	13	12	17	67	78	38
Bournemouth & Boscombe Ath.	42	15	7	20	54	71	37
Aldershot	42	13	10	19	50	75	36
Cardiff City	42	13	9	20	62	82	35
Gillingham	42	11	13	18	55	75	35
Southend United	42	11	9	22	65	78	31
Newport County	42	10	5	27	54	112	25

1935 F.A. Cup

Semi-finals

Sheffield Wednesday vs Burnley	3-0
Bolton Wanderers vs West Bromwich Albion	1-1, 0-2

Final

Wembley, 27th April 1935

Sheffield Wednesday 4 (Rimmer 2, Palethorpe, Hooper)

West Bromwich Albion 2 (Boyes, Sandford)

Attendance 93,204

DIVISION ONE 1935-36

SUNDERLAND	42	25	6	11	109	74	56
Derby County	42	18	12	12	61	52	48
Huddersfield Town	42	18	12	12	59	56	48
Stoke City	42	20	7	15	57	57	47
Brentford	42	17	12	13	81	60	46
Arsenal	42	15	15	12	78	48	45
Preston North End	42	18	8	16	67	64	44
Chelsea	42	15	13	14	65	72	43
Manchester City	42	17	8	17	68	60	42
Portsmouth	42	17	8	17	54	67	42
Leeds United	42	15	11	16	66	64	41
Birmingham	42	15	11	16	61	63	41
Bolton Wanderers	42	14	13	15	67	76	41
Middlesbrough	42	15	10	17	84	70	40
Wolverhampton Wanderers	42	15	10	17	77	76	40
Everton	42	13	13	16	89	89	39
Grimsby Town	42	17	5	20	65	73	39
West Bromwich Albion	42	16	6	20	89	88	38
Liverpool	42	13	12	17	60	64	38
Sheffield Wednesday	42	13	12	17	63	77	38
Aston Villa	*42*	*13*	*9*	*20*	*81*	*110*	*35*
Blackburn Rovers	*42*	*12*	*9*	*21*	*55*	*96*	*33*

DIVISION TWO 1935-36

Manchester United	42	22	12	8	85	43	56
Charlton Athletic	42	22	11	9	85	58	55
Sheffield United	42	20	12	10	79	50	52
West Ham United	42	22	8	12	90	68	52
Tottenham Hotspur	42	18	13	11	91	55	49
Leicester City	42	19	10	13	79	57	48
Plymouth Argyle	42	20	8	14	71	57	48
Newcastle United	42	20	6	16	88	79	46
Fulham	42	15	14	13	76	52	44
Blackpool	42	18	7	17	93	72	43
Norwich City	42	17	9	16	72	65	43
Bradford City	42	15	13	14	55	65	43
Swansea Town	42	15	9	18	67	76	39
Bury	42	13	12	17	66	84	38
Burnley	42	12	13	17	50	59	37
Bradford Park Avenue	42	14	9	19	62	84	37
Southampton	42	14	9	19	47	65	37
Doncaster Rovers	42	14	9	19	51	71	37
Nottingham Forest	42	12	11	19	69	76	35
Barnsley	42	12	9	21	54	80	33
Port Vale	*42*	*12*	*8*	*22*	*56*	*106*	*32*
Hull City	*42*	*5*	*10*	*27*	*47*	*111*	*20*

DIVISION THREE (N) 1935-36

Chesterfield	42	24	12	6	92	39	60
Chester	42	22	11	9	100	45	55
Tranmere Rovers	42	22	11	9	93	58	55
Lincoln City	42	22	9	11	91	51	53
Stockport County	42	20	8	14	65	49	48
Crewe Alexandra	42	19	9	14	80	76	47
Oldham Athletic	42	18	9	15	86	73	45
Hartlepools United	42	15	12	15	57	61	42
Accrington Stanley	42	17	8	17	63	72	42
Walsall	42	16	9	17	79	59	41
Rotherham United	42	16	9	17	69	66	41
Darlington	42	17	6	19	74	79	40
Carlisle United	42	14	12	16	56	62	40
Gateshead	42	13	14	15	56	76	40
Barrow	42	13	12	17	58	65	38
York City	42	13	12	17	62	95	38
Halifax Town	42	15	7	20	57	61	37
Wrexham	42	15	7	20	66	75	37
Mansfield Town	42	14	9	19	80	91	37
Rochdale	42	10	13	19	58	88	33
Southport	42	11	9	22	48	90	31
New Brighton	42	9	6	27	43	102	24

DIVISION THREE (S) 1935-36

Coventry City	42	24	9	9	102	45	57
Luton Town	42	22	12	8	81	45	56
Reading	42	26	2	14	87	62	54
Queen's Park Rangers	42	22	9	11	84	53	53
Watford	42	20	9	13	80	54	49
Crystal Palace	42	22	5	15	96	74	49
Brighton & Hove Albion	42	18	8	16	70	63	44
Bournemouth & Boscombe Ath.	42	16	11	15	60	56	43
Notts County	42	15	12	15	60	57	42
Torquay United	42	16	9	17	62	62	41
Aldershot	42	14	12	16	53	61	40
Millwall	42	14	12	16	58	71	40
Bristol City	42	15	10	17	48	59	40
Clapton Orient	42	16	6	20	55	61	38
Northampton Town	42	15	8	19	62	90	38
Gillingham	42	14	9	19	66	77	37
Bristol Rovers	42	14	9	19	69	95	37
Southend United	42	13	10	19	61	62	36
Swindon Town	42	14	8	20	64	73	36
Cardiff City	42	13	10	19	60	73	36
Newport County	42	11	9	22	60	111	31
Exeter City	42	8	11	23	59	93	27

1936 F.A. Cup

Semi-finals

Arsenal vs Grimsby Town	1-0
Fulham vs Sheffield United	1-2

Final

Wembley, 25th April 1936

Arsenal 1   (Drake)

Sheffield United 0

Attendance 93,384

DIVISION ONE 1936-37

	P	W	D	L	F	A	Pts
MANCHESTER CITY	42	22	13	7	107	61	57
Charlton Athletic	42	21	12	9	58	49	54
Arsenal	42	18	16	8	80	49	52
Derby County	42	21	7	14	96	90	49
Wolverhampton Wanderers	42	21	5	16	84	67	47
Brentford	42	18	10	14	82	78	46
Middlesbrough	42	19	8	15	74	71	46
Sunderland	42	19	6	17	89	87	44
Portsmouth	42	17	10	15	62	66	44
Stoke City	42	15	12	15	72	57	42
Birmingham	42	13	15	14	64	60	41
Grimsby Town	42	17	7	18	86	81	41
Chelsea	42	14	13	15	52	55	41
Preston North End	42	14	13	15	56	67	41
Huddersfield Town	42	12	15	15	62	64	39
West Bromwich Albion	42	16	6	20	77	98	38
Everton	42	14	9	19	81	78	37
Liverpool	42	12	11	19	62	84	35
Leeds United	42	15	4	23	60	80	34
Bolton Wanderers	42	10	14	18	43	66	34
Manchester United	42	10	12	20	55	78	32
Sheffield Wednesday	42	9	12	21	53	69	30

DIVISION TWO 1936-37

	P	W	D	L	F	A	Pts
Leicester City	42	24	8	10	89	57	56
Blackpool	42	24	7	11	88	53	55
Bury	42	22	8	12	74	55	52
Newcastle United	42	22	5	15	80	56	49
Plymouth Argyle	42	18	13	11	71	53	49
West Ham United	42	19	11	12	73	55	49
Sheffield United	42	18	10	14	66	54	46
Coventry City	42	17	11	14	66	54	45
Aston Villa	42	16	12	14	82	70	44
Tottenham Hotspur	42	17	9	16	88	66	43
Fulham	42	15	13	14	71	61	43
Blackburn Rovers	42	16	10	16	70	62	42
Burnley	42	16	10	16	57	61	42
Barnsley	42	16	9	17	50	64	41
Chesterfield	42	16	8	18	84	89	40
Swansea Town	42	15	7	20	50	65	37
Norwich City	42	14	8	20	63	71	36
Nottingham Forest	42	12	10	20	68	90	34
Southampton	42	11	12	19	53	77	34
Bradford Park Avenue	42	12	9	21	52	88	33
Bradford City	42	9	12	21	54	94	30
Doncaster Rovers	42	7	10	25	30	84	24

DIVISION THREE (N) 1936-37

	P	W	D	L	F	A	Pts
Stockport County	42	23	14	5	84	39	60
Lincoln City	42	25	7	10	103	57	57
Chester	42	22	9	11	87	57	53
Oldham Athletic	42	20	11	11	77	59	51
Hull City	42	17	12	13	68	69	46
Hartlepools United	42	19	7	16	75	69	45
Halifax Town	42	18	9	15	68	63	45
Wrexham	42	16	12	14	71	57	44
Mansfield Town	42	18	8	16	91	76	44
Carlisle United	42	18	8	16	65	68	44
Port Vale	42	17	10	15	58	64	44
York City	42	16	11	15	79	70	43
Accrington Stanley	42	16	9	17	76	69	41
Southport	42	12	13	17	73	87	37
New Brighton	42	13	11	18	55	70	37
Barrow	42	13	10	19	70	86	36
Rotherham United	42	14	7	21	78	91	35
Rochdale	42	13	9	20	69	86	35
Tranmere Rovers	42	12	9	21	71	88	33
Crewe Alexandra	42	10	12	20	55	83	32
Gateshead	42	11	10	21	63	98	32
Darlington	42	8	14	20	66	96	30

DIVISION THREE (S) 1936-37

	P	W	D	L	F	A	Pts
Luton Town	42	27	4	11	103	53	58
Notts County	42	23	10	9	74	52	56
Brighton & Hove Albion	42	24	5	14	74	43	53
Watford	42	19	11	12	85	60	49
Reading	42	19	11	12	76	60	49
Bournemouth & Boscombe Ath.	42	20	9	13	65	59	49
Northampton Town	42	20	6	16	85	68	46
Millwall	42	18	10	14	64	54	46
Queen's Park Rangers	42	18	9	15	73	52	45
Southend United	42	17	11	14	78	67	45
Gillingham	42	18	8	16	52	66	44
Clapton Orient	42	14	15	13	52	52	43
Swindon Town	42	14	11	17	75	73	39
Crystal Palace	42	13	12	17	62	61	38
Bristol Rovers	42	16	4	22	71	80	36
Bristol City	42	15	6	21	58	70	36
Walsall	42	13	10	19	62	84	36
Cardiff City	42	14	7	21	54	87	35
Newport County	42	12	10	20	67	98	34
Torquay United	42	11	10	21	57	80	32
Exeter City	42	10	12	20	59	88	32
Aldershot	42	7	9	26	50	89	23

1937 F.A. Cup

Semi-finals

Sunderland vs Millwall	2-1
Preston North End vs West Bromwich Albion	4-1

Final

Wembley, 1st May 1937

Sunderland 3 (Gurney, Carter, Burbanks)
Preston North End 1 (F. O'Donnell)

Attendance 93,495

DIVISION ONE 1937-38

ARSENAL	42	21	10	11	77	44	52
Wolverhampton Wanderers	42	20	11	11	72	49	51
Preston North End	42	16	17	9	64	44	49
Charlton Athletic	42	16	14	12	65	51	46
Middlesbrough	42	19	8	15	72	65	46
Brentford	42	18	9	15	69	59	45
Bolton Wanderers	42	15	15	12	64	60	45
Sunderland	42	14	16	12	55	57	44
Leeds United	42	14	15	13	64	69	43
Chelsea	42	14	13	15	65	65	41
Liverpool	42	15	11	16	65	71	41
Blackpool	42	16	8	18	61	66	40
Derby County	42	15	10	17	66	87	40
Everton	42	16	7	19	79	75	39
Huddersfield Town	42	17	5	20	55	68	39
Leicester City	42	14	11	17	54	75	39
Stoke City	42	13	12	17	58	59	38
Birmingham	42	10	18	14	58	62	38
Portsmouth	42	13	12	17	62	68	38
Grimsby Town	42	13	12	17	51	68	38
Manchester City	*42*	*14*	*8*	*20*	*80*	*77*	*36*
West Bromwich Albion	*42*	*14*	*8*	*20*	*74*	*91*	*36*

DIVISION THREE (N) 1937-38

Tranmere Rovers	42	23	10	9	81	41	56
Doncaster Rovers	42	21	12	9	74	49	54
Hull City	42	20	13	9	80	43	53
Oldham Athletic	42	19	13	10	67	46	51
Gateshead	42	20	11	11	84	59	51
Rotherham United	42	20	10	12	68	56	50
Lincoln City	42	19	8	15	66	50	46
Crewe Alexandra	42	18	9	15	71	53	45
Chester	42	16	12	14	77	72	44
Wrexham	42	16	11	15	58	63	43
York City	42	16	10	16	70	68	42
Carlisle United	42	15	9	18	57	67	39
New Brighton	42	15	8	19	60	61	38
Bradford City	42	14	10	18	66	69	38
Port Vale	42	12	14	16	65	73	38
Southport	42	12	14	16	53	82	38
Rochdale	42	13	11	18	67	78	37
Halifax Town	42	12	12	18	44	66	36
Darlington	42	11	10	21	54	79	32
Hartlepools United	42	10	12	20	53	80	32
Barrow	42	11	10	21	41	71	32
Accrington Stanley	42	11	7	24	45	75	29

DIVISION TWO 1937-38

Aston Villa	42	25	7	10	73	35	57
Manchester United	42	22	9	11	82	50	53
Sheffield United	42	22	9	11	73	56	53
Coventry City	42	20	12	10	66	45	52
Tottenham Hotspur	42	19	6	17	76	54	44
Burnley	42	17	10	15	54	54	44
Bradford Park Avenue	42	17	9	16	69	56	43
Fulham	42	16	11	15	61	57	43
West Ham United	42	14	14	14	53	52	42
Bury	42	18	5	19	63	60	41
Chesterfield	42	16	9	17	63	63	41
Luton Town	42	15	10	17	89	86	40
Plymouth Argyle	42	14	12	16	57	65	40
Norwich City	42	14	11	17	56	75	39
Southampton	42	15	9	18	55	77	39
Blackburn Rovers	42	14	10	18	71	80	38
Sheffield Wednesday	42	14	10	18	49	56	38
Swansea Town	42	13	12	17	45	73	38
Newcastle United	42	14	8	20	51	58	36
Nottingham Forest	42	14	8	20	47	60	36
Barnsley	*42*	*11*	*14*	*17*	*50*	*64*	*36*
Stockport County	*42*	*11*	*9*	*22*	*43*	*70*	*31*

DIVISION THREE (S) 1937-38

Millwall	42	23	10	9	83	37	56
Bristol City	42	21	13	8	68	40	55
Queen's Park Rangers	42	22	9	11	80	47	53
Watford	42	21	11	10	73	43	53
Brighton & Hove Albion	42	21	9	12	64	44	51
Reading	42	20	11	11	71	63	51
Crystal Palace	42	18	12	12	67	47	48
Swindon Town	42	17	10	15	49	49	44
Northampton Town	42	17	9	16	51	57	43
Cardiff City	42	15	12	15	67	54	42
Notts County	42	16	9	17	50	50	41
Southend United	42	15	10	17	70	68	40
Bournemouth & Boscombe Ath.	42	14	12	16	56	57	40
Mansfield Town	42	15	9	18	62	67	39
Bristol Rovers	42	13	13	16	46	61	39
Newport County	42	11	16	15	43	52	38
Exeter City	42	13	12	17	57	70	38
Aldershot	42	15	5	22	39	59	35
Clapton Orient	42	13	7	22	42	61	33
Torquay United	42	9	12	21	38	73	30
Walsall	42	11	7	24	52	88	29
Gillingham	*42*	*10*	*6*	*26*	*36*	*77*	*26*

1938 F.A. Cup

Semi-finals

Preston North End vs Aston Villa	2-1
Sunderland vs Huddersfield Town	1-3

Final

Wembley, 30th April 1938

Preston North End 1 (Mutch (pen))
Huddersfield Town 0 (aet.)

Attendance 93,497

DIVISION ONE 1938-39

EVERTON	42	27	5	10	88	52	59	
Wolverhampton Wanderers	42	22	11	9	88	39	55	
Charlton Athletic	42	22	6	14	75	59	50	
Middlesbrough	42	20	9	13	93	74	49	
Arsenal	42	19	9	14	55	41	47	
Derby County	42	19	8	15	66	55	46	
Stoke City	42	17	12	13	71	68	46	
Bolton Wanderers	42	15	15	12	67	58	45	
Preston North End	42	16	12	14	63	59	44	
Grimsby Town	42	16	11	15	61	69	43	
Liverpool	42	14	14	14	62	63	42	
Aston Villa	42	15	11	16	71	60	41	
Leeds United	42	16	9	17	59	67	41	
Manchester United	42	11	16	15	57	65	38	
Blackpool	42	12	14	16	56	68	38	
Sunderland	42	13	12	17	54	67	38	
Portsmouth	42	12	13	17	47	70	37	
Brentford	42	14	8	20	53	74	36	
Huddersfield Town	42	12	11	19	58	64	35	
Chelsea	42	12	9	21	64	80	33	
Birmingham	42	12	8	22	62	84	32	
Leicester City	42	9	11	22	48	82	29	

DIVISION THREE (N) 1938-39

Barnsley	42	30	7	5	94	34	67	
Doncaster Rovers	42	21	14	7	87	47	56	
Bradford City	42	22	8	12	89	56	52	
Southport	42	20	10	12	75	54	50	
Oldham Athletic	42	22	5	15	76	59	49	
Chester	42	20	9	13	88	70	49	
Hull City	42	18	10	14	83	74	46	
Crewe Alexandra	42	19	6	17	82	70	44	
Stockport County	42	17	9	16	91	77	43	
Gateshead	42	14	14	14	74	67	42	
Rotherham United	42	17	8	17	64	64	42	
Halifax Town	42	13	16	13	52	54	42	
Barrow	42	16	9	17	66	65	41	
Wrexham	42	17	7	18	66	79	41	
Rochdale	42	15	9	18	92	82	39	
New Brighton	42	15	9	18	68	73	39	
Lincoln City	42	12	9	21	66	92	33	
Darlington	42	13	7	22	62	92	33	
Carlisle United	42	13	7	22	64	111	33	
York City	42	12	9	21	66	92	33	
Hartlepools United	42	12	7	23	55	94	31	
Accrington Stanley	42	7	6	29	49	103	20	

DIVISION TWO 1938-39

Blackburn Rovers	42	25	5	12	94	60	55	
Sheffield United	42	20	14	8	69	41	54	
Sheffield Wednesday	42	21	11	10	88	59	53	
Coventry City	42	21	8	13	62	45	50	
Manchester City	42	21	7	14	96	72	49	
Chesterfield	42	20	9	13	69	52	49	
Luton Town	42	22	5	15	82	66	49	
Tottenham Hotspur	42	19	9	14	67	62	47	
Newcastle United	42	18	10	14	61	48	46	
West Bromwich Albion	42	18	9	15	89	72	45	
West Ham United	42	17	10	15	70	52	44	
Fulham	42	17	10	15	61	55	44	
Millwall	42	14	14	14	64	53	42	
Burnley	42	15	9	18	50	56	39	
Plymouth Argyle	42	15	8	19	49	55	38	
Bury	42	12	13	17	65	74	37	
Bradford Park Avenue	42	12	11	19	61	82	35	
Southampton	42	13	9	20	56	82	35	
Swansea Town	42	11	12	19	50	83	34	
Nottingham Forest	42	10	11	21	49	82	31	
Norwich City	42	13	5	24	50	91	31	
Tranmere Rovers	42	6	5	31	39	99	17	

DIVISION THREE (S) 1938-39

Newport County	42	22	11	9	58	45	55	
Crystal Palace	42	20	12	10	71	52	52	
Brighton & Hove Albion	42	19	11	12	68	49	49	
Watford	42	17	12	13	62	51	46	
Reading	42	16	14	12	69	59	46	
Queen's Park Rangers	42	15	15	14	68	49	44	
Ipswich Town	42	16	12	14	62	52	44	
Bristol City	42	16	12	14	61	63	44	
Swindon Town	42	18	8	16	72	77	44	
Aldershot	42	16	12	14	53	66	44	
Notts County	42	17	9	16	59	54	43	
Southend United	42	16	9	17	61	64	41	
Cardiff City	42	15	11	16	61	65	41	
Exeter City	42	13	14	15	65	82	40	
Bournemouth & Boscombe Ath.	42	13	13	16	52	58	39	
Mansfield Town	42	12	15	15	44	62	39	
Northampton Town	42	15	8	19	51	58	38	
Port Vale	42	14	9	19	52	58	37	
Torquay United	42	14	9	19	54	70	37	
Clapton Orient	42	11	13	18	53	55	35	
Walsall	42	11	11	20	68	69	33	
Bristol Rovers	42	10	13	19	55	61	33	

1939 F.A. Cup

Semi-finals

Portsmouth vs Huddersfield Town	2-1
Wolverhampton Wanderers vs Grimsby Town	5-0

Final

Wembley, 29th April 1939

Portsmouth 4   (Parker 2, Barlow, Anderson)
Wolverhampton Wanderers 1   (Dorsett)

Attendance 99,370

1946 F.A. Cup

Semi-finals

Bolton Wanderers vs Charlton Athletic	0-2
Derby County vs Birmingham City	1-1,4-0

Final

Wembley, 27th April 1946

Derby County 4   (H. Turner (og), Doherty, Stamps 2)
Charlton Athletic 1   (H. Turner)

Attendance 98,000

DIVISION ONE 1946-47

LIVERPOOL	42	25	7	10	84	52	57
Manchester United	42	22	12	8	95	54	56
Wolverhampton Wanderers	42	25	6	11	98	56	56
Stoke City	42	24	7	11	90	53	55
Blackpool	42	22	6	14	71	70	50
Sheffield United	42	21	7	14	89	75	49
Preston North End	42	18	11	13	76	74	47
Aston Villa	42	18	9	15	67	53	45
Sunderland	42	18	8	16	65	66	44
Everton	42	17	9	16	62	67	43
Middlesbrough	42	17	8	17	73	68	42
Portsmouth	42	16	9	17	66	60	41
Arsenal	42	16	9	17	72	70	41
Derby County	42	18	5	19	73	79	41
Chelsea	42	16	7	19	69	84	39
Grimsby Town	42	13	12	17	61	82	38
Blackburn Rovers	42	14	8	20	45	53	36
Bolton Wanderers	42	13	8	21	57	69	34
Charlton Athletic	42	11	12	19	57	71	34
Huddersfield Town	42	13	7	22	53	79	33
Brentford	*42*	*9*	*7*	*26*	*45*	*88*	*25*
Leeds United	*42*	*6*	*6*	*30*	*45*	*90*	*18*

DIVISION THREE (N) 1946-47

Doncaster Rovers	42	33	6	3	123	40	72
Rotherham United	42	29	6	7	114	53	64
Chester	42	25	6	11	95	51	56
Stockport County	42	24	2	16	78	53	50
Bradford City	42	20	10	12	62	47	50
Rochdale	42	19	10	13	80	64	48
Wrexham	42	17	12	13	65	51	46
Crewe Alexandra	42	17	9	16	70	74	43
Barrow	42	17	7	18	54	62	41
Tranmere Rovers	42	17	7	18	66	77	41
Hull City	42	16	8	18	49	53	40
Lincoln City	42	17	5	20	86	87	39
Hartlepools United	42	15	9	18	64	73	39
Gateshead	42	16	6	20	62	72	38
York City	42	14	9	19	67	81	37
Carlisle United	42	14	9	19	70	93	37
Darlington	42	15	6	21	68	80	36
New Brighton	42	14	8	20	57	77	36
Oldham Athletic	42	12	8	22	55	80	32
Accrington Stanley	42	14	4	24	56	92	32
Southport	42	7	11	24	53	85	25
Halifax Town	42	8	6	28	43	92	22

DIVISION TWO 1946-47

Manchester City	42	26	10	6	78	35	62
Burnley	42	22	14	6	65	29	58
Birmingham City	42	25	5	12	74	33	55
Chesterfield	42	18	14	10	58	44	50
Newcastle United	42	19	10	13	95	62	48
Tottenham Hotspur	42	17	14	11	65	53	48
West Bromwich Albion	42	20	8	14	88	75	48
Coventry City	42	16	13	13	66	59	45
Leicester City	42	18	7	17	69	64	43
Barnsley	42	17	8	17	84	86	42
Nottingham Forest	42	15	10	17	69	74	40
West Ham United	42	16	8	18	70	76	40
Luton Town	42	16	7	19	71	73	39
Southampton	42	15	9	18	69	76	39
Fulham	42	15	9	18	63	74	39
Bradford Park Avenue	42	14	11	17	65	77	39
Bury	42	12	12	18	80	78	36
Millwall	42	14	8	20	56	79	36
Plymouth Argyle	42	14	5	23	79	96	33
Sheffield Wednesday	42	12	8	22	67	88	32
Swansea Town	*42*	*11*	*7*	*24*	*55*	*83*	*29*
Newport County	*42*	*10*	*3*	*29*	*61*	*133*	*23*

DIVISION THREE (S) 1946-47

Cardiff City	42	30	6	6	93	30	66
Queen's Park Rangers	42	23	11	8	74	40	57
Bristol City	42	20	11	11	94	56	51
Swindon Town	42	19	11	12	84	73	49
Walsall	42	17	12	13	74	59	46
Ipswich Town	42	16	14	12	61	53	46
Bournemouth & Boscombe Ath.	42	18	8	16	72	54	44
Southend United	42	17	10	15	71	60	44
Reading	42	16	11	15	83	74	43
Port Vale	42	17	9	16	68	63	43
Torquay United	42	15	12	15	52	61	42
Notts County	42	15	10	17	63	63	40
Northampton Town	42	15	10	17	72	75	40
Bristol Rovers	42	16	8	18	59	69	40
Exeter City	42	15	9	18	60	69	39
Watford	42	17	5	20	61	76	39
Brighton & Hove Albion	42	13	12	17	54	72	38
Crystal Palace	42	13	11	18	49	62	37
Leyton Orient	42	12	8	22	54	75	32
Aldershot	42	10	12	20	48	78	32
Norwich City	42	10	8	24	64	100	28
Mansfield Town	42	9	10	23	48	96	28

1947 F.A. Cup

Semi-finals

Charlton Athletic vs Newcastle United	4-0
Burnley vs Liverpool	0-0, 1-0

Final

Wembley, 26th April 1947

Charlton Athletic 1 (Duffy)
Burnley 0 (aet.)

Attendance 99,000

DIVISION ONE 1947-48

ARSENAL	42	23	13	6	81	32	59
Manchester United	42	19	14	9	81	48	52
Burnley	42	20	12	10	56	43	52
Derby County	42	19	12	11	77	57	50
Wolverhampton Wanderers	42	19	9	14	83	70	47
Aston Villa	42	19	9	14	65	57	47
Preston North End	42	20	7	15	67	68	47
Portsmouth	42	19	7	16	68	50	45
Blackpool	42	17	10	15	57	41	44
Manchester City	42	15	12	15	52	47	42
Liverpool	42	16	10	16	65	61	42
Sheffield United	42	16	10	16	65	70	42
Charlton Athletic	42	17	6	19	57	66	40
Everton	42	17	6	19	52	66	40
Stoke City	42	14	10	18	41	55	38
Middlesbrough	42	14	9	19	71	73	37
Bolton Wanderers	42	16	5	21	46	58	37
Chelsea	42	14	9	19	53	71	37
Huddersfield Town	42	12	12	18	51	60	36
Sunderland	42	13	10	19	56	67	36
Blackburn Rovers	*42*	*11*	*10*	*21*	*54*	*72*	*32*
Grimsby Town	*42*	*8*	*6*	*28*	*45*	*111*	*22*

DIVISION THREE (N) 1947-48

Lincoln City	42	26	8	8	81	40	60
Rotherham United	42	25	9	8	95	49	59
Wrexham	42	21	8	13	74	54	50
Gateshead	42	19	11	12	75	57	49
Hull City	42	18	11	13	59	48	47
Accrington Stanley	42	20	6	16	62	59	46
Barrow	42	16	13	13	49	40	45
Mansfield Town	42	17	11	14	57	51	45
Carlisle United	42	18	7	17	88	77	43
Crewe Alexandra	42	18	7	17	61	63	43
Oldham Athletic	42	14	13	15	63	64	41
Rochdale	42	15	11	16	48	72	41
York City	42	13	14	15	65	60	40
Bradford City	42	15	10	17	65	66	40
Southport	42	14	11	17	60	63	39
Darlington	42	13	13	16	54	70	39
Stockport County	42	13	12	17	63	67	38
Tranmere Rovers	42	16	4	22	54	72	36
Hartlepools United	42	14	8	20	51	73	36
Chester	42	13	9	20	64	67	35
Halifax Town	42	7	13	22	43	76	27
New Brighton	42	8	9	25	38	81	25

DIVISION TWO 1947-48

Birmingham City	42	22	15	5	55	24	59
Newcastle United	42	24	8	10	72	41	56
Southampton	42	21	10	11	71	53	52
Sheffield Wednesday	42	20	11	11	66	53	51
Cardiff City	42	18	11	13	61	58	47
West Ham United	42	16	14	12	55	53	46
West Bromwich Albion	42	18	9	15	63	58	45
Tottenham Hotspur	42	15	14	13	56	43	44
Leicester City	42	16	11	15	60	57	43
Coventry City	42	14	13	15	59	52	41
Fulham	42	15	10	17	47	46	40
Barnsley	42	15	10	17	62	64	40
Luton Town	42	14	12	16	56	59	40
Bradford Park Avenue	42	16	8	18	68	72	40
Brentford	42	13	14	15	44	61	40
Chesterfield	42	16	7	19	54	55	39
Plymouth Argyle	42	9	20	13	40	58	38
Leeds United	42	14	8	20	62	72	36
Nottingham Forest	42	12	11	19	54	60	35
Bury	42	9	16	17	58	68	34
Doncaster Rovers	*42*	*9*	*11*	*22*	*40*	*66*	*29*
Millwall	*42*	*9*	*11*	*22*	*44*	*74*	*29*

DIVISION THREE (S) 1947-48

Queen's Park Rangers	42	26	9	7	74	37	61
Bournemouth & Boscombe Ath.	42	24	9	9	76	35	57
Walsall	42	21	9	12	70	40	51
Ipswich Town	42	23	3	16	67	61	49
Swansea Town	42	18	12	12	70	52	48
Notts County	42	19	8	15	68	59	46
Bristol City	42	18	7	17	77	65	43
Port Vale	42	16	11	15	63	54	43
Southend United	42	15	13	14	51	58	43
Reading	42	15	11	16	56	58	41
Exeter City	42	15	11	16	55	63	41
Newport County	42	14	13	15	61	73	41
Crystal Palace	42	13	13	16	49	49	39
Northampton Town	42	14	11	17	58	72	39
Watford	42	14	10	18	57	79	38
Swindon Town	42	10	16	16	41	46	36
Leyton Orient	42	13	10	19	51	73	36
Torquay United	42	11	13	18	63	62	35
Aldershot	42	10	15	17	45	67	35
Bristol Rovers	42	13	8	21	71	75	34
Norwich City	42	13	8	21	61	76	34
Brighton & Hove Albion	42	11	12	19	43	73	34

1948 F.A. Cup

Semi-finals

Derby County vs Manchester United	1-3
Blackpool vs Tottenham Hotspur	3-1

Final

Wembley, 24th April 1948

Manchester United 4 (Rowley 2, Pearson, Anderson)

Blackpool 2 (Shimwell (pen), Mortensen)

Attendance 99,000

DIVISION ONE 1948-49

PORTSMOUTH	42	25	8	9	84	42	58
Manchester United	42	21	11	10	77	44	53
Derby County	42	22	9	11	74	55	53
Newcastle United	42	20	12	10	70	56	52
Arsenal	42	18	13	11	74	44	49
Wolverhampton Wanderers	42	17	12	13	79	66	46
Manchester City	42	15	15	12	47	51	45
Sunderland	42	13	17	12	49	58	43
Charlton Athletic	42	15	12	15	63	67	42
Aston Villa	42	16	10	16	60	76	42
Stoke City	42	16	9	17	66	68	41
Liverpool	42	13	14	15	53	43	40
Chelsea	42	12	14	16	69	68	38
Bolton Wanderers	42	14	10	18	59	68	38
Burnley	42	12	14	16	43	50	38
Blackpool	42	11	16	15	54	67	38
Birmingham City	42	11	15	16	36	38	37
Everton	42	13	11	18	41	63	37
Middlesbrough	42	11	12	19	46	57	34
Huddersfield Town	42	12	10	20	40	69	34
Preston North End	*42*	*11*	*11*	*20*	*62*	*75*	*33*
Sheffield United	*42*	*11*	*11*	*20*	*57*	*78*	*33*

DIVISION TWO 1948-49

Fulham	42	24	9	9	77	37	57
West Bromwich Albion	42	24	8	10	69	39	56
Southampton	42	23	9	10	69	36	55
Cardiff City	42	19	13	10	62	47	51
Tottenham Hotspur	42	17	16	9	72	44	50
Chesterfield	42	15	17	10	51	45	47
West Ham United	42	18	10	14	56	58	46
Sheffield Wednesday	42	15	13	14	63	56	43
Barnsley	42	14	12	16	62	61	40
Luton Town	42	14	12	16	55	57	40
Grimsby Town	42	15	10	17	72	76	40
Bury	42	17	6	19	67	76	40
Queen's Park Rangers	42	14	11	17	44	62	39
Blackburn Rovers	42	15	8	19	53	63	38
Leeds United	42	12	13	17	55	63	37
Coventry City	42	15	7	20	55	64	37
Bradford Park Avenue	42	13	11	18	65	78	37
Brentford	42	11	14	17	42	53	36
Leicester City	42	10	16	16	62	79	36
Plymouth Argyle	42	12	12	18	49	64	36
Nottingham Forest	*42*	*14*	*7*	*21*	*50*	*54*	*35*
Lincoln City	*42*	*8*	*12*	*22*	*53*	*91*	*28*

DIVISION THREE (N) 1948-49

Hull City	42	27	11	4	93	28	65
Rotherham United	42	28	6	8	90	46	62
Doncaster Rovers	42	20	10	12	53	40	50
Darlington	42	20	6	16	83	74	46
Gateshead	42	16	13	13	69	58	45
Oldham Athletic	42	18	9	15	75	67	45
Rochdale	42	18	9	15	55	53	45
Stockport County	42	16	11	15	61	56	43
Wrexham	42	17	9	16	56	62	43
Mansfield Town	42	14	14	14	52	48	42
Tranmere Rovers	42	13	15	14	46	57	41
Crewe Alexandra	42	16	9	17	52	74	41
Barrow	42	14	12	16	41	48	40
York City	42	15	9	18	74	74	39
Carlisle United	42	14	11	17	60	77	39
Hartlepools United	42	14	10	18	45	58	38
New Brighton	42	14	8	20	46	58	36
Chester	42	11	13	18	57	56	35
Halifax Town	42	12	11	19	45	62	35
Accrington Stanley	42	12	10	20	55	64	34
Southport	42	11	9	22	45	64	31
Bradford City	42	10	9	23	48	77	29

DIVISION THREE (S) 1948-49

Swansea Town	42	27	8	7	87	34	62
Reading	42	25	5	12	77	50	55
Bournemouth & Boscombe Ath.	42	22	8	12	69	48	52
Swindon Town	42	18	15	9	64	56	51
Bristol Rovers	42	19	10	13	61	51	48
Brighton & Hove Albion	42	15	18	9	55	55	48
Ipswich Town	42	18	9	15	78	77	45
Millwall	42	17	11	14	63	64	45
Torquay United	42	17	11	14	65	70	45
Norwich City	42	16	12	14	67	49	44
Notts County	42	19	5	18	102	68	43
Exeter City	42	15	10	17	63	76	40
Port Vale	42	14	11	17	51	54	39
Walsall	42	15	8	19	56	64	38
Newport County	42	14	9	19	68	92	37
Bristol City	42	11	14	17	44	62	36
Watford	42	10	15	17	41	54	35
Southend United	42	9	16	17	41	46	34
Leyton Orient	42	11	12	19	58	80	34
Northampton Town	42	12	9	21	51	62	33
Aldershot	42	11	11	20	48	59	33
Crystal Palace	42	8	11	23	38	76	27

1949 F.A. Cup

Semi-finals

Manchester Utd. vs Wolverhampton Wanderers	1-1, 0-1
Leicester City vs Portsmouth	3-1

Final

Wembley, 30th April 1949

Wolverhampton Wanderers 3 (Pye 2, Smyth)
Leicester City 1 (Griffiths)

Attendance 99,500

DIVISION ONE 1949-50

PORTSMOUTH	**42**	**22**	**9**	**11**	**74**	**38**	**53**
Wolverhampton Wanderers	42	20	13	9	76	49	53
Sunderland	42	21	10	11	83	62	52
Manchester United	42	18	14	10	69	44	50
Newcastle United	42	19	12	11	77	55	50
Arsenal	42	19	11	12	79	55	49
Blackpool	42	17	15	10	46	35	49
Liverpool	42	17	14	11	64	54	48
Middlesbrough	42	20	7	15	59	48	47
Burnley	42	16	13	13	40	40	45
Derby County	42	17	10	15	69	61	44
Aston Villa	42	15	12	15	61	61	42
Chelsea	42	12	16	14	58	65	40
West Bromwich Albion	42	14	12	16	47	53	40
Huddersfield Town	42	14	9	19	52	73	37
Bolton Wanderers	42	10	14	18	45	59	34
Fulham	42	10	14	18	41	54	34
Everton	42	10	14	18	42	66	34
Stoke City	42	11	12	19	45	75	34
Charlton Athletic	42	13	6	23	53	65	32
Manchester City	*42*	*8*	*13*	*21*	*36*	*68*	*29*
Birmingham City	*42*	*7*	*14*	*21*	*31*	*67*	*28*

DIVISION TWO 1949-50

Tottenham Hotspur	**42**	**27**	**7**	**8**	**81**	**35**	**61**
Sheffield Wednesday	**42**	**18**	**16**	**8**	**67**	**48**	**52**
Sheffield United	42	19	14	9	68	49	52
Southampton	42	19	14	9	64	48	52
Leeds United	42	17	13	12	54	45	47
Preston North End	42	18	9	15	60	49	45
Hull City	42	17	11	14	64	72	45
Swansea Town	42	17	9	16	53	49	43
Brentford	42	15	13	14	44	49	43
Cardiff City	42	16	10	16	41	44	42
Grimsby Town	42	16	8	18	74	73	40
Coventry City	42	13	13	16	55	55	39
Barnsley	42	13	13	16	64	67	39
Chesterfield	42	15	9	18	43	47	39
Leicester City	42	12	15	15	55	65	39
Blackburn Rovers	42	14	10	18	55	60	38
Luton Town	42	10	18	14	41	51	38
Bury	42	14	9	19	60	65	37
West Ham United	42	12	12	18	53	61	36
Queen's Park Rangers	42	11	12	19	40	57	34
Plymouth Argyle	*42*	*8*	*16*	*18*	*44*	*65*	*32*
Bradford Park Avenue	*42*	*10*	*11*	*21*	*51*	*77*	*31*

DIVISION THREE (N) 1949-50

Doncaster Rovers	**42**	**19**	**17**	**6**	**66**	**38**	**55**
Gateshead	42	23	7	12	87	54	53
Rochdale	42	21	9	12	68	41	51
Lincoln City	42	21	9	12	60	39	51
Tranmere Rovers	42	19	11	12	51	48	49
Rotherham United	42	19	10	13	80	59	48
Crewe Alexandra	42	17	14	11	68	55	48
Mansfield Town	42	18	12	12	66	54	48
Carlisle United	42	16	15	11	68	51	47
Stockport County	42	19	7	16	55	52	45
Oldham Athletic	42	16	11	15	58	63	43
Chester	42	17	6	19	70	79	40
Accrington Stanley	42	16	7	19	57	62	39
New Brighton	42	14	10	18	45	63	38
Barrow	42	14	9	19	47	53	37
Southport	42	12	13	17	51	71	37
Darlington	42	11	13	18	56	69	35
Hartlepools United	42	14	5	23	52	79	33
Bradford City	42	12	8	22	61	76	32
Wrexham	42	10	12	20	39	54	32
Halifax Town	42	12	8	22	58	85	32
York City	42	9	13	20	52	70	31

DIVISION THREE (S) 1949-50

Notts County	**42**	**25**	**8**	**9**	**95**	**50**	**58**
Northampton Town	42	20	11	11	72	50	51
Southend United	42	19	13	10	66	48	51
Nottingham Forest	42	20	9	13	67	39	49
Torquay United	42	19	10	13	66	63	48
Watford	42	16	13	13	45	35	45
Crystal Palace	42	15	14	13	55	54	44
Brighton & Hove Albion	42	16	12	14	57	69	44
Bristol Rovers	42	19	5	18	51	51	43
Reading	42	17	8	17	70	64	42
Norwich City	42	16	10	16	65	63	42
Bournemouth & Boscombe Ath.	42	16	10	16	57	56	42
Port Vale	42	15	11	16	47	42	41
Swindon Town	42	15	11	16	59	62	41
Bristol City	42	15	10	17	60	61	40
Exeter City	42	14	11	17	63	75	39
Ipswich Town	42	12	11	19	57	86	35
Leyton Orient	42	12	11	19	53	85	35
Walsall	42	9	16	17	61	62	34
Aldershot	42	13	8	21	48	60	34
Newport County	42	13	8	21	67	98	34
Millwall	42	14	4	24	55	63	32

1950 F.A. Cup

Semi-final

Arsenal vs Chelsea	2-2, 1-0
Liverpool vs Everton	2-0

Final

Wembley, 29th April 1950

Arsenal 2   (Lewis 2)

Liverpool 0

Attendance 100,000

DIVISION ONE 1950-51

TOTTENHAM HOTSPUR	42	25	10	7	82	44	60
Manchester United	42	24	8	10	74	40	56
Blackpool	42	20	10	12	79	53	50
Newcastle United	42	18	13	11	62	53	49
Arsenal	42	19	9	14	73	56	47
Middlesbrough	42	18	11	13	76	65	47
Portsmouth	42	16	15	11	71	68	47
Bolton Wanderers	42	19	7	16	64	61	45
Liverpool	42	16	11	15	53	59	43
Burnley	42	14	14	14	48	43	42
Derby County	42	16	8	18	81	75	40
Sunderland	42	12	16	14	63	73	40
Stoke City	42	13	14	15	50	59	40
Wolverhampton Wanderers	42	15	8	19	74	61	38
Aston Villa	42	12	13	17	66	68	37
West Bromwich Albion	42	13	11	18	53	61	37
Charlton Athletic	42	14	9	19	63	80	37
Fulham	42	13	11	18	52	68	37
Huddersfield Town	42	15	6	21	64	92	36
Chelsea	42	12	8	22	53	65	32
Sheffield Wednesday	*42*	*12*	*8*	*22*	*64*	*83*	*32*
Everton	*42*	*12*	*8*	*22*	*48*	*86*	*32*

DIVISION TWO 1950-51

Preston North End	42	26	5	11	91	49	57
Manchester City	42	19	14	9	89	61	52
Cardiff City	42	17	16	9	53	45	50
Birmingham City	42	20	9	13	64	53	49
Leeds United	42	20	8	14	63	55	48
Blackburn Rovers	42	19	8	15	65	66	46
Coventry City	42	19	7	16	75	59	45
Sheffield United	42	16	12	14	72	62	44
Brentford	42	18	8	16	75	74	44
Hull City	42	16	11	15	74	70	43
Doncaster Rovers	42	15	13	14	64	68	43
Southampton	42	15	13	14	66	73	43
West Ham United	42	16	10	16	68	69	42
Leicester City	42	15	11	16	68	58	41
Barnsley	42	15	10	17	74	68	40
Queen's Park Rangers	42	15	10	17	71	82	40
Notts County	42	13	13	16	61	60	39
Swansea Town	42	16	4	22	54	77	36
Luton Town	42	9	14	19	57	70	32
Bury	42	12	8	22	60	86	32
Chesterfield	*42*	*9*	*12*	*21*	*44*	*69*	*30*
Grimsby Town	*42*	*8*	*12*	*22*	*61*	*95*	*28*

DIVISION THREE (N) 1950-51

Rotherham United	46	31	9	6	103	41	71
Mansfield Town	46	26	12	8	78	48	64
Carlisle United	46	25	12	9	79	50	62
Tranmere Rovers	46	24	11	11	83	62	59
Lincoln City	46	25	8	13	89	58	58
Bradford Park Avenue	46	23	8	15	90	72	54
Bradford City	46	21	10	15	90	63	52
Gateshead	46	21	8	17	84	62	50
Crewe Alexandra	46	19	10	17	61	60	48
Stockport County	46	20	8	18	63	63	48
Rochdale	46	17	11	18	69	62	45
Scunthorpe United	46	13	18	15	58	57	44
Chester	46	17	9	20	62	64	43
Wrexham	46	15	12	19	55	71	42
Oldham Athletic	46	16	8	22	73	73	40
Hartlepools United	46	16	7	23	64	66	39
York City	46	12	15	19	66	77	39
Darlington	46	13	13	20	59	77	39
Barrow	46	16	6	24	51	76	38
Shrewsbury Town	46	15	7	24	43	74	37
Southport	46	13	10	23	56	72	36
Halifax Town	46	11	12	23	50	69	34
Accrington Stanley	46	11	10	25	42	101	32
New Brighton	*46*	*11*	*8*	*27*	*40*	*90*	*30*

DIVISION THREE (S) 1950-51

Nottingham Forest	46	30	10	6	110	40	70
Norwich City	46	25	14	7	82	45	64
Reading	46	21	15	10	88	53	57
Plymouth Argyle	46	24	9	13	85	55	57
Millwall	46	23	10	13	80	57	56
Bristol Rovers	46	20	15	11	64	42	55
Southend United	46	21	10	15	92	69	52
Ipswich Town	46	23	6	17	69	58	52
Bournemouth & Boscombe Ath.	46	22	7	17	65	57	51
Bristol City	46	20	11	15	64	59	51
Newport County	46	19	9	18	77	70	47
Port Vale	46	16	13	17	60	65	45
Brighton & Hove Albion	46	13	17	16	71	79	43
Exeter City	46	18	6	22	62	85	42
Walsall	46	15	10	21	52	62	40
Colchester United	46	14	12	20	63	76	40
Swindon Town	46	18	4	24	55	67	40
Aldershot	46	15	10	21	56	88	40
Leyton Orient	46	15	8	23	53	75	38
Torquay United	46	14	9	23	64	81	37
Northampton Town	46	10	16	20	55	67	36
Gillingham	46	13	9	24	69	101	35
Watford	46	9	11	26	54	88	29
Crystal Palace	46	8	11	27	33	84	27

1951 F.A. Cup

Semi-final

Newcastle Utd. vs Wolverhampton Wanderers	0-0, 2-1
Blackpool vs Birmingham City	0-0, 2-1

Final

Wembley, 28th April 1951

Newcastle United 2 (Milburn 2)

Blackpool 0

Attendance 100,000

DIVISION ONE 1951-52

MANCHESTER UNITED	42	23	11	8	95	52	57
Tottenham Hotspur	42	22	9	11	76	51	53
Arsenal	42	21	11	10	80	61	53
Portsmouth	42	20	8	14	68	58	48
Bolton Wanderers	42	19	10	13	65	61	48
Aston Villa	42	19	9	14	79	70	47
Preston North End	42	17	12	13	74	54	46
Newcastle United	42	18	9	15	98	73	45
Blackpool	42	18	9	15	64	64	45
Charlton Athletic	42	17	10	15	68	63	44
Liverpool	42	12	19	11	57	61	43
Sunderland	42	15	12	15	70	61	42
West Bromwich Albion	42	14	13	15	74	77	41
Burnley	42	15	10	17	56	63	40
Manchester City	42	13	13	16	58	61	39
Wolverhampton Wanderers	42	12	14	16	73	73	38
Derby County	42	15	7	20	63	80	37
Middlesbrough	42	15	6	21	64	88	36
Chelsea	42	14	8	20	52	72	36
Stoke City	42	12	7	23	49	88	31
Huddersfield Town	42	10	8	24	49	82	28
Fulham	42	8	11	23	58	77	27

DIVISION TWO 1951-52

Sheffield Wednesday	42	21	11	10	100	66	53
Cardiff City	42	20	11	11	72	54	51
Birmingham City	42	21	9	12	67	56	51
Nottingham Forest	42	18	13	11	77	62	49
Leicester City	42	19	9	14	78	64	47
Leeds United	42	18	11	13	59	57	47
Everton	42	17	10	15	64	58	44
Luton Town	42	16	12	14	77	78	44
Rotherham United	42	17	8	17	73	71	42
Brentford	42	15	12	15	54	55	42
Sheffield United	42	18	5	19	90	76	41
West Ham United	42	15	11	16	67	77	41
Southampton	42	15	11	16	61	73	41
Blackburn Rovers	42	17	6	19	54	63	40
Notts County	42	16	7	19	71	68	39
Doncaster Rovers	42	13	12	17	55	60	38
Bury	42	15	7	20	67	69	37
Hull City	42	13	11	18	60	70	37
Swansea Town	42	12	12	18	72	76	36
Barnsley	42	11	14	17	59	72	36
Coventry City	42	14	6	22	59	82	34
Queen's Park Rangers	42	11	12	19	52	81	34

DIVISION THREE (N) 1951-52

Lincoln City	46	30	9	7	121	52	69
Grimsby Town	46	29	8	9	96	45	66
Stockport County	46	23	13	10	74	40	59
Oldham Athletic	46	24	9	13	90	61	57
Gateshead	46	21	11	14	66	49	53
Mansfield Town	46	22	8	16	73	60	52
Carlisle United	46	19	13	14	62	57	51
Bradford Park Avenue	46	19	12	15	74	64	50
Hartlepools United	46	21	8	17	71	65	50
York City	46	18	13	15	73	52	49
Tranmere Rovers	46	21	6	19	76	71	48
Barrow	46	17	12	17	57	61	46
Chesterfield	46	17	11	18	65	66	45
Scunthorpe United	46	14	16	16	65	74	44
Bradford City	46	16	10	20	61	68	42
Crewe Alexandra	46	17	8	21	63	82	42
Southport	46	15	11	20	53	71	41
Wrexham	46	15	9	22	63	73	39
Chester	46	15	9	22	72	85	39
Halifax Town	46	14	7	25	61	97	35
Rochdale	46	11	13	22	47	79	35
Accrington Stanley	46	10	12	24	61	92	32
Darlington	46	11	9	26	64	103	31
Workington	46	11	7	28	50	91	29

DIVISION THREE (S) 1951-52

Plymouth Argyle	46	29	8	9	107	53	66
Reading	46	29	3	14	112	60	61
Norwich City	46	26	9	11	89	50	61
Millwall	46	23	12	11	74	53	58
Brighton & Hove Albion	46	24	10	12	87	63	58
Newport County	46	21	12	13	77	76	54
Bristol Rovers	46	20	12	14	89	53	52
Northampton Town	46	22	5	19	93	74	49
Southend United	46	19	10	17	75	66	48
Colchester United	46	17	12	17	56	77	46
Torquay United	46	17	10	19	86	98	44
Aldershot	46	18	8	20	78	89	44
Port Vale	46	14	15	17	50	66	43
Bournemouth & Boscombe Ath.	46	16	10	20	69	75	42
Bristol City	46	15	12	19	58	69	42
Swindon Town	46	14	14	18	51	68	42
Ipswich Town	46	16	9	21	63	74	41
Leyton Orient	46	16	9	21	55	68	41
Crystal Palace	46	15	9	22	61	80	39
Shrewsbury Town	46	13	10	23	62	86	36
Watford	46	13	10	23	57	81	36
Gillingham	46	11	13	22	71	81	35
Exeter City	46	13	9	24	65	86	35
Walsall	46	13	5	28	55	94	31

1952 F.A. Cup

Semi-finals

Newcastle United vs Blackburn Rovers	0-0, 2-1
Arsenal vs Chelsea	1-1, 3-0

Final

Wembley, 3rd May 1952

Newcastle United 1   (G. Robledo)
Arsenal 0

Attendance 100,000

DIVISION ONE 1952-53

ARSENAL	42	21	12	9	97	64	54
Preston North End	42	21	12	9	85	60	54
Wolverhampton Wanderers	42	19	13	10	86	63	51
West Bromwich Albion	42	21	8	13	66	60	50
Charlton Athletic	42	19	11	12	77	63	49
Burnley	42	18	12	12	67	52	48
Blackpool	42	19	9	14	71	70	47
Manchester United	42	18	10	14	69	72	46
Sunderland	42	15	13	14	68	82	43
Tottenham Hotspur	42	15	11	16	78	69	41
Aston Villa	42	14	13	15	63	61	41
Cardiff City	42	14	12	16	54	46	40
Middlesbrough	42	14	11	17	70	77	39
Bolton Wanderers	42	15	9	18	61	69	39
Portsmouth	42	14	10	18	74	83	38
Newcastle United	42	14	9	19	59	70	37
Liverpool	42	14	8	20	61	82	36
Sheffield Wednesday	42	12	11	19	62	72	35
Chelsea	42	12	11	19	56	66	35
Manchester City	42	14	7	21	72	87	35
Stoke City	*42*	*12*	*10*	*20*	*53*	*66*	*34*
Derby County	*42*	*11*	*10*	*21*	*59*	*74*	*32*

DIVISION THREE (N) 1952-53

Oldham Athletic	46	22	15	9	77	45	59
Port Vale	46	20	18	8	67	35	58
Wrexham	46	24	8	14	86	66	56
York City	46	20	13	13	60	45	53
Grimsby Town	46	21	10	15	75	59	52
Southport	46	20	11	15	63	60	51
Bradford Park Avenue	46	19	12	15	75	61	50
Gateshead	46	17	15	14	76	60	49
Carlisle United	46	18	13	15	82	68	49
Crewe Alexandra	46	20	8	18	70	68	48
Stockport County	46	17	13	16	82	69	47
Chesterfield	46	18	11	17	65	63	47
Tranmere Rovers	46	21	5	20	65	63	47
Halifax Town	46	16	15	15	68	68	47
Scunthorpe United	46	16	14	16	62	56	46
Bradford City	46	14	18	14	75	80	46
Hartlepools United	46	16	14	16	57	61	46
Mansfield Town	46	16	14	16	55	62	46
Barrow	46	16	12	18	66	71	44
Chester	46	11	15	20	64	85	37
Darlington	46	14	6	26	58	96	34
Rochdale	46	14	5	27	62	83	33
Workington	46	11	10	25	55	91	32
Accrington Stanley	46	8	11	27	39	89	27

DIVISION TWO 1952-53

Sheffield United	42	25	10	7	97	55	60
Huddersfield Town	42	24	10	8	84	33	58
Luton Town	42	22	8	12	84	49	52
Plymouth Argyle	42	20	9	13	65	60	49
Leicester City	42	18	12	12	89	74	48
Birmingham City	42	19	10	13	71	66	48
Nottingham Forest	42	18	8	16	77	67	44
Fulham	42	17	10	15	81	71	44
Blackburn Rovers	42	18	8	16	68	65	44
Leeds United	42	14	15	13	71	63	43
Swansea Town	42	15	12	15	78	81	42
Rotherham United	42	16	9	17	75	74	41
Doncaster Rovers	42	12	16	14	58	64	40
West Ham United	42	13	13	16	58	60	39
Lincoln City	42	11	17	14	64	71	39
Everton	42	12	14	16	71	75	38
Brentford	42	13	11	18	59	76	37
Hull City	42	14	8	20	57	69	36
Notts County	42	14	8	20	60	88	36
Bury	42	13	9	20	53	81	35
Southampton	*42*	*10*	*13*	*19*	*68*	*85*	*33*
Barnsley	*42*	*5*	*8*	*29*	*47*	*108*	*18*

DIVISION THREE (S) 1952-53

Bristol Rovers	46	26	12	8	92	46	64
Millwall	46	24	14	8	82	44	62
Northampton Town	46	26	10	10	109	70	62
Norwich City	46	25	10	11	99	55	60
Bristol City	46	22	15	9	95	61	59
Coventry City	46	19	12	15	77	62	50
Brighton & Hove Albion	46	19	12	15	81	75	50
Southend United	46	18	13	15	69	74	49
Bournemouth & Boscombe Ath.	46	19	9	18	74	69	47
Watford	46	15	17	14	62	63	47
Reading	46	19	8	19	69	64	46
Torquay United	46	18	9	19	87	88	45
Crystal Palace	46	15	13	18	66	82	43
Leyton Orient	46	16	10	20	68	73	42
Newport County	46	16	10	20	70	82	42
Ipswich Town	46	13	15	18	60	69	41
Exeter City	46	13	14	19	61	71	40
Swindon Town	46	14	12	20	64	79	40
Aldershot	46	12	15	19	61	77	39
Queen's Park Rangers	46	12	15	19	61	82	39
Gillingham	46	12	15	19	55	74	39
Colchester United	46	12	14	20	59	76	38
Shrewsbury Town	46	12	12	22	68	91	36
Walsall	46	7	10	29	56	118	24

1953 F.A. Cup

Semi-finals

Blackpool vs Tottenham Hotspur	2-1
Bolton Wanderers vs Everton	4-3

Final

Wembley, 2nd May 1953

Blackpool 4 (Mortensen 3, Perry)

Bolton Wanderers 3 (Lofthouse, Moir, Bell)

Attendance 100,000

DIVISION ONE 1953-54

WOLVERHAMPTON WANDS.	**42**	**25**	**7**	**10**	**96**	**56**	**57**
West Bromwich Albion	42	22	9	11	86	63	53
Huddersfield Town	42	20	11	11	78	61	51
Manchester United	42	18	12	12	73	58	48
Bolton Wanderers	42	18	12	12	75	60	48
Blackpool	42	19	10	13	80	69	48
Burnley	42	21	4	17	78	67	46
Chelsea	42	16	12	14	74	68	44
Charlton Athletic	42	19	6	17	75	77	44
Cardiff City	42	18	8	16	51	71	44
Preston North End	42	19	5	18	87	58	43
Arsenal	42	15	13	14	75	73	43
Aston Villa	42	16	9	17	70	68	41
Portsmouth	42	14	11	17	81	89	39
Newcastle United	42	14	10	18	72	77	38
Tottenham Hotspur	42	16	5	21	65	76	37
Manchester City	42	14	9	19	62	77	37
Sunderland	42	14	8	20	81	89	36
Sheffield Wednesday	42	15	6	21	70	91	36
Sheffield United	42	11	11	20	69	90	33
Middlesbrough	*42*	*10*	*10*	*22*	*60*	*91*	*30*
Liverpool	*42*	*9*	*10*	*23*	*68*	*97*	*28*

DIVISION THREE (N) 1953-54

Port Vale	**46**	**26**	**17**	**3**	**74**	**21**	**69**
Barnsley	46	24	10	12	77	57	58
Scunthorpe United	46	21	15	10	77	56	57
Gateshead	46	21	13	12	74	55	55
Bradford City	46	22	9	15	60	55	53
Chesterfield	46	19	14	13	76	64	52
Mansfield Town	46	20	11	15	88	67	51
Wrexham	46	21	9	16	81	68	51
Bradford Park Avenue	46	18	14	14	77	68	50
Stockport County	46	18	11	17	77	67	47
Southport	46	17	12	17	63	60	46
Barrow	46	16	12	18	72	71	44
Carlisle United	46	14	15	17	83	71	43
Tranmere Rovers	46	18	7	21	59	70	43
Accrington Stanley	46	16	10	20	66	74	42
Crewe Alexandra	46	14	13	19	49	67	41
Grimsby Town	46	16	9	21	51	77	41
Hartlepools United	46	13	14	19	59	65	40
Rochdale	46	15	10	21	59	77	40
Workington	46	13	14	19	59	80	40
Darlington	46	12	14	20	50	71	38
York City	46	12	13	21	64	86	37
Halifax Town	46	12	10	24	44	73	34
Chester	46	11	10	25	48	67	32

DIVISION TWO 1953-54

Leicester City	**42**	**23**	**10**	**9**	**97**	**60**	**56**
Everton	**42**	**20**	**16**	**6**	**92**	**58**	**56**
Blackburn Rovers	42	23	9	10	86	50	55
Nottingham Forest	42	20	12	10	86	59	52
Rotherham United	42	21	7	14	80	67	49
Luton Town	42	18	12	12	64	59	48
Birmingham City	42	18	11	13	78	58	47
Fulham	42	17	10	15	98	85	44
Bristol Rovers	42	14	16	12	64	58	44
Leeds United	42	15	13	14	89	81	43
Stoke City	42	12	17	13	71	60	41
Doncaster Rovers	42	16	9	17	59	63	41
West Ham United	42	15	9	18	67	69	39
Notts County	42	13	13	16	54	74	39
Hull City	42	16	6	20	64	66	38
Lincoln City	42	14	9	19	65	83	37
Bury	42	11	14	17	54	72	36
Derby County	42	12	11	19	64	82	35
Plymouth Argyle	42	9	16	17	65	82	34
Swansea Town	42	13	8	21	58	82	34
Brentford	*42*	*10*	*11*	*21*	*40*	*78*	*31*
Oldham Athletic	*42*	*8*	*9*	*25*	*40*	*89*	*25*

DIVISION THREE (S) 1953-54

Ipswich Town	**46**	**27**	**10**	**9**	**82**	**51**	**64**
Brighton & Hove Albion	46	26	9	11	86	61	61
Bristol City	46	25	6	15	88	66	56
Watford	46	21	10	15	85	69	52
Northampton Town	46	20	11	15	82	55	51
Southampton	46	22	7	17	76	63	51
Norwich City	46	20	11	15	73	66	51
Reading	46	20	9	17	86	73	49
Exeter City	46	20	8	18	68	58	48
Gillingham	46	19	10	17	61	66	48
Leyton Orient	46	18	11	17	79	73	47
Millwall	46	19	9	18	74	77	47
Torquay United	46	17	12	17	81	88	46
Coventry City	46	18	9	19	61	56	45
Newport County	46	19	6	21	61	81	44
Southend United	46	18	7	21	69	71	43
Aldershot	46	17	9	20	74	86	43
Queen's Park Rangers	46	16	10	20	60	68	42
Bournemouth & Boscombe Ath.	46	16	8	22	67	70	40
Swindon Town	46	15	10	21	67	70	40
Shrewsbury Town	46	14	12	20	65	76	40
Crystal Palace	46	14	12	20	60	86	40
Colchester United	46	10	10	26	50	78	30
Walsall	46	9	8	29	40	87	26

1954 F.A. Cup

Semi-finals

West Bromwich Albion vs Port Vale	2-1
Sheffield Wednesday vs Preston North End	0-2

Final

Wembley, 1st May 1954

West Bromwich Albion 3   (Allen 2 (1 pen), Griffin)
Preston North End 2   (Morrison, Wayman)

Attendance 100,000

DIVISION ONE 1954-55

CHELSEA	42	20	12	10	81	57	52
Wolverhampton Wanderers	42	19	10	13	89	70	48
Portsmouth	42	18	12	12	74	62	48
Sunderland	42	15	18	9	64	54	48
Manchester United	42	20	7	15	84	74	47
Aston Villa	42	20	7	15	72	73	47
Manchester City	42	18	10	14	76	69	46
Newcastle United	42	17	9	16	89	77	43
Arsenal	42	17	9	16	69	63	43
Burnley	42	17	9	16	51	48	43
Everton	42	16	10	16	62	68	42
Huddersfield Town	42	14	13	15	63	68	41
Sheffield United	42	17	7	18	70	86	41
Preston North End	42	16	8	18	83	64	40
Charlton Athletic	42	15	10	17	76	75	40
Tottenham Hotspur	42	16	8	18	72	73	40
West Bromwich Albion	42	16	8	18	76	96	40
Bolton Wanderers	42	13	13	16	62	69	39
Blackpool	42	14	10	18	60	64	38
Cardiff City	42	13	11	18	62	76	37
Leicester City	*42*	*12*	*11*	*19*	*74*	*86*	*35*
Sheffield Wednesday	*42*	*8*	*10*	*24*	*63*	*100*	*26*

DIVISION TWO 1954-55

Birmingham City	42	22	10	10	92	47	54
Luton Town	42	23	8	11	88	53	54
Rotherham United	42	25	4	13	94	64	54
Leeds United	42	23	7	12	70	53	53
Stoke City	42	21	10	11	69	46	52
Blackburn Rovers	42	22	6	14	114	79	50
Notts County	42	21	6	15	74	71	48
West Ham United	42	18	10	14	74	70	46
Bristol Rovers	42	19	7	16	75	70	45
Swansea Town	42	17	9	16	86	83	43
Liverpool	42	16	10	16	92	96	42
Middlesbrough	42	18	6	18	73	82	42
Bury	42	15	11	16	77	72	41
Fulham	42	14	11	17	76	79	39
Nottingham Forest	42	16	7	19	58	62	39
Lincoln City	42	13	10	19	68	79	36
Port Vale	42	12	11	19	48	71	35
Doncaster Rovers	42	14	7	21	58	95	35
Hull City	42	12	10	20	44	69	34
Plymouth Argyle	42	12	7	23	57	82	31
Ipswich Town	*42*	*11*	*6*	*25*	*57*	*92*	*28*
Derby County	*42*	*7*	*9*	*26*	*53*	*82*	*23*

DIVISION THREE (N) 1954-55

Barnsley	46	30	5	11	86	46	65
Accrington Stanley	46	25	11	10	96	67	61
Scunthorpe United	46	23	12	11	81	53	58
York City	46	24	10	12	92	63	58
Hartlepools United	46	25	5	16	64	49	55
Chesterfield	46	24	6	16	81	70	54
Gateshead	46	20	12	14	65	69	52
Workington	46	18	14	14	68	55	50
Stockport County	46	18	12	16	84	70	48
Oldham Athletic	46	19	10	17	74	68	48
Southport	46	16	16	14	47	44	48
Rochdale	46	17	14	15	69	66	48
Mansfield Town	46	18	9	19	65	71	45
Halifax Town	46	15	13	18	63	67	43
Darlington	46	14	14	18	62	73	42
Bradford Park Avenue	46	15	11	20	56	70	41
Barrow	46	17	6	23	70	89	40
Wrexham	46	13	12	21	65	77	38
Tranmere Rovers	46	13	11	22	55	70	37
Carlisle United	46	15	6	25	78	89	36
Bradford City	46	13	10	23	47	55	36
Crewe Alexandra	46	10	14	22	68	91	34
Grimsby Town	46	13	8	25	47	78	34
Chester	46	12	9	25	44	77	33

DIVISION THREE (S) 1954-55

Bristol City	46	30	10	6	101	47	70
Leyton Orient	46	26	9	11	89	47	61
Southampton	46	24	11	11	75	51	59
Gillingham	46	20	15	11	77	66	55
Millwall	46	20	11	15	72	68	51
Brighton & Hove Albion	46	20	10	16	76	63	50
Watford	46	18	14	14	71	62	50
Torquay United	46	18	12	16	82	82	48
Coventry City	46	18	11	17	67	59	47
Southend United	46	17	12	17	83	80	46
Brentford	46	16	14	16	82	82	46
Norwich City	46	18	10	18	60	60	46
Northampton Town	46	19	8	19	73	81	46
Aldershot	46	16	13	17	75	71	45
Queen's Park Rangers	46	15	14	17	69	75	44
Shrewsbury Town	46	16	10	20	70	78	42
Bournemouth & Boscombe Ath.	46	12	18	16	57	65	42
Reading	46	13	15	18	65	73	41
Newport County	46	11	16	19	60	73	38
Crystal Palace	46	11	16	19	52	80	38
Swindon Town	46	11	15	20	46	64	37
Exeter City	46	11	15	20	47	73	37
Walsall	46	10	14	22	75	86	34
Colchester United	46	9	13	24	53	91	31

1955 F.A. Cup

Semi-finals

Newcastle United vs York City	1-1, 2-0
Sunderland vs Manchester City	0-1

Final

Wembley, 7th May 1955

Newcastle United 3 (Milburn, Mitchell, Hannah)

Manchester City 1 (Johnstone)

Attendance 100,000

DIVISION ONE 1955-56

MANCHESTER UNITED	42	25	10	7	83	51	60
Blackpool	42	20	9	13	86	62	49
Wolverhampton Wanderers	42	20	9	13	89	65	49
Manchester City	42	18	10	14	82	69	46
Arsenal	42	18	10	14	60	61	46
Birmingham City	42	18	9	15	75	57	45
Burnley	42	18	8	16	64	54	44
Bolton Wanderers	42	18	7	17	71	58	43
Sunderland	42	17	9	16	80	95	43
Luton Town	42	17	8	17	66	64	42
Newcastle United	42	17	7	18	85	70	41
Portsmouth	42	16	9	17	78	85	41
West Bromwich Albion	42	18	5	19	58	70	41
Charlton Athletic	42	17	6	19	75	81	40
Everton	42	15	10	17	55	69	40
Chelsea	42	14	11	17	64	77	39
Cardiff City	42	15	9	18	55	69	39
Tottenham Hotspur	42	15	7	20	61	71	37
Preston North End	42	14	8	20	73	72	36
Aston Villa	42	11	13	18	52	69	35
Huddersfield Town	*42*	*14*	*7*	*21*	*54*	*83*	*35*
Sheffield United	*42*	*12*	*9*	*21*	*63*	*77*	*33*

DIVISION TWO 1955-56

Sheffield Wednesday	42	21	13	8	101	62	55
Leeds United	42	23	6	13	80	60	52
Liverpool	42	21	6	15	85	63	48
Blackburn Rovers	42	21	6	15	84	65	48
Leicester City	42	21	6	15	94	78	48
Bristol Rovers	42	21	6	15	84	70	48
Nottingham Forest	42	19	9	14	68	63	47
Lincoln City	42	18	10	14	79	65	46
Fulham	42	20	6	16	89	79	46
Swansea Town	42	20	6	16	83	81	46
Bristol City	42	19	7	16	80	64	45
Port Vale	42	16	13	13	60	58	45
Stoke City	42	20	4	18	71	62	44
Middlesbrough	42	16	8	18	76	78	40
Bury	42	16	8	18	86	90	40
West Ham United	42	14	11	17	74	69	39
Doncaster Rovers	42	12	11	19	69	96	35
Barnsley	42	11	12	19	47	84	34
Rotherham United	42	12	9	21	56	75	33
Notts County	42	11	9	22	55	82	31
Plymouth Argyle	*42*	*10*	*8*	*24*	*54*	*87*	*28*
Hull City	*42*	*10*	*6*	*26*	*53*	*97*	*26*

DIVISION THREE (N) 1955-56

Grimsby Town	46	31	6	9	76	29	68
Derby County	46	28	7	11	110	55	63
Accrington Stanley	46	25	9	12	92	57	59
Hartlepools United	46	26	5	15	81	60	57
Southport	46	23	11	12	66	53	57
Chesterfield	46	25	4	17	94	66	54
Stockport County	46	21	9	16	90	61	51
Bradford City	46	18	13	15	78	64	49
Scunthorpe United	46	20	8	18	75	63	48
Workington	46	19	9	18	75	63	47
York City	46	19	9	18	85	72	47
Rochdale	46	17	13	16	66	84	47
Gateshead	46	17	11	18	77	84	45
Wrexham	46	16	10	20	66	73	42
Darlington	46	16	9	21	60	73	41
Tranmere Rovers	46	16	9	21	59	84	41
Chester	46	13	14	19	52	82	40
Mansfield Town	46	14	11	21	84	81	39
Halifax Town	46	14	11	21	66	76	39
Oldham Athletic	46	10	18	18	76	86	38
Carlisle United	46	15	8	23	71	95	38
Barrow	46	12	9	25	61	83	33
Bradford Park Avenue	46	13	7	26	61	122	33
Crewe Alexandra	46	9	10	27	50	105	28

DIVISION THREE (S) 1955-56

Leyton Orient	46	29	8	9	106	49	66
Brighton & Hove Albion	46	29	7	10	112	50	65
Ipswich Town	46	25	14	7	106	60	64
Southend United	46	21	11	14	88	80	53
Torquay United	46	20	12	14	86	63	52
Brentford	46	19	14	13	69	66	52
Norwich City	46	19	13	14	86	82	51
Coventry City	46	20	9	17	73	60	49
Bournemouth & Boscombe Ath.	46	19	10	17	63	51	48
Gillingham	46	19	10	17	69	71	48
Northampton Town	46	20	7	19	67	71	47
Colchester United	46	18	11	17	76	81	47
Shrewsbury Town	46	17	12	17	69	66	46
Southampton	46	18	8	20	91	81	44
Aldershot	46	12	16	18	70	90	40
Exeter City	46	15	10	21	58	77	40
Reading	46	15	9	22	70	79	39
Queen's Park Rangers	46	14	11	21	64	86	39
Newport County	46	15	9	22	58	79	39
Walsall	46	15	8	23	68	84	38
Watford	46	13	11	22	52	85	37
Millwall	46	15	6	25	83	100	36
Crystal Palace	46	12	10	24	54	83	34
Swindon Town	46	8	14	24	34	78	30

1956 F.A. Cup

Semi-finals

Tottenham Hotspur vs Manchester City	0-1
Birmingham City vs Sunderland	3-0

Final

Wembley, 5th May 1956

Manchester City 3 (Hayes, Dyson, Johnstone)
Birmingham City 1 (Kinsey)

Attendance 100,000

DIVISION ONE 1956-57

MANCHESTER UNITED	42	28	8	6	103	54	64
Tottenham Hotspur	42	22	12	8	104	56	56
Preston North End	42	23	10	9	84	56	56
Blackpool	42	22	9	11	93	65	53
Arsenal	42	21	8	13	85	69	50
Wolverhampton Wanderers	42	20	8	14	94	70	48
Burnley	42	18	10	14	56	50	46
Leeds United	42	15	14	13	72	63	44
Bolton Wanderers	42	16	12	14	65	65	44
Aston Villa	42	14	15	13	65	55	43
West Bromwich Albion	42	14	14	14	59	61	42
Birmingham City	42	15	9	18	69	69	39
Chelsea	42	13	13	16	73	73	39
Sheffield Wednesday	42	16	6	20	82	88	38
Everton	42	14	10	18	61	79	38
Luton Town	42	14	9	19	58	76	37
Newcastle United	42	14	8	20	67	87	36
Manchester City	42	13	9	20	78	88	35
Portsmouth	42	10	13	19	62	92	33
Sunderland	42	12	8	22	67	88	32
Cardiff City	*42*	*10*	*9*	*23*	*53*	*88*	*29*
Charlton Athletic	*42*	*9*	*4*	*29*	*62*	*120*	*22*

DIVISION THREE (N) 1956-57

Derby County	46	26	11	9	111	53	63
Hartlepools United	46	25	9	12	90	63	59
Accrington Stanley	46	25	8	13	95	64	58
Workington	46	24	10	12	93	63	58
Stockport County	46	23	8	15	91	75	54
Chesterfield	46	22	9	15	96	79	53
York City	46	21	10	15	75	61	52
Hull City	46	21	10	15	84	69	52
Bradford City	46	22	8	16	78	68	52
Barrow	46	21	9	16	76	62	51
Halifax Town	46	21	7	18	65	70	49
Wrexham	46	19	10	17	97	74	48
Rochdale	46	18	12	16	65	65	48
Scunthorpe United	46	15	15	16	71	69	45
Carlisle United	46	16	13	17	76	85	45
Mansfield Town	46	17	10	19	91	90	44
Gateshead	46	17	10	19	72	90	44
Darlington	46	17	8	21	82	95	42
Oldham Athletic	46	12	15	19	66	74	39
Bradford Park Avenue	46	16	3	27	66	93	35
Chester	46	10	13	23	55	84	33
Southport	46	10	12	24	52	94	32
Tranmere Rovers	46	7	13	26	51	91	27
Crewe Alexandra	46	6	9	31	43	110	21

DIVISION TWO 1956-57

Leicester City	42	25	11	6	109	67	61
Nottingham Forest	42	22	10	10	94	55	54
Liverpool	42	21	11	10	82	54	53
Blackburn Rovers	42	21	10	11	83	75	52
Stoke City	42	20	8	14	83	58	48
Middlesbrough	42	19	10	13	84	60	48
Sheffield United	42	19	8	15	87	76	46
West Ham United	42	19	8	15	59	63	46
Bristol Rovers	42	18	9	15	81	67	45
Swansea Town	42	19	7	16	90	90	45
Fulham	42	19	4	19	84	76	42
Huddersfield Town	42	18	6	18	68	74	42
Bristol City	42	16	9	17	74	79	41
Doncaster Rovers	42	15	10	17	77	77	40
Leyton Orient	42	15	10	17	66	84	40
Grimsby Town	42	17	5	20	61	62	39
Rotherham United	42	13	11	18	74	75	37
Lincoln City	42	14	6	22	54	80	34
Barnsley	42	12	10	20	59	89	34
Notts County	42	9	12	21	58	86	30
Bury	*42*	*8*	*9*	*25*	*60*	*96*	*25*
Port Vale	*42*	*8*	*6*	*28*	*57*	*101*	*22*

DIVISION THREE (S) 1956-57

Ipswich Town	46	25	9	12	101	54	59
Torquay United	46	24	11	11	89	64	59
Colchester United	46	22	14	10	84	56	58
Southampton	46	22	10	14	76	52	54
Bournemouth & Boscombe Ath.	46	19	14	13	88	62	52
Brighton & Hove Albion	46	19	14	13	86	65	52
Southend United	46	18	12	16	73	65	48
Brentford	46	16	16	14	78	76	48
Shrewsbury Town	46	15	18	13	72	79	48
Queen's Park Rangers	46	18	11	17	61	60	47
Watford	46	18	10	18	72	75	46
Newport County	46	16	13	17	65	62	45
Reading	46	18	9	19	80	81	45
Northampton Town	46	18	9	19	66	73	45
Walsall	46	16	12	18	80	74	44
Coventry City	46	16	12	18	74	84	44
Millwall	46	16	12	18	64	84	44
Plymouth Argyle	46	16	11	19	68	73	43
Aldershot	46	15	12	19	79	92	42
Crystal Palace	46	11	18	17	62	75	40
Exeter City	46	12	13	21	61	79	37
Gillingham	46	12	13	21	54	85	37
Swindon Town	46	15	6	25	66	96	36
Norwich City	46	8	15	23	61	94	31

1957 F.A. Cup

Semi-finals

Aston Villa vs West Bromwich Albion	2-2, 1-0
Manchester United vs Birmingham City	2-0

Final

Wembley, 4th May 1957

Aston Villa 2   (McParland 2)

Manchester United 1   (Taylor)

Attendance 100,000

DIVISION ONE 1957-58

WOLVERHAMPTON WANDS.	42	28	8	6	103	47	64
Preston North End	42	26	7	9	100	51	59
Tottenham Hotspur	42	21	9	12	93	77	51
West Bromwich Albion	42	18	14	10	92	70	50
Manchester City	42	22	5	15	104	100	49
Burnley	42	21	5	16	80	74	47
Blackpool	42	19	6	17	80	67	44
Luton Town	42	19	6	17	69	63	44
Manchester United	42	16	11	15	85	75	43
Nottingham Forest	42	16	10	16	69	63	42
Chelsea	42	15	12	15	83	79	42
Arsenal	42	16	7	19	73	85	39
Birmingham City	42	14	11	17	76	89	39
Aston Villa	42	16	7	19	73	86	39
Bolton Wanderers	42	14	10	18	65	87	38
Everton	42	13	11	18	65	75	37
Leeds United	42	14	9	19	51	63	37
Leicester City	42	14	5	23	91	112	33
Newcastle United	42	12	8	22	73	81	32
Portsmouth	42	12	8	22	73	88	32
Sunderland	*42*	*10*	*12*	*20*	*54*	*97*	*32*
Sheffield Wednesday	*42*	*12*	*7*	*23*	*69*	*92*	*31*

DIVISION TWO 1957-58

West Ham United	42	23	11	8	101	54	57
Blackburn Rovers	42	22	12	8	93	57	56
Charlton Athletic	42	24	7	11	107	69	55
Liverpool	42	22	10	10	79	54	54
Fulham	42	20	12	10	97	59	52
Sheffield United	42	21	10	11	75	50	52
Middlesbrough	42	19	7	16	83	74	45
Ipswich Town	42	16	12	14	68	69	44
Huddersfield Town	42	14	16	12	63	66	44
Bristol Rovers	42	17	8	17	85	80	42
Stoke City	42	18	6	18	75	73	42
Leyton Orient	42	18	5	19	77	79	41
Grimsby Town	42	17	6	19	86	83	40
Barnsley	42	14	12	16	70	74	40
Cardiff City	42	14	9	19	63	77	37
Derby County	42	14	8	20	60	81	36
Bristol City	42	13	9	20	63	88	35
Rotherham United	42	14	5	23	65	101	33
Swansea Town	42	11	9	22	72	99	31
Lincoln City	42	11	9	22	55	82	31
Notts County	*42*	*12*	*6*	*24*	*44*	*80*	*30*
Doncaster Rovers	*42*	*8*	*11*	*23*	*56*	*88*	*27*

DIVISION THREE (N) 1957-58

Scunthorpe United	46	29	8	9	88	50	66
Accrington Stanley	46	25	9	12	83	61	59
Bradford City	46	21	15	10	73	49	57
Bury	46	23	10	13	94	62	56
Hull City	46	19	15	12	78	67	53
Mansfield Town	46	22	8	16	100	92	52
Halifax Town	46	20	11	15	83	69	51
Chesterfield	46	18	15	13	71	69	51
Stockport County	46	18	11	17	74	67	47
Rochdale	46	19	8	19	79	67	46
Tranmere Rovers	46	18	10	18	82	76	46
Wrexham	46	17	12	17	61	63	46
York City	46	17	12	17	68	76	46
Gateshead	46	15	15	16	68	76	45
Oldham Athletic	46	14	17	15	72	84	45
Carlisle United	46	19	6	21	80	78	44
Hartlepools United	46	16	12	18	73	76	44
Barrow	46	13	15	18	66	74	41
Workington	46	14	13	19	72	81	41
Darlington	46	17	7	22	78	89	41
Chester	46	13	13	20	73	81	39
Bradford Park Avenue	46	13	11	22	68	95	37
Southport	46	11	6	29	52	88	28
Crewe Alexandra	46	8	7	31	47	93	23

DIVISION THREE (S) 1957-58

Brighton & Hove Albion	46	24	12	10	88	64	60
Brentford	46	24	10	12	82	56	58
Plymouth Argyle	46	25	8	13	67	48	58
Swindon Town	46	21	15	10	79	50	57
Reading	46	21	13	12	79	51	55
Southampton	46	22	10	14	112	72	54
Southend United	46	21	12	13	90	58	54
Norwich City	46	19	15	12	75	70	53
Bournemouth & Boscombe Ath.	46	21	9	16	81	74	51
Queen's Park Rangers	46	18	14	14	64	65	50
Newport County	46	17	14	15	73	67	48
Colchester United	46	17	13	16	77	79	47
Northampton Town	46	19	6	21	87	79	44
Crystal Palace	46	15	13	18	70	72	43
Port Vale	46	16	10	20	67	58	42
Watford	46	13	16	17	59	77	42
Shrewsbury Town	46	15	10	21	49	71	40
Aldershot	46	12	16	18	59	89	40
Coventry City	46	13	13	20	61	81	39
Walsall	46	14	9	23	61	75	37
Torquay United	46	11	13	22	49	74	35
Gillingham	46	13	9	24	52	81	35
Millwall	46	11	9	26	63	91	31
Exeter City	46	11	9	26	57	99	31

1958 F.A. Cup

Semi-finals

Blackburn Rovers vs Bolton Wanderers	1-2
Manchester United vs Fulham	2-2, 5-3

Final

Wembley, 3rd May 1958

Bolton Wanderers 2 (Lofthouse 2)

Manchester United 0

Attendance 100,000

DIVISION ONE 1958-59

WOLVERHAMPTON WANDS.	42	28	5	9	110	49	61
Manchester United	42	24	7	11	103	66	55
Arsenal	42	21	8	13	88	68	50
Bolton Wanderers	42	20	10	12	79	66	50
West Bromwich Albion	42	18	13	11	88	68	49
West Ham United	42	21	6	15	85	70	48
Burnley	42	19	10	13	81	70	48
Blackpool	42	18	11	13	66	49	47
Birmingham City	42	20	6	16	84	68	46
Blackburn Rovers	42	17	10	15	76	70	44
Newcastle United	42	17	7	18	80	80	41
Preston North End	42	17	7	18	70	77	41
Nottingham Forest	42	17	6	19	71	74	40
Chelsea	42	18	4	20	77	98	40
Leeds United	42	15	9	18	57	74	39
Everton	42	17	4	21	71	87	38
Luton Town	42	12	13	17	68	71	37
Tottenham Hotspur	42	13	10	19	85	95	36
Leicester City	42	11	10	21	67	98	32
Manchester City	42	11	9	22	64	95	31
Aston Villa	*42*	*11*	*8*	*23*	*58*	*87*	*30*
Portsmouth	*42*	*6*	*9*	*27*	*64*	*112*	*21*

DIVSION 2 1958-59

Sheffield Wednesday	42	28	6	8	106	48	62
Fulham	42	27	6	9	96	61	60
Sheffield United	42	23	7	12	82	48	53
Liverpool	42	24	5	13	87	62	53
Stoke City	42	21	7	14	72	58	49
Bristol Rovers	42	18	12	12	80	64	48
Derby County	42	20	8	14	74	71	48
Charlton Athletic	42	18	7	17	92	90	43
Cardiff City	42	18	7	17	65	65	43
Bristol City	42	17	7	18	74	70	41
Swansea Town	42	16	9	17	79	81	41
Brighton & Hove Albion	42	15	11	16	74	90	41
Middlesbrough	42	15	10	17	87	71	40
Huddersfield Town	42	16	8	18	62	55	40
Sunderland	42	16	8	18	64	75	40
Ipswich Town	42	17	6	19	62	77	40
Leyton Orient	42	14	8	20	71	78	36
Scunthorpe United	42	12	9	21	55	84	33
Lincoln City	42	11	7	24	63	93	29
Rotherham United	42	10	9	23	42	82	29
Grimsby Town	*42*	*9*	*10*	*23*	*62*	*90*	*28*
Barnsley	*42*	*10*	*7*	*25*	*55*	*91*	*27*

DIVISION THREE 1958-59

Plymouth Argyle	46	23	16	7	89	59	62
Hull City	46	26	9	11	90	55	61
Brentford	46	21	15	10	76	49	57
Norwich City	46	22	13	11	89	62	57
Colchester United	46	21	10	15	71	67	52
Reading	46	21	8	17	78	63	50
Tranmere Rovers	46	21	8	17	82	67	50
Southend United	46	21	8	17	85	80	50
Halifax Town	46	21	8	17	80	77	50
Bury	46	17	14	15	69	58	48
Bradford City	46	18	11	17	84	76	47
Bournemouth & Boscombe Ath.	46	17	12	17	69	69	46
Queen's Park Rangers	46	19	8	19	74	77	46
Southampton	46	17	11	18	88	80	45
Swindon Town	46	16	13	17	59	57	45
Chesterfield	46	17	10	19	67	64	44
Newport County	46	17	9	20	69	68	43
Wrexham	46	14	14	18	63	77	42
Accrington Stanley	46	15	12	19	71	87	42
Mansfield Town	46	14	13	19	73	98	41
Stockport County	*46*	*13*	*10*	*23*	*65*	*78*	*36*
Doncaster Rovers	*46*	*14*	*5*	*27*	*50*	*90*	*33*
Notts County	*46*	*8*	*13*	*25*	*55*	*96*	*29*
Rochdale	*46*	*8*	*12*	*26*	*37*	*79*	*28*

DIVISION FOUR 1958-59

Port Vale	46	26	12	8	110	58	64
Coventry City	46	24	12	10	84	47	60
York City	46	21	18	7	73	52	60
Shrewsbury Town	46	24	10	12	101	63	58
Exeter City	46	23	11	12	87	61	57
Walsall	46	21	10	15	95	64	52
Crystal Palace	46	20	12	14	90	71	52
Northampton Town	46	21	9	16	85	78	51
Millwall	46	20	10	16	76	69	50
Carlisle United	46	19	12	15	62	65	50
Gillingham	46	20	9	17	82	77	49
Torquay United	46	16	12	18	78	77	44
Chester	46	16	12	18	72	84	44
Bradford Park Avenue	46	18	7	21	75	77	43
Watford	46	16	10	20	81	79	42
Darlington	46	13	16	17	66	68	42
Workington	46	12	17	17	63	78	41
Crewe Alexandra	46	15	10	21	70	82	40
Hartlepools United	46	15	10	21	74	88	40
Gateshead	46	16	8	22	56	85	40
Oldham Athletic	46	16	4	26	59	84	36
Aldershot	46	14	7	25	63	97	35
Barrow	46	9	10	27	51	104	28
Southport	46	7	12	27	41	86	26

1959 F.A. Cup

Semi-finals

Nottingham Forest vs Aston Villa	1-0
Norwich City vs Luton Town	1-1, 0-1

Final

Wembley, 2nd May 1959

Nottingham Forest 2   (Dwight, Wilson)

Luton Town 1   (Pacey)

Attendance 100,000

DIVISION ONE 1959-60

BURNLEY	42	24	7	11	85	61	55
Wolverhampton Wanderers	42	24	6	12	106	67	54
Tottenham Hotspur	42	21	11	10	86	50	53
West Bromwich Albion	42	19	11	12	83	57	49
Sheffield Wednesday	42	19	11	12	80	59	49
Bolton Wanderers	42	20	8	14	59	51	48
Manchester United	42	19	7	16	102	80	45
Newcastle United	42	18	8	16	82	78	44
Preston North End	42	16	12	14	79	76	44
Fulham	42	17	10	15	73	80	44
Blackpool	42	15	10	17	59	71	40
Leicester City	42	13	13	16	66	75	39
Arsenal	42	15	9	18	68	80	39
West Ham United	42	16	6	20	75	91	38
Everton	42	13	11	18	73	78	37
Manchester City	42	17	3	22	78	84	37
Blackburn Rovers	42	16	5	21	60	70	37
Chelsea	42	14	9	19	76	91	37
Birmingham City	42	13	10	19	63	80	36
Nottingham Forest	42	13	9	20	50	74	35
Leeds United	*42*	*12*	*10*	*20*	*65*	*92*	*34*
Luton Town	*42*	*9*	*12*	*21*	*50*	*73*	*30*

DIVISION TWO 1959-60

Aston Villa	42	25	9	8	89	43	59
Cardiff City	42	23	12	7	90	62	58
Liverpool	42	20	10	12	90	66	50
Sheffield United	42	19	12	11	68	51	50
Middlesbrough	42	19	10	13	90	64	48
Huddersfield Town	42	19	9	14	73	52	47
Charlton Athletic	42	17	13	12	90	87	47
Rotherham United	42	17	13	12	61	60	47
Bristol Rovers	42	18	11	13	72	78	47
Leyton Orient	42	15	14	13	76	61	44
Ipswich Town	42	19	6	17	78	68	44
Swansea Town	42	15	10	17	82	84	40
Lincoln City	42	16	7	19	75	78	39
Brighton & Hove Albion	42	13	12	17	67	76	38
Scunthorpe United	42	13	10	19	57	71	36
Sunderland	42	12	12	18	52	65	36
Stoke City	42	14	7	21	66	83	35
Derby County	42	14	7	21	61	77	35
Plymouth Argyle	42	13	9	20	61	89	35
Portsmouth	42	10	12	20	59	77	32
Hull City	*42*	*10*	*10*	*22*	*48*	*76*	*30*
Bristol City	*42*	*11*	*5*	*26*	*60*	*97*	*27*

DIVISION THREE 1959-60

Southampton	46	26	9	11	106	75	61
Norwich City	46	24	11	11	82	54	59
Shrewsbury Town	46	18	16	12	97	75	52
Grimsby Town	46	18	16	12	87	70	52
Coventry City	46	21	10	15	78	63	52
Brentford	46	21	9	16	78	61	51
Bury	46	21	9	16	64	51	51
Queen's Park Rangers	46	18	13	15	73	54	49
Colchester United	46	18	11	17	83	74	47
Bournemouth & Boscombe Ath.	46	17	13	16	72	72	47
Reading	46	18	10	18	84	77	46
Southend United	46	19	8	19	76	74	46
Newport County	46	20	6	20	80	79	46
Port Vale	46	19	8	19	80	79	46
Halifax Town	46	18	10	18	70	72	46
Swindon Town	46	19	8	19	69	78	46
Barnsley	46	15	14	17	65	66	44
Chesterfield	46	18	7	21	71	84	43
Bradford City	46	15	12	19	66	74	42
Tranmere Rovers	46	14	13	19	72	75	41
York City	*46*	*13*	*12*	*21*	*57*	*73*	*38*
Mansfield Town	*46*	*15*	*6*	*25*	*81*	*112*	*36*
Wrexham	*46*	*14*	*8*	*24*	*68*	*101*	*36*
Accrington Stanley	*46*	*11*	*5*	*30*	*57*	*123*	*27*

DIVISION FOUR 1959-60

Walsall	46	28	9	9	102	60	65
Notts County	46	26	8	12	107	69	60
Torquay United	46	26	8	12	84	58	60
Watford	46	24	9	13	92	67	57
Millwall	46	18	17	11	84	61	53
Northampton Town	46	22	9	15	85	63	53
Gillingham	46	21	10	15	74	69	52
Crystal Palace	46	19	12	15	84	64	50
Exeter City	46	19	11	16	80	70	49
Stockport County	46	19	11	16	58	54	49
Bradford Park Avenue	46	17	15	14	70	68	49
Rochdale	46	18	10	18	65	60	46
Aldershot	46	18	9	19	77	74	45
Crewe Alexandra	46	18	9	19	79	88	45
Darlington	46	17	9	20	63	73	43
Workington	46	14	14	18	68	60	42
Doncaster Rovers	46	16	10	20	69	76	42
Barrow	46	15	11	20	77	87	41
Carlisle United	46	15	11	20	51	66	41
Chester	46	14	12	20	59	77	40
Southport	46	10	14	22	48	92	34
Gateshead	*46*	*12*	*9*	*25*	*58*	*86*	*33*
Oldham Athletic	46	8	12	26	41	83	28
Hartlepools United	46	10	7	29	59	109	27

1960 F.A. Cup

Semi-finals

Wolverhampton Wanderers vs Aston Villa	1-0
Sheffield Wednesday vs Blackburn Rovers	1-2

Final

Wembley, 7th May 1960

Wolverhampton Wands. 3 (McGrath (og), Deeley 2)

Blackburn Rovers 0

Attendance 100,000

DIVISION ONE 1960-61

TOTTENHAM HOTSPUR	42	31	4	7	115	55	66
Sheffield Wednesday	42	23	12	7	78	47	58
Wolverhampton Wanderers	42	25	7	10	103	75	57
Burnley	42	22	7	13	102	77	51
Everton	42	22	6	14	87	69	50
Leicester City	42	18	9	15	87	70	45
Manchester United	42	18	9	15	88	76	45
Blackburn Rovers	42	15	13	14	77	76	43
Aston Villa	42	17	9	16	78	77	43
West Bromwich Albion	42	18	5	19	67	71	41
Arsenal	42	15	11	16	77	85	41
Chelsea	42	15	7	20	98	100	37
Manchester City	42	13	11	18	79	90	37
Nottingham Forest	42	14	9	19	62	78	37
Cardiff City	42	13	11	18	60	85	37
West Ham United	42	13	10	19	77	88	36
Fulham	42	14	8	20	72	95	36
Bolton Wanderers	42	12	11	19	58	73	35
Birmingham City	42	14	6	22	62	84	34
Blackpool	42	12	9	21	68	73	33
Newcastle United	*42*	*11*	*10*	*21*	*86*	*109*	*32*
Preston North End	*42*	*10*	*10*	*22*	*43*	*71*	*30*

DIVISION TWO 1960-61

Ipswich Town	42	26	7	9	100	55	59
Sheffield United	42	26	6	10	81	51	58
Liverpool	42	21	10	11	87	58	52
Norwich City	42	20	9	13	70	53	49
Middlesbrough	42	18	12	12	83	74	48
Sunderland	42	17	13	12	75	60	47
Swansea Town	42	18	11	13	77	73	47
Southampton	42	18	8	16	84	81	44
Scunthorpe United	42	14	15	13	69	64	43
Charlton Athletic	42	16	11	15	97	91	43
Plymouth Argyle	42	17	8	17	81	82	42
Derby County	42	15	10	17	80	80	40
Luton Town	42	15	9	18	71	79	39
Leeds United	42	14	10	18	75	83	38
Rotherham United	42	12	13	17	65	64	37
Brighton & Hove Albion	42	14	9	19	61	75	37
Bristol Rovers	42	15	7	20	73	92	37
Stoke City	42	12	12	18	51	59	36
Leyton Orient	42	14	8	20	55	78	36
Huddersfield Town	42	13	9	20	62	71	35
Portsmouth	*42*	*11*	*11*	*20*	*64*	*91*	*33*
Lincoln City	*42*	*8*	*8*	*26*	*48*	*95*	*24*

DIVISION THREE 1960-61

Bury	46	30	8	8	108	45	68
Walsall	46	28	6	12	98	60	62
Queen's Park Rangers	46	25	10	11	93	60	60
Watford	46	20	12	14	85	72	52
Notts County	46	21	9	16	82	77	51
Grimsby Town	46	20	10	16	77	69	50
Port Vale	46	17	15	14	96	79	49
Barnsley	46	21	7	18	83	80	49
Halifax Town	46	16	17	13	71	78	49
Shrewsbury Town	46	15	16	15	83	75	46
Hull City	46	17	12	17	73	73	46
Torquay United	46	14	17	15	75	83	45
Newport County	46	17	11	18	81	90	45
Bristol City	46	17	10	19	70	68	44
Coventry City	46	16	12	18	80	83	44
Swindon Town	46	14	15	17	62	55	43
Brentford	46	13	17	16	56	70	43
Reading	46	14	12	20	72	83	40
Bournemouth & Boscombe Ath.	46	15	10	21	58	76	40
Southend United	46	14	11	21	60	76	39
Tranmere Rovers	*46*	*15*	*8*	*23*	*79*	*115*	*38*
Bradford City	*46*	*11*	*14*	*21*	*65*	*87*	*36*
Colchester United	*46*	*11*	*11*	*24*	*68*	*101*	*33*
Chesterfield	*46*	*10*	*12*	*24*	*67*	*87*	*32*

DIVISION FOUR 1960-61

Peterborough United	46	28	10	8	134	65	66
Crystal Palace	46	29	6	11	110	69	64
Northampton Town	46	25	10	11	90	62	60
Bradford Park Avenue	46	26	8	12	84	74	60
York City	46	21	9	16	80	60	51
Millwall	46	21	8	17	97	86	50
Darlington	46	18	13	15	78	70	49
Workington	46	21	7	18	74	76	49
Crewe Alexandra	46	20	9	17	61	67	49
Aldershot	46	18	9	19	79	69	45
Doncaster Rovers	46	19	7	20	76	78	45
Oldham Athletic	46	19	7	20	79	88	45
Stockport County	46	18	9	19	57	66	45
Southport	46	19	6	21	69	67	44
Gillingham	46	15	13	18	64	66	43
Wrexham	46	17	8	21	62	56	42
Rochdale	46	17	8	21	60	66	42
Accrington Stanley	46	16	8	22	74	88	40
Carlisle United	46	13	13	20	61	79	39
Mansfield Town	46	16	6	24	71	78	38
Exeter City	46	14	10	22	66	94	38
Barrow	46	13	11	22	52	79	37
Hartlepools United	46	12	8	26	71	103	32
Chester	46	11	9	26	61	104	31

1961 F.A. Cup

Semi-finals

Burnley vs Tottenham Hotspur — 0-3
Leicester City vs Sheffield United — 0-0, 0-0, 2-0

Final

Wembley, 6th May 1961

Tottenham Hotspur 2 (Smith, Dyson)
Leicester City 0

Attendance 100,000

1961 Football League Cup

Semi-finals

Rotherham United vs Shrewsbury Town (3-2, 1-1) — 4-3
Burnley vs Aston Villa (1-1, 2-2) — 3-3

Play-off

Burnley vs Aston Villa — 2-1

Final (1st leg)

Rotherham, 22nd August 1961

Rotherham United 2 (Webster, Kirkman)
Aston Villa 0

Attendance 12,226

Final (2nd leg)

Villa Park, 5th September 1961

Aston Villa 3 (O'Neill, Burrows, McParland)
Rotherham United 0 (aet.)

Attendance 27,000

Aston Villa won 3-2 on aggregate

DIVISION ONE 1961-62

IPSWICH TOWN	42	24	8	10	93	67	56
Burnley	42	21	11	10	101	67	53
Tottenham Hotspur	42	21	10	11	88	69	52
Everton	42	20	11	11	88	54	51
Sheffield United	42	19	9	14	61	69	47
Sheffield Wednesday	42	20	6	16	72	58	46
Aston Villa	42	18	8	16	65	56	44
West Ham United	42	17	10	15	76	82	44
West Bromwich Albion	42	15	13	14	83	67	43
Arsenal	42	16	11	15	71	72	43
Bolton Wanderers	42	16	10	16	62	66	42
Manchester City	42	17	7	18	78	81	41
Blackpool	42	15	11	16	70	75	41
Leicester City	42	17	6	19	72	71	40
Manchester United	42	15	9	18	72	75	39
Blackburn Rovers	42	14	11	17	50	58	39
Birmingham City	42	14	10	18	65	81	38
Wolverhampton Wanderers	42	13	10	19	73	86	36
Nottingham Forest	42	13	10	19	63	79	36
Fulham	42	13	7	22	66	74	33
Cardiff City	*42*	*9*	*14*	*19*	*50*	*81*	*32*
Chelsea	*42*	*9*	*10*	*23*	*63*	*94*	*28*

DIVISION THREE 1961-62

Portsmouth	46	27	11	8	87	47	65
Grimsby Town	46	28	6	12	80	56	62
Bournemouth & Boscombe Ath.	46	21	17	8	69	45	59
Queen's Park Rangers	46	24	11	11	111	73	59
Peterborough United	46	26	6	14	107	82	58
Bristol City	46	23	8	15	94	72	54
Reading	46	22	9	15	77	66	53
Northampton Town	46	20	11	15	85	57	51
Swindon Town	46	17	15	14	78	71	49
Hull City	46	20	8	18	67	54	48
Bradford Park Avenue	46	20	7	19	80	78	47
Port Vale	46	17	11	18	65	58	45
Notts County	46	17	9	20	67	74	43
Coventry City	46	16	11	19	64	71	43
Crystal Palace	46	14	14	18	83	80	42
Southend United	46	13	16	17	57	69	42
Watford	46	14	13	19	63	74	41
Halifax Town	46	15	10	21	62	84	40
Shrewsbury Town	46	13	12	21	73	84	38
Barnsley	46	13	12	21	71	95	38
Torquay United	*46*	*15*	*6*	*25*	*76*	*100*	*36*
Lincoln City	*46*	*9*	*17*	*20*	*57*	*87*	*35*
Brentford	*46*	*13*	*8*	*25*	*53*	*93*	*34*
Newport County	*46*	*7*	*8*	*31*	*46*	*102*	*22*

DIVISION TWO 1961-62

Liverpool	42	27	8	7	99	43	62
Leyton Orient	42	22	10	10	69	40	54
Sunderland	42	22	9	11	85	50	53
Scunthorpe United	42	21	7	14	86	71	49
Plymouth Argyle	42	19	8	15	75	75	46
Southampton	42	18	9	15	77	62	45
Huddersfield Town	42	16	12	14	67	59	44
Stoke City	42	17	8	17	55	57	42
Rotherham United	42	16	9	17	70	76	41
Preston North End	42	15	10	17	55	57	40
Newcastle United	42	15	9	18	64	58	39
Middlesbrough	42	16	7	19	76	72	39
Luton Town	42	17	5	20	69	71	39
Walsall	42	14	11	17	70	75	39
Charlton Athletic	42	15	9	18	69	75	39
Derby County	42	14	11	17	68	75	39
Norwich City	42	14	11	17	61	70	39
Bury	42	17	5	20	52	76	39
Leeds United	42	12	12	18	50	61	36
Swansea Town	42	12	12	18	61	83	36
Bristol Rovers	*42*	*13*	*7*	*22*	*53*	*81*	*33*
Brighton & Hove Albion	*42*	*10*	*11*	*21*	*42*	*86*	*31*

DIVISION FOUR 1961-62

Millwall	44	23	10	11	87	62	56
Colchester United	44	23	9	12	104	71	55
Wrexham	44	22	9	13	96	56	53
Carlisle United	44	22	8	14	64	63	52
Bradford City	44	21	9	14	94	86	51
York City	44	20	10	14	84	53	50
Aldershot	44	22	5	17	81	60	49
Workington	44	19	11	14	69	70	49
Barrow	44	17	14	13	74	58	48
Crewe Alexandra	44	20	6	18	79	70	46
Oldham Athletic	44	17	12	15	77	70	46
Rochdale	44	19	7	18	71	71	45
Darlington	44	18	9	17	61	73	45
Mansfield Town	44	19	6	19	77	66	44
Tranmere Rovers	44	20	4	20	70	81	44
Stockport County	44	17	9	18	70	69	43
Southport	44	17	9	18	61	71	43
Exeter City	44	13	11	20	62	77	37
Chesterfield	44	14	9	21	70	87	37
Gillingham	44	13	11	20	73	94	37
Doncaster Rovers	44	11	7	26	60	85	29
Hartlepools United	44	8	11	25	52	101	27
Chester	44	7	12	25	54	96	26

Accrington Stanley resigned from the League after 33 matches

1962 F.A. Cup

Semi-finals

Manchester United vs Tottenham Hotspur	1-3
Burnley vs Fulham	1-1, 2-1

Final

Wembley, 5th May 1962

Tottenham Hotspur 3 (Greaves, Smith, Blanchflower (pen))

Burnley 1 (Robson)

Attendance 100,000

1962 Football League Cup

Semi-finals

Norwich City vs Blackpool (4-1, 0-2)	4-3
Rochdale vs Blackburn Rovers (3-1, 1-2)	4-3

Final (1st leg)

Rochdale, 26th April 1962

Rochdale 0

Norwich City 3 (Lythgoe 2, Punton)

Attendance 11,123

Final (2nd leg)

Norwich, 1st May 1962

Norwich City 1 (Hill)

Rochdale 0

Attendance 19,708

Norwich City won 4-0 on aggregate

DIVISION ONE 1962-63

EVERTON	42	25	11	6	84	42	61
Tottenham Hotspur	42	23	9	10	111	62	55
Burnley	42	22	10	10	78	57	54
Leicester City	42	20	12	10	79	53	52
Wolverhampton Wanderers	42	20	10	12	93	65	50
Sheffield Wednesday	42	19	10	13	77	63	48
Arsenal	42	18	10	14	86	77	46
Liverpool	42	17	10	15	71	59	44
Nottingham Forest	42	17	10	15	67	69	44
Sheffield United	42	16	12	14	58	60	44
Blackburn Rovers	42	15	12	15	79	71	42
West Ham United	42	14	12	16	73	69	40
Blackpool	42	13	14	15	58	64	40
West Bromwich Albion	42	16	7	19	71	79	39
Aston Villa	42	15	8	19	62	68	38
Fulham	42	14	10	18	50	71	38
Ipswich Town	42	12	11	19	59	78	35
Bolton Wanderers	42	15	5	22	55	75	35
Manchester United	42	12	10	20	67	81	34
Birmingham City	42	10	13	19	63	90	33
Manchester City	*42*	*10*	*11*	*21*	*58*	*102*	*31*
Leyton Orient	*42*	*6*	*9*	*27*	*37*	*81*	*21*

DIVISION TWO 1962-63

Stoke City	42	20	13	9	73	50	53
Chelsea	42	24	4	14	81	42	52
Sunderland	42	20	12	10	84	55	52
Middlesbrough	42	20	9	13	86	85	49
Leeds United	42	19	10	13	79	53	48
Huddersfield Town	42	17	14	11	63	50	48
Newcastle United	42	18	11	13	79	59	47
Bury	42	18	11	13	51	47	47
Scunthorpe United	42	16	12	14	57	59	44
Cardiff City	42	18	7	17	83	73	43
Southampton	42	17	8	17	72	67	42
Plymouth Argyle	42	15	12	15	76	73	42
Norwich City	42	17	8	17	80	79	42
Rotherham United	42	17	6	19	67	74	40
Swansea Town	42	15	9	18	51	72	39
Portsmouth	42	13	11	18	63	79	37
Preston North End	42	13	11	18	59	74	37
Derby County	42	12	12	18	61	72	36
Grimsby Town	42	11	13	18	55	66	35
Charlton Athletic	42	13	5	24	62	94	31
Walsall	*42*	*11*	*9*	*22*	*53*	*89*	*31*
Luton Town	*42*	*11*	*7*	*24*	*61*	*84*	*29*

DIVISION THREE 1962-63

Northampton Town	46	26	10	10	109	60	62
Swindon Town	46	22	14	10	87	56	58
Port Vale	46	23	8	15	72	58	54
Coventry City	46	18	17	11	83	69	53
Bournemouth & Boscombe Ath.	46	18	16	12	63	46	52
Peterborough United	46	20	11	15	93	75	51
Notts County	46	19	13	14	73	74	51
Southend United	46	19	12	15	75	77	50
Wrexham	46	20	9	17	84	83	49
Hull City	46	19	10	17	74	69	48
Crystal Palace	46	17	13	16	68	58	47
Colchester United	46	18	11	17	73	93	47
Queen's Park Rangers	46	17	11	18	85	76	45
Bristol City	46	16	13	17	100	92	45
Shrewsbury Town	46	16	12	18	83	81	44
Millwall	46	15	13	18	82	87	43
Watford	46	17	8	21	82	85	42
Barnsley	46	15	11	20	63	74	41
Bristol Rovers	46	15	11	20	70	88	41
Reading	46	16	8	22	74	78	40
Bradford Park Avenue	*46*	*14*	*12*	*20*	*79*	*97*	*40*
Brighton & Hove Albion	*46*	*12*	*12*	*22*	*58*	*84*	*36*
Carlisle United	*46*	*13*	*9*	*24*	*61*	*89*	*35*
Halifax Town	*46*	*9*	*12*	*25*	*64*	*106*	*30*

DIVISION FOUR 1962-63

Brentford	46	27	8	11	98	64	62
Oldham Athletic	46	24	11	11	95	60	59
Crewe Alexandra	46	24	11	11	86	58	59
Mansfield Town	46	24	9	13	108	69	57
Gillingham	46	22	13	11	71	49	57
Torquay United	46	20	16	10	75	56	56
Rochdale	46	20	11	15	67	59	51
Tranmere Rovers	46	20	10	16	81	67	50
Barrow	46	19	12	15	82	80	50
Workington	46	17	13	16	76	68	47
Aldershot	46	15	17	14	73	69	47
Darlington	46	19	6	21	72	87	44
Southport	46	15	14	17	72	106	44
York City	46	16	11	19	67	62	43
Chesterfield	46	13	16	17	70	64	42
Doncaster Rovers	46	14	14	18	64	77	42
Exeter City	46	16	10	20	57	77	42
Oxford United	46	13	15	18	70	71	41
Stockport County	46	15	11	20	56	70	41
Newport County	46	14	11	21	76	90	39
Chester	46	15	9	22	51	66	39
Lincoln City	46	13	9	24	68	89	35
Bradford City	46	11	10	25	64	93	32
Hartlepools United	46	7	11	28	56	104	25

1963 F.A. Cup

Semi-finals

Leicester City vs Liverpool	1-0
Southampton vs Manchester United	0-1

Final

Wembley, 25th May 1963

Manchester United 3   (Law, Herd 2)
Leicester City 1   (Keyworth)

Attendance 100,000

1963 Football League Cup

Semi-finals

Birmingham City vs Bury (3-2, 1-1)	4-3
Sunderland vs Aston Villa (1-3, 0-0)	1-3

Final (1st leg)

St. Andrews, 23rd May 1963

Birmingham City 3   (Leek 2, Bloomfield)
Aston Villa 1   (Thomson)

Attendance 31,850

Final (2nd leg)

Villa Park, 27th May 1963

Aston Villa 0
Birmingham City 0

Attendance 37,920

Birmingham City won 3-1 on aggregate

DIVISION ONE 1963-64

LIVERPOOL	42	26	5	11	92	45	57
Manchester United	42	23	7	12	90	62	53
Everton	42	21	10	11	84	64	52
Tottenham Hotspur	42	22	7	13	97	81	51
Chelsea	42	20	10	12	72	56	50
Sheffield Wednesday	42	19	11	12	84	67	49
Blackburn Rovers	42	18	10	14	89	65	46
Arsenal	42	17	11	14	90	82	45
Burnley	42	17	10	15	71	64	44
West Bromwich Albion	42	16	11	15	70	61	43
Leicester City	42	16	11	15	61	58	43
Sheffield United	42	16	11	15	61	64	43
Nottingham Forest	42	16	9	17	64	68	41
West Ham United	42	14	12	16	69	74	40
Fulham	42	13	13	16	58	65	39
Wolverhampton Wanderers	42	12	15	15	70	80	39
Stoke City	42	14	10	18	77	78	38
Blackpool	42	13	9	20	52	73	35
Aston Villa	42	11	12	19	62	71	34
Birmingham City	42	11	7	24	54	92	29
Bolton Wanderers	*42*	*10*	*8*	*24*	*48*	*80*	*28*
Ipswich Town	*42*	*9*	*7*	*26*	*56*	*121*	*25*

DIVISION TWO 1963-64

Leeds United	42	24	15	3	71	34	63
Sunderland	42	25	11	6	81	37	61
Preston North End	42	23	10	9	79	54	56
Charlton Athletic	42	19	10	13	76	70	48
Southampton	42	19	9	14	100	73	47
Manchester City	42	18	10	14	84	66	46
Rotherham United	42	19	7	16	90	78	45
Newcastle United	42	20	5	17	74	69	45
Portsmouth	42	16	11	15	79	70	43
Middlesbrough	42	15	11	16	67	52	41
Northampton Town	42	16	9	17	58	60	41
Huddersfield Town	42	15	10	17	57	64	40
Derby County	42	14	11	17	56	67	39
Swindon Town	42	14	10	18	57	69	38
Cardiff City	42	14	10	18	56	81	38
Leyton Orient	42	13	10	19	54	72	36
Norwich City	42	11	13	18	64	80	35
Bury	42	13	9	20	57	73	35
Swansea Town	42	12	9	21	63	74	33
Plymouth Argyle	42	8	16	18	45	67	32
Grimsby Town	*42*	*9*	*14*	*19*	*47*	*75*	*32*
Scunthorpe United	*42*	*10*	*10*	*22*	*52*	*82*	*30*

DIVISION THREE 1963-64

Coventry City	46	22	16	8	98	61	60
Crystal Palace	46	23	14	9	73	51	60
Watford	46	23	12	11	79	59	58
Bournemouth & Boscombe Ath.	46	24	8	14	79	58	56
Bristol City	46	20	15	11	84	64	55
Reading	46	21	10	15	79	62	52
Mansfield Town	46	20	11	15	76	62	51
Hull City	46	16	17	13	73	68	49
Oldham Athletic	46	20	8	18	73	70	48
Peterborough United	46	18	11	17	75	70	47
Shrewsbury Town	46	18	11	17	73	80	47
Bristol Rovers	46	19	8	19	91	79	46
Port Vale	46	16	14	16	53	49	46
Southend United	46	15	15	16	77	78	45
Queen's Park Rangers	46	18	9	19	76	78	45
Brentford	46	15	14	17	87	80	44
Colchester United	46	12	19	15	70	68	43
Luton Town	46	16	10	20	64	80	42
Walsall	46	13	14	19	59	76	40
Barnsley	46	12	15	19	68	94	39
Milwall	*46*	*14*	*10*	*22*	*53*	*67*	*38*
Crewe Alexandra	*46*	*11*	*12*	*23*	*50*	*77*	*34*
Wrexham	*46*	*13*	*6*	*27*	*75*	*107*	*32*
Notts County	*46*	*9*	*9*	*28*	*45*	*92*	*27*

DIVISION FOUR 1963-64

Gillingham	46	23	14	9	59	30	60
Carlisle United	46	25	10	11	113	58	60
Workington	46	24	11	11	76	52	59
Exeter City	46	20	18	8	62	37	58
Bradford City	46	25	6	15	76	62	56
Torquay United	46	20	11	15	80	54	51
Tranmere Rovers	46	20	11	15	85	73	51
Brighton & Hove Albion	46	19	12	15	71	52	50
Aldershot	46	19	10	17	83	78	48
Halifax Town	46	17	14	15	77	77	48
Lincoln City	46	19	9	18	67	75	47
Chester	46	19	8	19	65	60	46
Bradford Park Avenue	46	18	9	19	75	81	45
Doncaster Rovers	46	15	12	19	70	75	42
Newport County	46	17	8	21	64	73	42
Chesterfield	46	15	12	19	57	71	42
Stockport County	46	15	12	19	50	68	42
Oxford United	46	14	13	19	59	63	41
Darlington	46	14	12	20	66	93	40
Rochdale	46	12	15	19	56	59	39
Southport	46	15	9	22	63	88	39
York City	46	14	7	25	52	66	35
Hartlepools United	46	12	9	25	54	93	33
Barrow	46	6	18	22	51	93	30

1964 F.A. Cup

Semi-finals

West Ham United vs Manchester United	3-1
Swansea Town vs Preston North End	1-2

Final

Wembley, 2nd May 1964

West Ham United 3   (Sissons, Hurst, Boyce)
Preston North End 2   (Holden, Dawson)

Attendance 100,000

1964 Football League Cup

Semi-finals

Leicester City vs West Ham United (4-3, 2-0)	6-3
Stoke City vs Manchester City (2-0, 0-1)	2-1

Final (1st leg)

Stoke, 15th April 1964

Stoke City 1   (Bebbington)
Leicester City 1   (Gibson)

Attendance 22,309

Final (2nd leg)

Leicester, 22nd April 1964

Leicester City 3   (Stringfellow, Gibson, Riley)
Stoke City 2   (Viollet, Kinnell)

Attendance 25,372

Leicester City won 4-3 on aggregate

DIVISION ONE 1964-65

MANCHESTER UNITED	42	26	9	7	89	39	61
Leeds United	42	26	9	7	83	52	61
Chelsea	42	24	8	10	89	54	56
Everton	42	17	15	10	69	60	49
Nottingham Forest	42	17	13	12	71	67	47
Tottenham Hotspur	42	19	7	16	87	71	45
Liverpool	42	17	10	15	67	73	44
Sheffield Wednesday	42	16	11	15	57	55	43
West Ham United	42	19	4	19	82	71	42
Blackburn Rovers	42	16	10	16	83	79	42
Stoke City	42	16	10	16	67	66	42
Burnley	42	16	10	16	70	70	42
Arsenal	42	17	7	18	69	75	41
West Bromwich Albion	42	13	13	16	70	65	39
Sunderland	42	14	9	19	64	74	37
Aston Villa	42	16	5	21	57	82	37
Blackpool	42	12	11	19	67	78	35
Leicester City	42	11	13	18	69	85	35
Sheffield United	42	12	11	19	50	64	35
Fulham	42	11	12	19	60	78	34
Wolverhampton Wanderers	*42*	*13*	*4*	*25*	*59*	*89*	*30*
Birmingham City	*42*	*8*	*11*	*23*	*64*	*96*	*27*

DIVISION TWO 1964-65

Newcastle United	42	24	9	9	81	45	57
Northampton Town	42	20	16	6	66	50	56
Bolton Wanderers	42	20	10	12	80	58	50
Southampton	42	17	14	11	83	63	48
Ipswich Town	42	15	17	10	74	67	47
Norwich City	42	20	7	15	61	57	47
Crystal Palace	42	16	13	13	55	51	45
Huddersfield Town	42	17	10	15	53	51	44
Derby County	42	16	11	15	84	79	43
Coventry City	42	17	9	16	72	70	43
Manchester City	42	16	9	17	63	62	41
Preston North End	42	14	13	15	76	81	41
Cardiff City	42	13	14	15	64	57	40
Rotherham United	42	14	12	16	70	69	40
Plymouth Argyle	42	16	8	18	63	79	40
Bury	42	14	10	18	60	66	38
Middlesbrough	42	13	9	20	70	76	35
Charlton Athletic	42	13	9	20	64	75	35
Leyton Orient	42	12	11	19	50	72	35
Portsmouth	42	12	10	20	56	77	34
Swindon Town	*42*	*14*	*5*	*23*	*63*	*81*	*33*
Swansea Town	*42*	*11*	*10*	*21*	*62*	*84*	*32*

DIVISION THREE 1964-65

Carlisle United	46	25	10	11	76	53	60
Bristol City	46	24	11	11	92	55	59
Mansfield Town	46	24	11	11	95	61	59
Hull City	46	23	12	11	91	57	58
Brentford	46	24	9	13	83	55	57
Bristol Rovers	46	20	15	11	82	58	55
Gillingham	46	23	9	14	70	50	55
Peterborough United	46	22	7	17	85	74	51
Watford	46	17	16	13	71	64	50
Grimsby Town	46	16	18	12	68	67	49
Bournemouth & Boscombe Ath.	46	18	11	17	72	63	47
Southend United	46	19	8	19	78	71	46
Reading	46	16	14	16	70	70	46
Queen's Park Rangers	46	17	12	17	72	80	46
Workington	46	17	12	17	58	69	46
Shrewsbury Town	46	15	12	19	76	84	42
Exeter City	46	12	17	17	51	52	41
Scunthorpe United	46	14	12	20	65	72	40
Walsall	46	15	7	24	55	80	37
Oldham Athletic	46	13	10	23	61	83	36
Luton Town	*46*	*11*	*11*	*24*	*51*	*94*	*33*
Port Vale	*46*	*9*	*14*	*23*	*41*	*76*	*32*
Colchester United	*46*	*10*	*10*	*26*	*50*	*89*	*30*
Barnsley	*46*	*9*	*11*	*26*	*54*	*90*	*29*

DIVISION FOUR 1964-65

Brighton & Hove Albion	46	26	11	9	102	57	63
Millwall	46	23	16	7	78	45	62
York City	46	28	6	12	91	56	62
Oxford United	46	23	15	8	87	44	61
Tranmere Rovers	46	27	6	13	99	56	60
Rochdale	46	22	14	10	74	53	58
Bradford Park Avenue	46	20	17	9	86	62	57
Chester	46	25	6	15	119	81	56
Doncaster Rovers	46	20	11	15	84	72	51
Crewe Alexandra	46	18	13	15	90	81	49
Torquay United	46	21	7	18	70	70	49
Chesterfield	46	20	8	18	58	70	48
Notts County	46	15	14	17	61	73	44
Wrexham	46	17	9	20	84	92	43
Hartlepools United	46	15	13	18	61	85	43
Newport County	46	17	8	21	85	81	42
Darlington	46	18	6	22	84	87	42
Aldershot	46	15	7	24	64	84	37
Bradford City	46	12	8	26	70	88	32
Southport	46	8	16	22	58	89	32
Barrow	46	12	6	28	59	105	30
Lincoln City	46	11	6	29	58	99	28
Halifax	46	11	6	29	54	103	28
Stockport County	46	10	7	29	44	87	27

1965 F.A. Cup

Semi-finals

Liverpool vs Chelsea	2-0
Manchester United vs Leeds United	0-0, 0-1

Final

Wembley, 1st May 1965

Liverpool 2 (Hunt, St. John)
Leeds United 1 (aet.) (Bremner)

Attendance 100,000

1965 Football League Cup

Semi-finals

Aston Villa vs Chelsea (2-3, 1-1)	3-4
Leicester City vs Plymouth Argyle (3-2, 1-0)	4-2

Final (1st leg)

Stamford Bridge, 15th March 1965

Chelsea 3 (Tambling, Venables (pen), McCreadie)
Leicester City 2 (Appleton, Goodfellow)

Attendance 20,690

Final (2nd leg)

Leicester, 5th April 1965

Leicester City 0
Chelsea 0

Attendance 26,958

Chelsea won 3-2 on aggregate

DIVISION ONE 1965-66

LIVERPOOL	42	26	9	7	79	34	61
Leeds United	42	23	9	10	79	38	55
Burnley	42	24	7	11	79	47	55
Manchester United	42	18	15	9	84	59	51
Chelsea	42	22	7	13	65	53	51
West Bromwich Albion	42	19	12	11	91	69	50
Leicester City	42	21	7	14	80	65	49
Tottenham Hotspur	42	16	12	14	75	66	44
Sheffield United	42	16	11	15	56	59	43
Stoke City	42	15	12	15	65	64	42
Everton	42	15	11	16	56	62	41
West Ham United	42	15	9	18	70	83	39
Blackpool	42	14	9	19	55	65	37
Arsenal	42	12	13	17	62	75	37
Newcastle United	42	14	9	19	50	63	37
Aston Villa	42	15	6	21	69	80	36
Sheffield Wednesday	42	14	8	20	56	66	36
Nottingham Forest	42	14	8	20	56	72	36
Sunderland	42	14	8	20	51	72	36
Fulham	42	14	7	21	67	85	35
Northampton Town	*42*	*10*	*13*	*19*	*55*	*92*	*33*
Blackburn Rovers	*42*	*8*	*4*	*30*	*57*	*88*	*20*

DIVISION THREE 1965-66

Hull City	46	31	7	8	109	62	69
Millwall	46	27	11	8	76	43	65
Queen's Park Rangers	46	24	9	13	95	65	57
Scunthorpe United	46	21	11	14	80	67	53
Workington	46	19	14	13	67	57	52
Gillingham	46	22	8	16	62	54	52
Swindon Town	46	19	13	14	74	48	51
Reading	46	19	13	14	70	63	51
Walsall	46	20	10	16	77	64	50
Shrewsbury Town	46	19	11	16	73	64	49
Grimsby Town	46	17	13	16	68	62	47
Watford	46	17	13	16	55	51	47
Peterborough United	46	17	12	17	80	66	46
Oxford United	46	19	8	19	70	74	46
Brighton & Hove Albion	46	16	11	19	67	65	43
Bristol Rovers	46	14	14	18	64	64	42
Swansea Town	46	15	11	20	81	96	41
Bournemouth & Boscombe Ath.	46	13	12	21	38	56	38
Mansfield Town	46	15	8	23	59	89	38
Oldham Athletic	46	12	13	21	55	81	37
Southend United	*46*	*16*	*4*	*26*	*54*	*83*	*36*
Exeter City	*46*	*12*	*11*	*23*	*53*	*79*	*35*
Brentford	*46*	*10*	*12*	*24*	*48*	*69*	*32*
York City	*46*	*9*	*9*	*28*	*53*	*106*	*27*

DIVISION TWO 1965-66

Manchester City	42	22	15	5	76	44	59
Southampton	42	22	10	10	85	56	54
Coventry City	42	20	13	9	73	53	53
Huddersfield Town	42	19	13	10	62	36	51
Bristol City	42	17	17	8	63	48	51
Wolverhampton Wanderers	42	20	10	12	87	61	50
Rotherham United	42	16	14	12	75	74	46
Derby County	42	16	11	15	71	68	43
Bolton Wanderers	42	16	9	17	62	59	41
Birmingham City	42	16	9	17	70	75	41
Crystal Palace	42	14	13	15	47	52	41
Portsmouth	42	16	8	18	74	78	40
Norwich City	42	12	15	15	52	52	39
Carlisle United	42	17	5	20	60	63	39
Ipswich Town	42	15	9	18	58	66	39
Charlton Athletic	42	12	14	16	61	70	38
Preston North End	42	11	15	16	62	70	37
Plymouth Argyle	42	12	13	17	54	63	37
Bury	42	14	7	21	62	76	35
Cardiff City	42	12	10	20	71	91	34
Middlesbrough	*42*	*10*	*13*	*19*	*58*	*86*	*33*
Leyton Orient	*42*	*5*	*13*	*24*	*38*	*80*	*23*

DIVISION FOUR 1965-66

Doncaster Rovers	46	24	11	11	85	54	59
Darlington	46	25	9	12	72	53	59
Torquay United	46	24	10	12	72	49	58
Colchester United	46	23	10	13	70	47	56
Tranmere Rovers	46	24	8	14	93	66	56
Luton Town	46	24	8	14	90	70	56
Chester	46	20	12	14	79	70	52
Notts County	46	19	12	15	61	53	50
Newport County	46	18	12	16	75	75	48
Southport	46	18	12	16	68	69	48
Bradford Park Avenue	46	21	5	20	102	92	47
Barrow	46	16	15	15	72	76	47
Stockport County	46	18	6	22	71	70	42
Crewe Alexandra	46	16	9	21	61	63	41
Halifax Town	46	15	11	20	67	75	41
Barnsley	46	15	10	21	74	78	40
Aldershot	46	15	10	21	75	84	40
Hartlepools United	46	16	8	22	63	75	40
Port Vale	46	15	9	22	48	59	39
Chesterfield	46	13	13	20	62	78	39
Rochdale	46	16	5	25	71	87	37
Lincoln City	46	13	11	22	57	82	37
Bradford City	46	12	13	21	63	94	37
Wrexham	46	13	9	24	72	104	35

1966 F.A. Cup

Semi-finals

Everton vs Manchester United	1-0
Sheffield Wednesday vs Chelsea	2-0

Final

Wembley, 14th May 1966

Everton 3 (Trebilcock 2, Temple)
Sheffield Wednesday 2 (McCalliog, Ford)

Attendance 100,000

1966 Football League Cup

Semi-finals

West Brom. Albion vs Peterborough Utd. (2-1, 4-2)	6-3
West Ham United vs Cardiff City (5-2, 5-1)	10-3

Final (1st leg)

Upton Park, 9th March 1966

West Ham United 2 (Moore, Byrne)
West Bromwich Albion 1 (Astle)

Attendance 28,341

Final (2nd leg)

The Hawthorns, 23rd March 1966

West Bromwich Albion 4 (Kaye, Brown, Clark, Williams)
West Ham United 1 (Peters)

Attendance 31,925

West Bromwich Albion won 5-3 on aggregate

DIVISION ONE 1966-67

MANCHESTER UNITED	42	24	12	6	84	45	60
Nottingham Forest	42	23	10	9	64	41	56
Tottenham Hotspur	42	24	8	10	71	48	56
Leeds United	42	22	11	9	62	42	55
Liverpool	42	19	13	10	64	47	51
Everton	42	19	10	13	65	46	48
Arsenal	42	16	14	12	58	47	46
Leicester City	42	18	8	16	78	71	44
Chelsea	42	15	14	13	67	62	44
Sheffield United	42	16	10	16	52	59	42
Sheffield Wednesday	42	14	13	15	56	47	41
Stoke City	42	17	7	18	63	58	41
West Bromwich Albion	42	16	7	19	77	73	39
Burnley	42	15	9	18	66	76	39
Manchester City	42	12	15	15	43	52	39
West Ham United	42	14	8	20	80	84	36
Sunderland	42	14	8	20	58	72	36
Fulham	42	11	12	19	71	83	34
Southampton	42	14	6	22	74	92	34
Newcastle United	42	12	9	21	39	81	33
Aston Villa	*42*	*11*	*7*	*24*	*54*	*85*	*29*
Blackpool	*42*	*6*	*9*	*27*	*41*	*76*	*21*

DIVISION TWO 1966-67

Coventry City	42	23	13	6	74	43	59
Wolverhampton Wanderers	42	25	8	9	88	48	58
Carlisle United	42	23	6	13	71	54	52
Blackburn Rovers	42	19	13	10	56	46	51
Ipswich Town	42	17	16	9	70	54	50
Huddersfield Town	42	20	9	13	58	46	49
Crystal Palace	42	19	10	13	61	55	48
Millwall	42	18	9	15	49	58	45
Bolton Wanderers	42	14	14	14	64	58	42
Birmingham City	42	16	8	18	70	66	40
Norwich City	42	13	14	15	49	55	40
Hull City	42	16	7	19	77	72	39
Preston North End	42	16	7	19	65	67	39
Portsmouth	42	13	13	16	59	70	39
Bristol City	42	12	14	16	56	62	38
Plymouth Argyle	42	14	9	19	59	58	37
Derby County	42	12	12	18	68	72	36
Rotherham United	42	13	10	19	61	70	36
Charlton Athletic	42	13	9	20	49	53	35
Cardiff City	42	12	9	21	61	87	33
Northampton Town	*42*	*12*	*6*	*24*	*47*	*84*	*30*
Bury	*42*	*11*	*6*	*25*	*49*	*83*	*28*

DIVISION THREE 1966-67

Queen's Park Rangers	46	26	15	5	103	38	67
Middlesbrough	46	23	9	14	87	64	55
Watford	46	20	14	12	61	46	54
Reading	46	22	9	15	76	57	53
Bristol Rovers	46	20	13	13	76	67	53
Shrewsbury Town	46	20	12	14	77	62	52
Torquay United	46	21	9	16	73	54	51
Swindon Town	46	20	10	16	81	59	50
Mansfield Town	46	20	9	17	84	79	49
Oldham Athletic	46	19	10	17	80	63	48
Gillingham	46	15	16	15	58	62	46
Walsall	46	18	10	18	65	72	46
Colchester United	46	17	10	19	76	73	44
Leyton Orient	46	13	18	15	58	68	44
Peterborough United	46	14	15	17	66	71	43
Oxford United	46	15	13	18	61	66	43
Grimsby Town	46	17	9	20	61	68	43
Scunthorpe United	46	17	8	21	58	73	42
Brighton & Hove Albion	46	13	15	18	61	71	41
Bournemouth & Boscombe Ath.	46	12	17	17	39	57	41
Swansea Town	*46*	*12*	*15*	*19*	*85*	*89*	*39*
Darlington	*46*	*13*	*11*	*22*	*47*	*81*	*37*
Doncaster Rovers	*46*	*12*	*8*	*26*	*58*	*117*	*32*
Workington	*46*	*12*	*7*	*27*	*55*	*89*	*31*

DIVISION FOUR 1966-67

Stockport County	46	26	12	8	69	42	64
Southport	46	23	13	10	69	42	59
Barrow	46	24	11	11	76	54	59
Tranmere Rovers	46	22	14	10	66	43	58
Crewe Alexandra	46	21	12	13	70	55	54
Southend United	46	22	9	15	70	49	53
Wrexham	46	16	20	10	76	62	52
Hartlepools United	46	22	7	17	66	64	51
Brentford	46	18	13	15	58	56	49
Aldershot	46	18	12	16	72	57	48
Bradford City	46	19	10	17	74	62	48
Halifax Town	46	15	14	17	59	68	44
Port Vale	46	14	15	17	55	58	43
Exeter City	46	14	15	17	50	60	43
Chesterfield	46	17	8	21	60	63	42
Barnsley	46	13	15	16	60	64	41
Luton Town	46	16	9	21	59	73	41
Newport County	46	12	16	18	56	63	40
Chester	46	15	10	21	54	78	40
Notts County	46	13	11	22	53	72	37
Rochdale	46	13	11	22	53	75	37
York City	46	12	11	23	65	79	35
Bradford Park Avenue	46	11	13	22	52	79	35
Lincoln City	46	9	13	24	58	82	31

1967 F.A. Cup

Semi-finals

Tottenham Hotspur vs Nottingham Forest	2-1
Chelsea vs Leeds United	1-0

Final

Wembley, 20th May 1967

Tottenham Hotspur 2   (Robertson, Saul)

Chelsea 1   (Tambling)

Attendance 100,000

1967 Football League Cup

Semi-finals

Birmingham City vs Queen's Park Rangers (1-4, 1-3)	2-7
West Bromwich Albion vs West Ham Utd. (4-0, 2-2)	6-2

Final

Wembley, 4th March 1967

Queen's Park Rangers 3   (R. Morgan, Marsh, Lazarus)

West Bromwich Albion 2   (Clark 2)

Attendance 97,952

DIVISION ONE 1967-68

	P	W	D	L	F	A	Pts
MANCHESTER CITY	42	26	6	10	86	43	58
Manchester United	42	24	8	10	89	55	56
Liverpool	42	22	11	9	71	40	55
Leeds United	42	22	9	11	71	41	53
Everton	42	23	6	13	67	40	52
Chelsea	42	18	12	12	62	68	48
Tottenham Hotspur	42	19	9	14	70	59	47
West Bromwich Albion	42	17	12	13	75	62	46
Arsenal	42	17	10	15	60	56	44
Newcastle United	42	13	15	14	54	67	41
Nottingham Forest	42	14	11	17	52	64	39
West Ham United	42	14	10	18	73	69	38
Leicester City	42	13	12	17	64	69	38
Burnley	42	14	10	18	64	71	38
Sunderland	42	13	11	18	51	61	37
Southampton	42	13	11	18	66	83	37
Wolverhampton Wanderers	42	14	8	20	66	75	36
Stoke City	42	14	7	21	50	73	35
Sheffield Wednesday	42	11	12	19	51	63	34
Coventry City	42	9	15	18	51	71	33
Sheffield United	42	11	10	21	49	70	32
Fulham	42	10	7	25	56	98	27

DIVISION TWO 1967-68

	P	W	D	L	F	A	Pts
Ipswich Town	42	22	15	5	79	44	59
Queen's Park Rangers	42	25	8	9	67	36	58
Blackpool	42	24	10	8	71	43	58
Birmingham City	42	19	14	9	83	51	52
Portsmouth	42	18	13	11	68	55	49
Middlesbrough	42	17	12	13	60	54	46
Millwall	42	14	17	11	62	50	45
Blackburn Rovers	42	16	11	15	56	49	43
Norwich City	42	16	11	15	60	65	43
Carlisle United	42	14	13	15	58	52	41
Crystal Palace	42	14	11	17	56	56	39
Bolton Wanderers	42	13	13	16	60	63	39
Cardiff City	42	13	12	17	60	66	38
Huddersfield Town	42	13	12	17	46	61	38
Charlton Athletic	42	12	13	17	63	68	37
Aston Villa	42	15	7	20	54	64	37
Hull City	42	12	13	17	58	73	37
Derby County	42	13	10	19	71	78	36
Bristol City	42	13	10	19	48	62	36
Preston North End	42	12	11	19	43	65	35
Rotherham United	42	10	11	21	42	76	31
Plymouth Argyle	42	9	9	24	38	72	27

DIVISION THREE 1967-68

	P	W	D	L	F	A	Pts
Oxford United	46	22	13	11	69	47	57
Bury	46	24	8	14	91	66	56
Shrewsbury Town	46	20	15	11	61	49	55
Torquay United	46	21	11	14	60	56	53
Reading	46	21	9	16	70	60	51
Watford	46	21	8	17	74	50	50
Walsall	46	19	12	15	74	61	50
Barrow	46	21	8	17	65	54	50
Swindon Town	46	16	17	13	74	51	49
Brighton & Hove Albion	46	16	16	14	57	55	48
Gillingham	46	18	12	16	59	63	48
Bournemouth & Boscombe Ath.	46	16	15	15	56	51	47
Stockport County	46	19	9	18	70	75	47
Southport	46	17	12	17	65	65	46
Bristol Rovers	46	17	9	20	72	78	43
Oldham Athletic	46	18	7	21	60	65	43
Northampton Town	46	14	13	19	58	72	41
Orient	46	12	17	17	46	62	41
Tranmere Rovers	46	14	12	20	62	74	40
Mansfield Town	46	12	13	21	51	67	37
Grimsby Town	46	14	9	23	52	69	37
Colchester United	46	9	15	22	50	87	33
Scunthorpe United	46	10	12	24	56	87	32
Peterborough United	46	20	10	16	79	67	31†

† Peterborough United were 'fined' 19 points and relegated for offering illegal bonuses.

DIVISION FOUR 1967-68

	P	W	D	L	F	A	Pts
Luton Town	46	27	12	7	87	44	66
Barnsley	46	24	13	9	68	46	61
Hartlepools United	46	25	10	11	60	46	60
Crewe Alexandra	46	20	18	8	74	49	58
Bradford City	46	23	11	12	72	51	57
Southend United	46	20	14	12	77	58	54
Chesterfield	46	21	11	14	71	50	53
Wrexham	46	20	13	13	72	53	53
Aldershot	46	18	17	11	70	55	53
Doncaster Rovers	46	18	15	13	66	56	51
Halifax Town	46	15	16	15	52	49	46
Newport County	46	16	13	17	58	63	45
Lincoln City	46	17	9	20	71	68	43
Brentford	46	18	7	21	61	64	43
Swansea Town	46	16	10	20	63	77	42
Darlington	46	12	17	17	47	53	41
Notts County	46	15	11	20	53	79	41
Port Vale	46	12	15	19	61	72	39
Rochdale	46	12	14	20	51	72	38
Exeter City	46	11	16	19	45	65	38
York City	46	11	14	21	65	68	36
Chester	46	9	14	23	57	78	32
Workington	46	10	11	25	54	87	31
Bradford Park Avenue	46	4	15	27	30	82	23

Port Vale was expelled from the League for financial irregularities but successfully applied for re-election for the 1968/69 season.

1968 F.A. Cup

Semi-finals

West Bromwich Albion vs Birmingham City	2-0
Everton vs Leeds United	1-0

Final

Wembley, 18th May 1968

West Bromwich Albion 1 (Astle)

Everton 0 (aet.)

Attendance 100,000

1968 Football League Cup

Semi-finals

Derby County vs Leeds United (0-1, 2-3)	2-4
Arsenal vs Huddersfield Town (3-2, 3-1)	6-3

Final

Wembley, 2nd March 1968

Leeds United 1 (Cooper)

Arsenal 0

Attendance 97,887

DIVISION ONE 1968-69

LEEDS UNITED	42	27	13	2	66	26	67
Liverpool	42	25	11	6	63	24	61
Everton	42	21	15	6	77	36	57
Arsenal	42	22	12	8	56	27	56
Chelsea	42	20	10	12	73	53	50
Tottenham Hotspur	42	14	17	11	61	51	45
Southampton	42	16	13	13	57	48	45
West Ham United	42	13	18	11	66	50	44
Newcastle United	42	15	14	13	61	55	44
West Bromwich Albion	42	16	11	15	64	67	43
Manchester United	42	15	12	15	57	53	42
Ipswich Town	42	15	11	16	59	60	41
Manchester City	42	15	10	17	64	55	40
Burnley	42	15	9	18	55	82	39
Sheffield Wednesday	42	10	16	16	41	54	36
Wolverhampton Wanderers	42	10	15	17	41	58	35
Sunderland	42	11	12	19	43	67	34
Nottingham Forest	42	10	13	19	45	57	33
Stoke City	42	9	15	18	40	63	33
Coventry City	42	10	11	21	46	64	31
Leicester City	*42*	*9*	*12*	*21*	*39*	*68*	*30*
Queen's Park Rangers	*42*	*4*	*10*	*28*	*39*	*95*	*18*

DIVISION TWO 1968-69

Derby County	42	26	11	5	65	32	63
Crystal Palace	42	22	12	8	70	47	56
Charlton Athletic	42	18	14	10	61	52	50
Middlesbrough	42	19	11	12	58	49	49
Cardiff City	42	20	7	15	67	54	47
Huddersfield Town	42	17	12	13	53	46	46
Birmingham City	42	18	8	16	73	59	44
Blackpool	42	14	15	13	51	41	43
Sheffield United	42	16	11	15	61	50	43
Millwall	42	17	9	16	57	49	43
Hull City	42	13	16	13	59	52	42
Carlisle United	42	16	10	16	46	49	42
Norwich City	42	15	10	17	53	56	40
Preston North End	42	12	15	15	38	44	39
Portsmouth	42	12	14	16	58	58	38
Bristol City	42	11	16	15	46	53	38
Bolton Wanderers	42	12	14	16	55	67	38
Aston Villa	42	12	14	16	37	48	38
Blackburn Rovers	42	13	11	18	52	63	37
Oxford United	42	12	9	21	34	55	33
Bury	*42*	*11*	*8*	*23*	*51*	*80*	*30*
Fulham	*42*	*7*	*11*	*24*	*40*	*81*	*25*

DIVISION THREE 1968-69

Watford	46	27	10	9	74	34	64
Swindon Town	46	27	10	9	71	35	64
Luton Town	46	25	11	10	74	38	61
Bournemouth & Boscombe Ath.	46	21	9	16	60	45	51
Plymouth Argyle	46	17	15	14	53	49	49
Torquay United	46	18	12	16	54	46	48
Tranmere Rovers	46	19	10	17	70	68	48
Southport	46	17	13	16	71	64	47
Stockport County	46	16	14	16	67	68	46
Barnsley	46	16	14	16	58	63	46
Rotherham United	46	16	13	17	56	50	45
Brighton & Hove Albion	46	16	13	17	72	65	45
Walsall	46	14	16	16	50	49	44
Reading	46	15	13	18	67	66	43
Mansfield Town	46	16	11	19	58	62	43
Bristol Rovers	46	16	11	19	63	71	43
Shrewsbury Town	46	16	11	19	51	67	43
Orient	46	14	14	18	51	58	42
Barrow	46	17	8	21	56	75	42
Gillingham	46	13	15	18	54	63	41
Northampton Town	*46*	*14*	*12*	*20*	*54*	*61*	*40*
Hartlepool	*46*	*10*	*19*	*17*	*40*	*70*	*39*
Crewe Alexandra	*46*	*13*	*9*	*24*	*52*	*76*	*35*
Oldham Athletic	*46*	*13*	*9*	*24*	*50*	*83*	*35*

DIVISION FOUR 1968-69

Doncaster Rovers	46	21	17	8	65	38	59
Halifax Town	46	20	17	9	53	37	57
Rochdale	46	18	20	8	68	35	56
Bradford City	46	18	20	8	65	46	56
Darlington	46	17	18	11	62	45	52
Colchester United	46	20	12	14	57	53	52
Southend United	46	19	13	14	78	61	51
Lincoln City	46	17	17	12	54	52	51
Wrexham	46	18	14	14	61	52	50
Swansea Town	46	19	11	16	58	54	49
Brentford	46	18	12	16	64	65	48
Workington	46	15	17	14	40	43	47
Port Vale	46	16	14	16	46	46	46
Chester	46	16	13	17	76	66	45
Aldershot	46	19	7	20	66	66	45
Scunthorpe United	46	18	8	20	61	60	44
Exeter City	46	16	11	19	66	65	43
Peterborough United	46	13	16	17	60	57	42
Notts County	46	12	18	16	48	57	42
Chesterfield	46	13	15	18	43	50	41
York City	46	14	11	21	53	75	39
Newport County	46	11	14	21	49	74	36
Grimsby Town	46	9	15	22	47	69	33
Bradford Park Avenue	46	5	10	31	32	106	20

1969 F.A. Cup

Semi-finals

Manchester City vs Everton	1-0
West Bromwich Albion vs Leicester City	0-1

Final

Wembley, 26th April 1969

Manchester City 1 (Young)

Leicester City 0

Attendance 100,000

1969 Football League Cup

Semi-finals

Arsenal vs Tottenham Hotspur (1-0, 1-1)	2-1
Burnley vs Swindon Town (1-2, 2-1)	3-3

Play-off

Burnley vs Swindon Town	2-3

Final

Wembley, 15th March 1969

Swindon Town 3 (Smart, Rogers 2)

Arsenal 1 (Gould)

Attendance 98,189

DIVISION ONE 1969-70

EVERTON	**42**	**29**	**8**	**5**	**72**	**34**	**66**
Leeds United	42	21	15	6	84	49	57
Chelsea	42	21	13	8	70	50	55
Derby County	42	22	9	11	64	37	53
Liverpool	42	20	11	11	65	42	51
Coventry City	42	19	11	12	58	48	49
Newcastle United	42	17	13	12	57	35	47
Manchester United	42	14	17	11	66	61	45
Stoke City	42	15	15	12	56	52	45
Manchester City	42	16	11	15	55	48	43
Tottenham Hotspur	42	17	9	16	54	55	43
Arsenal	42	12	18	12	51	49	42
Wolverhampton Wanderers	42	12	16	14	55	57	40
Burnley	42	12	15	15	56	61	39
Nottingham Forest	42	10	18	14	50	71	38
West Bromwich Albion	42	14	9	19	58	66	37
West Ham United	42	12	12	18	51	60	36
Ipswich Town	42	10	11	21	40	63	31
Southampton	42	6	17	19	46	67	29
Crystal Palace	42	6	15	21	34	68	27
Sunderland	*42*	*6*	*14*	*22*	*30*	*68*	*26*
Sheffield Wednesday	*42*	*8*	*9*	*25*	*40*	*71*	*25*

DIVISION THREE 1969-70

Orient	**46**	**25**	**12**	**9**	**67**	**36**	**62**
Luton Town	**46**	**23**	**14**	**9**	**77**	**43**	**60**
Bristol Rovers	46	20	16	10	80	59	56
Fulham	46	20	15	11	81	55	55
Brighton & Hove Albion	46	23	9	14	57	43	55
Mansfield Town	46	21	11	14	70	49	53
Barnsley	46	19	15	12	68	59	53
Reading	46	21	11	14	87	77	53
Rochdale	46	18	10	18	69	60	46
Bradford City	46	17	12	17	57	50	46
Doncaster Rovers	46	17	12	17	52	54	46
Walsall	46	17	12	17	54	67	46
Torquay United	46	14	17	15	62	59	45
Rotherham United	46	15	14	17	62	54	44
Shrewsbury Town	46	13	18	15	62	63	44
Tranmere Rovers	46	14	16	16	56	72	44
Plymouth Argyle	46	16	11	19	56	64	43
Halifax Town	46	14	15	17	47	63	43
Bury	46	15	11	20	75	80	41
Gillingham	46	13	13	20	52	64	39
Bournemouth & Boscombe Ath.	*46*	*12*	*15*	*19*	*48*	*71*	*39*
Southport	*46*	*14*	*10*	*22*	*48*	*66*	*38*
Barrow	*46*	*8*	*14*	*24*	*46*	*81*	*30*
Stockport County	*46*	*6*	*11*	*29*	*27*	*71*	*23*

DIVISION TWO 1969-70

Huddersfield Town	**42**	**24**	**12**	**6**	**68**	**37**	**60**
Blackpool	**42**	**20**	**13**	**9**	**56**	**45**	**53**
Leicester City	42	19	13	10	64	50	51
Middlesbrough	42	20	10	12	55	45	50
Swindon Town	42	17	16	9	57	47	50
Sheffield United	42	22	5	15	73	38	49
Cardiff City	42	18	13	11	61	41	49
Blackburn Rovers	42	20	7	15	54	50	47
Queen's Park Rangers	42	17	11	14	66	57	45
Millwall	42	15	14	13	56	56	44
Norwich City	42	16	11	15	49	46	43
Carlisle United	42	14	13	15	58	56	41
Hull City	42	15	11	16	72	70	41
Bristol City	42	13	13	16	54	50	39
Oxford United	42	12	15	15	35	42	39
Bolton Wanderers	42	12	12	18	54	61	36
Portsmouth	42	13	9	20	66	80	35
Birmingham City	42	11	11	20	51	78	33
Watford	42	9	13	20	44	57	31
Charlton Athletic	42	7	17	18	35	76	31
Aston Villa	*42*	*8*	*13*	*21*	*36*	*62*	*29*
Preston North End	*42*	*8*	*12*	*22*	*43*	*63*	*28*

DIVISION FOUR 1969-70

Chesterfield	**46**	**27**	**10**	**9**	**77**	**32**	**64**
Wrexham	**46**	**26**	**9**	**11**	**84**	**49**	**61**
Swansea City	**46**	**21**	**18**	**7**	**66**	**45**	**60**
Port Vale	**46**	**20**	**19**	**7**	**61**	**33**	**59**
Brentford	46	20	16	10	58	39	56
Aldershot	46	20	13	13	78	65	53
Notts County	46	22	8	16	73	62	52
Lincoln City	46	17	16	13	66	52	50
Peterborough United	46	17	14	15	77	69	48
Colchester United	46	17	14	15	64	63	48
Chester	46	21	6	19	58	66	48
Scunthorpe United	46	18	10	18	67	65	46
York City	46	16	14	16	55	62	46
Northampton Town	46	16	12	18	64	55	44
Crewe Alexandra	46	16	12	18	51	51	44
Grimsby Town	46	14	15	17	54	58	43
Southend United	46	15	10	21	59	85	40
Exeter City	46	14	11	21	57	59	39
Oldham Athletic	46	13	13	20	60	65	39
Workington	46	12	14	20	46	64	38
Newport County	46	13	11	22	53	74	37
Darlington	46	13	10	23	53	73	36
Hartlepool	46	10	10	26	42	82	30
Bradford Park Avenue	*46*	*6*	*11*	*29*	*41*	*96*	*23*

1970 F.A. Cup

Semi-finals

Chelsea vs Watford	5-1
Manchester United vs Leeds United	0-0, 0-0, 0-1

Final

Wembley, 11th April 1970

Chelsea 2 (Houseman, Hutchinson)
Leeds United 2 (aet.) (Charlton, Jones)

Attendance 100,000

Replay

Old Trafford, 29th April 1970

Chelsea 2 (Osgood, Webb)
Leeds United 1 (aet.) (Jones)

Attendance 62,000

1970 Football League Cup

Semi-finals

Manchester City vs Manchester United	(2-1, 2-2)	4-3
Carlisle United vs West Bromwich Albion	(1-0, 1-4)	2-4

Final

Wembley, 7th March 1970

Manchester City 2 (Doyle, Pardoe)
West Bromwich Albion 1 (Astle)

Attendance 97,963

DIVISION ONE 1970-71

ARSENAL	42	29	7	6	71	29	65
Leeds United	42	27	10	5	72	30	64
Tottenham Hotspur	42	19	14	9	54	33	52
Wolverhampton Wanderers	42	22	8	12	64	54	52
Liverpool	42	17	17	8	42	24	51
Chelsea	42	18	15	9	52	42	51
Southampton	42	17	12	13	56	44	46
Manchester United	42	16	11	15	65	66	43
Derby County	42	16	10	16	56	54	42
Coventry City	42	16	10	16	37	38	42
Manchester City	42	12	17	13	47	42	41
Newcastle United	42	14	13	15	44	46	41
Stoke City	42	12	13	17	44	48	37
Everton	42	12	13	17	54	60	37
Huddersfield Town	42	11	14	17	40	49	36
Nottingham Forest	42	14	8	20	42	61	36
West Bromwich Albion	42	10	15	17	58	75	35
Crystal Palace	42	12	11	19	39	57	35
Ipswich Town	42	12	10	20	42	48	34
West Ham United	42	10	14	18	47	60	34
Burnley	*42*	*7*	*13*	*22*	*29*	*63*	*27*
Blackpool	*42*	*4*	*15*	*23*	*34*	*66*	*23*

DIVISION TWO 1970-71

Leicester City	42	23	13	6	57	30	59
Sheffield United	42	21	14	7	73	39	56
Cardiff City	42	20	13	9	64	41	53
Carlisle United	42	20	13	9	65	43	53
Hull City	42	19	13	10	54	41	51
Luton Town	42	18	13	11	62	43	49
Middlesbrough	42	17	14	11	60	43	48
Millwall	42	19	9	14	59	42	47
Birmingham City	42	17	12	13	58	48	46
Norwich City	42	15	14	13	54	52	44
Queen's Park Rangers	42	16	11	15	58	53	43
Swindon Town	42	15	12	15	61	51	42
Sunderland	42	15	12	15	52	54	42
Oxford United	42	14	14	14	41	48	42
Sheffield Wednesday	42	12	12	18	51	69	36
Portsmouth	42	10	14	18	46	61	34
Orient	42	9	16	17	29	51	34
Watford	42	10	13	19	38	60	33
Bristol City	42	10	11	21	46	64	31
Charlton Athletic	42	8	14	20	41	65	30
Blackburn Rovers	*42*	*6*	*15*	*21*	*37*	*69*	*27*
Bolton Wanderers	*42*	*7*	*10*	*25*	*35*	*74*	*24*

DIVISION THREE 1970-71

Preston North End	46	22	17	7	63	39	61
Fulham	46	24	12	10	68	41	60
Halifax Town	46	22	12	12	74	55	56
Aston Villa	46	19	15	12	54	46	53
Chesterfield	46	17	17	12	66	38	51
Bristol Rovers	46	19	13	14	69	50	51
Mansfield Town	46	18	15	13	64	62	51
Rotherham United	46	17	16	13	64	60	50
Wrexham	46	18	13	15	72	65	49
Torquay United	46	19	11	16	54	57	49
Swansea City	46	15	16	15	59	56	46
Barnsley	46	17	11	18	49	52	45
Shrewsbury Town	46	16	13	17	58	62	45
Brighton & Hove Albion	46	14	16	16	50	47	44
Plymouth Argyle	46	12	19	15	63	63	43
Rochdale	46	14	15	17	61	68	43
Port Vale	46	15	12	19	52	59	42
Tranmere Rovers	46	10	22	14	45	55	42
Bradford City	46	13	14	19	49	62	40
Walsall	46	14	11	21	51	57	39
Reading	*46*	*14*	*11*	*21*	*48*	*85*	*39*
Bury	*46*	*12*	*13*	*21*	*52*	*60*	*37*
Doncaster Rovers	*46*	*13*	*9*	*24*	*45*	*66*	*35*
Gillingham	*46*	*10*	*13*	*23*	*42*	*67*	*33*

DIVISION FOUR 1970-71

Notts County	46	30	9	7	89	36	69
Bournemouth & Boscombe	46	24	12	10	81	46	60
Oldham Athletic	46	24	11	11	88	63	59
York City	46	23	10	13	78	54	56
Chester	46	24	7	15	69	55	55
Colchester United	46	21	12	13	70	54	54
Northampton Town	46	19	13	14	63	59	51
Southport	46	21	6	19	63	57	48
Exeter City	46	17	14	15	67	68	48
Workington	46	18	12	16	48	49	48
Stockport County	46	16	14	16	49	65	46
Darlington	46	17	11	18	58	57	45
Aldershot	46	14	17	15	66	71	45
Brentford	46	18	8	20	66	62	44
Crewe Alexandra	46	18	8	20	75	76	44
Peterborough United	46	18	7	21	70	71	43
Scunthorpe United	46	15	13	18	56	61	43
Southend United	46	14	15	17	53	66	43
Grimsby Town	46	18	7	21	57	71	43
Cambridge United	46	15	13	18	51	66	43
Lincoln City	46	13	13	20	70	71	39
Newport County	46	10	8	28	55	85	28
Hartlepool	46	8	12	26	34	74	28
Barrow	46	7	8	31	51	90	22

1971 F.A. Cup

Semi-finals

Stoke City vs Arsenal	2-2, 0-2
Liverpool vs Everton	2-1

Final

Wembley, 8th May 1971

Arsenal 2   (Kelly, George)

Liverpool 1 (aet.)   (Heighway)

Attendance 100,000

1971 Football League Cup

Semi-finals

Bristol City vs Tottenham Hotspur (1-1, 0-2)	1-3
Manchester United vs Aston Villa (1-1, 1-2)	2-3

Final

Wembley, 27th February 1971

Tottenham Hotspur 2   (Chivers 2)

Aston Villa 0

Attendance 100,000

DIVISION ONE 1971-72

DERBY COUNTY	42	24	10	8	69	33	58
Leeds United	42	24	9	9	73	31	57
Liverpool	42	24	9	9	64	30	57
Manchester City	42	23	11	8	77	45	57
Arsenal	42	22	8	12	58	40	52
Tottenham Hotspur	42	19	13	10	63	42	51
Chelsea	42	18	12	12	58	49	48
Manchester United	42	19	10	13	69	61	48
Wolverhampton Wanderers	42	18	11	13	65	57	47
Sheffield United	42	17	12	13	61	60	46
Newcastle United	42	15	11	16	49	52	41
Leicester City	42	13	13	16	41	46	39
Ipswich Town	42	11	16	15	39	53	38
West Ham United	42	12	12	18	47	51	36
Everton	42	9	18	15	37	48	36
West Bromwich Albion	42	12	11	19	42	54	35
Stoke City	42	10	15	17	39	56	35
Coventry City	42	9	15	18	44	67	33
Southampton	42	12	7	23	52	80	31
Crystal Palace	42	8	13	21	39	65	29
Nottingham Forest	*42*	*8*	*9*	*25*	*47*	*81*	*25*
Huddersfield Town	*42*	*6*	*13*	*23*	*27*	*59*	*25*

DIVISION THREE 1971-72

Aston Villa	46	32	6	8	85	32	70
Brighton & Hove Albion	46	27	11	8	82	47	65
Bournemouth & Boscombe Ath.	46	23	16	7	73	37	62
Notts County	46	25	12	9	74	44	62
Rotherham United	46	20	15	11	69	52	55
Bristol Rovers	46	21	12	13	75	56	54
Bolton Wanderers	46	17	16	13	51	41	50
Plymouth Argyle	46	20	10	16	74	64	50
Walsall	46	15	18	13	62	57	48
Blackburn Rovers	46	19	9	18	54	57	47
Oldham Athletic	46	17	11	18	59	63	45
Shrewsbury Town	46	17	10	19	73	65	44
Chesterfield	46	18	8	20	57	57	44
Swansea City	46	17	10	19	46	59	44
Port Vale	46	13	15	18	43	59	41
Wrexham	46	16	8	22	59	63	40
Halifax Town	46	13	12	21	48	61	38
Rochdale	46	12	13	21	57	83	37
York City	46	12	12	22	57	66	36
Tranmere Rovers	46	10	16	20	50	71	36
Mansfield Town	*46*	*8*	*20*	*18*	*41*	*63*	*36*
Barnsley	*46*	*9*	*18*	*19*	*32*	*64*	*36*
Torquay United	*46*	*10*	*12*	*24*	*41*	*69*	*32*
Bradford City	*46*	*11*	*10*	*25*	*45*	*77*	*32*

DIVISION TWO 1971-72

Norwich City	42	21	15	6	60	36	57
Birmingham City	42	19	18	5	60	31	56
Millwall	42	19	17	6	64	46	55
Queen's Park Rangers	42	20	14	8	57	28	54
Sunderland	42	17	16	9	67	57	50
Blackpool	42	20	7	15	70	50	47
Burnley	42	20	6	16	70	55	46
Bristol City	42	18	10	14	61	49	46
Middlesbrough	42	19	8	15	50	48	46
Carlisle United	42	17	9	16	61	57	43
Swindon Town	42	15	12	15	47	47	42
Hull City	42	14	10	18	49	53	38
Luton Town	42	10	18	14	43	48	38
Sheffield Wednesday	42	13	12	17	51	58	38
Oxford United	42	12	14	16	43	55	38
Portsmouth	42	12	13	17	59	68	37
Orient	42	14	9	19	50	61	37
Preston North End	42	12	12	18	52	58	36
Cardiff City	42	10	14	18	56	69	34
Fulham	42	12	10	20	45	68	34
Charlton Athletic	*42*	*12*	*9*	*21*	*55*	*77*	*33*
Watford	*42*	*5*	*9*	*28*	*24*	*75*	*19*

DIVISION FOUR 1971-72

Grimsby Town	46	28	7	11	88	56	63
Southend United	46	24	12	10	81	55	60
Brentford	46	24	11	11	76	44	59
Scunthorpe United	46	22	13	11	56	37	57
Lincoln City	46	21	14	11	77	59	56
Workington	46	16	19	11	50	34	51
Southport	46	18	14	14	66	46	50
Peterborough United	46	17	16	13	82	64	50
Bury	46	19	12	15	73	59	50
Cambridge United	46	17	14	15	62	60	48
Colchester United	46	19	10	17	70	69	48
Doncaster Rovers	46	16	14	16	56	63	46
Gillingham	46	16	13	17	61	67	45
Newport County	46	18	8	20	60	72	44
Exeter City	46	16	11	19	61	68	43
Reading	46	17	8	21	56	76	42
Aldershot	46	9	22	15	48	54	40
Hartlepool	46	17	6	23	58	69	40
Darlington	46	14	11	21	64	82	39
Chester	46	10	18	18	47	56	38
Northampton Town	46	12	13	21	66	79	37
Barrow	*46*	*13*	*11*	*22*	*40*	*71*	*37*
Stockport County	46	9	14	23	55	87	32
Crewe Alexandra	46	10	9	27	43	69	29

1972 F.A. Cup

Semi-finals

Leeds United vs Birmingham City	3-0
Arsenal vs Stoke City	1-1, 2-1

Final

Wembley, 6th May 1972

Leeds United 1 (Clarke)

Arsenal 0

Attendance 100,000

1972 Football League Cup

Semi-finals

Stoke City vs West Ham Utd. (1-2, 1-0, 0-0*, 3-2†)	5-4
Chelsea vs Tottenham Hotspur (3-2, 2-2)	5-4

* 1st play-off at Hillsborough; † 2nd play-off at Old Trafford

Final

Wembley, 4th March 1972

Stoke City 2 (Conroy, Eastham)

Chelsea 1 (Osgood)

Attendance 100,000

DIVISION ONE 1972-73

LIVERPOOL	42	25	10	7	72	42	60
Arsenal	42	23	11	8	57	43	57
Leeds United	42	21	11	10	71	45	53
Ipswich Town	42	17	14	11	55	45	48
Wolverhampton Wanderers	42	18	11	13	66	54	47
West Ham United	42	17	12	13	67	53	46
Derby County	42	19	8	15	56	54	46
Tottenham Hotspur	42	16	13	13	58	48	45
Newcastle United	42	16	13	13	60	51	45
Birmingham City	42	15	12	15	53	54	42
Manchester City	42	15	11	16	57	60	41
Chelsea	42	13	14	15	49	51	40
Southampton	42	11	18	13	47	52	40
Sheffield United	42	15	10	17	51	59	40
Stoke City	42	14	10	18	61	56	38
Leicester City	42	10	17	15	40	46	37
Everton	42	13	11	18	41	49	37
Manchester United	42	12	13	17	44	60	37
Coventry City	42	13	9	20	40	55	35
Norwich City	42	11	10	21	36	63	32
Crystal Palace	*42*	*9*	*12*	*21*	*41*	*58*	*30*
West Bromwich Albion	*42*	*9*	*10*	*23*	*38*	*62*	*28*

DIVISION THREE 1972-73

Bolton Wanderers	46	25	11	10	73	39	61
Notts County	46	23	11	12	67	47	57
Blackburn Rovers	46	20	15	11	57	47	55
Oldham Athletic	46	19	16	11	72	54	54
Bristol Rovers	46	20	13	13	77	56	53
Port Vale	46	21	11	14	56	69	53
Bournemouth	46	17	16	13	66	44	50
Plymouth Argyle	46	20	10	16	74	66	50
Grimsby Town	46	20	8	18	67	61	48
Tranmere Rovers	46	15	16	15	56	52	46
Charlton Athletic	46	17	11	18	69	67	45
Wrexham	46	14	17	15	55	54	45
Rochdale	46	14	17	15	48	54	45
Southend United	46	17	10	19	61	54	44
Shrewsbury Town	46	15	14	17	46	54	44
Chesterfield	46	17	9	20	57	61	43
Walsall	46	18	7	21	56	66	43
York City	46	13	15	18	42	46	41
Watford	46	12	17	17	43	48	41
Halifax Town	46	13	15	18	43	53	41
Rotherham United	*46*	*17*	*7*	*22*	*51*	*65*	*41*
Brentford	*46*	*15*	*7*	*24*	*51*	*69*	*37*
Swansea City	*46*	*14*	*9*	*23*	*51*	*73*	*37*
Scunthorpe United	*46*	*10*	*10*	*26*	*33*	*72*	*30*

DIVISION TWO 1972-73

Burnley	42	24	14	4	72	35	62
Queen's Park Rangers	42	24	13	5	81	37	61
Aston Villa	42	18	14	10	51	47	50
Middlesbrough	42	17	13	12	46	43	47
Bristol City	42	17	12	13	63	51	46
Sunderland	42	17	12	13	59	49	46
Blackpool	42	18	10	14	56	51	46
Oxford United	42	19	7	16	52	43	45
Fulham	42	16	12	14	58	49	44
Sheffield Wednesday	42	17	10	15	59	55	44
Millwall	42	16	10	16	55	47	42
Luton Town	42	15	11	16	44	53	41
Hull City	42	14	12	16	64	59	40
Nottingham Forest	42	14	12	16	47	52	40
Orient	42	12	12	18	49	53	36
Swindon Town	42	10	16	16	46	60	36
Portsmouth	42	12	11	19	42	59	35
Carlisle United	42	11	12	19	50	52	34
Preston North End	42	11	12	19	37	64	34
Cardiff City	42	11	11	20	43	58	33
Huddersfield Town	*42*	*8*	*17*	*17*	*36*	*56*	*33*
Brighton & Hove Albion	*42*	*8*	*13*	*21*	*46*	*83*	*29*

DIVISION FOUR 1972-73

Southport	46	26	10	10	71	48	62
Hereford United	46	23	12	11	56	38	58
Cambridge United	46	20	17	9	67	57	57
Aldershot	46	22	12	12	60	38	56
Newport County	46	22	12	12	64	44	56
Mansfield Town	46	20	14	12	78	51	54
Reading	46	17	18	11	51	38	52
Exeter City	46	18	14	14	57	51	50
Gillingham	46	19	11	16	63	58	49
Lincoln City	46	16	16	14	64	57	48
Stockport County	46	18	12	16	53	53	48
Bury	46	14	18	14	58	51	46
Workington	46	17	12	17	59	61	46
Barnsley	46	14	16	16	58	60	44
Chester	46	14	15	17	61	52	43
Bradford City	46	16	11	19	61	65	43
Doncaster Rovers	46	15	12	19	49	58	42
Torquay United	46	12	17	17	44	47	41
Peterborough United	46	14	13	19	71	76	41
Hartlepool	46	12	17	17	34	49	41
Crewe Alexandra	46	9	18	19	38	61	36
Colchester United	46	10	11	25	48	76	31
Northampton Town	46	10	11	25	40	73	31
Darlington	46	7	15	24	42	85	29

1973 F.A. Cup

Semi-finals

Arsenal vs Sunderland	1-2
Leeds United vs Wolverhampton Wanderers	1-0

Final

Wembley, 5th May 1973

Sunderland 1 (Porterfield)

Leeds United 0

Attendance 100,000

1973 Football League Cup

Semi-finals

Wolverhampton Wands. vs Tottenham H. (1-2, 2-2)	3-4
Chelsea vs Norwich City (0-2, 0-1)	0-3

Final

Wembley, 3rd March 1973

Tottenham Hotspur 1 (Coates)

Norwich City 0

Attendance 100,000

DIVISION ONE 1973-74

LEEDS UNITED	42	24	14	4	66	31	62
Liverpool	42	22	13	7	52	31	57
Derby County	42	17	14	11	52	42	48
Ipswich Town	42	18	11	13	67	58	47
Stoke City	42	15	16	11	54	42	46
Burnley	42	16	14	12	56	53	46
Everton	42	16	12	14	50	48	44
Queen's Park Rangers	42	13	17	12	56	52	43
Leicester City	42	13	16	13	51	41	42
Arsenal	42	14	14	14	49	51	42
Tottenham Hotspur	42	14	14	14	45	50	42
Wolverhampton Wanderers	42	13	15	14	49	49	41
Sheffield United	42	14	12	16	44	49	40
Manchester City	42	14	12	16	39	46	40
Newcastle United	42	13	12	17	49	48	38
Coventry City	42	14	10	18	43	54	38
Chelsea	42	12	13	17	56	60	37
West Ham United	42	11	15	16	55	60	37
Birmingham City	42	12	13	17	52	64	37
Southampton	*42*	*11*	*14*	*17*	*47*	*68*	*36*
Manchester United	*42*	*10*	*12*	*20*	*38*	*48*	*32*
Norwich City	*42*	*7*	*15*	*20*	*37*	*62*	*29*

DIVISION THREE 1973-74

Oldham Athletic	46	25	12	9	83	47	62
Bristol Rovers	46	22	17	7	65	33	61
York City	46	21	19	6	67	38	61
Wrexham	46	22	12	12	63	43	56
Chesterfield	46	21	14	11	55	42	56
Grimsby Town	46	18	15	13	67	50	51
Watford	46	19	12	15	64	56	50
Aldershot	46	19	11	16	65	52	49
Halifax Town	46	14	21	11	48	51	49
Huddersfield Town	46	17	13	16	56	55	47
Bournemouth	46	16	15	15	54	58	47
Southend United	46	16	14	16	62	62	46
Blackburn Rovers	46	18	10	18	62	64	46
Charlton Athletic	46	19	8	19	66	73	46
Walsall	46	16	13	17	57	48	45
Tranmere Rovers	46	15	15	16	50	44	45
Plymouth Argyle	46	17	10	19	59	54	44
Hereford United	46	14	15	17	53	57	43
Brighton & Hove Albion	46	16	11	19	52	58	43
Port Vale	46	14	14	18	52	58	42
Cambridge United	*46*	*13*	*9*	*24*	*48*	*81*	*35*
Shrewsbury Town	*46*	*10*	*11*	*25*	*41*	*62*	*31*
Southport	*46*	*6*	*16*	*24*	*35*	*82*	*28*
Rochdale	*46*	*2*	*17*	*27*	*38*	*94*	*21*

DIVISION TWO 1973-74

Middlesbrough	42	27	11	4	77	30	65
Luton Town	42	19	12	11	64	51	50
Carlisle United	42	20	9	13	61	48	49
Orient	42	15	18	9	55	42	48
Blackpool	42	17	13	12	57	40	47
Sunderland	42	19	9	14	58	44	47
Nottingham Forest	42	15	15	12	57	43	45
West Bromwich Albion	42	14	16	12	48	45	44
Hull City	42	13	17	12	46	47	43
Notts County	42	15	13	14	55	60	43
Bolton Wanderers	42	15	12	15	44	40	42
Millwall	42	14	14	14	51	51	42
Fulham	42	16	10	16	39	43	42
Aston Villa	42	13	15	14	48	45	41
Portsmouth	42	14	12	16	45	62	40
Bristol City	42	14	10	18	47	54	38
Cardiff City	42	10	16	16	49	62	36
Oxford United	42	10	16	16	35	46	36
Sheffield Wednesday	42	12	11	19	51	63	35
Crystal Palace	*42*	*11*	*12*	*19*	*43*	*56*	*34*
Preston North End	*42*	*9*	*14*	*19*	*40*	*62*	*31*
Swindon Town	*42*	*7*	*11*	*24*	*36*	*72*	*25*

Preston North End had one point deducted

DIVISION FOUR 1973-74

Peterborough United	46	27	11	8	75	38	65
Gillingham	46	25	12	9	90	49	62
Colchester United	46	24	12	10	73	36	60
Bury	46	24	11	11	81	49	59
Northampton Town	46	20	13	13	63	48	53
Reading	46	16	19	11	58	37	51
Chester	46	17	15	14	54	55	49
Bradford City	46	17	14	15	58	52	48
Newport County	46	16	14	16	56	65	45
Exeter City	45	18	8	19	58	55	44
Hartlepool	46	16	12	18	48	47	44
Lincoln City	46	16	12	18	63	67	44
Barnsley	46	17	10	19	58	64	44
Swansea City	46	16	11	19	45	46	43
Rotherham United	46	15	13	18	56	58	43
Torquay United	46	13	17	16	52	57	43
Mansfield Town	46	13	17	16	62	69	43
Scunthorpe United	45	14	12	19	47	64	42
Brentford	46	12	16	18	48	50	40
Darlington	46	13	13	20	40	62	39
Crewe Alexandra	46	14	10	22	43	71	38
Doncaster Rovers	46	12	11	23	47	80	35
Workington	46	11	13	22	43	74	35
Stockport County	46	7	20	19	44	69	34

Newport County had one point deducted
Scunthorpe United vs Exeter City match not played
Scunthorpe United were awarded two points

1974 F.A. Cup

Semi-finals

Burnley vs Newcastle United	0-2
Leicester City vs Liverpool	0-0, 1-3

Final

Wembley, 4th May 1974

Liverpool 3   (Keegan 2, Heighway)
Newcastle United 0

Attendance 100,000

1974 Football League Cup

Semi-finals

Norwich City vs Wolverhampton Wanderers (1-1, 0-1)	1-2
Plymouth Argyle vs Manchester City (1-1, 0-2)	1-3

Final

Wembley, 2nd March 1974

Wolverhampton Wanderers 2   (Hibbitt, Richards)
Manchester City 1   (Bell)

Attendance 100,000

DIVISION ONE 1974-75

DERBY COUNTY	42	21	11	10	67	49	53
Liverpool	42	20	11	11	60	39	51
Ipswich Town	42	23	5	14	66	44	51
Everton	42	16	18	8	56	42	50
Stoke City	42	17	15	10	64	48	49
Sheffield United	42	18	13	11	58	51	49
Middlesbrough	42	18	12	12	54	40	48
Manchester City	42	18	10	14	54	54	46
Leeds United	42	16	13	13	57	49	45
Burnley	42	17	11	14	68	67	45
Queen's Park Rangers	42	16	10	16	54	54	42
Wolverhampton Wanderers	42	14	11	17	57	54	39
West Ham United	42	13	13	16	58	59	39
Coventry City	42	12	15	15	51	62	39
Newcastle United	42	15	9	18	59	72	39
Arsenal	42	13	11	18	47	49	37
Birmingham City	42	14	9	19	53	61	37
Leicester City	42	12	12	18	46	60	36
Tottenham Hotspur	42	13	8	21	52	63	34
Luton Town	*42*	*11*	*11*	*20*	*47*	*65*	*33*
Chelsea	*42*	*9*	*15*	*18*	*42*	*72*	*33*
Carlisle United	*42*	*12*	*5*	*25*	*43*	*59*	*29*

DIVISION THREE 1974-75

Blackburn Rovers	46	22	16	8	68	45	60
Plymouth Argyle	46	24	11	11	79	58	59
Charlton Athletic	46	22	11	13	76	61	55
Swindon Town	46	21	11	14	64	58	53
Crystal Palace	46	18	15	13	66	57	51
Port Vale	46	18	15	13	61	54	51
Peterborough United	46	19	12	15	47	53	50
Walsall	46	18	13	15	67	52	49
Preston North End	46	19	11	16	63	56	49
Gillingham	46	17	14	15	65	60	48
Colchester United	46	17	13	16	70	63	47
Hereford United	46	16	14	16	64	66	46
Wrexham	46	15	15	16	65	55	45
Bury	46	16	12	18	53	50	44
Chesterfield	46	16	12	18	62	66	44
Grimsby Town	46	15	13	18	55	64	43
Halifax Town	46	13	17	16	49	65	43
Southend United	46	13	16	17	46	51	42
Brighton & Hove Albion	46	16	10	20	56	64	42
Aldershot	46	14	11	21	53	63	38
Bournemouth	*46*	*13*	*12*	*21*	*44*	*58*	*38*
Tranmere Rovers	*46*	*14*	*9*	*23*	*55*	*57*	*37*
Watford	*46*	*10*	*17*	*19*	*52*	*75*	*37*
Huddersfield Town	*46*	*11*	*10*	*25*	*47*	*76*	*32*

Aldershot had one point deducted

DIVISION TWO 1974-75

Manchester United	42	26	9	7	66	30	61
Aston Villa	42	25	8	9	79	32	58
Norwich City	42	20	13	9	58	37	53
Sunderland	42	19	13	10	65	35	51
Bristol City	42	21	8	13	47	33	50
West Bromwich Albion	42	18	9	15	54	42	45
Blackpool	42	14	17	11	38	33	45
Hull City	42	15	14	13	40	53	44
Fulham	42	13	16	13	44	39	42
Bolton Wanderers	42	15	12	15	45	41	42
Oxford United	42	15	12	15	41	51	42
Orient	42	11	20	11	28	39	42
Southampton	42	15	11	16	53	54	41
Notts County	42	12	16	14	49	59	40
York City	42	14	10	18	51	55	38
Nottingham Forest	42	12	14	16	43	55	38
Portsmouth	42	12	13	17	44	54	37
Oldham Athletic	42	10	15	17	40	48	35
Bristol Rovers	42	12	11	19	42	64	35
Millwall	*42*	*10*	*12*	*20*	*44*	*56*	*32*
Cardiff City	*42*	*9*	*14*	*19*	*36*	*62*	*32*
Sheffield Wednesday	*42*	*5*	*11*	*26*	*29*	*64*	*21*

DIVISION FOUR 1974-75

Mansfield Town	46	28	12	6	90	40	68
Shrewsbury Town	46	26	10	10	80	43	62
Rotherham United	46	22	15	9	71	41	59
Chester	46	23	11	12	64	38	57
Lincoln City	46	21	15	10	79	48	57
Cambridge United	46	20	14	12	62	44	54
Reading	46	21	10	15	63	47	52
Brentford	46	18	13	15	53	45	49
Exeter City	46	19	11	16	60	63	49
Bradford City	46	17	13	16	56	51	47
Southport	46	15	17	14	56	56	47
Newport County	46	19	9	18	68	75	47
Hartlepool	46	16	11	19	52	62	43
Torquay United	46	14	14	18	46	61	42
Barnsley	46	15	11	20	62	65	41
Northampton Town	46	15	11	20	67	73	41
Doncaster Rovers	46	14	12	20	65	79	40
Crewe Alexandra	46	11	18	17	34	47	40
Rochdale	46	13	13	20	59	75	39
Stockport County	46	12	14	20	43	70	38
Darlington	46	13	10	23	54	67	36
Swansea City	46	15	6	25	46	73	36
Workington	46	10	11	25	36	66	31
Scunthorpe United	46	7	15	24	41	78	29

1975 F.A. Cup

Semi-finals

West Ham United vs Ipswich Town	0-0, 2-1
Fulham vs Birmingham City	1-1, 1-0

Final

Wembley, 2nd May 1975

West Ham United 2 (A. Taylor 2)

Fulham 0

Attendance 100,000

1975 Football League Cup

Semi-finals

Chester vs Aston Villa (2-2, 2-3)	4-5
Manchester United vs Norwich City (2-2, 0-1)	2-3

Final

Wembley, 1st March 1975

Aston Villa 1 (Graydon)

Norwich City 0

Attendance 100,000

DIVISION ONE 1975-76

LIVERPOOL	42	23	14	5	66	31	60
Queen's Park Rangers	42	24	11	7	67	33	59
Manchester United	42	23	10	9	68	42	56
Derby County	42	21	11	10	75	58	53
Leeds United	42	21	9	12	65	46	51
Ipswich Town	42	16	14	12	54	48	46
Leicester City	42	13	19	10	48	51	45
Manchester City	42	16	11	15	64	46	43
Tottenham Hotspur	42	14	15	13	63	63	43
Norwich City	42	16	10	16	58	58	42
Everton	42	15	12	15	60	66	42
Stoke City	42	15	11	16	48	50	41
Middlesbrough	42	15	10	17	46	45	40
Coventry City	42	13	14	15	47	57	40
Newcastle United	42	15	9	18	71	62	39
Aston Villa	42	11	17	14	51	59	39
Arsenal	42	13	10	19	47	53	36
West Ham United	42	13	10	19	48	71	36
Birmingham City	42	13	7	22	57	75	33
Wolverhampton Wanderers	*42*	*10*	*10*	*22*	*51*	*68*	*30*
Burnley	*42*	*9*	*10*	*23*	*43*	*66*	*28*
Sheffield United	*42*	*6*	*10*	*26*	*33*	*82*	*22*

DIVISION THREE 1975-76

Hereford United	46	26	11	9	86	55	63
Cardiff City	46	22	13	11	69	48	57
Millwall	46	20	16	10	54	43	56
Brighton & Hove Albion	46	22	9	15	78	53	53
Crystal Palace	46	18	17	11	61	46	53
Wrexham	46	20	12	14	66	55	52
Walsall	46	18	14	14	74	61	50
Preston North End	46	19	10	17	62	57	48
Shrewsbury Town	46	19	10	17	61	59	48
Peterborough United	46	15	18	13	63	63	48
Mansfield Town	46	16	15	15	58	52	47
Port Vale	46	15	16	15	55	54	46
Bury	46	14	16	16	51	46	44
Chesterfield	46	17	9	20	69	69	43
Gillingham	46	12	19	15	58	68	43
Rotherham United	46	15	12	19	54	65	42
Chester	46	15	12	19	43	62	42
Grimsby Town	46	15	10	21	62	74	40
Swindon Town	46	16	8	22	62	75	40
Sheffield Wednesday	46	12	16	18	48	59	40
Aldershot	*46*	*13*	*13*	*20*	*59*	*75*	*39*
Colchester United	*46*	*12*	*14*	*20*	*41*	*65*	*38*
Southend United	*46*	*12*	*13*	*21*	*65*	*75*	*37*
Halifax Town	*46*	*11*	*13*	*22*	*41*	*61*	*35*

DIVISION TWO 1975-76

Sunderland	42	24	8	10	67	36	56
Bristol City	42	19	15	8	59	35	53
West Bromwich Albion	42	20	13	9	50	33	53
Bolton Wanderers	42	20	12	10	64	38	52
Notts County	42	19	11	12	60	41	49
Southampton	42	21	7	14	66	50	49
Luton Town	42	19	10	13	61	51	48
Nottingham Forest	42	17	12	13	55	40	46
Charlton Athletic	42	15	12	15	61	72	42
Blackpool	42	14	14	14	40	49	42
Chelsea	42	12	16	14	53	54	40
Fulham	42	13	14	15	45	47	40
Orient	42	13	14	15	37	39	40
Hull City	42	14	11	17	45	49	39
Blackburn Rovers	42	12	14	16	45	50	38
Plymouth Argyle	42	13	12	17	48	54	38
Oldham Athletic	42	13	12	17	57	68	38
Bristol Rovers	42	11	16	15	38	50	38
Carlisle United	42	12	13	17	45	59	37
Oxford United	*42*	*11*	*11*	*20*	*39*	*59*	*33*
York City	*42*	*10*	*8*	*24*	*39*	*71*	*28*
Portsmouth	*42*	*9*	*7*	*26*	*32*	*61*	*25*

DIVISION FOUR 1975-76

Lincoln City	46	32	10	4	111	39	74
Northampton Town	46	29	10	7	87	40	68
Reading	46	24	12	10	70	51	60
Tranmere Rovers	46	24	10	12	89	55	58
Huddersfield Town	46	21	14	11	56	41	56
Bournemouth	46	20	12	14	57	48	52
Exeter City	46	18	14	14	56	47	50
Watford	46	22	6	18	62	62	50
Torquay United	46	18	14	14	55	63	50
Doncaster Rovers	46	19	11	16	75	69	49
Swansea City	46	16	15	15	66	57	47
Barnsley	46	14	16	16	52	48	44
Cambridge United	46	14	15	17	58	62	43
Hartlepool	46	16	10	20	62	78	42
Rochdale	46	12	18	16	40	54	42
Crewe Alexandra	46	13	15	18	58	57	41
Bradford City	46	12	17	17	63	65	41
Brentford	46	14	13	19	56	60	41
Scunthorpe United	46	14	10	22	50	59	38
Darlington	46	14	10	22	48	57	38
Stockport County	46	13	12	21	43	76	38
Newport County	46	13	9	24	57	90	35
Southport	46	8	10	28	41	77	26
Workington	46	7	7	32	30	87	21

1976 F.A. Cup

Semi-finals

Southampton vs Crystal Palace	2-0
Manchester United vs Derby County	2-0

Final

Wembley, 1st May 1976

Southampton 1 (Stokes)

Manchester United 0

Attendance 100,000

1976 Football League Cup

Semi-finals

Middlesbrough vs Manchester City (1-0, 0-4)		1-4
Tottenham Hotspur vs Newcastle United (1-0, 1-3)		2-3

Final

Wembley, 28th February 1976

Manchester City 2 (Barnes, Tueart)

Newcastle United 1 (Gowling)

Attendance 100,000

DIVISION ONE 1976-77

LIVERPOOL	42	23	11	8	62	33	57
Manchester City	42	21	14	7	60	34	56
Ipswich Town	42	22	8	12	66	39	52
Aston Villa	42	22	7	13	76	50	51
Newcastle United	42	18	13	11	64	49	49
Manchester United	42	18	11	13	71	62	47
West Bromwich Albion	42	16	13	13	62	56	45
Arsenal	42	16	11	15	64	59	43
Everton	42	14	14	14	62	64	42
Leeds United	42	15	12	15	48	51	42
Leicester City	42	12	18	12	47	60	42
Middlesbrough	42	14	13	15	40	45	41
Birmingham City	42	13	12	17	63	61	38
Queen's Park Rangers	42	13	12	17	47	52	38
Derby County	42	9	19	14	50	55	37
Norwich City	42	14	9	19	47	64	37
West Ham United	42	11	14	17	46	65	36
Bristol City	42	11	13	18	38	48	35
Coventry City	42	10	15	17	48	59	35
Sunderland	*42*	*11*	*12*	*19*	*46*	*54*	*34*
Stoke City	*42*	*10*	*14*	*18*	*28*	*51*	*34*
Tottenham Hotspur	*42*	*12*	*9*	*21*	*48*	*72*	*33*

DIVISION TWO 1976-77

Wolverhampton Wanderers	42	22	13	7	84	45	57
Chelsea	42	21	13	8	73	53	55
Nottingham Forest	42	21	10	11	77	43	52
Bolton Wanderers	42	20	11	11	75	54	51
Blackpool	42	17	17	8	58	42	51
Luton Town	42	21	6	15	67	48	48
Charlton Athletic	42	16	16	10	71	58	48
Notts County	42	19	10	13	65	60	48
Southampton	42	17	10	15	72	67	44
Millwall	42	15	13	14	57	53	43
Sheffield United	42	14	12	16	54	63	40
Blackburn Rovers	42	15	9	18	42	54	39
Oldham Athletic	42	14	10	18	52	64	38
Hull City	42	10	17	15	45	53	37
Bristol Rovers	42	12	13	17	53	68	37
Burnley	42	11	14	17	46	64	36
Fulham	42	11	13	18	54	61	35
Cardiff City	42	12	10	20	56	67	34
Orient	42	9	16	17	37	55	34
Carlisle United	*42*	*11*	*12*	*19*	*49*	*75*	*34*
Plymouth Argyle	*42*	*8*	*16*	*18*	*46*	*65*	*32*
Hereford United	*42*	*8*	*15*	*19*	*57*	*78*	*31*

DIVISION THREE 1976-77

Mansfield Town	46	28	8	10	78	33	64
Brighton & Hove Albion	46	25	11	10	83	39	61
Crystal Palace	46	23	13	10	68	40	59
Rotherham United	46	22	15	9	69	44	59
Wrexham	46	24	10	12	80	54	58
Preston North End	46	21	12	13	64	43	54
Bury	46	23	8	15	64	59	54
Sheffield Wednesday	46	22	9	15	65	55	53
Lincoln City	46	19	14	13	77	70	52
Shrewsbury Town	46	18	11	17	65	59	47
Swindon Town	46	15	15	16	68	75	45
Gillingham	46	16	12	18	55	64	44
Chester	46	18	8	20	48	58	44
Tranmere Rovers	46	13	17	16	51	53	43
Walsall	46	13	15	18	57	65	41
Peterborough United	46	13	15	18	55	65	41
Oxford United	46	12	15	19	55	65	39
Chesterfield	46	14	10	22	56	64	38
Port Vale	46	11	16	19	47	71	38
Portsmouth	46	11	14	21	43	70	36
Reading	*46*	*13*	*9*	*24*	*49*	*73*	*35*
Northampton Town	*46*	*13*	*8*	*25*	*60*	*75*	*34*
Grimsby Town	*46*	*12*	*9*	*25*	*45*	*69*	*33*
York City	*46*	*10*	*12*	*24*	*50*	*89*	*32*

DIVISION FOUR 1976-77

Cambridge United	46	26	13	7	87	40	65
Exeter City	46	25	12	9	70	46	62
Colchester United	46	25	9	12	77	43	59
Bradford City	46	23	13	10	78	51	59
Swansea City	46	25	8	13	92	68	58
Barnsley	46	23	9	14	62	39	55
Watford	46	18	15	13	67	50	51
Doncaster Rovers	46	21	9	16	71	65	51
Huddersfield Town	46	19	12	15	60	49	50
Southend United	46	15	19	12	52	45	49
Darlington	46	18	13	15	59	64	49
Crewe Alexandra	46	19	11	16	47	60	49
Bournemouth	46	15	18	13	54	44	48
Stockport County	46	13	19	14	53	57	45
Brentford	46	18	7	21	77	76	43
Torquay United	46	17	9	20	59	67	43
Aldershot	46	16	11	19	49	59	43
Rochdale	46	13	12	21	50	59	38
Newport County	46	14	10	22	42	58	38
Scunthorpe United	46	13	11	22	49	73	37
Halifax Town	46	11	14	21	47	58	36
Hartlepool	46	10	12	24	47	73	32
Southport	46	3	19	24	33	77	25
Workington	*46*	*4*	*11*	*31*	*41*	*102*	*19*

1977 Football League Cup

Semi-finals

Queen's Park Rangers vs Aston Villa (0-0, 2-2, 0-3*)	2-5
Everton vs Bolton Wanderers (1-1, 1-0)	2-1

* Play-off at Highbury

Final

Wembley, 12th March 1977

Aston Villa 0
Everton 0

Attendance 100,000

Replay

Hillsborough, 16th March 1977

Aston Villa 1 (Kenyon (og))
Everton 1 (aet.) (Latchford)

Attendance 55,000

2nd Replay

* Old Trafford, 13th April 1977

Aston Villa 3 (Little 2, Nicholl)
Everton 2 (aet.) (Latchford, Lyons)

Attendance 54,749

1977 F.A. Cup

Semi-finals

Leeds United vs Manchester United	1-2
Everton vs Liverpool	2-2, 0-3

Final

Wembley, 21st May 1977

Manchester United 2 (Pearson, J. Greenhoff)
Liverpool 1 (Case)

Attendance 100,000

DIVISION ONE 1977-78

NOTTINGHAM FOREST	42	25	14	3	69	24	64
Liverpool	42	24	9	9	65	34	57
Everton	42	22	11	9	76	45	55
Manchester City	42	20	12	10	74	51	52
Arsenal	42	21	10	11	60	37	52
West Bromwich Albion	42	18	14	10	62	53	50
Coventry City	42	18	12	12	75	62	48
Aston Villa	42	18	10	14	57	42	46
Leeds United	42	18	10	14	63	53	46
Manchester United	42	16	10	16	67	63	42
Birmingham City	42	16	9	17	55	60	41
Derby County	42	14	13	15	54	59	41
Norwich City	42	11	18	13	52	66	40
Middlesbrough	42	12	15	15	42	54	39
Wolverhampton Wanderers	42	12	12	18	51	64	36
Chelsea	42	11	14	17	46	69	36
Bristol City	42	11	13	18	49	53	35
Ipswich Town	42	11	13	18	47	61	35
Queen's Park Rangers	42	9	15	18	47	64	33
West Ham United	*42*	*12*	*8*	*22*	*52*	*69*	*32*
Newcastle United	*42*	*6*	*10*	*26*	*42*	*78*	*22*
Leicester City	*42*	*5*	*12*	*25*	*26*	*70*	*22*

DIVISION THREE 1977-78

Wrexham	46	23	15	8	78	45	61
Cambridge United	46	23	12	11	72	51	58
Preston North End	46	20	16	10	63	38	56
Peterborough United	46	20	16	10	47	33	56
Chester	46	16	22	8	59	56	54
Walsall	46	18	17	11	61	50	53
Gillingham	46	15	20	11	67	60	50
Colchester United	46	15	18	13	55	44	48
Chesterfield	46	17	14	15	58	49	48
Swindon Town	46	16	16	14	67	60	48
Shrewsbury Town	46	16	16	15	63	57	47
Tranmere Rovers	46	16	15	15	57	52	47
Carlisle United	46	14	19	13	59	59	47
Sheffield Wednesday	46	15	15	16	50	52	46
Bury	46	13	19	14	62	56	45
Lincoln City	46	15	15	16	53	61	45
Exeter City	46	15	14	17	49	59	44
Oxford United	46	13	14	19	64	67	40
Plymouth Argyle	46	11	17	18	61	68	39
Rotherham United	46	13	13	20	51	68	39
Port Vale	*46*	*8*	*20*	*18*	*46*	*67*	*36*
Bradford City	*46*	*12*	*10*	*24*	*56*	*86*	*34*
Hereford United	*46*	*9*	*14*	*23*	*34*	*60*	*32*
Portsmouth	*46*	*7*	*17*	*22*	*41*	*75*	*31*

DIVISION TWO 1977-78

Bolton Wanderers	42	24	10	8	63	33	58
Southampton	42	22	13	7	70	39	57
Tottenham Hotspur	42	20	16	6	83	49	56
Brighton & Hove Albion	42	22	12	8	63	38	56
Blackburn Rovers	42	16	13	13	56	60	45
Sunderland	42	14	16	12	67	59	44
Stoke City	42	16	10	16	53	49	42
Oldham Athletic	42	13	16	13	54	58	42
Crystal Palace	42	13	15	14	50	47	41
Fulham	42	14	13	15	49	49	41
Burnley	42	15	10	17	56	64	40
Sheffield United	42	16	8	18	62	73	40
Luton Town	42	14	10	18	54	52	38
Orient	42	10	18	14	43	49	38
Notts County	42	11	16	15	54	62	38
Millwall	42	12	14	16	49	57	38
Charlton Athletic	42	13	12	17	55	68	38
Bristol Rovers	42	13	12	17	61	77	38
Cardiff City	42	13	12	17	51	71	38
Blackpool	*42*	*12*	*13*	*17*	*59*	*60*	*37*
Mansfield Town	*42*	*10*	*11*	*21*	*49*	*69*	*31*
Hull City	*42*	*8*	*12*	*22*	*34*	*52*	*28*

DIVISION FOUR 1977-78

Watford	46	30	11	5	85	38	71
Southend United	46	25	10	11	66	39	60
Swansea City	46	23	10	13	87	47	56
Brentford	46	21	14	11	86	54	56
Aldershot	46	19	16	11	67	47	54
Grimsby Town	46	21	11	14	57	51	53
Barnsley	46	18	14	14	61	49	50
Reading	46	18	14	14	55	52	50
Torquay United	46	16	15	15	57	56	47
Northampton Town	46	17	13	16	63	68	47
Huddersfield Town	46	15	15	16	63	55	45
Doncaster Rovers	46	14	17	15	52	65	45
Wimbledon	46	14	16	16	66	67	44
Scunthorpe United	46	14	16	16	50	55	44
Crewe Alexandra	46	15	14	17	50	69	44
Newport County	46	16	11	19	65	73	43
Bournemouth	46	14	15	17	41	51	43
Stockport County	46	16	10	20	56	56	42
Darlington	46	14	13	19	52	59	41
Halifax Town	46	10	21	15	52	62	41
Hartlepool United	46	15	7	24	51	84	37
York City	46	12	12	22	50	69	36
Southport	*46*	*6*	*19*	*21*	*52*	*76*	*31*
Rochdale	46	8	8	30	43	85	24

1978 F.A. Cup

Semi-finals

Ipswich Town vs West Bromwich Albion	3-1
Arsenal vs Orient	3-0

Final

Wembley, 6th May 1978

Ipswich Town 1   (Osborne)

Arsenal 0

Attendance 100,000

1978 Football League Cup

Semi-finals

Leeds United vs Nottingham Forest (1-3, 2-4)	3-7
Liverpool vs Arsenal (2-1, 0-0)	2-1

Final

Wembley, 18th March 1978

Nottingham Forest 0

Liverpool 0 (aet.)

Attendance 100,000

Replay

Old Trafford, 22nd March 1978

Nottingham Forest 1   (Robertson (penalty))

Liverpool 0

Attendance 54,375

DIVISION ONE 1978-79

LIVERPOOL	42	30	8	4	85	16	68
Nottingham Forest	42	21	18	3	61	26	60
West Bromwich Albion	42	24	11	7	72	35	59
Everton	42	17	17	8	52	40	51
Leeds United	42	18	14	10	70	52	50
Ipswich Town	42	20	9	13	63	49	49
Arsenal	42	17	14	11	61	48	48
Aston Villa	42	15	16	11	59	49	46
Manchester United	42	15	15	12	60	63	45
Coventry City	42	14	16	12	58	68	44
Tottenham Hotspur	42	13	15	14	48	61	41
Middlesbrough	42	15	10	17	57	50	40
Bristol City	42	15	10	17	47	51	40
Southampton	42	12	16	14	47	53	40
Manchester City	42	13	13	16	58	56	39
Norwich City	42	7	23	12	51	57	37
Bolton Wanderers	42	12	11	19	54	75	35
Wolverhampton Wanderers	42	13	8	21	44	68	34
Derby County	42	10	11	21	44	71	31
Queen's Park Rangers	*42*	*6*	*13*	*23*	*45*	*73*	*25*
Birmingham City	*42*	*6*	*10*	*26*	*37*	*64*	*22*
Chelsea	*42*	*5*	*10*	*27*	*44*	*92*	*20*

DIVISION THREE 1978-79

Shrewsbury Town	46	21	19	6	61	41	61
Watford	46	24	12	10	83	52	60
Swansea City	46	24	12	10	83	61	60
Gillingham	46	21	17	8	65	42	59
Swindon Town	46	25	7	14	74	52	57
Carlisle United	46	15	22	9	53	42	52
Colchester United	46	17	17	12	60	55	51
Hull City	46	19	11	16	66	61	49
Exeter City	46	17	15	14	61	56	49
Brentford	46	19	9	18	53	49	47
Oxford United	46	14	18	14	44	50	46
Blackpool	46	18	9	19	61	59	45
Southend United	46	15	15	16	51	49	45
Sheffield Wednesday	46	13	19	14	53	53	45
Plymouth Argyle	46	15	14	17	67	68	44
Chester	46	14	16	16	57	61	44
Rotherham United	46	17	10	19	49	55	44
Mansfield Town	46	12	19	15	51	52	43
Bury	46	11	20	15	59	65	42
Chesterfield	46	13	14	19	51	65	40
Peterborough United	*46*	*11*	*14*	*21*	*44*	*63*	*36*
Walsall	*46*	*10*	*12*	*24*	*56*	*71*	*32*
Tranmere Rovers	*46*	*6*	*16*	*24*	*45*	*78*	*28*
Lincoln City	*46*	*7*	*11*	*28*	*41*	*88*	*25*

DIVISION TWO 1978-79

Crystal Palace	42	19	19	4	51	24	57
Brighton & Hove Albion	42	23	10	9	72	39	56
Stoke City	42	20	16	6	58	31	56
Sunderland	42	22	11	9	70	44	55
West Ham United	42	18	14	10	70	39	50
Notts County	42	14	16	12	48	60	44
Preston North End	42	12	18	12	59	57	42
Newcastle United	42	17	8	17	51	55	42
Cardiff City	42	16	10	16	56	70	42
Fulham	42	13	15	14	50	47	41
Orient	42	15	10	17	51	51	40
Cambridge United	42	12	16	14	44	52	40
Burnley	42	14	12	16	51	62	40
Oldham Athletic	42	13	13	16	52	61	39
Wrexham	42	12	14	16	45	42	38
Bristol Rovers	42	14	10	18	48	60	38
Leicester City	42	10	17	15	43	52	37
Luton Town	42	13	10	19	60	57	36
Charlton Athletic	42	11	13	18	60	69	35
Sheffield United	*42*	*11*	*12*	*19*	*52*	*69*	*34*
Millwall	*42*	*11*	*10*	*21*	*42*	*61*	*32*
Blackburn Rovers	*42*	*10*	*10*	*22*	*41*	*72*	*30*

DIVISION FOUR 1978-79

Reading	46	26	13	7	76	35	65
Grimsby Town	46	26	9	11	82	49	61
Wimbledon	46	25	11	10	78	46	61
Barnsley	46	24	13	9	73	42	61
Aldershot	46	20	17	9	63	47	57
Wigan Athletic	46	21	13	12	63	48	55
Portsmouth	46	20	12	14	62	48	52
Newport County	46	21	10	15	66	55	52
Huddersfield Town	46	18	11	17	57	53	47
York City	46	18	11	17	51	55	47
Torquay United	46	19	8	19	58	65	46
Scunthorpe United	46	17	11	18	54	60	45
Hartlepool United	46	13	18	15	57	66	44
Hereford United	46	15	13	18	53	53	43
Bradford City	46	17	9	20	62	68	43
Port Vale	46	14	14	18	57	70	42
Stockport County	46	14	12	20	58	60	40
Bournemouth	46	14	11	21	47	48	39
Northampton Town	46	15	9	22	64	76	39
Rochdale	46	15	9	22	47	64	39
Darlington	46	11	15	20	49	66	37
Doncaster Rovers	46	13	11	22	50	73	37
Halifax Town	46	9	8	29	39	72	26
Crewe Alexandra	46	6	14	26	43	90	26

1979 F.A. Cup

Semi-finals

Arsenal vs Wolverhampton Wanderers	2-0
Manchester United vs Liverpool	2-2, 1-0

Final

Wembley, 12th May 1979

Arsenal 3 (Talbot, Stapleton, Sunderland)
Manchester United 2 (McQueen, McIlroy)

Attendance 100,000

1979 Football League Cup

Semi-finals

Nottingham Forest vs Watford (3-1, 0-0)	3-1
Leeds United vs Southampton (2-2, 0-1)	2-3

Final

Wembley, 17th March 1979

Nottingham Forest 3 (Birtles 2, Woodcock)
Southampton 2 (Peach, Holmes)

Attendance 100,000

DIVISION ONE 1979-80

Team	P	W	D	L	F	A	Pts
LIVERPOOL	42	25	10	7	81	30	60
Manchester United	42	24	10	8	65	35	58
Ipswich Town	42	22	9	11	68	39	53
Arsenal	42	18	16	8	52	36	52
Nottingham Forest	42	20	8	14	63	43	48
Wolverhampton Wanderers	42	19	9	14	58	47	47
Aston Villa	42	16	14	12	51	50	46
Southampton	42	18	9	15	65	53	45
Middlesbrough	42	16	12	14	50	44	44
West Bromwich Albion	42	11	19	12	54	50	41
Leeds United	42	13	14	15	46	50	40
Norwich City	42	13	14	15	58	66	40
Crystal Palace	42	12	16	14	41	50	40
Tottenham Hotspur	42	15	10	17	52	62	40
Coventry City	42	16	7	19	56	66	39
Brighton & Hove Albion	42	11	15	16	47	57	37
Manchester City	42	12	13	17	43	66	37
Stoke City	42	13	10	19	44	58	36
Everton	42	9	17	16	43	51	35
Bristol City	*42*	*9*	*13*	*20*	*37*	*66*	*31*
Derby County	*42*	*11*	*8*	*23*	*47*	*67*	*30*
Bolton Wanderers	*42*	*5*	*15*	*22*	*38*	*73*	*25*

DIVISION TWO 1979-80

Team	P	W	D	L	F	A	Pts
Leicester City	42	21	13	8	58	38	55
Sunderland	42	21	12	9	69	42	54
Birmingham City	42	21	11	10	58	38	53
Chelsea	42	23	7	12	66	52	53
Queen's Park Rangers	42	18	13	11	75	53	49
Luton Town	42	16	17	9	66	45	49
West Ham United	42	20	7	15	54	43	47
Cambridge United	42	14	16	12	61	53	44
Newcastle United	42	15	14	13	53	49	44
Preston North End	42	12	19	11	56	52	43
Oldham Athletic	42	16	11	15	49	53	43
Swansea City	42	17	9	16	48	53	43
Shrewsbury Town	42	18	5	19	60	53	41
Orient	42	12	17	13	48	54	41
Cardiff City	42	16	8	18	41	48	40
Wrexham	42	16	6	20	40	49	38
Notts County	42	11	15	16	51	52	37
Watford	42	12	13	17	39	46	37
Bristol Rovers	42	11	13	18	50	64	35
Fulham	*42*	*11*	*7*	*24*	*42*	*74*	*29*
Burnley	*42*	*6*	*15*	*21*	*39*	*73*	*27*
Charlton Athletic	*42*	*6*	*10*	*26*	*39*	*78*	*22*

DIVISION THREE 1979-80

Team	P	W	D	L	F	A	Pts
Grimsby Town	46	26	10	10	73	42	62
Blackburn Rovers	46	25	9	12	58	36	59
Sheffield Wednesday	46	21	16	9	81	47	58
Chesterfield	46	23	11	12	71	46	57
Colchester United	46	20	12	14	64	56	52
Carlisle United	46	18	12	16	66	56	48
Reading	46	16	16	14	66	65	48
Exeter City	46	19	10	17	60	68	48
Chester	46	17	13	16	49	57	47
Swindon Town	46	19	8	19	71	63	46
Barnsley	46	16	14	16	53	56	46
Sheffield United	46	18	10	18	60	66	46
Rotherham United	46	18	10	18	58	66	46
Millwall	46	16	13	17	65	59	45
Plymouth Argyle	46	16	12	18	59	55	44
Gillingham	46	14	14	18	49	51	42
Oxford United	46	14	13	19	57	62	41
Blackpool	46	15	11	20	62	74	41
Brentford	46	15	11	20	59	73	41
Hull City	46	12	16	18	51	69	40
Bury	*46*	*16*	*7*	*23*	*45*	*59*	*39*
Southend United	*46*	*14*	*10*	*22*	*47*	*58*	*38*
Mansfield Town	*46*	*10*	*16*	*20*	*47*	*58*	*36*
Wimbledon	*46*	*10*	*14*	*22*	*52*	*81*	*34*

DIVISION FOUR 1979-80

Team	P	W	D	L	F	A	Pts
Huddersfield Town	46	27	12	7	101	48	66
Walsall	46	23	18	5	75	47	64
Newport County	46	27	7	12	83	50	61
Portsmouth	46	24	12	10	91	49	60
Bradford City	46	24	12	10	77	50	60
Wigan Athletic	46	21	13	12	76	61	55
Lincoln City	46	18	17	11	64	42	53
Peterborough United	46	21	10	15	58	47	52
Torquay United	46	15	17	14	70	69	47
Aldershot	46	16	13	17	62	53	45
Bournemouth	46	13	18	15	52	51	44
Doncaster Rovers	46	15	14	17	62	63	44
Northampton Town	46	16	12	18	51	66	44
Scunthorpe United	46	14	15	17	58	75	43
Tranmere Rovers	46	14	13	19	50	56	41
Stockport County	46	14	12	20	48	72	40
York City	46	14	11	21	65	82	39
Halifax Town	46	13	13	20	46	72	39
Hartlepool United	46	14	10	22	59	64	38
Port Vale	46	12	12	22	56	70	36
Hereford United	46	11	14	21	38	52	36
Darlington	46	9	17	20	50	74	35
Crewe Alexandra	46	11	13	22	35	68	35
Rochdale	46	7	13	26	33	79	27

1980 F.A. Cup

Semi-finals

West Ham United vs Everton	1-1, 2-1
Arsenal vs Liverpool	0-0, 1-1, 1-1, 1-0

Final

Wembley, 10th May 1980

West Ham United 1 (Brooking)
Arsenal 0

Attendance 100,000

1980 Football League Cup

Semi-finals

Swindon Town vs Wolverhampton Wands. (2-1, 1-3)		3-4
Nottingham Forest vs Liverpool (1-0, 1-1)		2-1

Final

Wembley, 15th March 1980

Wolverhampton Wanderers 1 (Gray)
Nottingham Forest 0

Attendance 100,000

DIVISION ONE 1980-81

ASTON VILLA	42	26	8	8	72	40	60
Ipswich Town	42	23	10	9	77	43	56
Arsenal	42	19	15	8	61	45	53
West Bromwich Albion	42	20	12	10	60	42	52
Liverpool	42	17	17	8	62	42	51
Southampton	42	20	10	12	76	56	50
Nottingham Forest	42	19	12	11	62	44	50
Manchester United	42	15	18	9	51	36	48
Leeds United	42	17	10	15	39	47	44
Tottenham Hotspur	42	14	15	13	70	68	43
Stoke City	42	12	18	12	51	60	42
Manchester City	42	14	11	17	56	59	39
Birmingham City	42	13	12	17	50	61	38
Middlesbrough	42	16	5	21	53	61	37
Everton	42	13	10	19	55	58	36
Coventry City	42	13	10	19	48	68	36
Sunderland	42	14	7	21	52	53	35
Wolverhampton Wanderers	42	13	9	20	43	55	35
Brighton & Hove Albion	42	14	7	21	54	67	35
Norwich City	*42*	*13*	*7*	*22*	*49*	*73*	*33*
Leicester City	*42*	*13*	*6*	*23*	*40*	*67*	*32*
Crystal Palace	*42*	*6*	*7*	*29*	*47*	*83*	*19*

DIVISION THREE 1980-81

Rotherham United	46	24	13	9	62	32	61
Barnsley	46	21	17	8	72	45	59
Charlton Athletic	46	25	9	12	63	44	59
Huddersfield Town	46	21	14	11	71	40	56
Chesterfield	46	23	10	13	72	48	56
Portsmouth	46	22	9	15	55	47	53
Plymouth Argyle	46	19	14	13	56	44	52
Burnley	46	18	14	14	60	48	50
Brentford	46	14	19	13	52	49	47
Reading	46	18	10	18	62	62	46
Exeter City	46	16	13	17	62	66	45
Newport County	46	15	13	18	64	61	43
Fulham	46	15	13	18	57	64	43
Oxford United	46	13	17	16	39	47	43
Gillingham	46	12	18	16	48	58	42
Millwall	46	14	14	18	43	60	42
Swindon Town	46	13	15	18	51	56	41
Chester	46	15	11	20	38	48	41
Carlisle United	46	14	13	19	56	70	41
Walsall	46	13	15	18	59	74	41
Sheffield United	*46*	*14*	*12*	*20*	*65*	*63*	*40*
Colchester United	*46*	*14*	*11*	*21*	*45*	*65*	*39*
Blackpool	*46*	*9*	*14*	*23*	*45*	*75*	*32*
Hull City	*46*	*8*	*16*	*22*	*40*	*71*	*32*

DIVISION TWO 1980-81

West Ham United	42	28	10	4	79	29	66
Notts County	42	18	17	7	49	38	53
Swansea City	42	18	14	10	64	44	50
Blackburn Rovers	42	16	18	8	42	29	50
Luton Town	42	18	12	12	61	46	48
Derby County	42	15	15	12	57	52	45
Grimsby Town	42	15	15	12	44	42	45
Queen's Park Rangers	42	15	13	14	56	46	43
Watford	42	16	11	15	50	45	43
Sheffield Wednesday	42	17	8	17	53	51	42
Newcastle United	42	14	14	14	30	45	42
Chelsea	42	14	12	16	46	41	40
Cambridge United	42	17	6	19	53	65	40
Shrewsbury Town	42	11	17	14	46	47	39
Oldham Athletic	42	12	15	15	39	48	39
Wrexham	42	12	14	16	43	45	38
Orient	42	13	12	17	52	56	38
Bolton Wanderers	42	14	10	18	61	66	38
Cardiff City	42	12	12	18	44	60	36
Preston North End	*42*	*11*	*14*	*17*	*41*	*62*	*36*
Bristol City	*42*	*7*	*16*	*19*	*29*	*51*	*30*
Bristol Rovers	*42*	*5*	*13*	*24*	*34*	*65*	*23*

DIVISION FOUR 1980-81

Southend United	46	30	7	9	79	31	67
Lincoln City	46	25	15	6	66	25	65
Doncaster Rovers	46	22	12	12	59	49	56
Wimbledon	46	23	9	14	64	46	55
Peterborough United	46	17	18	11	68	54	52
Aldershot	46	18	14	14	43	41	50
Mansfield Town	46	20	9	17	58	44	49
Darlington	46	19	11	16	65	59	49
Hartlepool United	46	20	9	17	64	61	49
Northampton Town	46	18	13	15	65	67	49
Wigan Athletic	46	18	11	17	51	55	47
Bury	46	17	11	18	70	62	45
Bournemouth	46	16	13	17	47	48	45
Bradford City	46	14	16	16	53	60	44
Rochdale	46	14	15	17	60	70	43
Scunthorpe United	46	11	20	15	60	69	42
Torquay United	46	18	5	23	55	63	41
Crewe Alexandra	46	13	14	19	48	61	40
Port Vale	46	12	15	19	57	70	39
Stockport County	46	16	7	23	44	57	39
Tranmere Rovers	46	13	10	23	59	73	36
Hereford United	46	11	13	22	38	62	35
Halifax Town	46	11	12	23	44	71	34
York City	46	12	9	25	47	66	33

1981 F.A. Cup

Semi-finals

Tottenham Hotspur vs Wolverhampton Wanderers	2-2, 3-0
Ipswich Town vs Manchester City	0-1

Final

Wembley, 9th May 1981

Tottenham Hotspur 1 (Hutchinson (og))
Manchester City 1 (Hutchinson)

Attendance 100,000

Replay

Wembley, 14th May 1981

Tottenham Hotspur 3 (Villa 2, Crooks)
Manchester City 2 (MacKenzie, Reeves (pen))

Attendance 92,000

1981 Football League Cup

Semi-finals

Manchester City vs Liverpool (0-1, 1-1)		1-2
Coventry City vs West Ham United (3-2, 0-2)		3-4

Final

Wembley, 14th March 1981

Liverpool 1 (A. Kennedy)
West Ham United 1 (aet.) (Stewart)

Attendance 100,000

Replay

Villa Park, 1st April 1981

Liverpool 2 (Dalglish, R. Kennedy)
West Ham United 1 (Goddard)

Attendance 36,693

DIVISION ONE 1981-82

LIVERPOOL	42	26	9	7	80	32	87
Ipswich Town	42	26	5	11	75	53	83
Manchester United	42	22	12	8	59	29	78
Tottenham Hotspur	42	20	11	11	67	48	71
Arsenal	42	20	11	11	48	37	71
Swansea City	42	21	6	15	58	51	69
Southampton	42	19	9	14	72	67	66
Everton	42	17	13	12	56	50	64
West Ham United	42	14	16	12	66	57	58
Manchester City	42	15	13	14	49	50	58
Aston Villa	42	15	12	15	55	53	57
Nottingham Forest	42	15	12	15	42	48	57
Brighton & Hove Albion	42	13	13	16	43	52	52
Coventry City	42	13	11	18	56	62	50
Notts County	42	13	8	21	61	69	47
Birmingham City	42	10	14	18	53	61	44
West Bromwich Albion	42	11	11	20	46	57	44
Stoke City	42	12	8	22	44	63	44
Sunderland	42	11	11	20	38	58	44
Leeds United	*42*	*10*	*12*	*20*	*39*	*61*	*42*
Wolverhampton Wanderers	*42*	*10*	*10*	*22*	*32*	*63*	*40*
Middlesbrough	*42*	*8*	*15*	*19*	*34*	*52*	*39*

DIVISION THREE 1981-82

Burnley	46	21	17	8	66	45	80
Carlisle United	46	23	11	12	65	50	80
Fulham	46	21	15	10	77	51	78
Lincoln City	46	21	14	11	66	40	77
Oxford United	46	19	14	13	63	49	71
Gillingham	46	20	11	15	64	56	71
Southend United	46	18	15	13	63	51	69
Brentford	46	19	11	16	56	47	68
Millwall	46	18	13	15	62	62	67
Plymouth Argyle	46	18	11	17	64	56	65
Chesterfield	46	18	10	18	57	58	64
Reading	46	17	11	18	67	75	62
Portsmouth	46	14	19	13	56	51	61
Preston North End	46	16	13	17	50	56	61
Bristol Rovers	46	18	9	19	58	65	61
Newport County	46	14	16	16	54	54	58
Huddersfield Town	46	15	12	19	64	59	57
Exeter City	46	16	9	21	71	84	57
Doncaster Rovers	46	13	17	16	55	68	56
Walsall	46	13	14	19	51	55	53
Wimbledon	*46*	*14*	*11*	*21*	*61*	*75*	*53*
Swindon Town	*46*	*13*	*13*	*20*	*55*	*71*	*52*
Bristol City	*46*	*11*	*13*	*22*	*40*	*65*	*46*
Chester	*46*	*7*	*11*	*28*	*36*	*78*	*32*

Bristol Rovers had two points deducted

DIVISION TWO 1981-82

Luton Town	42	25	13	4	86	46	88
Watford	42	23	11	8	76	42	80
Norwich City	42	22	5	15	64	50	71
Sheffield Wednesday	42	20	10	12	55	51	70
Queen's Park Rangers	42	21	6	15	65	43	69
Barnsley	42	19	10	13	59	41	67
Rotherham United	42	20	7	15	66	54	67
Leicester City	42	18	12	12	56	48	66
Newcastle United	42	18	8	16	52	50	62
Blackburn Rovers	42	16	11	15	47	43	59
Oldham Athletic	42	15	14	13	50	51	59
Chelsea	42	15	12	15	60	60	57
Charlton Athletic	42	13	12	17	50	65	51
Cambridge United	42	13	9	20	48	53	48
Crystal Palace	42	13	9	20	34	45	48
Derby County	42	12	12	18	53	68	48
Grimsby Town	42	11	13	18	53	65	46
Shrewsbury Town	42	11	13	18	37	57	46
Bolton Wanderers	42	13	7	22	39	61	46
Cardiff City	*42*	*12*	*8*	*22*	*45*	*61*	*44*
Wrexham	*42*	*11*	*11*	*20*	*40*	*56*	*44*
Orient	*42*	*10*	*9*	*23*	*36*	*61*	*39*

DIVISION FOUR 1981-82

Sheffield United	46	27	15	4	94	41	96
Bradford City	46	26	13	7	88	45	91
Wigan Athletic	46	26	13	7	80	46	91
Bournemouth	46	23	19	4	62	30	88
Peterborough United	46	24	10	12	71	57	82
Colchester United	46	20	12	14	82	57	72
Port Vale	46	18	16	12	56	49	70
Hull City	46	19	12	15	70	61	69
Bury	46	17	17	12	80	59	68
Hereford United	46	16	19	11	64	58	67
Tranmere Rovers	46	14	18	14	51	56	60
Blackpool	46	15	13	18	66	60	58
Darlington	46	15	13	18	61	62	58
Hartlepool United	46	13	16	17	73	84	55
Torquay United	46	14	13	19	47	59	55
Aldershot	46	13	15	18	57	68	54
York City	46	14	8	24	69	91	50
Stockport County	46	12	13	21	48	67	49
Halifax Town	46	9	22	15	51	72	49
Mansfield Town	46	13	10	23	63	81	47
Rochdale	46	10	16	20	50	62	46
Northampton Town	46	11	9	26	57	84	42
Scunthorpe United	46	9	15	22	43	79	42
Crewe Alexandra	46	6	9	31	29	84	27

Mansfield Town had two points deducted

1982 F.A. Cup

Semi-finals

Tottenham Hotspur vs Leicester City	2-0
West Bromwich Albion vs Queen's Park Rangers	0-1

Final

Wembley, 22nd May 1982

Tottenham Hotspur 1   (Hoddle)

Queen's Park Rangers 1 (aet.)

Attendance 100,000

Replay

Wembley, 27th May 1982

Tottenham Hotspur 1   (Hoddle (pen))
Queen's Park Rangers 0

Attendance 90,000

1982 Football League Cup

Semi-finals

Ipswich Town vs Liverpool (0-2, 2-2)	2-4
West Brom. Albion vs Tottenham Hotspur (0-0, 0-1)	0-1

Final

Wembley, 13th March 1982

Liverpool 3   (Whelan 2, Rush)
Tottenham Hotspur 1 (aet.)   (Archibald)

Attendance 100,000

DIVISION ONE 1982-83

LIVERPOOL	42	24	10	8	87	37	82
Watford	42	22	5	15	74	57	71
Manchester United	42	19	13	10	56	38	70
Tottenham Hotspur	42	20	9	13	65	50	69
Nottingham Forest	42	20	9	13	62	50	69
Aston Villa	42	21	5	16	62	50	68
Everton	42	18	10	14	66	48	64
West Ham United	42	20	4	18	68	62	64
Ipswich Town	42	15	13	14	64	50	58
Arsenal	42	16	10	16	58	56	58
West Bromwich Albion	42	15	12	15	51	49	57
Southampton	42	15	12	15	54	58	57
Stoke City	42	16	9	17	53	64	57
Norwich City	42	14	12	16	52	58	54
Notts County	42	15	7	20	55	71	52
Sunderland	42	12	14	16	48	61	50
Birmingham City	42	12	14	16	40	55	50
Luton Town	42	12	13	17	65	84	49
Coventry City	42	13	9	20	48	59	48
Manchester City	*42*	*13*	*8*	*21*	*47*	*70*	*47*
Swansea City	*42*	*10*	*11*	*21*	*51*	*69*	*41*
Brighton & Hove Albion	*42*	*9*	*13*	*20*	*38*	*68*	*40*

DIVISION THREE 1982-83

Portsmouth	46	27	10	9	74	41	91
Cardiff City	46	25	11	10	76	50	86
Huddersfield Town	46	23	13	10	84	49	82
Newport County	46	23	9	14	76	54	78
Oxford United	46	22	12	12	71	53	78
Lincoln City	46	23	7	16	77	51	76
Bristol Rovers	46	22	9	15	84	58	75
Plymouth Argyle	46	19	8	19	61	66	65
Brentford	46	18	10	18	88	77	64
Walsall	46	17	13	16	64	63	64
Sheffield United	46	19	7	20	62	64	64
Bradford City	46	16	13	17	68	69	61
Gillingham	46	16	13	17	58	59	61
Bournemouth	46	16	13	17	59	68	61
Southend United	46	15	14	17	66	65	59
Preston North End	46	15	13	18	60	69	58
Millwall	46	14	13	19	64	77	55
Wigan Athletic	46	15	9	22	60	72	54
Exeter City	46	14	12	20	81	104	54
Orient	46	15	9	22	64	88	54
Reading	*46*	*12*	*17*	*17*	*64*	*79*	*53*
Wrexham	*46*	*12*	*15*	*19*	*56*	*76*	*51*
Doncaster Rovers	*46*	*9*	*11*	*26*	*57*	*97*	*38*
Chesterfield	*46*	*8*	*13*	*25*	*43*	*68*	*37*

DIVISION TWO 1982-83

Queen's Park Rangers	42	26	7	9	77	36	85
Wolverhampton Wanderers	42	20	15	7	68	44	75
Leicester City	42	20	10	12	72	44	70
Fulham	42	20	9	13	64	47	69
Newcastle United	42	18	13	11	75	53	67
Sheffield Wednesday	42	16	15	11	60	47	63
Oldham Athletic	42	14	19	9	64	47	61
Leeds United	42	13	21	8	51	46	60
Shrewsbury Town	42	15	14	13	48	48	59
Barnsley	42	14	15	13	57	55	57
Blackburn Rovers	42	15	12	15	58	58	57
Cambridge United	42	13	12	17	42	60	51
Derby County	42	10	19	13	49	58	49
Carlisle United	42	12	12	18	68	70	48
Crystal Palace	42	12	12	18	43	52	48
Middlesbrough	42	11	15	16	46	67	48
Charlton Athletic	42	13	9	20	63	86	48
Chelsea	42	11	14	17	51	61	47
Grimsby Town	42	12	11	19	45	70	47
Rotherham United	*42*	*10*	*15*	*17*	*45*	*68*	*45*
Burnley	*42*	*12*	*8*	*22*	*56*	*66*	*44*
Bolton Wanderers	*42*	*11*	*11*	*20*	*42*	*61*	*44*

DIVISION FOUR 1982-83

Wimbledon	46	29	11	6	96	45	98
Hull City	46	25	15	6	75	34	90
Port Vale	46	26	10	10	67	34	88
Scunthorpe United	46	23	14	9	71	42	83
Bury	46	23	12	11	74	46	81
Colchester United	46	24	9	13	75	55	81
York City	46	22	13	11	88	58	79
Swindon Town	46	19	11	16	61	54	68
Peterborough United	46	17	13	16	58	52	64
Mansfield Town	46	16	13	17	61	70	61
Halifax Town	46	16	12	18	59	66	60
Torquay United	46	17	7	22	56	65	58
Chester	46	15	11	20	55	60	56
Bristol City	46	13	17	16	59	70	56
Northampton Town	46	14	12	20	65	75	54
Stockport County	46	14	12	20	60	79	54
Darlington	46	13	13	20	61	71	52
Aldershot	46	12	15	19	61	82	51
Tranmere Rovers	46	13	11	22	49	71	50
Rochdale	46	11	16	19	55	73	49
Blackpool	46	13	12	21	55	74	49
Hartlepool United	46	13	9	24	46	76	48
Crewe Alexandra	46	11	8	27	53	71	41
Hereford United	46	11	8	27	42	79	41

Blackpool had two points deducted

1983 F.A. Cup

Semi-finals

Manchester United vs Arsenal	2-1
Brighton & Hove Albion vs Sheffield Wednesday	2-1

Final

Wembley, 21st May 1983

Manchester United 2 (Stapleton, Wilkins)
Brighton & Hove Albion 2 (Smith, Stevens)

Attendance 100,000

Replay

Wembley, 26th May 1983

Manchester United 4 (Robson 2, Whiteside, Muhren (pen))
Brighton & Hove Albion 0

Attendance 100,000

1983 Football League Cup

Semi-finals

Liverpool vs Burnley (3-0, 0-1)	3-1
Arsenal vs Manchester United (2-4, 1-2)	3-6

Final

Wembley, 26th March 1983

Liverpool 2 (Kennedy, Whelan)
Manchester United 1 (aet.) (Whiteside)

Attendance 100,000

DIVISION ONE 1983-84

LIVERPOOL	42	22	14	6	73	32	80
Southampton	42	22	11	9	66	38	77
Nottingham Forest	42	22	8	12	76	45	74
Manchester United	42	20	14	8	71	41	74
Queen's Park Rangers	42	22	7	13	67	37	73
Arsenal	42	18	9	15	74	60	63
Everton	42	16	14	12	44	42	62
Tottenham Hotspur	42	17	10	15	64	65	61
West Ham United	42	17	9	16	60	55	60
Aston Villa	42	17	9	16	59	61	60
Watford	42	16	9	17	68	77	57
Ipswich Town	42	15	8	19	55	57	53
Sunderland	42	13	13	16	42	53	52
Norwich City	42	12	15	15	48	49	51
Leicester City	42	13	12	17	65	68	51
Luton Town	42	14	9	19	53	66	51
West Bromwich Albion	42	14	9	19	48	62	51
Stoke City	42	13	11	18	44	63	50
Coventry City	42	13	11	18	57	77	50
Birmingham City	*42*	*12*	*12*	*18*	*39*	*50*	*48*
Notts County	*42*	*10*	*11*	*21*	*50*	*72*	*41*
Wolverhampton Wanderers	*42*	*6*	*11*	*25*	*27*	*80*	*29*

DIVISION TWO 1983-84

Chelsea	42	25	13	4	90	40	88
Sheffield Wednesday	42	26	10	6	72	34	88
Newcastle United	42	24	8	10	85	53	80
Manchester City	42	20	10	12	66	48	70
Grimsby Town	42	19	13	10	60	47	70
Blackburn Rovers	42	17	16	9	57	46	67
Carlisle United	42	16	16	10	48	41	64
Shrewsbury Town	42	17	10	15	49	53	61
Brighton & Hove Albion	42	17	9	16	69	60	60
Leeds United	42	16	12	14	55	56	60
Fulham	42	15	12	15	60	53	57
Huddersfield Town	42	14	15	13	56	49	57
Charlton Athletic	42	16	9	17	53	64	57
Barnsley	42	15	7	20	57	53	52
Cardiff City	42	15	6	21	53	66	51
Portsmouth	42	14	7	21	73	64	49
Middlesbrough	42	12	13	17	41	47	49
Crystal Palace	42	12	11	19	42	52	47
Oldham Athletic	42	13	8	21	47	73	47
Derby County	*42*	*11*	*9*	*22*	*36*	*72*	*42*
Swansea City	*42*	*7*	*8*	*27*	*36*	*85*	*29*
Cambridge United	*42*	*4*	*12*	*26*	*28*	*77*	*24*

DIVISION THREE 1983-84

Oxford United	46	28	11	7	91	50	95
Wimbledon	46	26	9	11	97	76	87
Sheffield United	46	24	11	11	86	53	83
Hull City	46	23	14	9	71	38	83
Bristol Rovers	46	22	13	11	68	54	79
Walsall	46	22	9	15	68	61	75
Bradford City	46	20	11	15	73	65	71
Gillingham	46	20	10	16	74	69	70
Millwall	46	18	13	15	71	65	67
Bolton Wanderers	46	18	10	18	56	60	64
Orient	46	18	9	19	71	81	63
Burnley	46	16	14	16	76	61	62
Newport County	46	16	14	16	58	75	62
Lincoln City	46	17	10	19	59	62	61
Wigan Athletic	46	16	13	17	46	56	61
Preston North End	46	15	11	20	66	66	56
Bournemouth	46	16	7	23	63	73	55
Rotherham United	46	15	9	22	57	64	54
Plymouth Argyle	46	13	12	21	56	62	51
Brentford	46	11	16	19	69	79	49
Scunthorpe United	*46*	*9*	*19*	*18*	*54*	*73*	*46*
Southend United	*46*	*10*	*14*	*22*	*55*	*76*	*44*
Port Vale	*46*	*11*	*10*	*25*	*51*	*83*	*43*
Exeter City	*46*	*6*	*15*	*25*	*50*	*84*	*33*

DIVISION FOUR 1983-84

York City	46	31	8	7	96	39	101
Doncaster Rovers	46	24	13	9	82	54	85
Reading	46	22	16	8	84	56	82
Bristol City	46	24	10	12	70	44	82
Aldershot	46	22	9	15	76	69	75
Blackpool	46	21	9	16	70	52	72
Peterborough United	46	18	14	14	72	48	68
Colchester United	46	17	16	13	69	53	67
Torquay United	46	18	13	15	59	64	67
Tranmere Rovers	46	17	15	14	53	53	66
Hereford United	46	16	15	15	54	53	63
Stockport County	46	17	11	18	60	64	62
Chesterfield	46	15	15	16	59	61	60
Darlington	46	17	8	21	49	50	59
Bury	46	15	14	17	61	64	59
Crewe Alexandra	46	16	11	19	56	67	59
Swindon Town	46	15	13	18	58	56	58
Northampton Town	46	13	14	19	53	78	53
Mansfield Town	46	13	13	20	66	70	52
Wrexham	46	11	15	20	59	74	48
Halifax Town	46	12	12	22	55	89	48
Rochdale	46	11	13	22	52	80	46
Hartlepool United	46	10	10	26	47	85	40
Chester City	46	7	13	26	45	82	34

1984 F.A. Cup

Semi-finals

Everton vs Southampton	1-0
Watford vs Plymouth Argyle	1-0

Final

Wembley, 19th May 1984

Everton 2 (Sharp, Gray)
Watford 0

Attendance 100,000

1984 Football League Cup

Semi-finals

Liverpool vs Walsall (2-2, 2-0)	4-2
Everton vs Aston Villa (2-0, 0-1)	2-1

Final

Wembley, 25th March 1984

Liverpool 0
Everton 0 (aet.)

Attendance 100,000

Replay

Maine Road, 28th March 1984

Liverpool 1 (Souness)
Everton 0

Attendance 52,089

DIVISION ONE 1984-85

EVERTON	42	28	6	8	88	43	90
Liverpool	42	22	11	9	68	35	77
Tottenham Hotspur	42	23	8	11	78	51	77
Manchester United	42	22	10	10	77	47	76
Southampton	42	19	11	12	56	47	68
Chelsea	42	18	12	12	63	48	66
Arsenal	42	19	9	14	61	49	66
Sheffield Wednesday	42	17	14	11	58	45	65
Nottingham Forest	42	19	7	16	56	48	64
Aston Villa	42	15	11	16	60	60	56
Watford	42	14	13	15	81	71	55
West Bromwich Albion	42	16	7	19	58	62	55
Luton Town	42	15	9	18	57	61	54
Newcastle United	42	13	13	16	55	70	52
Leicester City	42	15	6	21	65	73	51
West Ham United	42	13	12	17	51	68	51
Ipswich Town	42	13	11	18	46	57	50
Coventry City	42	15	5	22	47	64	50
Queen's Park Rangers	42	13	11	18	53	72	50
Norwich City	*42*	*13*	*10*	*19*	*46*	*64*	*49*
Sunderland	*42*	*10*	*10*	*22*	*40*	*62*	*40*
Stoke City	*42*	*3*	*8*	*31*	*24*	*91*	*17*

DIVISION THREE 1984-85

Bradford City	46	28	10	8	77	45	94
Millwall	46	26	12	8	73	42	90
Hull City	46	25	12	9	78	49	87
Gillingham	46	25	8	13	80	62	83
Bristol City	46	24	9	13	74	47	81
Bristol Rovers	46	21	12	13	66	48	75
Derby County	46	19	13	14	65	54	70
York City	46	20	9	17	70	57	69
Reading	46	19	12	15	68	62	69
Bournemouth	46	19	11	16	57	46	68
Walsall	46	18	13	15	58	52	67
Rotherham United	46	18	11	17	55	55	65
Brentford	46	16	14	16	62	64	62
Doncaster Rovers	46	17	8	21	72	74	59
Plymouth Argyle	46	15	14	17	62	65	59
Wigan Athletic	46	15	14	17	60	64	59
Bolton Wanderers	46	16	6	24	69	75	54
Newport County	46	13	13	20	55	67	52
Lincoln City	46	11	18	17	50	51	51
Swansea City	46	12	11	23	53	80	47
Burnley	*46*	*11*	*13*	*22*	*60*	*73*	*46*
Orient	*46*	*11*	*13*	*22*	*51*	*76*	*46*
Preston North End	*46*	*13*	*7*	*26*	*51*	*100*	*46*
Cambridge United	*46*	*4*	*9*	*33*	*37*	*95*	*21*

DIVISION TWO 1984-85

Oxford United	42	25	9	8	84	36	84
Birmingham City	42	25	7	10	59	33	82
Manchester City	42	21	11	10	66	40	74
Portsmouth	42	20	14	8	69	50	74
Blackburn Rovers	42	21	10	11	66	41	73
Brighton & Hove Albion	42	20	12	10	54	34	72
Leeds United	42	19	12	11	66	43	69
Shrewsbury Town	42	18	11	13	66	53	65
Fulham	42	19	8	15	68	64	65
Grimsby Town	42	18	8	16	72	64	62
Barnsley	42	14	16	12	42	42	58
Wimbledon	42	16	10	16	71	75	58
Huddersfield Town	42	15	10	17	52	64	55
Oldham Athletic	42	15	8	19	49	67	53
Crystal Palace	42	12	12	18	46	65	48
Carlisle United	42	13	8	21	50	67	47
Charlton Athletic	42	11	12	19	51	63	45
Sheffield United	42	10	14	18	54	66	44
Middlesbrough	42	10	10	22	41	57	40
Notts County	*42*	*10*	*7*	*25*	*45*	*73*	*37*
Cardiff City	*42*	*9*	*8*	*25*	*47*	*79*	*35*
Wolverhampton Wanderers	*42*	*8*	*9*	*25*	*37*	*79*	*33*

DIVISION FOUR 1984-85

Chesterfield	46	26	13	7	64	35	91
Blackpool	46	24	14	8	73	39	86
Darlington	46	24	13	9	66	49	85
Bury	46	24	12	10	76	50	84
Hereford United	46	22	11	13	65	47	77
Tranmere Rovers	46	24	3	19	83	66	75
Colchester United	46	20	14	12	87	65	74
Swindon Town	46	21	9	16	62	58	72
Scunthorpe United	46	19	14	13	83	62	71
Crewe Alexandra	46	18	12	16	65	69	66
Peterborough United	46	16	14	16	54	53	62
Port Vale	46	14	18	14	61	59	60
Aldershot	46	17	8	21	56	63	59
Mansfield Town	46	13	18	15	41	38	57
Wrexham	46	15	9	22	67	70	54
Chester City	46	15	9	22	60	72	54
Rochdale	46	13	14	19	55	69	53
Exeter City	46	13	14	19	57	79	53
Hartlepool United	46	14	10	22	54	67	52
Southend United	46	13	11	22	58	83	50
Halifax Town	46	15	5	26	42	69	50
Stockport County	46	13	8	25	58	79	47
Northampton Town	46	14	5	27	53	74	47
Torquay United	46	9	14	23	38	63	41

1985 F.A.Cup

Semi-finals

Luton Town vs Everton	1-2
Manchester United vs Liverpool	2-2, 2-1

Final

Wembley, 18 May 1985

Everton 0
Manchester United 1   (Whiteside)

Attendance 100,000

1985 Football League Cup

Semi-finals

Sunderland vs Chelsea (2-0, 3-2)	5-2
Ipswich Town vs Norwich City (1-0, 0-2)	1-2

Final

Wembley, 24th March 1985

Norwich City 1   (Chisholm (og))
Sunderland 0

Attendance 100,000

DIVISION ONE 1985-86

LIVERPOOL	42	26	10	6	89	37	88
Everton	42	26	8	8	87	41	86
West Ham United	42	26	6	10	74	40	84
Manchester United	42	22	10	10	70	36	76
Sheffield Wednesday	42	21	10	11	63	54	73
Chelsea	42	20	11	11	57	56	71
Arsenal	42	20	9	13	49	47	69
Nottingham Forest	42	19	11	12	69	53	68
Luton Town	42	18	12	12	61	44	66
Tottenham Hotspur	42	19	8	15	74	52	65
Newcastle United	42	17	12	13	67	72	63
Watford	42	16	11	15	69	62	59
Queen's Park Rangers	42	15	7	20	53	64	52
Southampton	42	12	10	20	51	62	46
Manchester City	42	11	12	19	43	57	45
Aston Villa	42	10	14	18	51	67	44
Coventry City	42	11	10	21	48	71	43
Oxford United	42	10	12	20	62	80	42
Leicester City	42	10	12	20	54	76	42
Ipswich Town	*42*	*11*	*8*	*23*	*32*	*55*	*41*
Birmingham City	*42*	*8*	*5*	*29*	*30*	*73*	*29*
West Bromwich Albion	*42*	*4*	*12*	*26*	*35*	*89*	*24*

DIVISION THREE 1985-86

Reading	46	29	7	10	67	51	94
Plymouth Argyle	46	26	9	11	88	53	87
Derby County	46	23	15	8	80	41	84
Wigan Athletic	46	23	14	9	82	48	83
Gillingham	46	22	13	11	81	54	79
Walsall	46	22	9	15	90	64	75
York City	46	20	11	15	77	58	71
Notts County	46	19	14	13	71	60	71
Bristol City	46	18	14	14	69	60	68
Brentford	46	18	12	16	58	61	66
Doncaster Rovers	46	16	16	14	45	52	64
Blackpool	46	17	12	17	66	55	63
Darlington	46	15	13	18	61	78	58
Rotherham United	46	15	12	19	61	59	57
Bournemouth	46	15	9	22	65	72	54
Bristol Rovers	46	14	12	20	51	75	54
Chesterfield	46	13	14	19	61	64	53
Bolton Wanderers	46	15	8	23	54	68	53
Newport County	46	11	18	17	52	65	51
Bury	46	12	13	21	63	65	49
Lincoln City	*46*	*10*	*16*	*20*	*55*	*77*	*46*
Cardiff City	*46*	*12*	*9*	*25*	*53*	*83*	*45*
Wolverhampton Wanderers	*46*	*11*	*10*	*25*	*57*	*98*	*43*
Swansea City	*46*	*11*	*10*	*25*	*43*	*87*	*43*

DIVISION TWO 1985-86

Norwich City	42	25	9	8	84	37	84
Charlton Athletic	42	22	11	9	78	45	77
Wimbledon	42	21	13	8	58	37	76
Portsmouth	42	22	7	13	69	41	73
Crystal Palace	42	19	9	14	57	52	66
Hull City	42	17	13	12	65	55	64
Sheffield United	42	17	11	14	64	63	62
Oldham Athletic	42	17	9	16	62	61	60
Millwall	42	17	8	17	64	65	59
Stoke City	42	14	15	13	48	50	57
Brighton & Hove Albion	42	16	8	18	64	64	56
Barnsley	42	14	14	14	47	50	56
Bradford City	42	16	6	20	51	63	54
Leeds United	42	15	8	19	56	72	53
Grimsby Town	42	14	10	18	58	62	52
Huddersfield Town	42	14	10	18	51	67	52
Shrewsbury Town	42	14	9	19	52	64	51
Sunderland	42	13	11	18	47	61	50
Blackburn Rovers	42	12	13	17	53	62	49
Carlisle United	*42*	*13*	*7*	*22*	*47*	*71*	*46*
Middlesbrough	*42*	*12*	*9*	*21*	*44*	*53*	*45*
Fulham	*42*	*10*	*6*	*26*	*45*	*69*	*36*

DIVISION FOUR 1985-86

Swindon Town	46	32	6	8	82	43	102
Chester City	46	23	15	8	83	50	84
Mansfield Town	46	23	12	11	74	47	81
Port Vale	46	21	16	9	67	37	79
Orient	46	20	12	14	79	64	72
Colchester United	46	19	13	14	88	63	70
Hartlepool United	46	20	10	16	68	67	70
Northampton Town	46	18	10	18	79	58	64
Southend United	46	18	10	18	69	67	64
Hereford United	46	18	10	18	74	73	64
Stockport County	46	17	13	16	63	71	64
Crewe Alexandra	46	18	9	19	54	61	63
Wrexham	46	17	9	20	68	80	60
Burnley	46	16	11	19	60	65	59
Scunthorpe United	46	15	14	17	50	55	59
Aldershot	46	17	7	22	66	74	58
Peterborough United	46	13	17	16	52	64	56
Rochdale	46	14	13	19	57	77	55
Tranmere Rovers	46	15	9	22	74	73	54
Halifax Town	46	14	12	20	60	71	54
Exeter City	46	13	15	18	47	59	54
Cambridge United	46	15	9	22	65	80	54
Preston North End	46	11	10	25	54	89	43
Torquay United	46	9	10	27	43	88	37

1986 F.A. Cup

Semi-finals

Everton vs Sheffield Wednesday	2-1
Liverpool vs Southampton	2-0

Final

Wembley, 10th May 1986

Everton 1   (Lineker)

Liverpool 3   (Rush 2, Johnston)

Attendance 98,000

1986 Football League Cup

Semi-finals

Queen's Park Rangers vs Liverpool (1-0, 2-2)		3-2
Aston Villa vs Oxford United (2-2, 1-2)		3-4

Final

Wembley, 20 April 1985

Oxford United 3   (Hebberd, Houghton, Charles)

Queen's Park Rangers 0

Attendance 90,396

DIVISION ONE 1986-87

EVERTON	42	26	8	8	76	31	86
Liverpool	42	23	8	11	72	42	77
Tottenham Hotspur	42	21	8	13	68	43	71
Arsenal	42	20	10	12	58	35	70
Norwich City	42	17	17	8	53	51	68
Wimbledon	42	19	9	14	57	50	66
Luton Town	42	18	12	12	47	45	66
Nottingham Forest	42	18	11	13	64	51	65
Watford	42	18	9	15	67	54	63
Coventry City	42	17	12	13	50	45	63
Manchester United	42	14	14	14	52	45	56
Southampton	42	14	10	18	69	68	52
Sheffield Wednesday	42	13	13	16	58	59	52
Chelsea	42	13	13	16	53	64	52
West Ham United	42	14	10	18	52	67	52
Queen's Park Rangers	42	13	11	18	48	64	50
Newcastle United	42	12	11	19	47	65	47
Oxford United	42	11	13	18	44	69	46
Charlton Athletic	42	11	11	20	45	55	44
Leicester City	*42*	*11*	*9*	*22*	*54*	*76*	*42*
Manchester City	*42*	*8*	*15*	*19*	*36*	*57*	*39*
Aston Villa	*42*	*8*	*12*	*22*	*45*	*79*	*36*

Division One/Division Two Play-offs

Ipswich Town vs Charlton Athletic	0-0, 1-2
Leeds United vs Oldham Athletic	1-0, 1-2
(Leeds United won on away goals)	
Charlton Athletic vs Leeds United	1-0, 0-1, 2-1
(Third game was played at Leeds)	

DIVISION TWO 1986-87

Derby County	42	25	9	8	64	38	84
Portsmouth	42	23	9	10	53	28	78
Oldham Athletic	42	22	9	11	65	44	75
Leeds United	42	19	11	12	58	44	68
Ipswich Town	42	17	13	12	59	43	64
Crystal Palace	42	19	5	18	51	53	62
Plymouth Argyle	42	16	13	13	62	57	61
Stoke City	42	16	10	16	63	53	58
Sheffield United	42	15	13	14	50	49	58
Bradford City	42	15	10	17	62	62	55
Barnsley	42	14	13	15	49	52	55
Blackburn Rovers	42	15	10	17	45	55	55
Reading	42	14	11	17	52	59	53
Hull City	42	13	14	15	41	55	53
West Bromwich Albion	42	13	12	17	51	49	51
Millwall	42	14	9	19	39	45	51
Huddersfield Town	42	13	12	17	54	61	51
Shrewsbury Town	42	15	6	21	41	53	51
Birmingham City	42	11	17	14	47	59	50
Sunderland	*42*	*12*	*12*	*18*	*49*	*59*	*48*
Grimsby Town	*42*	*10*	*14*	*18*	*39*	*59*	*44*
Brighton & Hove Albion	*42*	*9*	*12*	*21*	*37*	*54*	*39*

Division Two/Division Three Play-offs

Gillingham vs Sunderland	3-2, 3-4
(Gillingham won on away goals)	
Wigan Athletic vs Swindon Town	2-3, 0-0
Gillingham vs Swindon Town	1-0, 1-2, 0-2
(Third game was played at Swindon)	

DIVISION THREE 1986-87

Bournemouth	46	29	10	7	76	40	97
Middlesbrough	46	28	10	8	67	30	94
Swindon Town	46	25	12	9	77	47	87
Wigan Athletic	46	25	10	11	83	60	85
Gillingham	46	23	9	14	65	48	78
Bristol City	46	21	14	11	63	36	77
Notts County	46	21	13	12	77	56	76
Walsall	46	22	9	15	80	67	75
Blackpool	46	16	16	14	74	59	64
Mansfield Town	46	15	16	15	52	55	61
Brentford	46	15	15	16	64	66	60
Port Vale	46	15	12	19	76	70	57
Doncaster Rovers	46	14	15	17	56	62	57
Rotherham United	46	15	12	19	48	57	57
Chester City	46	13	17	16	61	59	56
Bury	46	14	13	19	54	60	55
Chesterfield	46	13	15	18	56	69	54
Fulham	46	12	17	17	59	77	53
Bristol Rovers	46	13	12	21	49	75	51
York City	46	12	13	21	55	79	49
Bolton Wanderers	*46*	*10*	*15*	*21*	*46*	*58*	*45*
Carlisle United	*46*	*10*	*8*	*28*	*39*	*78*	*38*
Darlington	*46*	*7*	*16*	*23*	*45*	*77*	*37*
Newport County	*46*	*8*	*13*	*25*	*49*	*86*	*37*

Division Three/Division Four Play-offs

Aldershot vs Bolton Wanderers	1-0, 2-2
Colchester United vs Wolverhampton Wanderers	0-2, 0-0
Aldershot vs Wolverhampton Wanderers	2-0, 1-0

DIVISION FOUR 1986-87

Northampton Town	46	30	9	7	103	53	99
Preston North End	46	26	12	8	72	47	90
Southend United	46	25	5	16	68	55	80
Wolverhampton Wanderers	46	24	7	15	69	50	79
Colchester United	46	21	7	18	64	56	70
Aldershot	*46*	*20*	*10*	*16*	*64*	*57*	*70*
Orient	46	20	9	17	64	61	69
Scunthorpe United	46	18	12	16	73	57	66
Wrexham	46	15	20	11	70	51	65
Peterborough United	46	17	14	15	57	50	65
Cambridge United	46	17	11	18	60	62	62
Swansea City	46	17	11	18	56	61	62
Cardiff City	46	15	16	15	48	50	61
Exeter City	46	11	23	12	53	49	56
Halifax Town	46	15	10	21	59	74	55
Hereford United	46	14	11	21	60	61	53
Crewe Alexandra	46	13	14	19	70	72	53
Hartlepool United	46	11	18	17	44	65	51
Stockport County	46	13	12	21	40	69	51
Tranmere Rovers	46	11	17	18	54	72	50
Rochdale	46	11	17	18	54	73	50
Burnley	46	12	13	21	53	74	49
Torquay United	46	10	18	18	56	72	48
Lincoln City	*46*	*12*	*12*	*22*	*45*	*65*	*48*

1987 F.A. Cup

Semi-finals

Tottenham Hotspur vs Watford	4-1
Coventry City vs Leeds United	3-2

Final

Wembley, 16th May 1987

Coventry City 3　(Bennett, Houchen, Mabbutt (og))
Tottenham Hotspur 2　(C. Allen, Mabbutt)

Attendance 98,000

1987 Football League Cup

Semi-finals

Arsenal vs Tottenham Hotspur (0-1, 2-1, 2-1*)	4-3
Southampton vs Liverpool (0-0, 0-3)	0-3
* Play-off	

Final

Wembley, 5th April 1987

Arsenal 2　(Nicholas 2)
Liverpool 1　(Rush)

Attendance 96,000

DIVISION ONE 1987-88

LIVERPOOL	40	26	12	2	87	24	90
Manchester United	40	23	12	5	71	38	81
Nottingham Forest	40	20	13	7	67	39	73
Everton	40	19	13	8	53	27	70
Queen's Park Rangers	40	19	10	11	48	38	67
Arsenal	40	18	12	10	58	39	66
Wimbledon	40	14	15	11	58	47	57
Newcastle United	40	14	14	12	55	53	56
Luton Town	40	14	11	15	57	58	53
Coventry City	40	13	14	13	46	53	53
Sheffield Wednesday	40	15	8	17	52	66	53
Southampton	40	12	14	14	49	53	50
Tottenham Hotspur	40	12	11	17	38	48	47
Norwich City	40	12	9	19	40	52	45
Derby County	40	10	13	17	35	45	43
West Ham United	40	9	15	16	40	52	42
Charlton Athletic	40	9	15	16	38	52	42
Chelsea	*40*	*9*	*15*	*16*	*50*	*68*	*42*
Portsmouth	*40*	*7*	*14*	*19*	*36*	*66*	*35*
Watford	*40*	*7*	*11*	*22*	*27*	*51*	*32*
Oxford United	*40*	*6*	*13*	*21*	*44*	*80*	*31*

Division One/Division Two Play-offs

Blackburn Rovers vs Chelsea	0-2, 1-4
Bradford City vs Middlesbrough	2-1, 0-2
Middlesbrough vs Chelsea	2-0, 0-1

DIVISION TWO 1987-88

Millwall	44	25	7	12	72	52	82
Aston Villa	44	22	12	10	68	41	78
Middlesbrough	44	22	12	10	63	36	78
Bradford City	44	22	11	11	74	54	77
Blackburn Rovers	44	21	14	9	68	52	77
Crystal Palace	44	22	9	13	86	59	75
Leeds United	44	19	12	13	61	51	69
Ipswich Town	44	19	9	16	61	52	66
Manchester City	44	19	8	17	80	60	65
Oldham Athletic	44	18	11	15	72	64	65
Stoke City	44	17	11	16	50	57	62
Swindon Town	44	16	11	17	73	60	59
Leicester City	44	16	11	17	62	61	59
Barnsley	44	15	12	17	61	62	57
Hull City	44	14	15	15	54	60	57
Plymouth Argyle	44	16	8	20	65	67	56
Bournemouth	44	13	10	21	56	68	49
Shrewsbury Town	44	11	16	17	42	54	49
Birmingham City	44	11	15	18	41	66	48
West Bromwich Albion	44	12	11	21	50	69	47
Sheffield United	*44*	*13*	*7*	*24*	*45*	*74*	*46*
Reading	*44*	*10*	*12*	*22*	*44*	*70*	*42*
Huddersfield Town	*44*	*6*	*10*	*28*	*41*	*100*	*28*

Division Two/Division Three Play-offs

Bristol City vs Sheffield United	1-0, 1-1
Notts County vs Walsall	1-3, 1-1
Bristol City vs Walsall	1-3, 2-0, 0-4
(Third game played at Walsall)	

1988 F.A. Cup

Semi-finals

Liverpool vs Nottingham Forest	2-1
Luton Town vs Wimbledon	1-2

Final

Wembley, 14th May 1988

Wimbledon 1   (Sanchez)

Liverpool 0

Attendance 98,203

DIVISION THREE 1987-88

Sunderland	46	27	12	7	92	48	93
Brighton & Hove Albion	46	23	15	8	69	47	84
Walsall	46	23	13	10	68	50	82
Notts County	46	23	12	11	82	49	81
Bristol City	46	21	12	13	77	62	75
Northampton Town	46	18	19	9	70	51	73
Wigan Athletic	46	20	12	14	70	61	72
Bristol Rovers	46	18	12	16	68	56	66
Fulham	46	19	9	18	69	60	66
Blackpool	46	17	14	15	71	62	65
Port Vale	46	18	11	17	58	56	65
Brentford	46	16	14	16	53	59	62
Gillingham	46	14	17	15	77	61	59
Bury	46	15	14	17	58	57	59
Chester City	46	14	16	16	51	62	58
Preston North End	46	15	13	18	48	59	58
Southend United	46	14	13	19	65	83	55
Chesterfield	46	15	10	21	41	70	55
Mansfield Town	46	14	12	20	48	59	54
Aldershot	46	15	8	23	64	74	53
Rotherham United	*46*	*12*	*16*	*18*	*50*	*66*	*52*
Grimsby Town	*46*	*12*	*14*	*20*	*48*	*58*	*50*
York City	*46*	*8*	*9*	*29*	*48*	*91*	*33*
Doncaster Rovers	*46*	*8*	*9*	*29*	*40*	*84*	*33*

Division Three/Division Four Play-offs

Swansea City vs Rotherham United	1-0, 1-1
Torquay United vs Scunthorpe United	2-1, 1-1
Swansea City vs Torquay United	2-1, 3-3

DIVISION FOUR 1987-88

Wolverhampton Wanderers	46	27	9	10	82	43	90
Cardiff City	46	24	13	9	66	41	85
Bolton Wanderers	46	22	12	12	66	42	78
Scunthorpe United	46	20	17	9	76	51	77
Torquay United	46	21	14	11	66	41	77
Swansea City	46	20	10	16	62	56	70
Peterborough United	46	20	10	16	52	53	70
Leyton Orient	46	19	12	15	85	63	69
Colchester United	46	19	10	17	47	51	67
Burnley	46	20	7	19	57	62	67
Wrexham	46	20	6	20	69	58	66
Scarborough	46	17	14	15	56	48	65
Darlington	46	18	11	17	71	69	65
Tranmere Rovers	46	19	9	18	61	53	64
Cambridge United	46	16	13	17	50	52	61
Hartlepool United	46	15	14	17	50	57	59
Crewe Alexandra	46	13	19	14	57	53	58
Halifax Town	46	14	14	18	54	59	55
Hereford United	46	14	12	20	41	59	54
Stockport County	46	12	15	19	44	58	51
Rochdale	46	11	15	20	47	76	48
Exeter City	46	11	13	22	53	68	46
Carlisle United	46	12	8	26	57	86	44
Newport County	*46*	*6*	*7*	*33*	*35*	*105*	*25*

Tranmere Rovers had 2 points deducted
Halifax Town had 1 point deducted

1988 Football League Cup

Semi-finals

Oxford United vs Luton Town (1-1, 0-2)		1-3
Everton vs Arsenal (0-1, 1-3)		1-4

Final

Wembley, 24th April 1988

Luton Town 3   (B. Stein 2, Wilson)

Arsenal 2   (Hayes, Smith)

Attendance 95,732

DIVISION ONE 1988-89

ARSENAL	38	22	10	6	73	36	76
Liverpool	38	22	10	6	65	28	76
Nottingham Forest	38	17	13	8	64	43	64
Norwich City	38	17	11	10	48	45	62
Derby County	38	17	7	14	40	38	58
Tottenham Hotspur	38	15	12	11	60	46	57
Coventry City	38	14	13	11	47	42	55
Everton	38	14	12	12	50	45	54
Queen's Park Rangers	38	14	11	13	43	37	53
Millwall	38	14	11	13	47	52	53
Manchester United	38	13	12	13	45	35	51
Wimbledon	38	14	9	15	50	46	51
Southampton	38	10	15	13	52	66	45
Charlton Athletic	38	10	12	16	44	58	42
Sheffield Wednesday	38	10	12	16	34	51	42
Luton Town	38	10	11	17	42	52	41
Aston Villa	38	9	13	16	45	56	40
Middlesbrough	38	9	12	17	44	61	39
West Ham United	38	10	8	20	37	62	38
Newcastle United	38	7	10	21	32	63	31

DIVISION TWO 1988-89

Chelsea	46	29	12	5	96	50	99
Manchester City	46	23	13	10	77	53	82
Crystal Palace	46	23	12	11	71	49	81
Watford	46	22	12	12	74	48	78
Blackburn Rovers	46	22	11	13	74	59	77
Swindon Town	46	20	16	10	68	53	76
Barnsley	46	20	14	12	66	58	74
Ipswich Town	46	22	7	17	71	61	73
West Bromwich Albion	46	18	18	10	65	41	72
Leeds United	46	17	16	13	59	50	67
Sunderland	46	16	15	15	60	60	63
Bournemouth	46	18	8	20	53	62	62
Stoke City	46	15	14	17	57	72	59
Bradford City	46	13	17	16	52	59	56
Leicester City	46	13	16	17	56	63	55
Oldham Athletic	46	11	21	14	75	72	54
Oxford United	46	14	12	20	62	70	54
Plymouth Argyle	46	14	12	20	55	66	54
Brighton & Hove Albion	46	14	9	23	57	66	51
Portsmouth	46	13	12	21	53	62	51
Hull City	46	11	14	21	52	68	47
Shrewsbury Town	46	8	18	20	40	67	42
Birmingham City	46	8	11	27	31	76	35
Walsall	46	5	16	25	41	80	31

Division Two Play-offs

Blackburn Rovers vs Watford	0-0, 1-1
(Blackburn Rovers won on away goals)	
Swindon Town vs Crystal Palace	1-0, 0-2
Blackburn Rovers vs Crystal Palace	3-1, 0-3

DIVISION THREE 1988-89

Wolverhampton Wanderers	46	26	14	6	96	49	92
Sheffield United	46	25	9	12	93	54	84
Port Vale	46	24	12	10	78	48	84
Fulham	46	22	9	15	69	67	75
Bristol Rovers	46	19	17	10	67	51	74
Preston North End	46	19	15	12	79	60	72
Brentford	46	18	14	14	66	61	68
Chester City	46	19	11	16	64	61	68
Notts County	46	18	13	15	64	54	67
Bolton Wanderers	46	16	16	14	58	54	64
Bristol City	46	18	9	19	53	55	63
Swansea City	46	15	16	15	51	53	61
Bury	46	16	13	17	55	67	61
Huddersfield Town	46	17	9	20	63	73	60
Mansfield Town	46	14	17	15	48	52	59
Cardiff City	46	14	15	17	44	56	57
Wigan Athletic	46	14	14	18	55	53	56
Reading	46	15	11	20	68	72	56
Blackpool	46	14	13	19	56	59	55
Northampton Town	46	16	6	24	66	76	54
Southend United	46	13	15	18	56	75	54
Chesterfield	46	14	7	25	51	86	49
Gillingham	46	12	4	30	47	81	40
Aldershot	46	8	13	25	48	78	37

Division Three Play-offs

Bristol Rovers vs Fulham	1-0, 4-0
Preston North End vs Port Vale	1-1, 1-3
Bristol Rovers vs Port Vale	1-1, 0-1

DIVISION FOUR 1988-89

Rotherham United	46	22	16	8	76	35	82
Tranmere Rovers	46	21	17	8	62	43	80
Crewe Alexandra	46	21	15	10	67	48	78
Scunthorpe United	46	21	14	11	77	57	77
Scarborough	46	21	14	11	67	52	77
Leyton Orient	46	21	12	13	86	50	75
Wrexham	46	19	14	13	77	63	71
Cambridge United	46	18	14	14	71	62	68
Grimsby Town	46	17	15	14	65	59	66
Lincoln City	46	18	10	18	64	60	64
York City	46	17	13	16	62	63	64
Carlisle United	46	15	15	16	53	52	60
Exeter City	46	18	6	22	65	68	60
Torquay United	46	17	8	21	45	60	59
Hereford United	46	14	16	16	66	72	58
Burnley	46	14	13	19	52	61	55
Peterborough United	46	14	12	20	52	74	54
Rochdale	46	13	14	19	56	82	53
Hartlepool United	46	14	10	22	50	78	52
Stockport County	46	10	21	15	54	52	51
Halifax Town	46	13	11	22	69	75	50
Colchester United	46	12	14	20	60	78	50
Doncaster Rovers	46	13	10	23	49	78	49
Darlington	46	8	18	20	53	76	42

Division Four Play-offs

Leyton Orient vs Scarborough	2-0, 0-1
Wrexham vs Scunthorpe United	3-1, 2-0
Wrexham vs Leyton Orient	0-0, 1-2

1989 F.A. Cup

Semi-finals

Liverpool vs Nottingham Forest	
(abandoned after 6 minutes)	0-0
Everton vs Norwich City	1-0

Replay

Liverpool vs Nottingham Forest	3-1

Final

Wembley, 20 May 1989

Liverpool 3 (aet.)   (Aldridge, Rush 2)
Everton 2   (McCall 2)

Attendance 82,800

1989 Football League Cup

Semi-finals

West Ham United vs Luton Town (0-3, 0-2)	0-5
Nottingham Forest vs Bristol City (1-1, 1-0)	2-1

Final

Wembley, 9th April 1989

Nottingham Forest 3   (Clough 2 (1 pen), Webb)
Luton Town 1   (Harford)

Attendance 76,130

DIVISION ONE 1989-90

LIVERPOOL	**38**	**23**	**10**	**5**	**78**	**37**	**79**
Aston Villa	38	21	7	10	57	38	70
Tottenham Hotspur	38	19	6	13	59	47	63
Arsenal	38	18	8	12	54	38	62
Chelsea	38	16	12	10	58	50	60
Everton	38	17	8	13	57	46	59
Southampton	38	15	10	13	71	63	55
Wimbledon	38	13	16	9	47	40	55
Nottingham Forest	38	15	9	14	55	47	54
Norwich City	38	13	14	11	44	42	53
Queen's Park Rangers	38	13	11	14	45	44	50
Coventry City	38	14	7	17	39	59	49
Manchester United	38	13	9	16	46	47	48
Manchester City	38	12	12	14	43	52	48
Crystal Palace	38	13	9	16	42	66	48
Derby County	38	13	7	18	43	40	46
Luton Town	38	10	13	15	43	57	43
Sheffield Wednesday	*38*	*11*	*10*	*17*	*35*	*51*	*43*
Charlton Athletic	*38*	*7*	*9*	*22*	*31*	*57*	*30*
Millwall	*38*	*5*	*11*	*22*	*39*	*65*	*26*

DIVISION TWO 1989-90

Leeds United	**46**	**24**	**13**	**9**	**79**	**52**	**85**
Sheffield United	**46**	**24**	**13**	**9**	**78**	**58**	**85**
Newcastle United	46	22	14	10	80	55	80
Swindon Town	46	20	14	12	79	59	74
Blackburn Rovers	46	19	17	10	74	59	74
Sunderland	**46**	**20**	**14**	**12**	**70**	**64**	**74**
West Ham United	46	20	12	14	80	57	72
Oldham Athletic	46	19	14	13	70	57	71
Ipswich Town	46	19	12	15	67	66	69
Wolverhampton Wanderers	46	18	13	15	67	60	67
Port Vale	46	15	16	15	62	57	61
Portsmouth	46	15	16	15	62	65	61
Leicester City	46	15	14	17	67	79	59
Hull City	46	14	16	16	58	65	58
Watford	46	14	15	17	58	60	57
Plymouth Argyle	46	14	13	19	58	63	55
Oxford United	46	15	9	22	57	66	54
Brighton & Hove Albion	46	15	9	22	56	72	54
Barnsley	46	13	15	18	49	71	54
West Bromwich Albion	46	12	15	19	67	71	51
Middlesbrough	46	13	11	22	52	63	50
Bournemouth	*46*	*12*	*12*	*22*	*57*	*76*	*48*
Bradford City	*46*	*9*	*14*	*23*	*44*	*68*	*41*
Stoke City	*46*	*6*	*19*	*21*	*35*	*63*	*37*

Swindon Town were promoted through the play-offs. However, they were then immediately relegated for financial irregularities and their promotion place was taken by Sunderland.

Division Two Play-offs

Blackburn Rovers vs Swindon Town	1-2, 1-2
Sunderland vs Newcastle United	0-0, 2-0
Swindon Town vs Sunderland	1-0

1990 F.A. Cup

Semi-finals

Crystal Palace vs Liverpool	4-3
Manchester United vs Oldham Athletic	3-3, 2-1

Final

Wembley, 12th May 1990

Manchester United 3 (Robson, Hughes 2)
Crystal Palace 3 (aet.) (O'Reilly, Wright 2)

Attendance 80,000

Replay

Wembley, 17th May 1990

Manchester United 1 (Martin)
Crystal Palace 0

Attendance 80,000

DIVISION THREE 1989-90

Bristol Rovers	**46**	**26**	**15**	**5**	**71**	**35**	**93**
Bristol City	**46**	**27**	**10**	**9**	**76**	**40**	**91**
Notts County	**46**	**25**	**12**	**9**	**73**	**53**	**87**
Tranmere Rovers	46	23	11	12	86	49	80
Bury	46	21	11	14	70	49	74
Bolton Wanderers	46	18	15	13	59	48	69
Birmingham City	46	18	12	16	60	59	66
Huddersfield Town	46	17	14	15	61	62	65
Rotherham United	46	17	13	16	71	62	64
Reading	46	15	19	12	57	53	64
Shrewsbury Town	46	16	15	15	59	54	63
Crewe Alexandra	46	15	17	14	56	53	62
Brentford	46	18	7	21	66	66	61
Leyton Orient	46	16	10	20	52	56	58
Mansfield Town	46	16	7	23	50	65	55
Chester City	46	13	15	18	43	55	54
Swansea City	46	14	12	20	45	63	54
Wigan Athletic	46	13	14	19	48	64	53
Preston North End	46	14	10	22	65	79	52
Fulham	46	12	15	19	55	66	51
Cardiff City	*46*	*12*	*14*	*20*	*51*	*70*	*50*
Northampton Town	*46*	*11*	*14*	*21*	*51*	*68*	*47*
Blackpool	*46*	*10*	*16*	*20*	*49*	*73*	*46*
Walsall	*46*	*9*	*14*	*23*	*40*	*72*	*41*

Division Three Play-offs

Bolton Wanderers vs Notts County	1-1, 0-2
Bury vs Tranmere Rovers	0-0, 0-2
Notts County vs Tranmere Rovers	2-0

DIVISION FOUR 1989-90

Exeter City	**46**	**28**	**5**	**13**	**83**	**48**	**89**
Grimsby Town	**46**	**22**	**13**	**11**	**70**	**47**	**79**
Southend United	**46**	**22**	**9**	**15**	**61**	**48**	**75**
Stockport County	46	21	11	14	68	62	74
Maidstone United	46	22	7	17	77	61	73
Cambridge United	**46**	**21**	**10**	**15**	**76**	**66**	**73**
Chesterfield	46	19	14	13	63	50	71
Carlisle United	46	21	8	17	61	60	71
Peterborough United	46	17	17	12	59	46	68
Lincoln City	46	18	14	14	48	48	68
Scunthorpe United	46	17	15	14	69	54	66
Rochdale	46	20	6	20	52	55	66
York City	46	16	16	14	55	53	64
Gillingham	46	17	11	18	46	48	62
Torquay United	46	15	12	19	53	66	57
Burnley	46	14	14	18	45	55	56
Hereford United	46	15	10	21	56	62	55
Scarborough	46	15	10	21	60	73	55
Hartlepool United	46	15	10	21	66	88	55
Doncaster Rovers	46	14	9	23	53	60	51
Wrexham	46	13	12	21	51	67	51
Aldershot	46	12	14	20	49	69	50
Halifax Town	46	12	13	21	57	65	49
Colchester United	*46*	*11*	*10*	*25*	*48*	*75*	*43*

Division Four Play-offs

Cambridge United vs Maidstone United	1-1, 2-0
Chesterfield vs Stockport County	4-0, 2-0
Cambridge United vs Chesterfield	1-0

1990 Football League Cup

Semi-finals

Nottingham Forest vs Coventry City (2-1, 0-0)	2-1
Oldham Athletic vs West Ham United (6-0, 0-3)	6-3

Final

Wembley, 29th April 1990

Nottingham Forest 1 (Jemson)
Oldham Athletic 0

Attendance 74,343

DIVISION ONE 1990-91

ARSENAL	38	24	13	1	74	18	83
Liverpool	38	23	7	8	77	40	76
Crystal Palace	38	20	9	9	50	41	69
Leeds United	38	19	7	12	65	47	64
Manchester City	38	17	11	10	64	53	62
Manchester United	38	16	12	10	58	45	60
Wimbledon	38	14	14	10	53	46	56
Nottingham Forest	38	14	12	12	65	50	54
Everton	38	13	12	13	50	46	51
Tottenham Hotspur	38	11	16	11	51	50	49
Chelsea	38	13	10	15	58	69	49
Queen's Park Rangers	38	12	10	16	44	53	46
Sheffield United	38	13	7	18	36	55	46
Southampton	38	12	9	17	58	69	45
Norwich City	38	13	6	19	41	64	45
Coventry City	38	11	11	16	42	49	44
Aston Villa	38	9	14	15	46	58	41
Luton Town	*38*	*10*	*7*	*21*	*42*	*61*	*37*
Sunderland	*38*	*8*	*10*	*20*	*38*	*60*	*34*
Derby County	*38*	*5*	*9*	*24*	*37*	*75*	*24*

Arsenal had 2 points deducted
Manchester United had 1 point deducted

DIVISION TWO 1990-91

Oldham Athletic	46	25	13	8	83	53	88
West Ham United	46	24	15	7	60	34	87
Sheffield Wednesday	46	22	16	8	80	51	82
Notts County	46	23	11	12	76	55	80
Millwall	46	20	13	13	70	51	73
Brighton & Hove Albion	46	21	7	18	63	69	70
Middlesbrough	46	20	9	17	66	47	69
Barnsley	46	19	12	15	63	48	69
Bristol City	46	20	7	19	68	71	67
Oxford United	46	14	19	13	69	66	61
Newcastle United	46	14	17	15	49	56	59
Wolverhampton Wanderers	46	13	19	14	63	63	58
Bristol Rovers	46	15	13	18	56	59	58
Ipswich Town	46	13	18	15	60	68	57
Port Vale	46	15	12	19	56	64	57
Charlton Athletic	46	13	17	16	57	61	56
Portsmouth	46	14	11	21	58	70	53
Plymouth Argyle	46	12	17	17	54	68	53
Blackburn Rovers	46	14	10	22	51	66	52
Watford	46	12	15	19	45	59	51
Swindon Town	46	12	14	20	65	73	50
Leicester City	46	14	8	24	60	83	50
West Bromwich Albion	*46*	*10*	*18*	*18*	*52*	*61*	*48*
Hull City	*46*	*10*	*15*	*21*	*57*	*85*	*45*

Division Two Play-offs

Brighton & Hove Albion vs Millwall	4-1, 2-1
Middlesbrough vs Notts County	1-1, 0-1
Notts County vs Brighton & Hove Albion	3-1

1991 F.A. Cup

Semi-finals

Arsenal vs Tottenham Hotspur	1-3
Nottingham Forest vs West Ham United	4-0

Final

Wembley, 18th May 1991

Tottenham Hotspur 2　(Stewart, Walker (og))
Nottingham Forest 1　(Pearce)

Attendance 80,000

DIVISION THREE 1990-91

Cambridge United	46	25	11	10	75	45	86
Southend United	46	26	7	13	67	51	85
Grimsby Town	46	24	11	11	66	34	83
Bolton Wanderers	46	24	11	11	64	50	83
Tranmere Rovers	46	23	9	14	64	46	78
Brentford	46	21	13	12	59	47	76
Bury	46	20	13	13	67	56	73
Bradford City	46	20	10	16	62	54	70
Bournemouth	46	19	13	14	58	58	70
Wigan Athletic	46	20	9	17	71	54	69
Huddersfield Town	46	18	13	15	57	51	67
Birmingham City	46	16	17	13	45	49	65
Leyton Orient	46	18	10	18	55	58	64
Stoke City	46	16	12	18	55	59	60
Reading	46	17	8	21	53	66	59
Exeter City	46	16	9	21	58	52	57
Preston North End	46	15	11	20	54	67	56
Shrewsbury Town	46	14	10	22	61	68	52
Chester City	46	14	9	23	46	58	51
Swansea City	46	13	9	24	49	72	48
Fulham	46	16	10	20	41	56	46
Crewe Alexandra	*46*	*11*	*11*	*24*	*62*	*80*	*44*
Rotherham United	*46*	*10*	*12*	*24*	*50*	*87*	*42*
Mansfield Town	*46*	*8*	*14*	*24*	*42*	*63*	*38*

Division Three Play-offs

Brentford vs Tranmere Rovers	2-2, 0-1
Bury vs Bolton Wanderers	1-1, 0-1
Tranmere Rovers vs Bolton Wanderers	1-0

DIVISION FOUR 1990-91

Darlington	46	22	17	7	68	38	83
Stockport County	46	23	13	10	84	47	82
Hartlepool United	46	24	10	12	67	48	82
Peterborough United	46	21	17	8	67	45	80
Blackpool	46	23	10	13	78	47	79
Burnley	46	23	10	13	70	51	79
Torquay United	46	18	18	10	64	47	72
Scunthorpe United	46	20	11	15	71	62	71
Scarborough	46	19	12	15	59	56	69
Northampton Town	46	18	13	15	57	58	67
Doncaster Rovers	46	17	14	15	56	46	65
Rochdale	46	15	17	14	50	53	62
Cardiff City	46	15	15	16	43	54	60
Lincoln City	46	14	17	15	50	61	59
Gillingham	46	12	18	16	57	60	54
Walsall	46	12	17	17	48	51	53
Hereford United	46	13	14	19	53	58	53
Chesterfield	46	13	14	19	47	62	53
Maidstone United	46	13	12	21	66	71	51
Carlisle United	46	13	9	24	47	89	48
York City	46	11	13	22	45	57	46
Halifax Town	46	12	10	24	59	79	46
Aldershot	46	10	11	25	61	101	41
Wrexham	46	10	10	26	48	74	40

Division Four Play-offs

Scunthorpe United vs Blackpool	1-1, 1-2
Torquay United vs Burnley	2-0, 0-1
Torquay United vs Blackpool	2-2
Torquay United won 5-4 on penalties	

1991 Football League Cup

Semi-finals

Manchester United vs Leeds United (2-1, 1-0)	3-1
Chelsea vs Sheffield Wednesday (0-2, 1-3)	1-5

Final

Wembley, 21st April 1991

Sheffield Wednesday 1　(Sheridan)
Manchester United 0

Attendance 80,000

DIVISION ONE 1991-92

LEEDS UNITED	**42**	**22**	**16**	**4**	**74**	**37**	**82**
Manchester United	42	21	15	6	63	33	78
Sheffield Wednesday	42	21	12	9	62	49	75
Arsenal	42	19	15	8	81	46	72
Manchester City	42	20	10	12	61	48	70
Liverpool	42	16	16	10	47	40	64
Aston Villa	42	17	9	16	48	44	60
Nottingham Forest	42	16	11	15	60	58	59
Sheffield United	42	16	9	17	65	63	57
Crystal Palace	42	14	15	13	53	61	57
Queen's Park Rangers	42	12	18	12	48	47	54
Everton	42	13	14	15	52	51	53
Wimbledon	42	13	14	15	53	53	53
Chelsea	42	13	14	15	50	60	53
Tottenham Hotspur	42	15	7	20	58	63	52
Southampton	42	14	10	18	39	55	52
Oldham Athletic	42	14	9	19	63	67	51
Norwich City	42	11	12	19	47	63	45
Coventry City	42	11	11	20	35	44	44
Luton Town	*42*	*10*	*12*	*20*	*38*	*71*	*42*
Notts County	*42*	*10*	*10*	*22*	*40*	*62*	*40*
West Ham United	*42*	*9*	*11*	*22*	*37*	*59*	*38*

DIVISION TWO 1991-92

Ipswich Town	**46**	**24**	**12**	**10**	**70**	**50**	**84**
Middlesbrough	**46**	**23**	**11**	**12**	**58**	**41**	**80**
Derby County	46	23	9	14	69	51	78
Leicester City	46	23	8	15	62	55	77
Cambridge United	46	19	17	10	65	47	74
Blackburn Rovers	**46**	**21**	**11**	**14**	**70**	**53**	**74**
Charlton Athletic	46	20	11	15	54	48	71
Swindon Town	46	18	15	13	69	55	69
Portsmouth	46	19	12	15	65	51	69
Watford	46	18	11	17	51	48	65
Wolverhampton Wanderers	46	18	10	18	61	54	64
Southend United	46	17	11	18	63	63	62
Bristol Rovers	46	16	14	16	60	63	62
Tranmere Rovers	46	14	19	13	56	56	61
Millwall	46	17	10	19	64	71	61
Barnsley	46	16	11	19	46	57	59
Bristol City	46	13	15	18	55	71	54
Sunderland	46	14	11	21	61	65	53
Grimsby Town	46	14	11	21	47	62	53
Newcastle United	46	13	13	20	66	84	52
Oxford United	46	13	11	22	66	73	50
Plymouth Argyle	*46*	*13*	*9*	*24*	*42*	*64*	*48*
Brighton & Hove Albion	*46*	*12*	*11*	*23*	*56*	*77*	*47*
Port Vale	*46*	*10*	*15*	*21*	*42*	*59*	*45*

Division Two Play-offs

Blackburn Rovers vs Derby County	4-2, 1-2
Cambridge United vs Leicester City	1-1, 0-5
Blackburn Rovers vs Leicester City	1-0

1992 F.A. Cup

Semi-finals

Liverpool vs Portsmouth	1-1, 0-0
Liverpool won 3-1 on penalties	
Sunderland vs Norwich	1-0

Final

Wembley, 9th May 1992

Liverpool 2   (Thomas, I. Rush)

Sunderland 0

Attendance 79,544

DIVISION THREE 1991-92

Brentford	**46**	**25**	**7**	**14**	**81**	**55**	**82**
Birmingham City	**46**	**23**	**12**	**11**	**69**	**52**	**81**
Huddersfield Town	46	22	12	12	59	38	78
Stoke City	46	21	14	11	69	49	77
Stockport County	46	22	10	14	75	51	76
Peterborough United	**46**	**20**	**14**	**12**	**65**	**58**	**74**
West Bromwich Albion	46	19	14	13	64	49	71
Bournemouth	46	20	11	15	52	48	71
Fulham	46	19	13	14	57	53	70
Leyton Orient	46	18	11	17	62	52	65
Hartlepool United	46	18	11	17	57	57	65
Reading	46	16	13	17	59	62	61
Bolton Wanderers	46	14	17	15	57	56	59
Hull City	46	16	11	19	54	54	59
Wigan Athletic	46	15	14	17	58	64	59
Bradford City	46	13	19	14	62	61	58
Preston North End	46	15	12	19	61	72	57
Chester City	46	14	14	18	56	59	56
Swansea City	46	14	14	18	55	65	56
Exeter City	46	14	11	21	57	80	53
Bury	*46*	*13*	*12*	*21*	*55*	*74*	*51*
Shrewsbury Town	*46*	*12*	*11*	*23*	*53*	*68*	*47*
Torquay United	*46*	*13*	*8*	*25*	*42*	*68*	*47*
Darlington	*46*	*10*	*7*	*29*	*56*	*90*	*37*

Division Three Play-offs

Stockport County vs Stoke City	1-0, 1-1	
Peterborough United vs Huddersfield Town	2-2, 2-1	
Peterborough United vs Stockport County		2-1

DIVISION FOUR 1991-92

Burnley	**42**	**25**	**8**	**9**	**79**	**43**	**83**
Rotherham United	**42**	**22**	**11**	**9**	**70**	**37**	**77**
Mansfield Town	**42**	**23**	**8**	**11**	**75**	**53**	**77**
Blackpool	**42**	**22**	**10**	**10**	**71**	**45**	**76**
Scunthorpe United	42	21	9	12	64	59	72
Crewe Alexandra	42	20	10	12	66	51	70
Barnet	42	21	6	15	81	61	69
Rochdale	42	18	13	11	57	53	67
Cardiff City	42	17	15	10	66	53	66
Lincoln City	42	17	11	14	50	44	62
Gillingham	42	15	12	15	63	53	57
Scarborough	42	15	12	15	64	68	57
Chesterfield	42	14	11	17	49	61	53
Wrexham	42	14	9	19	52	73	51
Walsall	42	12	13	17	48	58	49
Northampton Town	42	11	13	18	46	57	46
Hereford United	42	12	8	22	44	57	44
Maidstone United	42	8	18	16	45	56	42
York City	42	8	16	18	42	58	40
Halifax Town	42	10	8	24	34	75	38
Doncaster Rovers	42	9	8	25	40	65	35
Carlisle United	42	7	13	22	41	67	34

Aldershot were declared bankrupt and obliged to resign from
the League after playing 36 matches, the results of which were
declared void.

Division Four Play-offs

Barnet vs Blackpool	1-0, 0-2	
Crewe Alexandra vs Scunthorpe United	2-2, 0-2	
Blackpool vs Scunthorpe United		1-1
Blackpool won 4-3 on penalties		

1992 Football League Cup

Semi-finals

Nottingham Forest vs Tottenham Hotspur (1-1, 2-1)		3-2
Middlesbrough vs Manchester United (0-0, 1-2)		1-2

Final

Wembley, 12th April 1992

Manchester United 1   (McClair)

Nottingham Forest 0

Attendance 76,810

F.A. PREMIER LEAGUE 1992-93

MANCHESTER UNITED	42	24	12	6	67	31	84
Aston Villa	42	21	11	10	57	40	74
Norwich City	42	21	9	12	61	65	72
Blackburn Rovers	42	20	11	11	68	46	71
Queen's Park Rangers	42	17	12	13	63	55	63
Liverpool	42	16	11	15	62	55	59
Sheffield Wednesday	42	15	14	13	55	51	59
Tottenham Hotspur	42	16	11	15	60	66	59
Manchester City	42	15	12	15	56	51	57
Arsenal	42	15	11	16	40	38	56
Chelsea	42	14	14	14	51	54	56
Wimbledon	42	14	12	16	56	55	54
Everton	42	15	8	19	53	55	53
Sheffield United	42	14	10	18	54	53	52
Coventry City	42	13	13	16	52	57	52
Ipswich Town	42	12	16	14	50	55	52
Leeds United	42	12	15	15	57	62	51
Southampton	42	13	11	18	54	61	50
Oldham Athletic	42	13	10	19	63	74	49
Crystal Palace	*42*	*11*	*16*	*15*	*48*	*61*	*49*
Middlesbrough	*42*	*11*	*11*	*20*	*54*	*75*	*44*
Nottingham Forest	*42*	*10*	*10*	*22*	*41*	*62*	*40*

DIVISION ONE 1992-93

Newcastle United	46	29	9	8	92	38	96
West Ham United	46	26	10	10	81	41	88
Portsmouth	46	26	10	10	80	46	88
Tranmere Rovers	46	23	10	13	72	56	79
Swindon Town	46	21	13	12	74	59	76
Leicester City	46	22	10	14	71	64	76
Millwall	46	18	16	12	65	53	70
Derby County	46	19	9	18	68	57	66
Grimsby Town	46	19	7	20	58	57	64
Peterborough United	46	16	14	16	55	63	62
Wolverhampton Wanderers	46	16	13	17	57	56	61
Charlton Athletic	46	16	13	17	49	46	61
Barnsley	46	17	9	20	56	60	60
Oxford United	46	14	14	18	53	56	56
Bristol City	46	14	14	18	49	67	56
Watford	46	14	13	19	57	71	55
Notts County	46	12	16	18	55	70	52
Southend United	46	13	13	20	54	64	52
Birmingham City	46	13	12	21	50	72	51
Luton Town	46	10	21	15	48	62	51
Sunderland	46	13	11	22	50	64	50
Brentford	*46*	*13*	*10*	*23*	*52*	*71*	*49*
Cambridge United	*46*	*11*	*16*	*19*	*48*	*69*	*49*
Bristol Rovers	*46*	*10*	*11*	*25*	*55*	*87*	*41*

Division One Play-offs

Leicester City vs Portsmouth	1-0, 2-2
Swindon Town vs Tranmere Rovers	3-1, 2-3
Swindon Town vs Leicester City	4-3

1993 F.A. Cup

Semi-finals

Sheffield United vs Sheffield Wednesday	1-2
Arsenal vs Tottenham Hotspur	1-0

Final

Wembley, 15th May 1993

Arsenal 1 (Wright)
Sheffield Wednesday 1 (aet.) (Hirst)

Attendance 79,347

Replay

Wembley, 20th May 1993

Arsenal 2 (Wright, Linighan)
Sheffield Wednesday 1 (aet.) (Waddle)

Attendance 62,267

DIVISION TWO 1992-93

Stoke City	46	27	12	7	73	34	93
Bolton Wanderers	46	27	9	10	80	41	90
Port Vale	46	26	11	9	79	44	89
West Bromwich Albion	46	25	10	11	88	54	85
Swansea City	46	20	13	13	65	47	73
Stockport County	46	19	15	12	81	57	72
Leyton Orient	46	21	9	16	69	53	72
Reading	46	18	15	13	66	51	69
Brighton & Hove Albion	46	20	9	17	63	59	69
Bradford City	46	18	14	14	69	67	68
Rotherham United	46	17	14	15	60	60	65
Fulham	46	16	17	13	57	55	65
Burnley	46	15	16	15	57	59	61
Plymouth Argyle	46	16	12	18	59	64	60
Huddersfield Town	46	17	9	20	54	61	60
Hartlepool United	46	14	12	20	42	60	54
Bournemouth	46	12	17	17	45	52	53
Blackpool	46	12	15	19	63	75	51
Exeter City	46	11	17	18	54	69	50
Hull City	46	13	11	22	46	69	50
Preston North End	*46*	*13*	*8*	*25*	*65*	*94*	*47*
Mansfield Town	*46*	*11*	*11*	*24*	*52*	*80*	*44*
Wigan Athletic	*46*	*10*	*11*	*25*	*43*	*72*	*41*
Chester City	*46*	*8*	*5*	*33*	*49*	*102*	*29*

Division Two Play-offs

Stockport County vs Port Vale	1-1, 0-1
Swansea City vs West Bromwich Albion	2-1, 0-2
West Bromwich Albion vs Port Vale	3-0

DIVISION THREE 1992-93

Cardiff City	42	25	8	9	77	47	83
Wrexham	42	23	11	8	75	52	80
Barnet	42	23	10	9	66	48	79
York City	42	21	12	9	72	45	75
Walsall	42	22	7	13	76	61	73
Crewe Alexandra	42	21	7	14	75	56	70
Bury	42	18	9	15	63	55	63
Lincoln City	42	18	9	15	57	53	63
Shrewsbury Town	42	17	11	14	57	52	62
Colchester United	42	18	5	19	67	76	59
Rochdale	42	16	10	16	70	70	58
Chesterfield	42	15	11	16	59	63	56
Scarborough	42	15	9	18	66	71	54
Scunthorpe United	42	14	12	16	57	54	54
Darlington	42	12	14	16	48	53	50
Doncaster Rovers	42	11	14	17	42	57	47
Hereford United	42	10	15	17	47	60	45
Carlisle United	42	11	11	20	51	65	44
Torquay United	42	12	7	23	45	67	43
Northampton Town	42	11	8	23	48	74	41
Gillingham	42	9	13	20	48	64	40
Halifax Town	*42*	*9*	*9*	*24*	*45*	*68*	*36*

Maidstone United were declared bankrupt

Division Three Play-offs

Bury vs York City	0-0, 0-1
Crewe Alexandra vs Walsall	5-1, 4-2
York City vs Crewe Alexandra	1-1

York City won 5-3 on penalties

1993 Football League Cup

Semi-finals

Crystal Palace vs Arsenal (1-3, 0-2)	1-5
Blackburn Rovers vs Sheffield Wednesday (2-4, 1-2)	3-6

Final

Wembley, 18th April 1993

Arsenal 2 (Merson, Morrow)
Sheffield Wednesday 1 (Harkes)

Attendance 74,007

F.A. PREMIER LEAGUE 1993-94

MANCHESTER UNITED	42	27	11	4	80	38	92
Blackburn Rovers	42	25	9	8	63	36	84
Newcastle United	42	23	8	11	82	41	77
Arsenal	42	18	17	7	53	28	71
Leeds United	42	18	16	8	65	39	70
Wimbledon	42	18	11	13	56	53	65
Sheffield Wednesday	42	16	16	10	76	54	64
Liverpool	42	17	9	16	59	55	60
Queen's Park Rangers	42	16	12	14	62	61	60
Aston Villa	42	15	12	15	46	50	57
Coventry City	42	14	14	14	43	45	56
Norwich City	42	12	17	13	65	61	53
West Ham United	42	13	13	16	47	58	52
Chelsea	42	13	12	17	49	53	51
Tottenham Hotspur	42	11	12	19	54	59	45
Manchester City	42	9	18	15	38	49	45
Everton	42	12	8	22	42	63	44
Southampton	42	12	7	23	49	66	43
Ipswich Town	42	9	16	17	35	58	43
Sheffield United	*42*	*8*	*18*	*16*	*42*	*60*	*42*
Oldham Athletic	*42*	*9*	*13*	*20*	*42*	*68*	*40*
Swindon Town	*42*	*5*	*15*	*22*	*47*	*100*	*30*

DIVISION ONE 1993-94

Crystal Palace	46	27	9	10	73	46	90
Nottingham Forest	46	23	14	9	74	49	83
Millwall	46	19	17	10	58	49	74
Leicester City	46	19	16	11	72	59	73
Tranmere Rovers	46	21	9	16	69	53	72
Derby County	46	20	11	15	73	68	71
Notts County	46	20	8	18	65	69	68
Wolverhampton Wanderers	46	17	17	12	60	47	68
Middlesbrough	46	18	13	15	66	54	67
Stoke City	46	18	13	15	57	59	67
Charlton Athletic	46	19	8	19	61	58	65
Sunderland	46	19	8	19	54	57	65
Bristol City	46	16	16	14	47	50	64
Bolton Wanderers	46	15	14	17	63	64	59
Southend United	46	17	8	21	63	67	59
Grimsby Town	46	13	20	13	52	47	59
Portsmouth	46	15	13	18	52	58	58
Barnsley	46	16	7	23	55	67	55
Watford	46	15	9	22	66	80	54
Luton Town	46	14	11	21	56	60	53
West Bromwich Albion	46	13	12	21	60	69	51
Birmingham City	*46*	*13*	*12*	*21*	*52*	*69*	*51*
Oxford United	*46*	*13*	*10*	*23*	*54*	*75*	*49*
Peterborough United	*46*	*8*	*13*	*25*	*48*	*76*	*37*

Division One Play-offs

Derby County vs Millwall	2-0, 3-1
Tranmere Rovers vs Leicester City	0-0, 1-2
Leicester City vs Derby County	2-1

DIVISION TWO 1993-94

Reading	46	26	11	9	81	44	89
Port Vale	46	26	10	10	79	46	88
Plymouth Argyle	46	25	10	11	88	56	85
Stockport County	46	24	13	9	74	44	85
York City	46	21	12	13	64	40	75
Burnley	46	21	10	15	79	58	73
Bradford City	46	19	13	14	61	53	70
Bristol Rovers	46	20	10	16	60	59	70
Hull City	46	18	14	14	62	54	68
Cambridge United	46	19	9	18	79	73	66
Huddersfield Town	46	17	14	15	58	61	65
Wrexham	46	17	11	18	66	77	62
Swansea City	46	16	12	18	56	58	60
Brighton & Hove Albion	46	15	14	17	60	67	59
Rotherham United	46	15	13	18	63	60	58
Brentford	46	13	19	14	57	55	58
Bournemouth	46	14	15	17	51	59	57
Leyton Orient	46	14	14	18	57	71	56
Cardiff City	46	13	15	18	66	79	54
Blackpool	46	16	5	25	63	75	53
Fulham	46	14	10	22	50	63	52
Exeter City	46	11	12	23	52	83	45
Hartlepool United	46	9	9	28	41	87	36
Barnet	46	5	13	28	41	86	28

Division Two Play-offs

Burnley vs Plymouth Argyle	0-0, 3-1
York City vs Stockport County	0-0, 0-1
Burnley vs Stockport County	2-1

DIVISION THREE 1993-94

Shrewsbury Town	42	22	13	7	63	39	79
Chester City	42	21	11	10	69	46	74
Crewe Alexandra	42	21	10	11	80	61	73
Wycombe Wanderers	42	19	13	10	67	53	70
Preston North End	42	18	13	11	79	60	67
Torquay United	42	17	16	9	64	56	67
Carlisle United	42	18	10	14	57	42	64
Chesterfield	42	16	14	12	55	48	62
Rochdale	42	16	12	14	63	51	60
Walsall	42	17	9	16	48	53	60
Scunthorpe United	42	15	14	13	64	56	59
Mansfield Town	42	15	10	17	53	62	55
Bury	42	14	11	17	55	56	53
Scarborough	42	15	8	19	55	61	53
Doncaster Rovers	42	14	10	18	44	57	52
Gillingham	42	12	15	15	44	51	51
Colchester United	42	13	10	19	56	71	49
Lincoln City	42	12	11	19	52	63	47
Wigan Athletic	42	11	12	19	51	70	45
Hereford United	42	12	6	24	60	79	42
Darlington	42	10	11	21	42	64	41
Northampton Town	42	9	11	22	44	66	38

Division Three Play-offs

Carlisle United vs Wycombe Wanderers	0-2, 1-2
Torquay United vs Preston North End	2-0, 1-4
Wycombe Wanderers vs Preston North End	4-2

1994 F.A. Cup

Semi-finals

Chelsea vs Luton Town	2-0
Manchester United vs Oldham Athletic	1-1, 4-1

Final

Wembley, 14th May 1994

Manchester United 4 (Cantona 2 (2 pens), Hughes, McClair)

Chelsea 0

Attendance 79,634

1994 Football League Cup

Semi-finals

Manchester Utd. vs Sheffield Wednesday (1-0, 4-1)	5-1
Tranmere Rovers vs Aston Villa (3-1, 1-3)	4-4
Aston Villa won 5-4 on penalties	

Final

Wembley, 27th March 1994

Aston Villa 3 (Atkinson, Saunders 2 (1 pen))

Manchester United 1 (Hughes)

Attendance 77,231

F.A. PREMIER LEAGUE 1994-95

BLACKBURN ROVERS	42	27	8	7	80	39	89
Manchester United	42	26	10	6	77	28	88
Nottingham Forest	42	22	11	9	72	43	77
Liverpool	42	21	11	10	65	37	74
Leeds United	42	20	13	9	59	38	73
Newcastle United	42	20	12	10	67	47	72
Tottenham Hotspur	42	16	14	12	66	58	62
Queen's Park Rangers	42	17	9	16	61	59	60
Wimbledon	42	15	11	16	48	65	56
Southampton	42	12	18	12	61	63	54
Chelsea	42	13	15	14	50	55	54
Arsenal	42	13	12	17	52	49	51
Sheffield Wednesday	42	13	12	17	49	57	51
West Ham United	42	13	11	18	44	48	50
Everton	42	11	17	14	44	51	50
Coventry City	42	12	14	16	44	62	50
Manchester City	42	12	13	17	53	64	49
Aston Villa	42	11	15	16	51	56	48
Crystal Palace	*42*	*11*	*12*	*19*	*34*	*49*	*45*
Norwich City	*42*	*10*	*13*	*19*	*37*	*54*	*43*
Leicester City	*42*	*6*	*11*	*25*	*45*	*80*	*29*
Ipswich Town	*42*	*7*	*6*	*29*	*36*	*93*	*27*

DIVISION ONE 1994-95

Middlesbrough	46	23	13	10	67	40	82
Reading	46	23	10	13	58	44	79
Bolton Wanderers	46	21	14	11	67	45	77
Wolverhampton Wanderers	46	21	13	12	77	61	76
Tranmere Rovers	46	22	10	14	67	58	76
Barnsley	46	20	12	14	63	52	72
Watford	46	19	13	14	52	46	70
Sheffield United	46	17	17	12	74	55	68
Derby County	46	18	12	16	66	51	66
Grimsby Town	46	17	14	15	62	56	65
Stoke City	46	16	15	15	50	53	63
Millwall	46	16	14	16	60	60	62
Southend United	46	18	8	20	54	73	62
Oldham Athletic	46	16	13	17	60	60	61
Charlton Athletic	46	16	11	19	58	66	59
Luton Town	46	15	13	18	61	64	58
Port Vale	46	15	13	18	58	64	58
Portsmouth	46	15	13	18	53	63	58
West Bromwich Albion	46	16	10	20	51	57	58
Sunderland	46	12	18	16	41	45	54
Swindon Town	*46*	*12*	*12*	*22*	*54*	*73*	*48*
Burnley	*46*	*11*	*13*	*22*	*49*	*74*	*46*
Bristol City	*46*	*11*	*12*	*23*	*42*	*63*	*45*
Notts County	*46*	*9*	*13*	*24*	*45*	*66*	*40*

Division One Play-offs

Tranmere Rovers vs Reading	1-3, 0-0
Wolverhampton Wanderers vs Bolton Wanderers	2-1, 0-2
Bolton Wanderers vs Reading	4-3

1995 F.A. Cup

Semi-finals

Crystal Palace vs Manchester United	2-2, 0-2
Everton vs Tottenham Hotspur	4-1

Final

Wembley, 20th May 1995

Everton 1 (Rideout)

Manchester United 0

Attendance 79,592

DIVISION TWO 1994-95

Birmingham City	46	25	14	7	84	37	89
Brentford	46	25	10	11	81	39	85
Crewe Alexandra	46	25	8	13	80	68	84
Bristol Rovers	46	22	16	8	70	40	82
Huddersfield Town	46	22	15	9	79	49	81
Wycombe Wanderers	46	21	15	10	60	46	78
Oxford United	46	21	12	13	66	52	75
Hull City	46	21	11	14	70	57	74
York City	46	21	9	16	67	51	72
Swansea City	46	19	14	13	57	45	71
Stockport County	46	19	8	19	63	60	65
Blackpool	46	18	10	18	64	70	64
Wrexham	46	16	15	15	65	64	63
Bradford City	46	16	12	18	57	64	60
Peterborough United	46	14	18	14	54	69	60
Brighton & Hove Albion	46	14	17	15	54	53	59
Rotherham United	46	14	14	18	57	61	56
Shrewsbury Town	46	13	14	19	54	62	53
Bournemouth	46	13	11	22	49	69	50
Cambridge United	*46*	*11*	*15*	*20*	*52*	*69*	*48*
Plymouth Argyle	*46*	*12*	*10*	*24*	*45*	*83*	*46*
Cardiff City	*46*	*9*	*11*	*26*	*46*	*74*	*38*
Chester City	*46*	*6*	*11*	*29*	*37*	*84*	*29*
Leyton Orient	*46*	*6*	*8*	*32*	*30*	*75*	*26*

Division Two Play-offs

Bristol Rovers vs Crewe Alexandra	0-0, 1-1
Bristol Rovers won on away goals	
Huddersfield Town vs Brentford	1-1, 1-1
Huddersfield Town won 4-3 on penalties	
Huddersfield Town vs Bristol Rovers	2-1

DIVISION THREE 1994-95

Carlisle United	42	27	10	5	67	31	91
Walsall	42	24	11	7	75	40	83
Chesterfield	42	23	12	7	62	37	81
Bury	42	23	11	8	73	36	80
Preston North End	42	19	10	13	58	41	67
Mansfield Town	42	18	11	13	84	59	65
Scunthorpe United	42	18	8	16	68	63	62
Fulham	42	16	14	12	60	54	62
Doncaster Rovers	42	17	10	15	58	43	61
Colchester United	42	16	10	16	56	64	58
Barnet	42	15	11	16	56	63	56
Lincoln City	42	15	11	16	54	55	56
Torquay United	42	14	13	15	54	57	55
Wigan Athletic	42	14	10	18	53	60	52
Rochdale	42	12	14	16	44	67	50
Hereford United	42	12	13	17	45	62	49
Northampton Town	42	10	14	18	45	67	44
Hartlepool United	42	11	10	21	43	69	43
Gillingham	42	10	11	21	46	64	41
Darlington	42	11	8	23	43	57	41
Scarborough	42	8	10	24	49	70	34
Exeter City	42	8	10	24	36	70	34

Division Three Play-offs

Mansfield Town vs Chesterfield	1-1, 2-5
Preston North End vs Bury	0-1, 0-1
Chesterfield vs Bury	2-0

1995 Football League Cup

Semi-finals

Liverpool vs Crystal Palace (1-0, 1-0)	2-0
Swindon Town vs Bolton Wanderers (2-1, 1-3)	3-4

Final

Wembley, 2nd April 1995

Liverpool 2 (McManaman 2)

Bolton Wanderers 1 (Thompson)

Attendance 75,595

F.A. PREMIER LEAGUE 1995-96

MANCHESTER UNITED	38	25	7	6	73	35	82
Newcastle United	38	24	6	8	66	37	78
Liverpool	38	20	11	7	70	34	71
Aston Villa	38	18	9	11	52	35	63
Arsenal	38	17	12	9	49	32	63
Everton	38	17	10	11	64	44	61
Blackburn Rovers	38	18	7	13	61	47	61
Tottenham Hotspur	38	16	13	9	50	38	61
Nottingham Forest	38	15	13	10	50	54	58
West Ham United	38	14	9	15	43	52	51
Chelsea	38	12	14	12	46	44	50
Middlesbrough	38	11	10	17	35	50	43
Leeds United	38	12	7	19	40	57	43
Wimbledon	38	10	11	17	55	70	41
Sheffield Wednesday	38	10	10	18	48	61	40
Coventry City	38	8	14	16	42	60	38
Southampton	38	9	11	18	34	52	38
Manchester City	*38*	*9*	*11*	*18*	*33*	*58*	*38*
Queen's Park Rangers	*38*	*9*	*6*	*23*	*38*	*57*	*33*
Bolton Wanderers	*38*	*8*	*5*	*25*	*39*	*71*	*29*

DIVISION ONE 1995-96

Sunderland	46	22	17	7	59	33	83
Derby County	46	21	16	9	71	51	79
Crystal Palace	46	20	15	11	67	48	75
Stoke City	46	20	13	13	60	49	73
Leicester City	46	19	14	13	66	60	71
Charlton Athletic	46	17	20	9	57	45	71
Ipswich Town	46	19	12	15	79	69	69
Huddersfield Town	46	17	12	17	61	58	63
Sheffield United	46	16	14	16	57	54	62
Barnsley	46	14	18	14	60	66	60
West Bromwich Albion	46	16	12	18	60	68	60
Port Vale	46	15	15	16	59	66	60
Tranmere Rovers	46	14	17	15	64	60	59
Southend United	46	15	14	17	52	61	59
Birmingham City	46	15	13	18	61	64	58
Norwich City	46	14	15	17	59	55	57
Grimsby Town	46	14	14	18	55	69	56
Oldham Athletic	46	14	14	18	54	50	56
Reading	46	13	17	16	54	63	56
Wolverhampton Wanderers	46	13	16	17	56	62	55
Portsmouth	46	13	13	20	61	69	52
Millwall	*46*	*13*	*13*	*20*	*43*	*63*	*52*
Watford	*46*	*10*	*18*	*18*	*62*	*70*	*48*
Luton Town	*46*	*11*	*12*	*23*	*40*	*64*	*45*

Division One Play-offs

Charlton Athletic vs Crystal Palace	1-2, 0-1
Leicester City vs Stoke City	0-0, 1-0
Leicester City vs Crystal Palace	2-1

DIVISION TWO 1995-96

Swindon Town	46	25	17	4	71	34	92
Oxford United	46	24	11	11	76	39	83
Blackpool	46	23	13	10	67	40	82
Notts County	46	21	15	10	63	39	78
Crewe Alexandra	46	22	7	17	77	60	73
Bradford City	46	22	7	17	71	69	73
Chesterfield	46	20	12	14	56	51	72
Wrexham	46	18	16	12	76	55	70
Stockport County	46	19	13	14	61	47	70
Bristol Rovers	46	20	10	16	57	60	70
Walsall	46	19	12	15	60	45	69
Wycombe Wanderers	46	15	15	16	63	59	60
Bristol City	46	15	15	16	55	60	60
Bournemouth	46	16	10	20	51	70	58
Brentford	46	15	13	18	43	49	58
Rotherham United	46	14	14	18	54	62	56
Burnley	46	14	13	19	56	68	55
Shrewsbury Town	46	13	14	19	58	70	53
Peterborough United	46	13	13	20	59	66	52
York City	46	13	13	20	58	73	52
Carlisle United	*46*	*12*	*13*	*21*	*57*	*72*	*49*
Swansea City	*46*	*11*	*14*	*21*	*43*	*79*	*47*
Brighton & Hove Albion	*46*	*10*	*10*	*26*	*46*	*69*	*40*
Hull City	*46*	*5*	*16*	*25*	*36*	*78*	*31*

Division Two Play-offs

Bradford City vs Blackpool	0-2, 3-0
Crewe Alexandra vs Notts County	2-2, 0-1
Bradford City vs Notts County	2-0

DIVISION THREE 1995-96

Preston North End	46	23	17	6	78	38	86
Gillingham	46	22	17	7	49	20	83
Bury	46	22	13	11	66	48	79
Plymouth Argyle	46	22	12	12	68	49	78
Darlington	46	20	18	8	60	42	78
Hereford United	46	20	14	12	65	47	74
Colchester United	46	18	18	10	61	51	72
Chester City	46	18	16	12	72	53	70
Barnet	46	18	16	12	65	45	70
Wigan Athletic	46	20	10	16	62	56	70
Northampton Town	46	18	13	15	51	44	67
Scunthorpe United	46	15	15	16	67	61	60
Doncaster Rovers	46	16	11	19	49	60	59
Exeter City	46	13	18	15	46	53	57
Rochdale	46	14	13	19	57	61	55
Cambridge United	46	14	12	20	61	71	54
Fulham	46	12	17	17	57	63	53
Lincoln City	46	13	14	19	57	73	53
Mansfield Town	46	11	20	15	54	64	53
Hartlepool United	46	12	13	21	47	67	49
Leyton Orient	46	12	11	23	44	63	47
Cardiff City	46	11	12	23	41	64	45
Scarborough	46	8	16	22	39	69	40
Torquay United	46	5	14	27	30	84	29

Division Three Play-offs

Colchester United vs Plymouth Argyle	1-0, 1-3
Hereford United vs Darlington	1-2, 1-2
Plymouth Argyle vs Darlington	1-0

1996 F.A. Cup

Semi-finals

Chelsea vs Manchester United	1-2
Aston Villa vs Liverpool	0-3

Final

Wembley, 11th May 1996

Manchester United 1   (Cantona)

Liverpool 0

Attendance 79,007

1996 Football League Cup

Semi-finals

Birmingham City vs Leeds United (1-2, 0-3)	1-5
Arsenal vs Aston Villa (2-2, 0-0)	2-2

Aston Villa won on the away goals rule

Final

Wembley, 24th March 1996

Aston Villa 3   (Milosevic, Taylor, Yorke)

Leeds United 0

Attendance 77,056

F.A. PREMIER LEAGUE 1996-97

MANCHESTER UNITED	38	21	12	5	76	44	75
Newcastle United	38	19	11	8	73	40	68
Arsenal	38	19	11	8	62	32	68
Liverpool	38	19	11	8	62	37	68
Aston Villa	38	17	10	11	47	34	61
Chelsea	38	16	11	11	58	55	59
Sheffield Wednesday	38	14	15	9	50	51	57
Wimbledon	38	15	11	12	49	46	56
Leicester City	38	12	11	15	46	54	47
Tottenham Hotspur	38	13	7	18	44	51	46
Leeds United	38	11	13	14	28	38	46
Derby County	38	11	13	14	45	58	46
Blackburn Rovers	38	9	15	14	42	43	42
West Ham United	38	10	12	16	39	48	42
Everton	38	10	12	16	44	57	42
Southampton	38	10	11	17	50	56	41
Coventry City	38	9	14	15	38	54	41
Sunderland	*38*	*10*	*10*	*18*	*35*	*53*	*40*
Middlesbrough	*38*	*10*	*12*	*16*	*51*	*60*	*39*
Nottingham Forest	*38*	*6*	*16*	*16*	*31*	*59*	*34*

Middlesbrough had 3 points deducted

DIVISION ONE 1996-97

Bolton Wanderers	46	28	14	4	100	53	98
Barnsley	46	22	14	10	76	55	80
Wolverhampton Wanderers	46	22	10	14	68	51	76
Ipswich Town	46	20	14	12	68	50	74
Sheffield United	46	20	13	13	75	52	73
Crystal Palace	46	19	14	13	78	48	71
Portsmouth	46	20	8	18	59	53	68
Port Vale	46	17	16	13	58	55	67
Queen's Park Rangers	46	18	12	16	64	60	66
Birmingham City	46	17	15	14	52	48	66
Tranmere Rovers	46	17	14	15	63	56	65
Stoke City	46	18	10	18	51	57	64
Norwich City	46	17	12	17	63	68	63
Manchester City	46	17	10	19	59	60	61
Charlton Athletic	46	16	11	19	52	66	59
West Bromwich Albion	46	14	15	17	68	72	57
Oxford United	46	16	9	21	64	68	57
Reading	46	15	12	19	58	67	57
Swindon Town	46	15	9	22	52	71	54
Huddersfield Town	46	13	15	18	48	61	54
Bradford City	46	12	12	22	47	72	48
Grimsby Town	*46*	*11*	*13*	*22*	*60*	*81*	*46*
Oldham Athletic	*46*	*10*	*13*	*23*	*51*	*66*	*43*
Southend United	*46*	*8*	*15*	*23*	*42*	*86*	*39*

Division One Play-offs

Crystal Palace vs Wolverhampton Wanderers	3-1, 1-2
Sheffield United vs Ipswich Town	1-1, 2-2

Sheffield United won on away goals

Crystal Palace vs Sheffield United	1-0

1997 F.A. Cup

Semi-finals

Middlesbrough vs Chesterfield	3-3, 3-0
Wimbledon vs Chelsea	0-3

Final

Wembley, 17th May 1997

Chelsea 2 (Di Matteo, Newton)
Middlesbrough 0

Attendance 79,160

1997 Football League Cup

Semi-finals

Leicester City vs Wimbledon (0-0, 1-1)	1-1

Leicester City won on the away goals rule

Stockport County vs Middlesbrough (0-2, 1-0)	1-2

DIVISION TWO 1996-97

Bury	46	24	12	10	62	38	84
Stockport County	46	23	13	10	59	41	82
Luton Town	46	21	15	10	71	45	78
Brentford	46	20	14	12	56	43	74
Bristol City	46	21	10	15	69	51	73
Crewe Alexandra	46	22	7	17	56	47	73
Blackpool	46	18	15	13	60	47	69
Wrexham	46	17	18	11	54	50	69
Burnley	46	19	11	16	71	55	68
Chesterfield	46	18	14	14	42	39	68
Gillingham	46	19	10	17	60	59	67
Walsall	46	19	10	17	54	53	67
Watford	46	16	19	11	45	38	67
Millwall	46	16	13	17	50	55	61
Preston North End	46	18	7	21	49	55	61
Bournemouth	46	15	15	16	43	45	60
Bristol Rovers	46	15	11	20	47	50	56
Wycombe Wanderers	46	15	10	21	51	56	55
Plymouth Argyle	46	12	18	16	47	58	54
York City	46	13	13	20	47	68	52
Peterborough United	*46*	*11*	*14*	*21*	*55*	*73*	*47*
Shrewsbury Town	*46*	*11*	*13*	*22*	*49*	*74*	*46*
Rotherham United	*46*	*7*	*14*	*25*	*39*	*70*	*35*
Notts County	*46*	*7*	*14*	*25*	*33*	*59*	*35*

Division Two Play-offs

Bristol City vs Brentford	1-2, 1-2
Crewe Alexandra vs Luton Town	2-1, 2-2
Crewe Alexandra vs Brentford	1-0

DIVISION THREE 1996-97

Wigan Athletic	46	26	9	11	84	51	87
Fulham	46	25	12	9	72	38	87
Carlisle United	46	24	12	10	67	44	84
Northampton Town	46	20	12	14	67	44	72
Swansea City	46	21	8	17	62	58	71
Chester City	46	18	16	12	55	43	70
Cardiff City	46	20	9	17	56	54	69
Colchester United	46	17	17	12	62	51	68
Lincoln City	46	18	12	16	70	69	66
Cambridge United	46	18	11	17	53	59	65
Mansfield Town	46	16	16	14	47	45	64
Scarborough	46	16	15	15	65	68	63
Scunthorpe United	46	18	9	19	59	62	63
Rochdale	46	14	16	16	58	58	58
Barnet	46	14	16	16	46	51	58
Leyton Orient	46	15	12	19	50	58	57
Hull City	46	13	18	15	44	50	57
Darlington	46	14	10	22	64	78	52
Doncaster Rovers	46	14	10	22	52	66	52
Hartlepool United	46	14	9	23	53	66	51
Torquay United	46	13	11	22	46	62	50
Exeter City	46	12	12	22	48	73	48
Brighton & Hove Albion	46	13	10	23	53	70	47
Hereford United	*46*	*11*	*14*	*21*	*50*	*65*	*47*

Brighton & Hove Albion had two points deducted

Division Three Play-offs

Cardiff City vs Northampton Town	0-1, 2-3
Chester City vs Swansea City	0-0, 0-3
Northampton Town vs Swansea City	1-0

Final

Wembley, 6th April 1997

Leicester City 1 (Heskey)
Middlesbrough 1 (aet.) (Ravanelli)

Attendance 76,757

Replay

Hillsborough, 16th April 1997

Leicester City 1 (Claridge)
Middlesbrough 0

Attendance 39,428

F.A. PREMIER LEAGUE 1997-98

ARSENAL	38	23	9	6	68	33	78
Manchester United	38	23	8	7	73	26	77
Liverpool	38	18	11	9	68	42	65
Chelsea	38	20	3	15	71	43	63
Leeds United	38	17	8	13	57	46	59
Blackburn Rovers	38	16	10	12	57	52	58
Aston Villa	38	17	6	15	49	48	57
West Ham United	38	16	8	14	56	57	56
Derby County	38	16	7	15	52	49	55
Leicester City	38	13	14	11	51	41	53
Coventry City	38	12	16	10	46	44	52
Southampton	38	14	6	18	50	55	48
Newcastle United	38	11	11	16	35	44	44
Tottenham Hotspur	38	11	11	16	44	56	44
Wimbledon	38	10	14	14	34	46	44
Sheffield Wednesday	38	12	8	18	52	67	44
Everton	38	9	13	16	41	56	40
Bolton Wanderers	*38*	*9*	*13*	*16*	*41*	*61*	*40*
Barnsley	*38*	*10*	*5*	*23*	*37*	*82*	*35*
Crystal Palace	*38*	*8*	*9*	*21*	*37*	*71*	*33*

DIVISION ONE 1997-98

Nottingham Forest	46	28	10	8	82	42	94
Middlesbrough	46	27	10	9	77	41	91
Sunderland	46	26	12	8	86	50	90
Charlton Athletic	46	26	10	10	80	49	88
Ipswich Town	46	23	14	9	77	43	83
Sheffield United	46	19	17	10	69	54	74
Birmingham City	46	19	17	10	60	35	74
Stockport County	46	19	8	19	71	69	65
Wolverhampton Wanderers	46	18	11	17	57	53	65
West Bromwich Albion	46	16	13	17	50	56	61
Crewe Alexandra	46	18	5	23	58	65	59
Oxford United	46	16	10	20	60	64	58
Bradford City	46	14	15	17	46	59	57
Tranmere Rovers	46	14	14	18	54	57	56
Norwich City	46	14	13	19	52	69	55
Huddersfield Town	46	14	11	21	50	72	53
Bury	46	11	19	16	42	58	52
Swindon Town	46	14	10	22	42	73	52
Port Vale	46	13	10	23	56	66	49
Portsmouth	46	13	10	23	51	63	49
Queen's Park Rangers	46	10	19	17	51	63	49
Manchester City	*46*	*12*	*12*	*22*	*56*	*57*	*48*
Stoke City	*46*	*11*	*13*	*22*	*44*	*74*	*46*
Reading	*46*	*11*	*9*	*26*	*39*	*78*	*42*

Division One Play-offs

Ipswich Town vs Charlton Athletic	0-1, 0-1
Sheffield United vs Sunderland	2-1, 0-2
Charlton Athletic vs Sunderland	4-4
Charlton Athletic won 7-6 on penalties	

1998 F.A. Cup

Semi-finals

Sheffield United vs Newcastle United	0-1
Wolverhampton Wanderers vs Arsenal	0-1

Final

Wembley, 16th May 1998

Arsenal 2 (Overmars, Anelka)
Newcastle United 0

Attendance 79,183

DIVISION TWO 1997-98

Watford	46	24	16	6	67	41	88
Bristol City	46	25	10	11	69	39	85
Grimsby Town	46	19	15	12	55	37	72
Northampton Town	46	18	17	11	52	37	71
Bristol Rovers	46	20	10	16	70	64	70
Fulham	46	20	10	16	60	43	70
Wrexham	46	18	16	12	55	51	70
Gillingham	46	19	13	14	52	47	70
Bournemouth	46	18	12	16	57	52	66
Chesterfield	46	16	17	13	46	44	65
Wigan Athletic	46	17	11	18	64	66	62
Blackpool	46	17	11	18	59	67	62
Oldham Athletic	46	15	16	15	62	54	61
Wycombe Wanderers	46	14	18	14	51	53	60
Preston North End	46	15	14	17	56	56	59
York City	46	14	17	15	52	58	59
Luton Town	46	14	15	17	60	64	57
Millwall	46	14	13	19	43	54	55
Walsall	46	14	12	20	43	52	54
Burnley	46	13	13	20	55	65	52
Brentford	*46*	*11*	*17*	*18*	*50*	*71*	*50*
Plymouth Argyle	*46*	*12*	*13*	*21*	*55*	*70*	*49*
Carlisle United	*46*	*12*	*8*	*26*	*57*	*73*	*44*
Southend United	*46*	*11*	*10*	*25*	*47*	*79*	*43*

Division Two Play-offs

Fulham vs Grimsby Town		1-1, 0-1
Bristol Rovers vs Northampton Town		3-1, 0-3
Grimsby Town vs Northampton Town		1-0

DIVISION THREE 1997-98

Notts County	46	29	12	5	82	43	99
Macclesfield Town	46	23	13	10	63	44	82
Lincoln City	46	20	15	11	60	51	75
Colchester United	46	21	11	14	72	60	74
Torquay United	46	21	11	14	68	59	74
Scarborough	46	19	15	12	67	58	72
Barnet	46	19	13	14	61	51	70
Scunthorpe United	46	19	12	15	56	52	69
Rotherham United	46	16	19	11	67	61	67
Peterborough United	46	18	13	15	63	51	67
Leyton Orient	46	19	12	15	62	47	66
Mansfield Town	46	16	17	13	64	55	65
Shrewsbury Town	46	16	13	17	61	62	61
Chester City	46	17	10	19	60	61	61
Exeter City	46	15	15	16	68	63	60
Cambridge United	46	14	18	14	63	57	60
Hartlepool United	46	12	23	11	61	53	59
Rochdale	46	17	7	22	56	55	58
Darlington	46	14	12	20	56	72	54
Swansea City	46	13	11	22	49	62	50
Cardiff City	46	9	23	14	48	52	50
Hull City	46	11	8	27	56	83	41
Brighton & Hove Albion	46	6	17	23	38	66	35
Doncaster Rovers	*46*	*4*	*8*	*34*	*30*	*113*	*20*

Leyton Orient had 3 points deducted

Division Three Play-offs

Barnet vs Colchester United		1-0, 1-3
Scarborough vs Torquay United		1-3, 1-4
Colchester United vs Torquay United		1-0

1998 Football League Cup

Semi-finals

Liverpool vs Middlesbrough (2-1, 0-2)	2-3
Arsenal vs Chelsea (2-1, 1-3)	3-4

Final

Wembley, 29th March 1998

Chelsea 2 (Sinclair, Di Matteo)
Middlesbrough 0 (aet.)

Attendance 77,698

F.A. PREMIER LEAGUE 1998-99

MANCHESTER UNITED	38	22	13	3	80	37	79
Arsenal	38	22	12	4	59	17	78
Chelsea	38	20	15	3	57	30	75
Leeds United	38	18	13	7	62	34	67
West Ham United	38	16	9	13	46	53	57
Aston Villa	38	15	10	13	51	46	55
Liverpool	38	15	9	14	68	49	54
Derby County	38	13	13	12	40	45	52
Middlesbrough	38	12	15	11	48	54	51
Leicester City	38	12	13	13	40	46	49
Tottenham Hotspur	38	11	14	13	47	50	47
Sheffield Wednesday	38	13	7	18	41	42	46
Newcastle United	38	11	13	14	48	54	46
Everton	38	11	10	17	42	47	43
Coventry City	38	11	9	18	39	51	42
Wimbledon	38	10	12	16	40	63	42
Southampton	38	11	8	19	37	64	41
Charlton Athletic	*38*	*8*	*12*	*18*	*41*	*56*	*36*
Blackburn Rovers	*38*	*7*	*14*	*17*	*38*	*52*	*35*
Nottingham Forest	*38*	*7*	*9*	*22*	*35*	*69*	*30*

DIVISION ONE 1998-99

Sunderland	46	31	12	3	91	28	105
Bradford City	46	26	9	11	82	47	87
Ipswich Town	46	26	8	12	69	32	86
Birmingham City	46	23	12	11	66	37	81
Watford	46	21	14	11	65	56	77
Bolton Wanderers	46	20	16	10	78	59	76
Wolverhampton Wanderers	46	19	16	11	64	43	73
Sheffield United	46	18	13	15	71	66	67
Norwich City	46	15	17	14	62	61	62
Huddersfield Town	46	15	16	15	62	71	61
Grimsby Town	46	17	10	19	40	52	61
West Bromwich Albion	46	16	11	19	69	76	59
Barnsley	46	14	17	15	59	56	59
Crystal Palace	46	14	16	16	58	71	58
Tranmere Rovers	46	12	20	14	63	61	56
Stockport County	46	12	17	17	49	60	53
Swindon Town	46	13	11	22	59	81	50
Crewe Alexandra	46	12	12	22	54	78	48
Portsmouth	46	11	14	21	57	73	47
Queen's Park Rangers	46	12	11	23	52	61	47
Port Vale	46	13	8	25	45	75	47
Bury	*46*	*10*	*17*	*19*	*35*	*60*	*47*
Oxford United	*46*	*10*	*14*	*22*	*48*	*71*	*44*
Bristol City	*46*	*9*	*15*	*22*	*57*	*80*	*42*

Division One Play-offs

Bolton Wanderers vs Ipswich Town	1-0, 3-4
Bolton Wanderers won on away goals	
Watford vs Birmingham City	1-0, 0-1
Watford won 7-6 on penalties	
Watford vs Bolton Wanderers	2-0

1999 F.A. Cup

Semi-finals

Newcastle United vs Tottenham Hotspur	2-0 (aet)
Manchester United vs Arsenal	0-0, 2-1 (aet)

Final

Wembley, 22nd May 1999

Manchester United 2   (Sheringham, Scholes)
Newcastle United 0

Attendance 79,101

DIVISION TWO 1998-99

Fulham	46	31	8	7	79	32	101
Walsall	46	26	9	11	63	47	87
Manchester City	46	22	16	8	69	33	82
Gillingham	46	22	14	10	75	44	80
Preston North End	46	22	13	11	78	50	79
Wigan Athletic	46	22	10	14	75	48	76
Bournemouth	46	21	13	12	63	41	76
Stoke City	46	21	6	19	59	63	69
Chesterfield	46	17	13	16	46	44	64
Millwall	46	17	11	18	52	59	62
Reading	46	16	13	17	54	63	61
Luton Town	46	16	10	20	51	60	58
Bristol Rovers	46	13	17	16	65	56	56
Blackpool	46	14	14	18	44	54	56
Burnley	46	13	16	17	54	73	55
Notts County	46	14	12	20	52	61	54
Wrexham	46	13	14	19	43	62	53
Colchester United	46	12	16	18	52	70	52
Wycombe Wanderers	46	13	12	21	52	58	51
Oldham Athletic	46	14	9	23	48	66	51
York City	*46*	*13*	*11*	*22*	*56*	*80*	*50*
Northampton Town	*46*	*10*	*18*	*18*	*43*	*57*	*48*
Lincoln City	*46*	*13*	*7*	*26*	*42*	*74*	*46*
Macclesfield Town	*46*	*11*	*10*	*25*	*43*	*63*	*43*

Division Two Play-offs

Wigan Athletic vs Manchester City	1-1, 0-1
Preston North End vs Gillingham	1-1, 0-1
Manchester City vs Gillingham	2-2
Manchester City won 3-1 on penalties	

DIVISION THREE 1998-99

Brentford	46	26	7	13	79	56	85
Cambridge United	46	23	12	11	78	48	81
Cardiff City	46	22	14	10	60	39	80
Scunthorpe United	46	22	8	16	69	58	74
Rotherham United	46	20	13	13	79	61	73
Leyton Orient	46	19	15	12	68	59	72
Swansea City	46	19	14	13	56	48	71
Mansfield Town	46	19	10	17	60	58	67
Peterborough United	46	18	12	16	72	56	66
Halifax Town	46	17	15	14	58	56	66
Darlington	46	18	11	17	69	58	65
Exeter City	46	17	12	17	47	50	63
Plymouth Argyle	46	17	10	19	58	54	61
Chester City	46	13	18	15	57	66	57
Shrewsbury Town	46	14	14	18	52	63	56
Barnet	46	14	13	19	54	71	55
Brighton & Hove Albion	46	16	7	23	49	66	55
Southend United	46	14	12	20	52	58	54
Rochdale	46	13	15	18	42	55	54
Torquay United	46	12	17	17	47	58	53
Hull City	46	14	11	21	44	62	53
Hartlepool United	46	13	12	21	52	65	51
Carlisle United	46	11	16	19	43	53	49
Scarborough	*46*	*14*	*6*	*26*	*50*	*77*	*48*

Division Three Play-offs

Leyton Orient vs Rotherham United	0-0, 0-0
Leyton Orient won 4-2 on penalties	
Swansea City vs Scunthorpe United	1-0, 1-3
Scunthorpe United vs Leyton Orient	1-0

1999 Football League Cup

Semi-finals

Sunderland vs Leicester City (1-2, 1-1)	2-3
Tottenham Hotspur vs Wimbledon (0-0, 1-0)	1-0

Final

Wembley, 21st March 1999

Tottenham Hotspur 1   (Nielsen)
Leicester City 0

Attendance 77,892

F.A. PREMIER LEAGUE 1999-2000

MANCHESTER UNITED	38	28	7	3	97	45	91
Arsenal	38	22	7	9	73	43	73
Leeds United	38	21	6	11	58	43	69
Liverpool	38	19	10	9	51	30	67
Chelsea	38	18	11	9	53	34	65
Aston Villa	38	15	13	10	46	35	58
Sunderland	38	16	10	12	57	56	58
Leicester City	38	16	7	15	55	55	55
West Ham United	38	15	10	13	52	53	55
Tottenham Hotspur	38	15	8	15	57	49	53
Newcastle United	38	14	10	14	63	54	52
Middlesbrough	38	14	10	14	46	52	52
Everton	38	12	14	12	59	49	50
Coventry City	38	12	8	18	47	54	44
Southampton	38	12	8	18	45	62	44
Derby County	38	9	11	18	44	57	38
Bradford City	38	9	9	20	38	68	36
Wimbledon	*38*	*7*	*12*	*19*	*46*	*74*	*33*
Sheffield Wednesday	*38*	*8*	*7*	*23*	*38*	*70*	*31*
Watford	*38*	*6*	*6*	*26*	*35*	*77*	*24*

DIVISION ONE 1999-2000

Charlton Athletic	46	27	10	9	79	45	91
Manchester City	46	26	11	9	78	40	89
Ipswich Town	46	25	12	9	71	42	87
Barnsley	46	24	10	12	88	67	82
Birmingham City	46	22	11	13	65	44	77
Bolton Wanderers	46	21	13	12	69	50	76
Wolverhampton Wanderers	46	21	11	14	64	48	74
Huddersfield Town	46	21	11	14	62	49	74
Fulham	46	17	16	13	49	41	67
Queen's Park Rangers	46	16	18	12	62	53	66
Blackburn Rovers	46	15	17	14	55	51	62
Norwich City	46	14	15	17	45	50	57
Tranmere Rovers	46	15	12	19	57	68	57
Nottingham Forest	46	14	14	18	53	55	56
Crystal Palace	46	13	15	18	57	67	54
Sheffield United	46	13	15	18	59	71	54
Stockport County	46	13	15	18	55	67	54
Portsmouth	46	13	12	21	55	66	51
Crewe Alexandra	46	14	9	23	46	67	51
Grimsby Town	46	13	12	21	41	67	51
West Bromwich Albion	46	10	19	17	43	60	49
Walsall	*46*	*11*	*13*	*22*	*52*	*77*	*46*
Port Vale	*46*	*7*	*15*	*24*	*48*	*69*	*36*
Swindon Town	*46*	*8*	*12*	*26*	*38*	*77*	*36*

Division One Play-offs

Birmingham City vs Barnsley	0-4, 2-1
Bolton Wanderers vs Ipswich Town	2-2, 3-5
Ipswich Town vs Barnsley	4-2

2000 F.A. Cup

Semi-finals

Bolton Wanderers vs Aston Villa	0-0

Aston Villa won 4-1 on penalties

Newcastle United vs Chelsea	1-2

Final

Wembley, 20th May 2000

Chelsea 1 (Di Matteo)

Aston Villa 0

Attendance 78,217

DIVISION TWO 1999-2000

Preston North End	46	28	11	7	74	37	95
Burnley	46	25	13	8	69	47	88
Gillingham	46	25	10	11	79	48	85
Wigan Athletic	46	22	17	7	72	38	83
Millwall	46	23	13	10	76	50	82
Stoke City	46	23	13	10	68	42	82
Bristol Rovers	46	23	11	12	69	45	80
Notts County	46	18	11	17	61	55	65
Bristol City	46	15	19	12	59	57	64
Reading	46	16	14	16	57	63	62
Wrexham	46	17	11	18	52	61	62
Wycombe Wanderers	46	16	13	17	56	53	61
Luton Town	46	17	10	19	61	65	61
Oldham Athletic	46	16	12	18	50	55	60
Bury	46	13	18	15	61	64	57
Bournemouth	46	16	9	21	59	62	57
Brentford	46	13	13	20	47	61	52
Colchester United	46	14	10	22	59	82	52
Cambridge United	46	12	12	22	64	65	48
Oxford United	46	12	9	25	43	73	45
Cardiff City	*46*	*9*	*17*	*20*	*45*	*67*	*44*
Blackpool	*46*	*8*	*17*	*21*	*49*	*77*	*41*
Scunthorpe United	*46*	*9*	*12*	*25*	*40*	*74*	*39*
Chesterfield	*46*	*7*	*15*	*24*	*34*	*63*	*36*

Division Two Play-offs

Millwall vs Wigan Athletic	0-0, 0-1
Stoke City vs Gillingham	3-2, 0-3
Gillingham vs Wigan Athletic	3-2

DIVISION THREE 1999-2000

Swansea City	46	24	13	9	51	30	85
Rotherham United	46	24	12	10	72	36	84
Northampton Town	46	25	7	14	63	45	82
Darlington	46	21	16	9	66	36	79
Peterborough United	46	22	12	12	63	54	78
Barnet	46	21	12	13	59	53	75
Hartlepool United	46	21	9	16	60	49	72
Cheltenham Town	46	20	10	16	50	42	70
Torquay United	46	19	12	15	62	52	69
Rochdale	46	18	14	14	57	54	68
Brighton & Hove Albion	46	17	16	13	64	46	67
Plymouth Argyle	46	16	18	12	55	51	66
Macclesfield Town	46	18	11	17	66	61	65
Hull City	46	15	14	17	43	43	59
Lincoln City	46	15	14	17	67	69	59
Southend United	46	15	11	20	53	61	56
Mansfield Town	46	16	8	22	50	65	56
Halifax Town	46	15	9	22	44	58	54
Leyton Orient	46	13	13	20	47	52	52
York City	46	12	16	18	39	53	52
Exeter City	46	11	11	24	46	72	44
Shrewsbury Town	46	9	13	24	40	67	40
Carlisle United	46	9	12	25	42	75	39
Chester City	*46*	*10*	*9*	*27*	*44*	*79*	*39*

Division Three Play-offs

Barnet vs Peterborough United	1-2, 0-3
Hartlepool United vs Darlington	0-2, 0-1
Peterborough United vs Darlington	1-0

2000 Football League Cup

Semi-finals

Bolton Wanderers vs Tranmere Rovers (0-1, 0-3)	0-4
Aston Villa vs Leicester City (0-0, 0-1)	0-1

Final

Wembley, 27th February 2000

Leicester City 2 (Elliott 2)

Tranmere Rovers 1 (Kelly)

Attendance 74,313

F.A. PREMIER LEAGUE 2000-2001

MANCHESTER UNITED	38	24	8	6	79	31	80
Arsenal	38	20	10	8	63	38	70
Liverpool	38	20	9	9	71	39	69
Leeds United	38	20	8	10	64	43	68
Ipswich Town	38	20	6	12	57	42	66
Chelsea	38	17	10	11	68	45	61
Sunderland	38	15	12	11	46	41	57
Aston Villa	38	13	15	10	46	43	54
Charlton Athletic	38	14	10	14	50	57	52
Southampton	38	14	10	14	40	48	52
Newcastle United	38	14	9	15	44	50	51
Tottenham Hotspur	38	13	10	15	47	54	49
Leicester City	38	14	6	18	39	51	48
Middlesbrough	38	9	15	14	44	44	42
West Ham United	38	10	12	16	45	50	42
Everton	38	11	9	18	45	59	42
Derby County	38	10	12	16	37	59	42
Manchester City	*38*	*8*	*10*	*20*	*41*	*65*	*34*
Coventry City	*38*	*8*	*10*	*20*	*36*	*63*	*34*
Bradford City	*38*	*5*	*11*	*22*	*30*	*70*	*26*

DIVISION ONE 2000-2001

Fulham	46	30	11	5	90	32	101
Blackburn Rovers	46	26	13	7	76	39	91
Bolton Wanderers	46	24	15	7	76	45	87
Preston North End	46	23	9	14	64	52	78
Birmingham City	46	23	9	14	59	48	78
West Bromwich Albion	46	21	11	14	60	52	74
Burnley	46	21	9	16	50	54	72
Wimbledon	46	17	18	11	71	50	69
Watford	46	20	9	17	76	67	69
Sheffield United	46	19	11	16	52	49	68
Nottingham Forest	46	20	8	18	55	53	68
Wolverhampton Wanderers	46	14	13	19	45	48	55
Gillingham	46	13	16	17	61	66	55
Crewe Alexandra	46	15	10	21	47	62	55
Norwich City	46	14	12	20	46	58	54
Barnsley	46	15	9	22	49	62	54
Sheffield Wednesday	46	15	8	23	52	71	53
Grimsby Town	46	14	10	22	43	62	52
Stockport County	46	11	18	17	58	65	51
Portsmouth	46	10	19	17	47	59	49
Crystal Palace	46	12	13	21	57	70	49
Huddersfield Town	*46*	*11*	*15*	*20*	*48*	*57*	*48*
Queen's Park Rangers	*46*	*7*	*19*	*20*	*45*	*75*	*40*
Tranmere Rovers	*46*	*9*	*11*	*26*	*46*	*77*	*38*

Division One Play-offs

Birmingham City vs Preston North End	1-0, 1-2
Preston North End won 4-2 on penalties	
West Bromwich Albion vs Bolton Wands.	2-2, 0-3
Bolton Wanderers vs Preston North End	3-0

2001 F.A. Cup

Semi-finals

Arsenal vs Tottenham Hotspur	2-1
Wycombe Wanderers vs Liverpool	1-2

Final

The Millennium Stadium, Cardiff, 12th May 2001

Arsenal 1 (Ljungberg)
Liverpool 2 (Owen 2)

Attendance 72,500

DIVISION TWO 2000-2001

Millwall	46	28	9	9	89	38	93
Rotherham United	46	27	10	9	79	55	91
Reading	46	25	11	10	86	52	86
Walsall	46	23	12	11	79	50	81
Stoke City	46	21	14	11	74	49	77
Wigan Athletic	46	19	18	9	53	42	75
Bournemouth	46	20	13	13	79	55	73
Notts County	46	19	12	15	62	66	69
Bristol City	46	18	14	14	70	56	68
Wrexham	46	17	12	17	65	71	63
Port Vale	46	16	14	16	55	49	62
Peterborough United	46	15	14	17	61	66	59
Wycombe Wanderers	46	15	14	17	46	53	59
Brentford	46	14	17	15	56	70	59
Oldham Athletic	46	15	13	18	53	65	58
Bury	46	16	10	20	45	59	58
Colchester United	46	15	12	19	55	59	57
Northampton Town	46	15	12	19	46	59	57
Cambridge United	46	14	11	21	61	77	53
Swindon Town	46	13	13	20	47	65	52
Bristol Rovers	*46*	*12*	*15*	*19*	*53*	*57*	*51*
Luton Town	*46*	*9*	*13*	*24*	*52*	*80*	*40*
Swansea City	*46*	*8*	*13*	*25*	*47*	*73*	*37*
Oxford United	*46*	*7*	*6*	*33*	*53*	*100*	*27*

Division Two Play-offs

Stoke City vs Walsall	0-0, 2-4
Wigan Athletic vs Reading	0-0, 1-2
Walsall vs Reading	3-2

DIVISION THREE 2000-2001

Brighton & Hove Albion	46	28	8	10	73	35	92
Cardiff City	46	23	13	10	95	58	82
Chesterfield	46	25	14	7	79	42	80
Hartlepool United	46	21	14	11	71	54	77
Leyton Orient	46	20	15	11	59	51	75
Hull City	46	19	17	10	47	39	74
Blackpool	46	22	6	18	74	58	72
Rochdale	46	18	17	11	59	48	71
Cheltenham Town	46	18	14	14	59	52	68
Scunthorpe United	46	18	11	17	62	52	65
Southend United	46	15	18	13	55	53	63
Mansfield Town	46	15	13	18	64	72	58
Plymouth Argyle	46	15	13	18	54	61	58
Macclesfield Town	46	14	14	18	51	62	56
Shrewsbury Town	46	15	10	21	49	65	55
Kidderminster Harriers	46	13	14	19	47	61	53
York City	46	13	13	20	42	63	52
Lincoln City	46	12	15	19	58	66	51
Exeter City	46	12	14	20	40	58	50
Darlington	46	12	13	21	44	56	49
Torquay United	46	12	13	21	52	77	49
Carlisle United	46	11	15	20	42	65	48
Halifax Town	46	12	11	23	54	68	47
Barnet	*46*	*12*	*9*	*25*	*67*	*81*	*45*

Chesterfield had 9 points deducted

Division Three Play-offs

Blackpool vs Hartlepool United	2-0, 3-1
Hull City vs Leyton Orient	1-0, 0-2
Blackpool vs Leyton Orient	4-2

2001 Football League Cup

Semi-finals

Ipswich Town vs Birmingham City (1-0, 1-4)	2-4
Crystal Palace vs Liverpool (2-1, 0-5)	2-6

Final

The Millennium Stadium, Cardiff, 25th February 2001

Birmingham City 1 (Purse (pen))
Liverpool 1 (aet.) (Fowler)

Attendance 73,500

Liverpool won on 5-4 on penalties.

F.A. PREMIER LEAGUE 2001-2002

ARSENAL	38	26	9	3	79	36	87
Liverpool	38	24	8	6	67	30	80
Manchester United	38	24	5	9	87	45	77
Newcastle United	38	21	8	9	74	52	71
Leeds United	38	18	12	8	53	37	66
Chelsea	38	17	13	8	66	38	64
West Ham United	38	15	8	15	48	57	53
Aston Villa	38	12	14	12	46	47	50
Tottenham Hotspur	38	14	8	16	49	53	50
Blackburn Rovers	38	12	10	16	55	51	46
Southampton	38	12	9	17	46	54	45
Middlesbrough	38	12	9	17	35	47	45
Fulham	38	10	14	14	36	44	44
Charlton Athletic	38	10	14	14	38	49	44
Everton	38	11	10	17	45	57	43
Bolton Wanderers	38	9	13	16	44	62	40
Sunderland	38	10	10	18	29	51	40
Ipswich Town	38	9	9	20	41	64	36
Derby County	38	8	6	24	33	63	30
Leicester City	38	5	13	20	30	64	28

DIVISION ONE 2001-2002

Manchester City	46	31	6	9	108	52	99
West Bromwich Albion	46	27	8	11	61	29	89
Wolverhampton Wanderers	46	25	11	10	76	43	86
Millwall	46	22	11	13	69	48	77
Birmingham City	46	21	13	12	70	49	76
Norwich City	46	22	9	15	60	51	75
Burnley	46	21	12	13	70	62	75
Preston North End	46	20	12	14	71	59	72
Wimbledon	46	18	13	15	63	57	67
Crystal Palace	46	20	6	20	70	62	66
Coventry City	46	20	6	20	59	53	66
Gillingham	46	18	10	18	64	67	64
Sheffield United	46	15	15	16	53	54	60
Watford	46	16	11	19	62	56	59
Bradford City	46	15	10	21	69	76	55
Nottingham Forest	46	12	18	16	50	51	54
Portsmouth	46	13	14	19	60	72	53
Walsall	46	13	12	21	51	71	51
Grimsby Town	46	12	14	20	50	72	50
Sheffield Wednesday	46	12	14	20	49	71	50
Rotherham United	46	10	19	17	52	66	49
Crewe Alexandra	46	12	13	21	47	76	49
Barnsley	46	11	15	20	59	86	48
Stockport County	46	6	8	32	42	102	26

Division One Play-offs

Birmingham City vs Millwall	1-1, 1-0
Norwich City vs Wolverhampton Wanderers	3-1, 0-1
Birmingham City vs Norwich City	1-1
Birmingham won 4-2 on penalties	

DIVISION TWO 2001-2002

Brighton & Hove Albion	46	25	15	6	66	42	90
Reading	46	23	15	8	70	43	84
Brentford	46	24	11	11	77	43	83
Cardiff City	46	23	14	9	75	50	83
Stoke City	46	23	11	12	67	40	80
Huddersfield Town	46	21	15	10	65	47	78
Bristol City	46	21	10	15	68	53	73
Queen's Park Rangers	46	19	14	13	60	49	71
Oldham Athletic	46	18	16	12	77	65	70
Wigan Athletic	46	16	16	14	66	51	64
Wycombe Wanderers	46	17	13	16	58	64	64
Tranmere Rovers	46	16	15	15	63	60	63
Swindon Town	46	15	14	17	46	56	59
Port Vale	46	16	10	20	51	62	58
Colchester United	46	15	12	19	65	76	57
Blackpool	46	14	14	18	66	69	56
Peterborough United	46	15	10	21	64	59	55
Chesterfield	46	13	13	20	53	65	52
Notts County	46	13	11	22	59	71	50
Northampton Town	46	14	7	25	54	79	49
Bournemouth	46	10	14	22	56	71	44
Bury	46	11	11	24	43	75	44
Wrexham	46	11	10	25	56	89	43
Cambridge United	46	7	13	26	47	93	34

Division Two Play-offs

Huddersfield Town vs Brentford	0-0, 1-2
Stoke City vs Cardiff City	1-2, 2-0
Stoke City vs Brentford	2-0

DIVISION THREE 2001-2002

Plymouth Argyle	46	31	9	6	71	28	102
Luton Town	46	30	7	9	96	48	97
Mansfield Town	46	24	7	15	72	60	79
Cheltenham Town	46	21	15	10	66	49	78
Rochdale	46	21	15	10	65	52	78
Rushden & Diamonds	46	20	13	13	69	53	73
Hartlepool United	46	20	11	15	74	48	71
Scunthorpe United	46	19	14	13	74	56	71
Shrewsbury Town	46	20	10	16	64	53	70
Kidderminster Harriers	46	19	9	18	56	47	66
Hull City	46	16	13	17	57	51	61
Southend United	46	15	13	18	51	54	58
Macclesfield Town	46	15	13	18	41	52	58
York City	46	16	9	21	54	67	57
Darlington	46	15	11	20	60	71	56
Exeter City	46	14	13	19	48	73	55
Carlisle United	46	12	16	18	49	56	52
Leyton Orient	46	13	13	20	55	71	52
Torquay United	46	12	15	19	46	63	51
Swansea City	46	13	12	21	53	77	51
Oxford United	46	11	14	21	53	62	47
Lincoln City	46	10	16	20	44	62	46
Bristol Rovers	46	11	12	23	40	60	45
Halifax Town	46	8	12	26	39	84	36

Division Three Play-offs

Hartlepool United vs Cheltenham Town	1-1, 1-1
Cheltenham Town won 5-4 on penalties	
Rushden & Diamonds vs Rochdale	2-2, 2-1
Cheltenham Town vs Rushden & Diamonds	3-1

2002 F.A. Cup

Semi-finals

Fulham vs Chelsea	0-1
Middlesbrough vs Arsenal	0-1

Final

The Millennium Stadium, Cardiff, 4th May 2002

Arsenal 2 (Parlour, Ljungberg)

Chelsea 0

Attendance 73,963

2002 Football League Cup

Semi-finals

Chelsea vs Tottenham Hotspur (2-1, 1-5)	3-6
Sheffield Wednesday vs Blackburn Rovers (1-2, 2-4)	3-6

Final

The Millennium Stadium, Cardiff, 24th February 2002

Blackburn Rovers 2 (Jansen, Cole)

Tottenham Hotspur 1 (Ziege)

Attendance 72,500

F.A. PREMIER LEAGUE 2002-2003

MANCHESTER UNITED	38	25	8	5	74	34	83
Arsenal	38	23	9	6	85	42	78
Newcastle United	38	21	6	11	63	48	69
Chelsea	38	19	10	9	68	38	67
Liverpool	38	18	10	10	61	41	64
Blackburn Rovers	38	16	12	10	52	43	60
Everton	38	17	8	13	48	49	59
Southampton	38	13	13	12	43	46	52
Manchester City	38	15	6	17	47	54	51
Tottenham Hotspur	38	14	8	16	51	62	50
Middlesbrough	38	13	10	15	48	44	49
Charlton Athletic	38	14	7	17	45	56	49
Birmingham City	38	13	9	16	41	49	48
Fulham	38	13	9	16	41	50	48
Leeds United	38	14	5	19	58	57	47
Aston Villa	38	12	9	17	42	47	45
Bolton Wanderers	38	10	14	14	41	51	44
West Ham United	*38*	*10*	*12*	*16*	*42*	*59*	*42*
West Bromwich Albion	*38*	*6*	*8*	*24*	*29*	*65*	*26*
Sunderland	*38*	*4*	*7*	*27*	*21*	*65*	*19*

DIVISION ONE 2002-2003

Portsmouth	**46**	**29**	**11**	**6**	**97**	**45**	**98**
Leicester City	**46**	**26**	**14**	**6**	**73**	**40**	**92**
Sheffield United	46	23	11	12	72	52	80
Reading	46	25	4	17	61	46	79
Wolverhampton Wanderers	**46**	**20**	**16**	**10**	**81**	**44**	**76**
Nottingham Forest	46	20	14	12	82	50	74
Ipswich Town	46	19	13	14	80	64	70
Norwich City	46	19	12	15	60	49	69
Millwall	46	19	9	18	59	69	66
Wimbledon	46	18	11	17	76	73	65
Gillingham	46	16	14	16	56	65	62
Preston North End	46	16	13	17	68	70	61
Watford	46	17	9	20	54	70	60
Crystal Palace	46	14	17	15	59	52	59
Rotherham United	46	15	14	17	62	62	59
Burnley	46	15	10	21	65	89	55
Walsall	46	15	9	22	57	69	54
Derby County	46	15	7	24	55	74	52
Bradford City	46	14	10	22	51	73	52
Coventry City	46	12	14	20	46	62	50
Stoke City	46	12	14	20	45	69	50
Sheffield Wednesday	*46*	*10*	*16*	*20*	*56*	*73*	*46*
Brighton & Hove Albion	*46*	*11*	*12*	*23*	*49*	*67*	*45*
Grimsby Town	*46*	*9*	*12*	*25*	*48*	*85*	*39*

Division One Play-offs

Nottingham Forest vs Sheffield United	1-1, 3-4
Wolverhampton Wanderers vs Reading	2-1, 1-0
Wolverhampton Wanderers vs Sheffield United	3-0

2003 F.A. Cup

Semi-finals

Arsenal vs Sheffield United	1-0
Southampton vs Watford	2-1

Final

The Millennium Stadium, Cardiff, 17th May 2003

Arsenal 1   (Pires)
Southampton 0

Attendance 73,726

DIVISION TWO 2002-2003

Wigan Athletic	**46**	**29**	**13**	**4**	**68**	**25**	**100**
Crewe Alexandra	**46**	**25**	**11**	**10**	**76**	**40**	**86**
Bristol City	46	24	11	11	79	48	83
Queen's Park Rangers	46	24	11	11	69	45	83
Oldham Athletic	46	22	16	8	68	38	82
Cardiff City	**46**	**23**	**12**	**11**	**68**	**43**	**81**
Tranmere Rovers	46	23	11	12	66	57	80
Plymouth Argyle	46	17	14	15	63	52	65
Luton Town	46	17	14	15	67	62	65
Swindon Town	46	16	12	18	59	63	60
Peterborough United	46	14	16	16	51	54	58
Colchester United	46	14	16	16	52	56	58
Blackpool	46	15	13	18	56	64	58
Stockport County	46	15	10	21	65	70	55
Notts County	46	13	16	17	62	70	55
Brentford	46	14	12	20	47	56	54
Port Vale	46	14	11	21	54	70	53
Wycombe Wanderers	46	13	13	20	59	66	52
Barnsley	46	13	13	20	51	64	52
Chesterfield	46	14	8	24	43	73	50
Cheltenham Town	*46*	*10*	*18*	*18*	*53*	*68*	*48*
Huddersfield Town	*46*	*11*	*12*	*23*	*39*	*61*	*45*
Mansfield Town	*46*	*12*	*8*	*26*	*66*	*97*	*44*
Northampton Town	*46*	*10*	*9*	*27*	*40*	*79*	*39*

Division Two Play-offs

Cardiff City vs Bristol City	1-0, 0-0
Oldham Athletic vs Queen's Park Rangers	1-1, 0-1
Cardiff City vs Queen's Park Rangers	1-0

DIVISION THREE 2002-2003

Rushden & Diamonds	**46**	**24**	**15**	**7**	**73**	**47**	**87**
Hartlepool United	**46**	**24**	**13**	**9**	**71**	**51**	**85**
Wrexham	**46**	**23**	**15**	**8**	**84**	**50**	**84**
Bournemouth	**46**	**20**	**14**	**12**	**60**	**48**	**74**
Scunthorpe United	46	19	15	12	68	49	72
Lincoln City	46	18	16	12	46	37	70
Bury	46	18	16	12	57	56	70
Oxford United	46	19	12	15	57	47	69
Torquay United	46	16	18	12	71	71	66
York City	46	17	15	14	52	53	66
Kidderminster Harriers	46	16	15	15	62	63	63
Cambridge United	46	16	13	17	67	70	61
Hull City	46	14	17	15	58	53	59
Darlington	46	12	18	16	58	59	54
Boston United	46	15	13	18	55	56	54
Macclesfield Town	46	14	12	20	57	63	54
Southend United	46	17	3	26	47	59	54
Leyton Orient	46	14	11	21	51	61	53
Rochdale	46	12	16	18	63	70	52
Bristol Rovers	46	12	15	19	50	57	51
Swansea City	46	12	13	21	48	65	49
Carlisle United	46	13	10	23	52	78	49
Exeter City	*46*	*11*	*15*	*20*	*50*	*64*	*48*
Shrewsbury Town	*46*	*9*	*14*	*23*	*62*	*92*	*41*

Boston United had 4 points deducted

Division Three Play-offs

Bury vs Bournemouth	0-0, 1-3
Lincoln City vs Scunthorpe United	5-3, 1-0
Bournemouth vs Lincoln City	5-2

2003 Football League Cup

Semi-finals

Manchester United vs Blackburn Rovers (1-1, 3-1)	4-2
Sheffield United vs Liverpool (2-1, 0-2 aet)	2-3

Final

The Millennium Stadium, Cardiff, 2nd March 2003

Liverpool 2   (Gerrard, Owen)
Manchester United 0

Attendance 74,500

F.A. PREMIER LEAGUE 2003-2004

ARSENAL	38	26	12	0	73	26	90
Chelsea	38	24	7	7	67	30	79
Manchester United	38	23	6	9	64	35	75
Liverpool	38	16	12	10	55	37	60
Newcastle United	38	13	17	8	52	40	56
Aston Villa	38	15	11	12	48	44	56
Charlton Athletic	38	14	11	13	51	51	53
Bolton Wanderers	38	14	11	13	48	56	53
Fulham	38	14	10	14	52	46	52
Birmingham City	38	12	14	12	43	48	50
Middlesbrough	38	13	9	16	44	52	48
Southampton	38	12	11	15	44	45	47
Portsmouth	38	12	9	17	47	54	45
Tottenham Hotspur	38	13	6	19	47	57	45
Blackburn Rovers	38	12	8	18	51	59	44
Manchester City	38	9	14	15	55	54	41
Everton	38	9	12	17	45	57	39
Leicester City	*38*	*6*	*15*	*17*	*48*	*65*	*33*
Leeds United	*38*	*8*	*9*	*21*	*40*	*79*	*33*
Wolverhampton Wanderers	*38*	*7*	*12*	*19*	*38*	*77*	*33*

DIVISION ONE 2003-2004

Norwich City	46	28	10	8	79	39	94
West Bromwich Albion	46	25	11	10	64	42	86
Sunderland	46	22	13	11	62	45	79
West Ham United	46	19	17	10	67	45	74
Ipswich Town	46	21	10	15	84	72	73
Crystal Palace	46	21	10	15	72	61	73
Wigan Athletic	46	18	17	11	60	45	71
Sheffield United	46	20	11	15	65	56	71
Reading	46	20	10	16	55	57	70
Millwall	46	18	15	13	55	48	69
Stoke City	46	18	12	16	58	55	66
Coventry City	46	17	14	15	67	54	65
Cardiff City	46	17	14	15	68	58	65
Nottingham Forest	46	15	15	16	61	58	60
Preston North End	46	15	14	17	69	71	59
Watford	46	15	12	19	54	68	57
Rotherham United	46	13	15	18	53	61	54
Crewe Alexandra	46	14	11	21	57	66	53
Burnley	46	13	14	19	60	77	53
Derby County	46	13	13	20	53	67	52
Gillingham	46	14	9	23	48	67	51
Walsall	*46*	*13*	*12*	*21*	*45*	*65*	*51*
Bradford City	*46*	*10*	*6*	*30*	*38*	*69*	*36*
Wimbledon	*46*	*8*	*5*	*33*	*41*	*89*	*29*

Division One Play-offs

Crystal Palace vs Sunderland	3-2, 1-2
Crystal Palace won 5-4 on penalties	
Ipswich Town vs West Ham United	1-0, 0-2
Crystal Palace vs West Ham United	1-0

DIVISION TWO 2003-2004

Plymouth Argyle	46	26	12	8	85	41	90
Queen's Park Rangers	46	22	17	7	80	45	83
Bristol City	46	23	13	10	58	37	82
Brighton & Hove Albion	46	22	11	13	64	43	77
Swindon Town	46	20	13	13	76	58	73
Hartlepool United	46	20	13	13	76	61	73
Port Vale	46	21	10	15	73	63	73
Tranmere Rovers	46	17	16	13	59	56	67
AFC Bournemouth	46	17	15	14	56	51	66
Luton Town	46	17	15	14	69	66	66
Colchester United	46	17	13	16	52	56	64
Barnsley	46	15	17	14	54	58	62
Wrexham	46	17	9	20	50	60	60
Blackpool	46	16	11	19	58	65	59
Oldham Athletic	46	12	21	13	66	60	57
Sheffield Wednesday	46	13	14	19	48	64	53
Brentford	46	14	11	21	52	69	53
Peterborough United	46	12	16	18	58	58	52
Stockport County	46	11	19	16	62	70	52
Chesterfield	46	12	15	19	49	71	51
Grimsby Town	*46*	*13*	*11*	*22*	*55*	*81*	*50*
Rushden & Diamonds	*46*	*13*	*9*	*24*	*60*	*74*	*48*
Notts County	*46*	*10*	*12*	*24*	*50*	*78*	*42*
Wycombe Wanderers	*46*	*6*	*19*	*21*	*50*	*75*	*37*

Division Two Play-offs

Hartlepool United vs Bristol City	1-1, 1-2
Swindon Town vs Brighton & Hove Albion	0-1, 2-1
Brighton & Hove Albion won 4-3 on penalties	
Brighton & Hove Albion vs Bristol City	1-0

DIVISION THREE 2003-2004

Doncaster Rovers	46	27	11	8	79	37	92
Hull City	46	25	13	8	82	44	88
Torquay United	46	23	12	11	68	44	81
Huddersfield Town	46	23	12	11	68	52	81
Mansfield Town	46	22	9	15	76	62	75
Northampton Town	46	22	9	15	58	51	75
Lincoln City	46	19	17	10	68	47	74
Yeovil Town	46	23	5	18	70	57	74
Oxford United	46	18	17	11	55	44	71
Swansea City	46	15	14	17	58	61	59
Boston United	46	16	11	19	50	54	59
Bury	46	15	11	20	54	64	56
Cambridge United	46	14	14	18	55	67	56
Cheltenham Town	46	14	14	18	57	71	56
Bristol Rovers	46	14	13	19	50	61	55
Kidderminster Harriers	46	14	13	19	45	59	55
Southend United	46	14	12	20	51	63	54
Darlington	46	14	11	21	53	61	53
Leyton Orient	46	13	14	19	48	65	53
Macclesfield Town	46	13	13	20	54	69	52
Rochdale	46	12	14	20	49	58	50
Scunthorpe United	46	11	16	19	69	72	49
Carlisle United	*46*	*12*	*9*	*25*	*46*	*69*	*45*
York City	*46*	*10*	*14*	*22*	*35*	*66*	*44*

Division Three Play-offs

Lincoln City vs Huddersfield Town	1-2, 2-2
Northampton Town vs Mansfield Town	0-2, 3-1
Mansfield Town won 5-4 on penalties	
Huddersfield Town vs Mansfield Town	0-0
Huddersfield won 4-1 on penalties	

2004 F.A. Cup

Semi-finals

Arsenal vs Manchester United	0-1
Sunderland vs Millwall	0-1

Final

The Millennium Stadium, Cardiff, 22nd May 2004

Manchester United 3 (Ronaldo, Van Nistelrooy 2)
Millwall 0

Attendance 71,350

2004 Football League Cup

Semi-finals

Arsenal vs Middlesbrough (0-1, 1-2)	1-3
Bolton vs Aston Villa (5-2, 0-2)	5-4

Final

The Millennium Stadium, Cardiff, 29th February 2004

Bolton Wanderers 1 (Davies)
Middlesbrough 2 (Job, Zenden)

Attendance 72,634

F.A. PREMIER LEAGUE 2004-2005

CHELSEA	38	29	8	1	72	15	95
Arsenal	38	25	8	5	87	36	83
Manchester United	38	22	11	5	58	26	77
Everton	38	18	7	13	45	46	61
Liverpool	38	17	7	14	52	41	58
Bolton Wanderers	38	16	10	12	49	44	58
Middlesbrough	38	14	13	11	53	46	55
Manchester City	38	13	13	12	47	39	52
Tottenham Hotspur	38	14	10	14	47	41	52
Aston Villa	38	12	11	15	45	52	47
Charlton Athletic	38	12	10	16	42	58	46
Birmingham City	38	11	12	15	40	46	45
Fulham	38	12	8	18	52	60	44
Newcastle United	38	10	14	14	47	57	44
Blackburn Rovers	38	9	15	14	32	43	42
Portsmouth	38	10	9	19	43	59	39
West Bromwich Albion	38	6	16	16	36	61	34
Crystal Palace	*38*	*7*	*12*	*19*	*41*	*62*	*33*
Norwich City	*38*	*7*	*12*	*19*	*42*	*77*	*33*
Southampton	*38*	*6*	*14*	*18*	*45*	*66*	*32*

THE CHAMPIONSHIP 2004-2005

Sunderland	46	29	7	10	76	41	94
Wigan Athletic	46	25	12	9	79	35	87
Ipswich Town	46	24	13	9	85	56	85
Derby County	46	22	10	14	71	60	76
Preston North End	46	21	12	13	67	58	75
West Ham United	46	21	10	15	66	56	73
Reading	46	19	13	14	51	44	70
Sheffield United	46	18	13	15	57	56	67
Wolverhampton Wanderers	46	15	21	10	72	59	66
Millwall	46	18	12	16	51	45	66
Queens Park Rangers	46	17	11	18	54	58	62
Stoke City	46	17	10	19	36	38	61
Burnley	46	15	15	16	38	39	60
Leeds United	46	14	18	14	49	52	60
Leicester City	46	12	21	13	49	46	57
Cardiff City	46	13	15	18	48	51	54
Plymouth Argyle	46	14	11	21	52	64	53
Watford	46	12	16	18	52	59	52
Coventry City	46	13	13	20	61	73	52
Brighton & Hove Albion	46	13	12	21	40	65	51
Crewe Alexandra	46	12	14	20	66	86	50
Gillingham	*46*	*12*	*14*	*20*	*45*	*66*	*50*
Nottingham Forest	*46*	*9*	*17*	*20*	*42*	*66*	*44*
Rotherham United	*46*	*5*	*14*	*27*	*35*	*69*	*29*

The Championship Play-offs

West Ham United vs Ipswich Town	2-2, 2-0
Preston North End vs Derby County	2-0, 0-0
West Ham United vs Preston North End	1-0

2005 F.A. Cup

Semi-finals

Arsenal vs Blackburn Rovers	3-0
Manchester United vs Newcastle United	4-1

Final

The Millennium Stadium, Cardiff, 21st May 2005

Arsenal 0
Manchester United 0 (aet.)

Attendance 71,876

Arsenal won 5-4 on penalties

LEAGUE ONE 2004-2005

Luton Town	46	29	11	6	87	48	98
Hull City	46	26	8	12	80	53	86
Tranmere Rovers	46	22	13	11	73	55	79
Brentford	46	22	9	15	57	60	75
Sheffield Wednesday	46	19	15	12	77	59	72
Hartlepool United	46	21	8	17	76	66	71
Bristol City	46	18	16	12	74	57	70
AFC Bournemouth	46	20	10	16	77	64	70
Huddersfield Town	46	20	10	16	74	65	70
Doncaster Rovers	46	16	18	12	65	60	66
Bradford City	46	17	14	15	64	62	65
Swindon Town	46	17	12	17	66	68	63
Barnsley	46	14	19	13	69	64	61
Walsall	46	16	12	18	65	69	60
Colchester United	46	14	17	15	60	50	59
Blackpool	46	15	12	19	54	59	57
Chesterfield	46	14	15	17	55	62	57
Port Vale	46	17	5	24	49	59	56
Oldham Athletic	46	14	10	22	60	73	52
Milton Keynes Dons	46	12	15	19	54	68	51
Torquay United	*46*	*12*	*15*	*19*	*55*	*79*	*51*
Wrexham	*46*	*13*	*14*	*19*	*62*	*80*	*43*
Peterborough United	*46*	*9*	*12*	*25*	*49*	*73*	*39*
Stockport County	*46*	*6*	*8*	*32*	*49*	*98*	*26*

Wrexham had 10 points deducted

League One Play-offs

Sheffield Wednesday vs Brentford	1-0, 2-1
Hartlepool United vs Tranmere Rovers	2-0, 0-2
Hartlepool United won 6-5 on penalties	
Sheffield Wednesday vs Hartlepool United	4-2

LEAGUE TWO 2004-2005

Yeovil Town	46	25	8	13	90	65	83
Scunthorpe United	46	22	14	10	69	42	80
Swansea City	46	24	8	14	62	43	80
Southend United	46	22	12	12	65	46	78
Macclesfield Town	46	22	9	15	60	49	75
Lincoln City	46	20	12	14	64	47	72
Northampton Town	46	20	12	14	62	51	72
Darlington	46	20	12	14	57	49	72
Rochdale	46	16	18	12	54	48	66
Wycombe Wanderers	46	17	14	15	58	52	65
Leyton Orient	46	16	15	15	65	67	63
Bristol Rovers	46	13	21	12	60	57	60
Mansfield Town	46	15	15	16	56	56	60
Cheltenham Town	46	16	12	18	51	54	60
Oxford United	46	16	11	19	50	63	59
Boston United	46	14	16	16	62	58	58
Bury	46	14	16	16	54	54	58
Grimsby Town	46	13	17	16	47	51	56
Notts County	46	13	13	20	46	62	52
Chester City	46	12	16	18	43	69	52
Shrewsbury Town	46	11	16	19	48	53	49
Rushden & Diamonds	46	10	14	22	42	63	44
Kidderminster Harriers	*46*	*10*	*9*	*27*	*38*	*81*	*39*
Cambridge United	*46*	*8*	*16*	*22*	*39*	*62*	*30*

Cambridge United had 10 points deducted

League Two Play-offs

Lincoln City vs Macclesfield Town	1-0, 1-1
Northampton Town vs Southend United	0-0, 0-1
Southend United vs Lincoln City	2-0

2005 Football League Cup

Semi-finals

Chelsea vs Manchester United (0-0, 2-1)	2-1
Liverpool vs Watford (1-0, 1-0)	2-0

Final

The Millennium Stadium, Cardiff, 27th February 2005

Chelsea 3   (Gerrard (og), Drogba, Kezman)
Liverpool 2 (aet.)   (Riise, Nunez)

Attendance 78,000

F.A. PREMIER LEAGUE 2005-2006

CHELSEA	38	29	4	5	72	22	91
Manchester United	38	25	8	5	72	34	83
Liverpool	38	25	7	6	57	25	82
Arsenal	38	20	7	11	68	31	67
Tottenham Hotspur	38	18	11	9	53	38	65
Blackburn Rovers	38	19	6	13	51	42	63
Newcastle United	38	17	7	14	47	42	58
Bolton Wanderers	38	15	11	12	49	41	56
West Ham United	38	16	7	15	52	55	55
Wigan Athletic	38	15	6	17	45	52	51
Everton	38	14	8	16	34	49	50
Fulham	38	14	6	18	48	58	48
Charlton Athletic	38	13	8	17	41	55	47
Middlesbrough	38	12	9	17	48	58	45
Manchester City	38	13	4	21	43	48	43
Aston Villa	38	10	12	16	42	55	42
Portsmouth	38	10	8	20	37	62	38
Birmingham City	*38*	*8*	*10*	*20*	*28*	*50*	*34*
West Bromwich Albion	*38*	*7*	*9*	*22*	*31*	*58*	*30*
Sunderland	*38*	*3*	*6*	*29*	*26*	*69*	*15*

THE CHAMPIONSHIP 2005-2006

Reading	46	31	13	2	99	32	106
Sheffield United	46	26	12	8	76	46	90
Watford	46	22	15	9	77	53	81
Preston North End	46	20	20	6	59	30	80
Leeds United	46	21	15	10	57	38	78
Crystal Palace	46	21	12	13	67	48	75
Wolverhampton Wanderers	46	16	19	11	50	42	67
Coventry City	46	16	15	15	62	65	63
Norwich City	46	18	8	20	56	65	62
Luton Town	46	17	10	19	66	67	61
Cardiff City	46	16	12	18	58	59	60
Southampton	46	13	19	14	49	50	58
Stoke City	46	17	7	22	54	63	58
Plymouth Argyle	46	13	17	16	39	46	56
Ipswich Town	46	14	14	18	53	66	56
Leicester City	46	13	15	18	51	59	54
Burnley	46	14	12	20	46	54	54
Hull City	46	12	16	18	49	55	52
Sheffield Wednesday	46	13	13	20	39	52	52
Derby County	46	10	20	16	53	67	50
Queens Park Rangers	46	12	14	20	50	65	50
Crewe Alexandra	*46*	*9*	*15*	*22*	*57*	*86*	*42*
Millwall	*46*	*8*	*16*	*22*	*35*	*62*	*40*
Brighton & Hove Albion	*46*	*7*	*17*	*22*	*39*	*71*	*38*

The Championship Play-offs

Leeds United vs Preston North End	1-1, 2-0
Crystal Palace vs Watford	0-3, 0-0
Watford vs Leeds United	3-0

2006 F.A. Cup

Semi-finals

Chelsea vs Liverpool	1-2
Middlesbrough vs West Ham United	0-1

Final

The Millennium Stadium, Cardiff, 13th May 2006

Liverpool 3 (Cisse, Gerrard 2)

West Ham United 3 (aet.) (Carragher (og), Ashton, Konchesky)

Attendance 74,000

Liverpool won 3-1 on penalties

LEAGUE ONE 2005-2006

Southend United	46	23	13	10	72	43	82
Colchester United	46	22	13	11	58	40	79
Brentford	46	20	16	10	72	52	76
Huddersfield Town	46	19	16	11	72	59	73
Barnsley	46	18	18	10	62	44	72
Swansea City	46	18	17	11	78	55	71
Nottingham Forest	46	19	12	15	67	52	69
Doncaster Rovers	46	20	9	17	55	51	69
Bristol City	46	18	11	17	66	62	65
Oldham Athletic	46	18	11	17	58	60	65
Bradford City	46	14	19	13	51	49	61
Scunthorpe United	46	15	15	16	68	73	60
Port Vale	46	16	12	18	49	54	60
Gillingham	46	16	12	18	50	64	60
Yeovil Town	46	15	11	20	54	62	56
Chesterfield	46	14	14	18	63	73	56
AFC Bournemouth	46	12	19	15	49	53	55
Tranmere Rovers	46	13	15	18	50	52	54
Blackpool	46	12	17	17	56	64	53
Rotherham United	46	12	16	18	52	62	52
Hartlepool United	*46*	*11*	*17*	*18*	*44*	*59*	*50*
Milton Keynes Dons	*46*	*12*	*14*	*20*	*45*	*66*	*50*
Swindon Town	*46*	*11*	*15*	*20*	*46*	*65*	*48*
Walsall	*46*	*11*	*14*	*21*	*47*	*70*	*47*

League One Play-offs

Barnsley vs Huddersfield Town	0-1, 3-1
Swansea City vs Brentford	1-1, 2-0
Swansea City vs Barnsley	2-2

Barnsley won 4-3 on penalties

LEAGUE TWO 2005-2006

Carlisle United	46	25	11	10	84	42	86
Northampton Town	46	22	17	7	63	37	83
Leyton Orient	46	22	15	9	67	51	81
Grimsby Town	46	22	12	12	64	44	78
Cheltenham Town	46	19	15	12	65	53	72
Wycombe Wanderers	46	18	17	11	72	56	71
Lincoln City	46	15	21	10	65	53	66
Darlington	46	16	15	15	58	52	63
Peterborough United	46	17	11	18	57	49	62
Shrewsbury Town	46	16	13	17	55	55	61
Boston United	46	15	16	15	50	60	61
Bristol Rovers	46	17	9	20	59	67	60
Wrexham	46	15	14	17	61	54	59
Rochdale	46	14	14	18	66	69	56
Chester City	46	14	12	20	53	59	54
Mansfield Town	46	13	15	18	59	66	54
Macclesfield Town	46	12	18	16	60	71	54
Barnet	46	12	18	16	44	57	54
Bury (-1)	46	12	17	17	45	57	52
Torquay United	46	13	13	20	53	66	52
Notts County	46	12	16	18	48	63	52
Stockport County	46	11	19	16	57	78	52
Oxford United	*46*	*11*	*16*	*19*	*43*	*57*	*49*
Rushden & Diamonds	*46*	*11*	*12*	*23*	*44*	*76*	*45*

Bury had one point deducted

League Two Play-offs

Lincoln City vs Grimsby Town	0-1, 1-2
Wycombe Wanderers vs Cheltenham Town	1-2, 0-0
Cheltenham Town vs Grimsby Town	1-0

2006 Football League Cup

Semi-finals

Blackburn Rovers vs Manchester United	(1-1, 1-2)	2-3
Wigan Athletic vs Arsenal	(1-0, 1-2 aet)	2-2

Wigan Athletic won on the away goals rule

Final

The Millennium Stadium, Cardiff, 26th February 2006

Manchester United 4 (Rooney 2, Saha, Ronaldo)

Wigan Athletic 0

Attendance 66,866

F.A. PREMIER LEAGUE 2006-2007

MANCHESTER UNITED	38	28	5	5	83	27	89
Chelsea	38	24	11	3	64	24	83
Liverpool	38	20	8	10	57	27	68
Arsenal	38	19	11	8	63	35	68
Tottenham Hotspur	38	17	9	12	57	54	60
Everton	38	15	13	10	52	36	58
Bolton Wanderers	38	16	8	14	47	52	56
Reading	38	16	7	15	52	47	55
Portsmouth	38	14	12	12	45	42	54
Blackburn Rovers	38	15	7	16	52	54	52
Aston Villa	38	11	17	10	43	41	50
Middlesbrough	38	12	10	16	44	49	46
Newcastle United	38	11	10	17	38	47	43
Manchester City	38	11	9	18	29	44	42
West Ham United	38	12	5	21	35	59	41
Fulham	38	8	15	15	38	60	39
Wigan Athletic	38	10	8	20	37	59	38
Sheffield United	38	10	8	20	32	55	38
Charlton Athletic	38	8	10	20	34	60	34
Watford	38	5	13	20	29	59	28

THE CHAMPIONSHIP 2006-2007

Sunderland	46	27	7	12	76	47	88
Birmingham City	46	26	8	12	67	42	86
Derby County	46	25	9	12	62	46	84
West Bromwich Albion	46	22	10	14	81	55	76
Wolverhampton Wndrs	46	22	10	14	59	56	76
Southampton	46	21	12	13	77	53	75
Preston North End	46	22	8	16	64	53	74
Stoke City	46	19	16	11	62	41	73
Sheffield Wednesday	46	20	11	15	70	66	71
Colchester United	46	20	9	17	70	56	69
Plymouth Argyle	46	17	16	13	63	62	67
Crystal Palace	46	18	11	17	59	51	65
Cardiff City	46	17	13	16	57	53	64
Ipswich Town	46	18	8	20	64	59	62
Burnley	46	15	12	19	52	49	57
Norwich City	46	16	9	21	56	71	57
Coventry City	46	16	8	22	47	62	56
Queens Park Rangers	46	14	11	21	54	68	53
Leicester City	46	13	14	19	49	64	53
Barnsley	46	15	5	26	53	85	50
Hull City	46	13	10	23	51	67	49
Southend United	46	10	12	24	47	80	42
Luton Town	46	10	10	26	53	81	40
Leeds United	46	13	7	26	46	72	36

Leeds United had 10 points deducted

The Championship Play-offs

Southampton vs Derby County	1-2, 3-2
Derby County won 4-3 on penalties	
Wolverhampton Wands. vs West Bromwich Albion	2-3, 0-1
Derby County vs West Bromwich Albion	1-0

2007 F.A. Cup

Semi-finals

Blackburn Rovers vs Chelsea	1-2
Watford vs Manchester United	1-4

Final

Wembley, 19th May 2007

Chelsea 1 (Drogba)
Manchester United 0 **(aet.)**

Attendance 89,826

LEAGUE ONE 2006-2007

Scunthorpe United	46	26	13	7	73	35	91
Bristol City	46	25	10	11	63	39	85
Blackpool	46	24	11	11	76	49	83
Nottingham Forest	46	23	13	10	65	41	82
Yeovil Town	46	23	10	13	55	39	79
Oldham Athletic	46	21	12	13	69	47	75
Swansea City	46	20	12	14	69	53	72
Carlisle United	46	19	11	16	54	55	68
Tranmere Rovers	46	18	13	15	58	53	67
Millwall	46	19	9	18	59	62	66
Doncaster Rovers	46	16	15	15	52	47	63
Port Vale	46	18	6	22	64	65	60
Crewe Alexandra	46	17	9	20	66	72	60
Northampton Town	46	15	14	17	48	51	59
Huddersfield Town	46	14	17	15	60	69	59
Gillingham	46	17	8	21	56	77	59
Cheltenham Town	46	15	9	22	49	61	54
Brighton & Hove Albion	46	14	11	21	49	58	53
AFC Bournemouth	46	13	13	20	50	64	52
Leyton Orient	46	12	15	19	61	77	51
Chesterfield	46	12	11	23	45	53	47
Bradford City	46	11	14	21	47	65	47
Rotherham United	46	13	9	24	58	75	38
Brentford	46	8	13	25	40	79	37

Rotherham United had 10 points deducted

League One Play-offs

Yeovil Town vs Nottingham Forest	0-2, 5-2
Oldham Athletic vs Blackpool	1-2, 1-3
Blackpool vs Yeovil Town	2-0

LEAGUE TWO 2006-2007

Walsall	46	25	14	7	66	34	89
Hartlepool United	46	26	10	10	65	40	88
Swindon Town	46	25	10	11	58	38	85
Milton Keynes Dons	46	25	9	12	76	58	84
Lincoln City	46	21	11	14	70	59	74
Bristol Rovers	46	20	12	14	49	42	72
Shrewsbury Town	46	18	17	11	68	46	71
Stockport County	46	21	8	17	65	54	71
Rochdale	46	18	12	16	70	50	66
Peterborough United	46	18	11	17	70	61	65
Darlington	46	17	14	15	52	56	65
Wycombe Wanderers	46	16	14	16	52	47	62
Notts County	46	16	14	16	55	53	62
Barnet	46	16	11	19	55	70	59
Grimsby Town	46	17	8	21	57	73	59
Hereford United	46	14	13	19	45	53	55
Mansfield Town	46	14	12	20	58	63	54
Chester City	46	13	14	19	40	48	53
Wrexham	46	13	12	21	43	65	51
Accrington Stanley	46	13	11	22	70	81	50
Bury	46	13	11	22	46	61	50
Macclesfield Town	46	12	12	22	55	77	48
Boston United	46	12	10	24	51	80	46
Torquay United	46	7	14	25	36	63	35

League Two Play-offs

Bristol Rovers vs Lincoln City	2-1, 5-3
Shrewsbury Town vs Milton Keynes Dons	0-0, 2-1
Bristol Rovers vs Shrewsbury Town	3-1

2007 Football League Cup

Semi-finals

Tottenham Hotspur vs Arsenal (2-2, 1-3 aet)	3-5
Wycombe Wanderers vs Chelsea (1-1, 0-4)	1-5

Final

The Millennium Stadium, Cardiff, 25th February 2007

Chelsea 2 (Drogba 2)
Arsenal 1 (Walcott)

Attendance 70,073

F.A. PREMIER LEAGUE 2007-2008

MANCHESTER UNITED	38	27	6	5	80	22	87
Chelsea	38	25	10	3	65	26	85
Arsenal	38	24	11	3	74	31	83
Liverpool	38	21	13	4	67	28	76
Everton	38	19	8	11	55	33	65
Aston Villa	38	16	12	10	71	51	60
Blackburn Rovers	38	15	13	10	50	48	58
Portsmouth	38	16	9	13	48	40	57
Manchester City	38	15	10	13	45	53	55
West Ham United	38	13	10	15	42	50	49
Tottenham Hotspur	38	11	13	14	66	61	46
Newcastle United	38	11	10	17	45	65	43
Middlesbrough	38	10	12	16	43	53	42
Wigan Athletic	38	10	10	18	34	51	40
Sunderland	38	11	6	21	36	59	39
Bolton Wanderers	38	9	10	19	36	54	37
Fulham	38	8	12	18	38	60	36
Reading	*38*	*10*	*6*	*22*	*41*	*66*	*36*
Birmingham City	*38*	*8*	*11*	*19*	*46*	*62*	*35*
Derby County	*38*	*1*	*8*	*29*	*20*	*89*	*11*

THE CHAMPIONSHIP 2007-2008

West Bromwich Albion	46	23	12	11	88	55	81
Stoke City	46	21	16	9	69	55	79
Hull City	46	21	12	13	65	47	75
Bristol City	46	20	14	12	54	53	74
Crystal Palace	46	18	17	11	58	42	71
Watford	46	18	16	12	62	56	70
Wolverhampton Wanderers	46	18	16	12	53	48	70
Ipswich Town	46	18	15	13	65	56	69
Sheffield United	46	17	15	14	56	51	66
Plymouth Argyle	46	17	13	16	60	50	64
Charlton Athletic	46	17	13	16	63	58	64
Cardiff City	46	16	16	14	59	55	64
Burnley	46	16	14	16	60	67	62
Queens Park Rangers	46	14	16	16	60	66	58
Preston North End	46	15	11	20	50	56	56
Sheffield Wednesday	46	14	13	19	54	55	55
Norwich City	46	15	10	21	49	59	55
Barnsley	46	14	13	19	52	65	55
Blackpool	46	12	18	16	59	64	54
Southampton	46	13	15	18	56	72	54
Coventry City	46	14	11	21	52	64	53
Leicester City	*46*	*12*	*16*	*18*	*42*	*45*	*52*
Scunthorpe United	*46*	*11*	*13*	*22*	*46*	*69*	*46*
Colchester United	*46*	*7*	*17*	*22*	*62*	*86*	*38*

The Championship Play-offs

Watford vs Hull City	0-2, 1-4
Crystal Palace vs Bristol City	1-2, 1-2
Hull City vs Bristol City	1-0

2008 F.A. Cup

Semi-finals

Barnsley vs Cardiff City	0-1
West Bromwich Albion vs Portsmouth	0-1

Final

Wembley, 17th May 2008

Portsmouth 1 (Kanu)
Cardiff City 0

Attendance 89,874

LEAGUE ONE 2007-2008

Swansea City	46	27	11	8	82	42	92
Nottingham Forest	46	22	16	8	64	32	82
Doncaster Rovers	46	23	11	12	65	41	80
Carlisle United	46	23	11	12	64	46	80
Leeds United	46	27	10	9	72	38	76
Southend United	46	22	10	14	70	55	76
Brighton & Hove Albion	46	19	12	15	58	50	69
Oldham Athletic	46	18	13	15	58	46	67
Northampton Town	46	17	15	14	60	55	66
Huddersfield Town	46	20	6	20	50	62	66
Tranmere Rovers	46	18	11	17	52	47	65
Walsall	46	16	16	14	52	46	64
Swindon Town	46	16	13	17	63	56	61
Leyton Orient	46	16	12	18	49	63	60
Hartlepool United	46	15	9	22	63	66	54
Bristol Rovers	46	12	17	17	45	53	53
Millwall	46	14	10	22	45	60	52
Yeovil Town	46	14	10	22	38	59	52
Cheltenham Town	46	13	12	21	42	64	51
Crewe Alexandra	46	12	14	20	47	65	50
AFC Bournemouth	*46*	*17*	*7*	*22*	*62*	*72*	*48*
Gillingham	*46*	*11*	*13*	*22*	*44*	*73*	*46*
Port Vale	*46*	*9*	*11*	*26*	*47*	*81*	*38*
Luton Town	*46*	*11*	*10*	*25*	*43*	*63*	*33*

Leeds United had 15 points deducted
AFC Bournemouth and Luton Town had 10 points deducted

League One Play-offs

Southend United vs Doncaster Rovers	0-0, 1-5
Leeds United vs Carlisle United	1-2, 2-0
Doncaster Rovers vs Leeds United	1-0

LEAGUE TWO 2007-2008

Milton Keynes Dons	46	29	10	7	82	37	97
Peterborough United	46	28	8	10	84	43	92
Hereford United	46	26	10	10	72	41	88
Stockport County	46	24	10	12	72	54	82
Rochdale	46	23	11	12	77	54	80
Darlington	46	22	12	12	67	40	78
Wycombe Wanderers	46	22	12	12	56	42	78
Chesterfield	46	19	12	15	76	56	69
Rotherham United	46	21	11	14	62	58	64
Bradford City	46	17	11	18	63	61	60
Morecambe	46	16	12	18	59	63	60
Barnet	46	16	12	18	56	63	60
Bury	46	16	11	19	58	61	59
Brentford	46	17	8	21	52	70	59
Lincoln City	46	18	4	24	61	77	58
Grimsby Town	46	15	10	21	55	66	55
Accrington Stanley	46	16	3	27	49	83	51
Shrewsbury Town	46	12	14	20	56	65	50
Macclesfield Town	46	11	17	18	47	64	50
Dagenham & Redbridge	46	13	10	23	49	70	49
Notts County	46	10	18	18	37	53	48
Chester City	46	12	11	23	51	68	47
Mansfield Town	*46*	*11*	*9*	*26*	*48*	*68*	*42*
Wrexham	*46*	*10*	*10*	*26*	*38*	*70*	*40*

Rotherham United had 10 points deducted

League Two Play-offs

Wycombe Wanderers vs Stockport County	1-1, 0-1
Darlington vs Rochdale	2-1, 1-2
Rochdale won 5-4 on penalties	
Rochdale vs Stockport County	2-3

2008 Football League Cup

Semi-finals

Chelsea vs Everton (2-1, 1-0)	3-1
Arsenal vs Tottenham Hotspur (1-1, 1-5)	2-6

Final

Wembley, 24th February 2008

Chelsea 1 (Drogba)
Tottenham Hotspur 2 (aet.) (Berbatov (pen), Woodgate)

Attendance 87,660

F.A. PREMIER LEAGUE 2008-2009

MANCHESTER UNITED	38	28	6	4	68	24	90
Liverpool	38	25	11	2	77	27	86
Chelsea	38	25	8	5	68	24	83
Arsenal	38	20	12	6	68	37	72
Everton	38	17	12	9	55	37	63
Aston Villa	38	17	11	10	54	48	62
Fulham	38	14	11	13	39	34	53
Tottenham Hotspur	38	14	9	15	45	45	51
West Ham United	38	14	9	15	42	45	51
Manchester City	38	15	5	18	58	50	50
Wigan Athletic	38	12	9	17	34	45	45
Stoke City	38	12	9	17	38	55	45
Bolton Wanderers	38	11	8	19	41	53	41
Portsmouth	38	10	11	17	38	57	41
Blackburn Rovers	38	10	11	17	40	60	41
Sunderland	38	9	9	20	34	54	36
Hull City	38	8	11	19	39	64	35
Newcastle United	*38*	*7*	*13*	*18*	*40*	*59*	*34*
Middlesbrough	*38*	*7*	*11*	*20*	*28*	*57*	*32*
West Bromwich Albion	*38*	*8*	*8*	*22*	*36*	*67*	*32*

The Championship Play-offs

Preston North End vs Sheffield United	1-1, 0-1
Burnley vs Reading	1-0, 2-0
Sheffield United vs Burnley	0-1

THE CHAMPIONSHIP 2008-2009

Wolverhampton Wanderers	46	27	9	10	80	52	90
Birmingham City	46	23	14	9	54	37	83
Sheffield United	46	22	14	10	64	39	80
Reading	46	21	14	11	72	40	77
Burnley	46	21	13	12	72	60	76
Preston North End	46	21	11	14	66	54	74
Cardiff City	46	19	17	10	65	53	74
Swansea City	46	16	20	10	63	50	68
Ipswich Town	46	17	15	14	62	53	66
Bristol City	46	15	16	15	54	54	61
Queen's Park Rangers	46	15	16	15	42	44	61
Sheffield Wednesday	46	16	13	17	51	58	61
Watford	46	16	10	20	68	72	58
Doncaster Rovers	46	17	7	22	42	53	58
Crystal Palace	46	15	12	19	52	55	57
Blackpool	46	13	17	16	47	58	56
Coventry City	46	13	15	18	47	58	54
Derby County	46	14	12	20	55	67	54
Nottingham Forest	46	13	14	19	50	65	53
Barnsley	46	13	13	20	45	58	52
Plymouth Argyle	46	13	12	21	44	57	51
Norwich City	*46*	*12*	*10*	*24*	*57*	*70*	*46*
Southampton	*46*	*10*	*15*	*21*	*46*	*69*	*45*
Charlton Athletic	*46*	*8*	*15*	*23*	*52*	*74*	*39*

League One Play-offs

Scunthorpe United vs Milton Keynes Dons	1-1, 0-0
Scunthorpe United won 7-6 on penalties	
Millwall vs Leeds United	1-0, 1-1
Scunthorpe United vs Millwall	3-2

2009 F.A. Cup

Semi-finals

Arsenal vs Chelsea	1-2
Manchester United vs Everton	0-1 (aet)
Everton won 4-2 on penalties	

Final

Wembley, 30th May 2009

Chelsea 2 (Drogba, Lampard)
Everton 1 (Saha)

Attendance 89,391

LEAGUE ONE 2008-2009

Leicester City	46	27	15	4	84	39	96
Peterborough United	46	26	11	9	78	54	89
Milton Keynes Dons	46	26	9	11	83	47	87
Leeds United	46	26	6	14	77	49	84
Millwall	46	25	7	14	63	53	82
Scunthorpe United	46	22	10	14	82	63	76
Tranmere Rovers	46	21	11	14	62	49	74
Southend United	46	21	8	17	58	61	71
Huddersfield Town	46	18	14	14	62	65	68
Oldham Athletic	46	16	17	13	66	65	65
Bristol Rovers	46	17	12	17	79	61	63
Colchester United	46	18	9	19	58	58	63
Walsall	46	17	10	19	61	66	61
Leyton Orient	46	15	11	20	45	57	56
Swindon Town	46	12	17	17	68	71	53
Brighton & Hove Albion	46	13	13	20	55	70	52
Yeovil Town	46	12	15	19	41	66	51
Stockport County	46	16	12	18	59	57	50
Hartlepool United	46	13	11	22	66	79	50
Carlisle United	46	12	14	20	56	69	50
Northampton Town	*46*	*12*	*13*	*21*	*61*	*65*	*49*
Crewe Alexandra	*46*	*12*	*10*	*24*	*59*	*82*	*46*
Cheltenham Town	*46*	*9*	*12*	*25*	*51*	*91*	*39*
Hereford United	*46*	*9*	*7*	*30*	*42*	*79*	*34*

Stockport County had 10 points deducted

LEAGUE TWO 2008-2009

Brentford	46	23	16	7	65	36	85
Exeter City	46	22	13	11	65	50	79
Wycombe Wanderers	46	20	18	8	54	33	78
Bury	46	21	15	10	63	43	78
Gillingham	46	21	12	13	58	55	75
Rochdale	46	19	13	14	70	59	70
Shrewsbury Town	46	17	18	11	61	44	69
Dagenham & Redbridge	46	19	11	16	77	53	68
Bradford City	46	18	13	15	66	55	67
Chesterfield	46	16	15	15	62	57	63
Morecambe	46	15	18	13	53	56	63
Darlington	46	20	12	14	61	44	62
Lincoln City	46	14	17	15	53	52	59
Rotherham United	46	21	12	13	60	46	58
Aldershot Town	46	14	12	20	59	80	54
Accrington Stanley	46	13	11	22	42	59	50
Barnet	46	11	15	20	56	74	48
Port Vale	46	13	9	24	44	66	48
Notts County	46	11	14	21	49	69	47
Macclesfield Town	46	13	8	25	45	77	47
AFC Bournemouth	46	17	12	17	59	51	46
Grimsby Town	46	9	14	23	51	69	41
Chester City	*46*	*8*	*13*	*25*	*43*	*81*	*37*
Luton Town	*46*	*13*	*17*	*16*	*58*	*65*	*26*

Darlington had 10 points deducted
Rotherham United had 17 points deducted
AFC Bournemouth had 17 points deducted
Luton Town had 30 points deducted

League Two Play-offs

Shrewsbury Town vs Bury	0-1, 1-0
Shrewsbury Town won 4-3 on penalties	
Rochdale vs Gillingham	0-0, 1-2
Gillingham vs Shrewsbury Town	1-0

2009 Football League Cup

Semi-finals

Derby County vs Manchester United (1-0, 2-4)	3-4
Tottenham Hotspur vs Burnley (4-1, 2-3)	6-4

Final

Wembley, 1st March 2009

Manchester United 0
Tottenham Hotspur 0 (aet.)

Attendance 88,217

Manchester United won 4-1 on penalties

F.A. PREMIER LEAGUE 2009-2010

CHELSEA	38	27	5	6	103	32	86
Manchester United	38	27	4	7	86	28	85
Arsenal	38	23	6	9	83	41	75
Tottenham Hotspur	38	21	7	10	67	41	70
Manchester City	38	18	13	7	73	45	67
Aston Villa	38	17	13	8	52	39	64
Liverpool	38	18	9	11	61	35	63
Everton	38	16	13	9	60	49	61
Birmingham City	38	13	11	14	38	47	50
Blackburn Rovers	38	13	11	14	41	55	50
Stoke City	38	11	14	13	34	48	47
Fulham	38	12	10	16	39	46	46
Sunderland	38	11	11	16	48	56	44
Bolton Wanderers	38	10	9	19	42	67	39
Wolverhampton Wanderers	38	9	11	18	32	56	38
Wigan Athletic	38	9	9	20	37	79	36
West Ham United	38	8	11	19	47	66	35
Burnley	*38*	*8*	*6*	*24*	*42*	*82*	*30*
Hull City	*38*	*6*	*12*	*20*	*34*	*75*	*30*
Portsmouth	*38*	*7*	*7*	*24*	*34*	*66*	*19*

Portsmouth had 9 points deducted

THE CHAMPIONSHIP 2009-2010

Newcastle United	46	30	12	4	90	35	102
West Bromwich Albion	46	26	13	7	89	48	91
Nottingham Forest	46	22	13	11	65	40	79
Cardiff City	46	22	10	14	73	54	76
Leicester City	46	21	13	12	61	45	76
Blackpool	46	19	13	14	74	58	70
Swansea City	46	17	18	11	40	37	69
Sheffield United	46	17	14	15	62	55	65
Reading	46	17	12	17	68	63	63
Bristol City	46	15	18	13	56	65	63
Middlesbrough	46	16	14	16	58	50	62
Doncaster Rovers	46	15	15	16	59	58	60
Queen's Park Rangers	46	14	15	17	58	65	57
Derby County	46	15	11	20	53	63	56
Ipswich Town	46	12	20	14	50	61	56
Watford	46	14	12	20	61	68	54
Preston North End	46	13	15	18	58	73	54
Barnsley	46	14	12	20	53	69	54
Coventry City	46	13	15	18	47	64	54
Scunthorpe United	46	14	10	22	62	84	52
Crystal Palace	46	14	17	15	50	53	49
Sheffield Wednesday	*46*	*11*	*14*	*21*	*49*	*69*	*47*
Plymouth Argyle	*46*	*11*	*8*	*27*	*43*	*68*	*41*
Peterborough United	*46*	*8*	*10*	*28*	*46*	*80*	*34*

Crystal Palace had 10 points deducted

The Championship Play-offs

Blackpool vs Nottingham Forest	2-1, 4-3
Leicester City vs Cardiff City	0-1, 3-2
Cardiff City won 4-3 on penalties	
Blackpool vs Cardiff City	3-2

2010 F.A. Cup

Semi-finals

Aston Villa vs Chelsea	0-3
Tottenham Hotspur vs Portsmouth	0-2 (aet)

Final

Wembley, 15th May 2010

Chelsea 1   (Drogba)

Portsmouth 0

Attendance 88,335

LEAGUE ONE 2009-2010

Norwich City	46	29	8	9	89	47	95
Leeds United	46	25	11	10	77	44	86
Millwall	46	24	13	9	76	44	85
Charlton Athletic	46	23	15	8	73	57	84
Swindon Town	46	22	16	8	71	48	82
Huddersfield Town	46	23	11	12	82	56	80
Southampton	46	23	14	9	85	47	73
Colchester United	46	20	12	14	64	52	72
Brentford	46	14	20	12	55	52	62
Walsall	46	16	14	16	60	63	62
Bristol Rovers	46	19	5	22	59	70	62
Milton Keynes Dons	46	17	9	20	60	68	60
Brighton & Hove Albion	46	15	14	17	56	60	59
Carlisle United	46	15	13	18	63	66	58
Yeovil Town	46	13	14	19	55	59	53
Oldham Athletic	46	13	13	20	39	57	52
Leyton Orient	46	13	12	21	53	63	51
Exeter City	46	11	18	17	48	60	51
Tranmere Rovers	46	14	9	23	45	72	51
Hartlepool United	46	14	11	21	59	67	50
Gillingham	*46*	*12*	*14*	*20*	*48*	*64*	*50*
Wycombe Wanderers	*46*	*10*	*15*	*21*	*56*	*76*	*45*
Southend United	*46*	*10*	*13*	*23*	*51*	*72*	*43*
Stockport County	*46*	*5*	*10*	*31*	*35*	*95*	*25*

Southampton had 10 points deducted
Hartlepool United had 3 points deducted

League One Play-offs

Swindon Town vs Charlton Athletic	2-1, 1-2
Swindon Town won 5-4 on penalties	
Huddersfield Town vs Millwall	0-0, 0-2
Millwall vs Swindon Town	1-0

LEAGUE TWO 2009-2010

Notts County	46	27	12	7	96	31	93
Bournemouth	46	25	8	13	61	44	83
Rochdale	46	25	7	14	82	48	82
Morecambe	46	20	13	13	73	64	73
Rotherham United	46	21	10	15	55	52	73
Aldershot Town	46	20	12	14	69	56	72
Dagenham & Redbridge	46	20	12	14	69	58	72
Chesterfield	46	21	7	18	61	62	70
Bury	46	19	12	15	54	59	69
Port Vale	46	17	17	12	61	50	68
Northampton Town	46	18	13	15	62	53	67
Shrewsbury Town	46	17	12	17	55	54	63
Burton Albion	46	17	11	18	71	71	62
Bradford City	46	16	14	16	59	62	62
Accrington Stanley	46	18	7	21	62	74	61
Hereford United	46	17	8	21	54	65	59
Torquay United	46	14	15	17	64	55	57
Crewe Alexandra	46	15	10	21	68	73	55
Macclesfield Town	46	12	18	16	49	58	54
Lincoln City	46	13	11	22	42	65	50
Barnet	46	12	12	22	47	63	48
Cheltenham Town	46	10	18	18	54	71	48
Grimsby Town	*46*	*9*	*17*	*20*	*45*	*71*	*44*
Darlington	*46*	*8*	*6*	*32*	*33*	*87*	*30*

League Two Play-offs

Aldershot Town vs Rotherham United	0-1, 0-2
Dagenham & Redbridge vs Morecambe	6-0, 1-2
Dagenham & Redbridge vs Rotherham United	3-2

2010 Football League Cup

Semi-finals

Blackburn Rovers vs Aston Villa (0-1, 4-6)	4-7
Manchester City vs Manchester United (2-1, 1-3)	3-4

Final

Wembley, 28th February 2010

Aston Villa 1   (Milner pen)

Manchester United 2   (Owen, Rooney)

Attendance 88,596

F.A. PREMIER LEAGUE 2010-2011

Team	P	W	D	L	F	A	Pts
MANCHESTER UNITED	38	23	11	4	78	37	80
Chelsea	38	21	8	9	69	33	71
Manchester City	38	21	8	9	60	33	71
Arsenal	38	19	11	8	72	43	68
Tottenham Hotspur	38	16	14	8	55	46	62
Liverpool	38	17	7	14	59	44	58
Everton	38	13	15	10	51	45	54
Fulham	38	11	16	11	49	43	49
Aston Villa	38	12	12	14	48	59	48
Sunderland	38	12	11	15	45	56	47
West Bromwich Albion	38	12	11	15	56	71	47
Newcastle United	38	11	13	14	56	57	46
Stoke City	38	13	7	18	46	48	46
Bolton Wanderers	38	12	10	16	52	56	46
Blackburn Rovers	38	11	10	17	46	59	43
Wigan Athletic	38	9	15	14	40	61	42
Wolverhampton Wanderers	38	11	7	20	46	66	40
Birmingham City	*38*	*8*	*15*	*15*	*37*	*58*	*39*
Blackpool	*38*	*10*	*9*	*19*	*55*	*78*	*39*
West Ham United	*38*	*7*	*12*	*19*	*43*	*70*	*33*

The Championship Play-offs

Nottingham Forest vs Swansea City	0-0, 1-3
Reading vs Cardiff City	0-0, 3-0
Swansea City vs Reading	4-2

THE CHAMPIONSHIP 2010-2011

Team	P	W	D	L	F	A	Pts
Queen's Park Rangers	46	24	16	6	71	32	88
Norwich City	46	23	15	8	83	58	84
Swansea City	46	24	8	14	69	42	80
Cardiff City	46	23	11	12	76	54	80
Reading	46	20	17	9	77	51	77
Nottingham Forest	46	20	15	11	69	50	75
Leeds United	46	19	15	12	81	70	72
Burnley	46	18	14	14	65	61	68
Millwall	46	18	13	15	62	48	67
Leicester City	46	19	10	17	76	71	67
Hull City	46	16	17	13	52	51	65
Middlesbrough	46	17	11	18	68	68	62
Ipswich Town	46	18	8	20	62	68	62
Watford	46	16	13	17	77	71	61
Bristol City	46	17	9	20	62	65	60
Portsmouth	46	15	13	18	53	60	58
Barnsley	46	14	14	18	55	66	56
Coventry City	46	14	13	19	54	58	55
Derby County	46	13	10	23	58	71	49
Crystal Palace	46	12	12	22	44	69	48
Doncaster Rovers	46	11	15	20	55	81	48
Preston North End	*46*	*10*	*12*	*24*	*54*	*79*	*42*
Sheffield United	*46*	*11*	*9*	*26*	*44*	*79*	*42*
Scunthorpe United	*46*	*12*	*6*	*28*	*43*	*87*	*42*

League One Play-offs

AFC Bournemouth vs Huddersfield Town	1-1, 3-3
Huddersfield Town won 4-2 on penalties	
Milton Keynes Dons vs Peterborough United	3-2, 0-2
Peterborough United vs Huddersfield Town	3-0

2011 F.A. Cup

Semi-finals

Bolton Wanderers vs Stoke City	0-5
Manchester City vs Manchester United	1-0

Final

Wembley, 14th May 2011

Manchester City 1   (Yaya Touré)
Stoke City 0

Attendance 88,643

LEAGUE ONE 2010-2011

Team	P	W	D	L	F	A	Pts
Brighton & Hove Albion	46	28	11	7	85	40	95
Southampton	46	28	8	10	86	38	92
Huddersfield Town	46	25	12	9	77	48	87
Peterborough United	46	23	10	13	106	75	79
Milton Keynes Dons	46	23	8	15	67	60	77
Bournemouth	46	19	14	13	75	54	71
Leyton Orient	46	19	13	14	71	62	70
Exeter City	46	20	10	16	66	71	70
Rochdale	46	18	14	14	63	55	68
Colchester United	46	16	14	16	57	63	62
Brentford	46	17	10	19	55	62	61
Carlisle United	46	16	11	19	60	62	59
Charlton Athletic	46	15	14	17	62	66	59
Yeovil Town	46	16	11	19	56	66	59
Sheffield Wednesday	46	16	10	20	67	67	58
Hartlepool United	46	15	12	19	47	65	57
Tranmere Rovers	46	15	11	20	53	60	56
Oldham Athletic	46	13	17	16	53	62	56
Notts County	46	14	8	24	46	60	50
Walsall	46	12	12	22	56	75	48
Dagenham & Redbridge	*46*	*12*	*11*	*23*	*52*	*70*	*47*
Bristol Rovers	*46*	*11*	*12*	*23*	*48*	*82*	*45*
Plymouth Argyle	*46*	*15*	*7*	*24*	*51*	*74*	*42*
Swindon Town	*46*	*9*	*14*	*23*	*50*	*72*	*41*

Plymouth Argyle had 10 points deducted

LEAGUE TWO 2010-2011

Team	P	W	D	L	F	A	Pts
Chesterfield	46	24	14	8	85	51	86
Bury	46	23	12	11	82	50	81
Wycombe Wanderers	46	22	14	10	69	50	80
Shrewsbury Town	46	22	13	11	72	49	79
Accrington Stanley	46	18	19	9	73	55	73
Stevenage	46	18	15	13	62	45	69
Torquay United	46	17	18	11	74	53	68
Gillingham	46	17	17	12	67	57	68
Rotherham United	46	17	15	14	75	60	66
Crewe Alexandra	46	18	11	17	87	65	65
Port Vale	46	17	14	15	54	49	65
Oxford United	46	17	12	17	58	60	63
Southend United	46	16	13	17	62	56	61
Aldershot Town	46	14	19	13	54	54	61
Macclesfield Town	46	14	13	19	59	73	55
Northampton Town	46	11	19	16	63	71	52
Cheltenham Town	46	13	13	20	56	77	52
Bradford City	46	15	7	24	43	68	52
Burton Albion	46	12	15	19	56	70	51
Morecambe	46	13	12	21	54	73	51
Hereford United	46	12	17	17	50	66	50
Barnet	46	12	12	22	58	77	48
Lincoln City	*46*	*13*	*8*	*25*	*45*	*81*	*47*
Stockport County	*46*	*9*	*14*	*23*	*48*	*96*	*41*

Torquay United had 1 point deducted
Hereford United had 3 points deducted

League Two Play-offs

Torquay United vs Shrewsbury Town	2-0, 0-0
Stevenage Borough vs Accrington Stanley	2-0, 1-0
Stevenage Borough vs Torquay United	1-0

2011 Football League Cup

Semi-finals

Ipswich Town vs Arsenal (1-0, 0-3)	1-3
West Ham United vs Birmingham City (2-1, 1-3 aet)	3-4

Final

Wembley, 27th February 2011

Arsenal 1   (Van Persie)
Birmingham City 2   (Zigic, Martins)

Attendance 88,851

F.A. PREMIER LEAGUE 2011-2012

MANCHESTER CITY	38	28	5	5	93	29	89
Manchester United	38	28	5	5	89	33	89
Arsenal	38	21	7	10	74	49	70
Tottenham Hotspur	38	20	9	9	66	41	69
Newcastle United	38	19	8	11	56	51	65
Chelsea	38	18	10	10	65	46	64
Everton	38	15	11	12	50	40	56
Liverpool	38	14	10	14	47	40	52
Fulham	38	14	10	14	48	51	52
West Bromwich Albion	38	13	8	17	45	52	47
Swansea City	38	12	11	15	44	51	47
Norwich City	38	12	11	15	52	66	47
Sunderland	38	11	12	15	45	46	45
Stoke City	38	11	12	15	36	53	45
Wigan Athletic	38	11	10	17	42	62	43
Aston Villa	38	7	17	14	37	53	38
Queens Park Rangers	38	10	7	21	43	66	37
Bolton Wanderers	*38*	*10*	*6*	*22*	*46*	*77*	*36*
Blackburn Rovers	*38*	*8*	*7*	*23*	*48*	*78*	*31*
Wolverhampton Wanderers	*38*	*5*	*10*	*23*	*40*	*82*	*25*

The Championship Play-offs

West Ham United vs Cardiff City	2-0, 3-0
Birmingham City vs Blackpool	0-1, 2-2
West Ham United vs Blackpool	2-1

THE CHAMPIONSHIP 2011-2012

Reading	46	27	8	11	69	41	89
Southampton	46	26	10	10	85	46	88
West Ham United	46	24	14	8	81	48	86
Birmingham City	46	20	16	10	78	51	76
Blackpool	46	20	15	11	79	59	75
Cardiff City	46	19	18	9	66	53	75
Middlesbrough	46	18	16	12	52	51	70
Hull City	46	19	11	16	47	44	68
Leicester City	46	18	12	16	66	55	66
Brighton & Hove Albion	46	17	15	14	52	52	66
Watford	46	16	16	14	56	64	64
Derby County	46	18	10	18	50	58	64
Burnley	46	17	11	18	61	58	62
Leeds United	46	17	10	19	65	68	61
Ipswich Town	46	17	10	19	69	77	61
Millwall	46	15	12	19	55	57	57
Crystal Palace	46	13	17	16	46	51	56
Peterborough United	46	13	11	22	67	77	50
Nottingham Forest	46	14	8	24	48	63	50
Bristol City	46	12	13	21	44	68	49
Barnsley	46	13	9	24	49	74	48
Portsmouth	*46*	*13*	*11*	*22*	*50*	*59*	*40*
Coventry City	*46*	*9*	*13*	*24*	*41*	*65*	*40*
Doncaster Rovers	*46*	*8*	*12*	*26*	*43*	*80*	*36*

Portsmouth had 10 points deducted

League One Play-offs

Sheffield United vs Stevenage	0-0, 1-0
Huddersfield Town vs Milton Keynes Dons	2-0, 1-2
Sheffield United vs Huddersfield Town	0-0
Huddersfield Town won 8-7 on penalties	

2012 F.A. Cup

Semi-finals

Liverpool vs Everton	2-1
Tottenham Hotspur vs Chelsea	1-5

Final

Wembley, 5th May 2012

Chelsea 2   (Ramires, Drogba)

Liverpool 1   (Carroll)

Attendance 89,102

LEAGUE ONE 2011-2012

Charlton Athletic	46	30	11	5	82	36	101
Sheffield Wednesday	46	28	9	9	81	48	93
Sheffield United	46	27	9	10	92	51	90
Huddersfield Town	46	21	18	7	79	47	81
Milton Keynes Dons	46	22	14	10	84	47	80
Stevenage	46	21	10	15	69	44	73
Notts County	46	18	19	9	75	63	73
Carlisle United	46	18	15	13	65	66	69
Brentford	46	18	13	15	63	52	67
Colchester United	46	13	20	13	61	66	59
Bournemouth	46	15	13	18	48	52	58
Tranmere Rovers	46	14	14	18	49	53	56
Hartlepool United	46	14	14	18	50	55	56
Bury	46	15	11	20	60	79	56
Preston North End	46	13	15	18	54	68	54
Oldham Athletic	46	14	12	20	50	66	54
Yeovil Town	46	14	12	20	59	80	54
Scunthorpe United	46	10	22	14	55	59	52
Walsall	46	10	20	16	51	57	50
Leyton Orient	46	13	11	22	48	75	50
Wycombe Wanderers	*46*	*11*	*10*	*25*	*65*	*88*	*43*
Chesterfield	*46*	*10*	*12*	*24*	*55*	*81*	*42*
Exeter City	*46*	*10*	*12*	*24*	*46*	*75*	*42*
Rochdale	*46*	*8*	*14*	*24*	*47*	*81*	*38*

LEAGUE TWO 2011-2012

Swindon Town	46	29	6	11	75	32	93
Shrewsbury Town	46	26	10	10	66	41	88
Crawley Town	46	23	15	8	76	54	84
Southend United	46	25	8	13	77	48	83
Torquay United	46	23	12	11	63	50	81
Cheltenham Town	46	23	8	15	66	50	77
Crewe Alexandra	46	20	12	14	67	59	72
Gillingham	46	20	10	16	79	62	70
Oxford United	46	17	17	12	59	48	68
Rotherham United	46	18	13	15	67	63	67
Aldershot Town	46	19	9	18	54	52	66
Port Vale	46	20	9	17	68	60	59
Bristol Rovers	46	15	12	19	60	70	57
Accrington Stanley	46	14	15	17	54	66	57
Morecambe	46	14	14	18	63	57	56
AFC Wimbledon	46	15	9	22	62	78	54
Burton Albion	46	14	12	20	54	81	54
Bradford City	46	12	14	20	54	59	50
Dagenham & Redbridge	46	14	8	24	50	72	50
Northampton Town	46	12	11	23	56	79	47
Plymouth Argyle	46	10	16	20	47	64	46
Barnet	46	12	10	24	52	79	46
Hereford United	*46*	*10*	*14*	*22*	*50*	*70*	*44*
Macclesfield Town	*46*	*8*	*13*	*25*	*39*	*64*	*37*

Port Vale had 10 points deducted

League Two Play-offs

Southend United vs Crewe Alexandra	0-1, 2-2
Torquay United vs Cheltenham Town	0-2, 1-2
Cheltenham Town vs Crewe Alexandra	0-2

2012 Football League Cup

Semi-finals

Crystal Palace vs Cardiff City (1-0, 0-1 aet)	1-1
Cardiff City won 3-1 on penalties	
Manchester City vs Liverpool (0-1, 2-2)	2-3

Final

Wembley, 26th February 2012

Cardiff City 2   (Mason, Turner)

Liverpool 2 (aet.)   (Skrtel, Kuyt)

Attendance 88,851

Liverpool won 3-2 on penalties

F.A. PREMIER LEAGUE 2012-2013

MANCHESTER UNITED	38	28	5	5	86	43	89
Manchester City	38	23	9	6	66	34	78
Chelsea	38	22	9	7	75	39	75
Arsenal	38	21	10	7	72	37	73
Tottenham Hotspur	38	21	9	8	66	46	72
Everton	38	16	15	7	55	40	63
Liverpool	38	16	13	9	71	43	61
West Bromwich Albion	38	14	7	17	53	57	49
Swansea City	38	11	13	14	47	51	46
West Ham United	38	12	10	16	45	53	46
Norwich City	38	10	14	14	41	58	44
Fulham	38	11	10	17	50	60	43
Stoke City	38	9	15	14	34	45	42
Southampton	38	9	14	15	49	60	41
Aston Villa	38	10	11	17	47	69	41
Newcastle United	38	11	8	19	45	68	41
Sunderland	38	9	12	17	41	54	39
Wigan Athletic	*38*	*9*	*9*	*20*	*47*	*73*	*36*
Reading	*38*	*6*	*10*	*22*	*43*	*73*	*28*
Queen's Park Rangers	*38*	*4*	*13*	*21*	*30*	*60*	*25*

The Championship Play-offs

Watford vs Leicester City	0-1, 3-1
Brighton & Hove Albion vs Crystal Palace	0-0, 0-2
Crystal Palace vs Watford	1-0 (aet)

THE CHAMPIONSHIP 2012-2013

Cardiff City	46	25	12	9	72	45	87
Hull City	46	24	7	15	61	52	79
Watford	46	23	8	15	85	58	77
Brighton & Hove Albion	46	19	18	9	69	43	75
Crystal Palace	46	19	15	12	73	62	72
Leicester City	46	19	11	16	71	48	68
Bolton Wanderers	46	18	14	14	69	61	68
Nottingham Forest	46	17	16	13	63	59	67
Charlton Athletic	46	17	14	15	65	59	65
Derby County	46	16	13	17	65	62	61
Burnley	46	16	13	17	62	60	61
Birmingham City	46	15	16	15	63	69	61
Leeds United	46	17	10	19	57	66	61
Ipswich Town	46	16	12	18	48	61	60
Blackpool	46	14	17	15	62	63	59
Middlesbrough	46	18	5	23	61	70	59
Blackburn Rovers	46	14	16	16	55	62	58
Sheffield Wednesday	46	16	10	20	53	61	58
Huddersfield Town	46	15	13	18	53	73	58
Millwall	46	15	11	20	51	62	56
Barnsley	46	14	13	19	56	70	55
Peterborough United	*46*	*15*	*9*	*22*	*66*	*75*	*54*
Wolverhampton Wanderers	*46*	*14*	*9*	*23*	*55*	*69*	*51*
Bristol City	*46*	*11*	*8*	*27*	*59*	*84*	*41*

League One Play-offs

Brentford vs Swindon Town	1-1, 3-3 (aet)
Brentford won 5-4 on penalties	
Yeovil Town vs Sheffield United	0-1, 2-0
Yeovil Town vs Brentford	2-1

LEAGUE ONE 2012-2013

Doncaster Rovers	46	25	9	12	62	44	84
Bournemouth	46	24	11	11	76	53	83
Brentford	46	21	16	9	62	47	79
Yeovil Town	46	23	8	15	71	56	77
Sheffield United	46	19	18	9	56	42	75
Swindon Town	46	20	14	12	72	39	74
Leyton Orient	46	21	8	17	55	48	71
Milton Keynes Dons	46	19	13	14	62	45	70
Walsall	46	17	17	12	65	58	68
Crawley Town	46	18	14	14	59	58	68
Tranmere Rovers	46	19	10	17	58	48	67
Notts County	46	16	17	13	61	49	65
Crewe Alexandra	46	18	10	18	54	62	64
Preston North End	46	14	17	15	54	49	59
Coventry City	46	18	11	17	66	59	55
Shrewsbury Town	46	13	16	17	54	60	55
Carlisle United	46	14	13	19	56	77	55
Stevenage	46	15	9	22	47	64	54
Oldham Athletic	46	14	9	23	46	59	51
Colchester United	46	14	9	23	47	68	51
Scunthorpe United	*46*	*13*	*9*	*24*	*49*	*73*	*48*
Bury	*46*	*9*	*14*	*23*	*45*	*73*	*41*
Hartlepool United	*46*	*9*	*14*	*23*	*39*	*67*	*41*
Portsmouth	*46*	*10*	*12*	*24*	*51*	*69*	*32*

Coventry City had 10 points deducted
Portsmouth had 10 points deducted

LEAGUE TWO 2012-2013

Gillingham	46	23	14	9	66	39	83
Rotherham United	46	24	7	15	74	59	79
Port Vale	46	21	15	10	87	52	78
Burton Albion	46	22	10	14	71	65	76
Cheltenham Town	46	20	15	11	58	51	75
Northampton Town	46	21	10	15	64	55	73
Bradford City	46	18	15	13	63	52	69
Chesterfield	46	18	13	15	60	45	67
Oxford United	46	19	8	19	59	60	65
Exeter City	46	18	10	18	63	62	64
Southend United	46	16	13	17	61	55	61
Rochdale	46	16	13	17	68	70	61
Fleetwood Town	46	15	15	16	55	57	60
Bristol Rovers	46	16	12	18	60	69	60
Wycombe Wanderers	46	17	9	20	50	60	60
Morecambe	46	15	13	18	55	61	58
York City	46	12	19	15	50	60	55
Accrington Stanley	46	14	12	20	51	67	54
Torquay United	46	13	14	19	55	62	53
AFC Wimbledon	46	14	11	21	54	76	53
Plymouth Argyle	46	13	13	20	46	55	52
Dagenham & Redbridge	46	13	12	21	55	62	51
Barnet	*46*	*13*	*12*	*21*	*47*	*59*	*51*
Aldershot Town	*46*	*11*	*15*	*20*	*42*	*60*	*48*

League Two Play-offs

Burton Albion vs Bradford City	3-2, 1-3
Cheltenham Town vs Northampton Town	0-1, 0-1
Bradford City vs Northampton Town	3-0

2013 F.A. Cup

Semi-finals

Millwall vs Wigan Athletic	0-2
Chelsea vs Manchester City	1-2

Final

Wembley, 11th May 2013

Manchester City 0
Wigan Athletic 1   (Watson)

Attendance 86,254

2013 Football League Cup

Semi-finals

Bradford City vs Aston Villa (3-1, 1-2)	4-3
Chelsea vs Swansea City (0-2, 0-0)	0-2

Final

Wembley, 24th February 2013

Swansea City 5   (Dyer 2, Michu, De Guzmán 2)
Bradford City 0

Attendance 82,597

F.A. PREMIER LEAGUE 2013-2014

	P	W	D	L	F	A	Pts
MANCHESTER CITY	38	27	5	6	102	37	86
Liverpool	38	26	6	6	101	50	84
Chelsea	38	25	7	6	71	27	82
Arsenal	38	24	7	7	68	41	79
Everton	38	21	9	8	61	39	72
Tottenham Hotspur	38	21	6	11	55	51	69
Manchester United	38	19	7	12	64	43	64
Southampton	38	15	11	12	54	46	56
Stoke City	38	13	11	14	45	52	50
Newcastle United	38	15	4	19	43	59	49
Crystal Palace	38	13	6	19	33	48	45
Swansea City	38	11	9	18	54	54	42
West Ham United	38	11	7	20	40	51	40
Sunderland	38	10	8	20	41	60	38
Aston Villa	38	10	8	20	39	61	38
Hull City	38	10	7	21	38	53	37
West Bromwich Albion	38	7	15	16	43	59	36
Norwich City	38	8	9	21	28	62	33
Fulham	38	9	5	24	40	85	32
Cardiff City	38	7	9	22	32	74	30

The Championship Play-offs

Derby County vs Brighton & Hove Albion	2-1, 4-1
Queen's Park Rangers vs Wigan Athletic	0-0, 2-1 (aet)
Derby County vs Queen's Park Rangers	0-1

THE CHAMPIONSHIP 2013-2014

	P	W	D	L	F	A	Pts
Leicester City	46	31	9	6	83	43	102
Burnley	46	26	15	5	72	37	93
Derby County	46	25	10	11	84	52	85
Queen's Park Rangers	46	23	11	12	60	44	80
Wigan Athletic	46	21	10	15	61	48	73
Brighton & Hove Albion	46	19	15	12	55	40	72
Reading	46	19	14	13	70	56	71
Blackburn Rovers	46	18	16	12	70	62	70
Ipswich Town	46	18	14	14	60	54	68
Bournemouth	46	18	12	16	67	66	66
Nottingham Forest	46	16	17	13	67	64	65
Middlesbrough	46	16	16	14	62	50	64
Watford	46	15	15	16	74	64	60
Bolton Wanderers	46	14	17	15	59	60	59
Leeds United	46	16	9	21	59	67	57
Sheffield Wednesday	46	13	14	19	63	65	53
Huddersfield Town	46	14	11	21	58	65	53
Charlton Athletic	46	13	12	21	41	61	51
Millwall	46	11	15	20	46	74	48
Blackpool	46	11	13	22	38	66	46
Birmingham City	46	11	11	24	58	74	44
Doncaster Rovers	46	11	11	24	39	70	44
Barnsley	46	9	12	25	44	77	39
Yeovil Town	46	8	13	25	44	75	37

League One Play-offs

Leyton Orient vs Peterborough United	1-1, 2-1
Rotherham United vs Preston North End	1-1, 3-1
Leyton Orient vs Rotherham United	2-2 (aet)
Rotherham United won 4-3 on penalties.	

LEAGUE ONE 2013-2014

	P	W	D	L	F	A	Pts
Wolverhampton Wanderers	46	31	10	5	89	31	103
Brentford	46	28	10	8	72	43	94
Leyton Orient	46	25	11	10	85	45	86
Rotherham United	46	24	14	8	86	58	86
Preston North End	46	23	16	7	72	46	85
Peterborough United	46	23	5	18	72	58	74
Sheffield United	46	18	13	15	48	46	67
Swindon Town	46	19	9	18	63	59	66
Port Vale	46	18	7	21	59	73	61
Milton Keynes Dons	46	17	9	20	63	65	60
Bradford City	46	14	17	15	57	54	59
Bristol City	46	13	19	14	70	67	58
Walsall	46	14	16	16	49	49	58
Crawley Town	46	14	15	17	48	54	57
Oldham Athletic	46	14	14	18	50	59	56
Colchester United	46	13	14	19	53	61	53
Gillingham	46	15	8	23	60	79	53
Coventry City	46	16	13	17	74	77	51
Crewe Alexandra	46	13	12	21	54	80	51
Notts County	46	15	5	26	64	77	50
Tranmere Rovers	46	12	11	23	52	79	47
Carlisle United	46	11	12	23	43	76	45
Shrewsbury Town	46	9	15	22	44	65	42
Stevenage	46	11	9	26	46	72	42

Coventry City had 10 points deducted after exiting administration without a CVA.

LEAGUE TWO 2013-2014

	P	W	D	L	F	A	Pts
Chesterfield	46	23	15	8	71	40	84
Scunthorpe United	46	20	21	5	68	44	81
Rochdale	46	24	9	13	69	48	81
Fleetwood Town	46	22	10	14	66	52	76
Southend United	46	19	15	12	56	39	72
Burton Albion	46	19	15	12	47	42	72
York City	46	18	17	11	52	41	71
Oxford United	46	16	14	16	53	50	62
Dagenham & Redbridge	46	15	15	16	53	59	60
Plymouth Argyle	46	16	12	18	51	58	60
Mansfield Town	46	15	15	16	49	58	60
Bury	46	13	20	13	59	51	59
Portsmouth	46	14	17	15	56	66	59
Newport County	46	14	16	16	56	59	58
Accrington Stanley	46	14	15	17	54	56	57
Exeter City	46	14	13	19	54	57	55
Cheltenham Town	46	13	16	17	53	63	55
Morecambe	46	13	15	18	52	64	54
Hartlepool United	46	14	11	21	50	56	53
AFC Wimbledon	46	14	14	18	49	57	53
Northampton Town	46	13	14	19	42	57	53
Wycombe Wanderers	46	12	14	20	46	54	50
Bristol Rovers	46	12	14	20	43	54	50
Torquay United	46	12	9	25	42	66	45

AFC Wimbledon had 3 points deducted for fielding an ineligible player.

League Two Play-offs

Fleetwood Town vs York City	1-0, 0-0
Southend United vs Burton Albion	0-1, 2-2
Burton Albion vs Fleetwood Town	0-1

2014 F.A. Cup

Semi-finals

Hull City vs Sheffield United	5-3
Wigan Athletic vs Arsenal	1-1 (aet)
Arsenal won 4-2 on penalties	

Final

Wembley, 17th May 2014

Arsenal 3　(Cazorla, Koscielny, Ramsey)
Hull City 2 (aet.)　(Chester, Davies)

Attendance 89,345

2014 Football League Cup

Semi-finals

Sunderland vs Manchester United (2-1, 1-1 (aet))		3-2
Manchester City vs West Ham United (6-0, 1-1)		7-1

Final

Wembley, 2nd March 2014

Manchester City 3　(Touré, Nasri, Navas)
Sunderland 1　(Borini)

Attendance 84,697

F.A. PREMIER LEAGUE 2014-2015

CHELSEA	38	26	9	3	73	32	87
Manchester City	38	24	7	7	83	38	79
Arsenal	38	22	9	7	71	36	75
Manchester United	38	20	10	8	62	37	70
Tottenham Hotspur	38	19	7	12	58	53	64
Liverpool	38	18	8	12	52	48	62
Southampton	38	18	6	14	54	33	60
Swansea City	38	16	8	14	46	49	56
Stoke City	38	15	9	14	48	45	54
Crystal Palace	38	13	9	16	47	51	48
Everton	38	12	11	15	48	50	47
West Ham United	38	12	11	15	44	47	47
West Bromwich Albion	38	11	11	16	38	51	44
Leicester City	38	11	8	19	46	55	41
Newcastle United	38	10	9	19	40	63	39
Sunderland	38	7	17	14	31	53	38
Aston Villa	38	10	8	20	31	57	38
Hull City	*38*	*8*	*11*	*19*	*33*	*51*	*35*
Burnley	*38*	*7*	*12*	*19*	*28*	*53*	*33*
Queen's Park Rangers	*38*	*8*	*6*	*24*	*42*	*73*	*30*

The Championship Play-offs

Brentford vs Middlesbrough	1-2, 0-3
Ipswich Town vs Norwich City	1-1, 1-3
Middlesbrough vs Norwich City	0-2

THE CHAMPIONSHIP 2014-2015

Bournemouth	46	26	12	8	98	45	90
Watford	46	27	8	11	91	50	89
Norwich City	46	25	11	10	88	48	86
Middlesbrough	46	25	10	11	68	37	85
Brentford	46	23	9	14	78	59	78
Ipswich Town	46	22	12	12	72	54	78
Wolverhampton Wanderers	46	22	12	12	70	56	78
Derby County	46	21	14	11	85	56	77
Blackburn Rovers	46	17	16	13	66	59	67
Birmingham City	46	16	15	15	54	64	63
Cardiff City	46	16	14	16	57	61	62
Charlton Athletic	46	14	18	14	54	60	60
Sheffield Wednesday	46	14	18	14	43	49	60
Nottingham Forest	46	15	14	17	71	69	59
Leeds United	46	15	11	20	50	61	56
Huddersfield Town	45	13	16	17	58	75	55
Fulham	46	14	10	22	62	83	52
Bolton Wanderers	46	13	12	21	54	67	51
Reading	46	13	11	22	48	69	50
Brighton & Hove Albion	46	10	17	19	44	54	47
Rotherham United	46	11	16	19	46	67	46
Millwall	*46*	*9*	*14*	*23*	*42*	*76*	*41*
Wigan Athletic	*46*	*9*	*12*	*25*	*39*	*64*	*39*
Blackpool	*46*	*4*	*14*	*28*	*36*	*91*	*26*

Rotherham United had 3 points deducted for fielding an ineligible player.

League One Play-offs

Chesterfield vs Preston North End	0-1, 0-3
Sheffield United vs Swindon Town	1-2, 5-5
Preston North End vs Swindon Town	4-0

LEAGUE ONE 2014-2015

Bristol City	46	29	12	5	96	38	99
Milton Keynes Dons	46	27	10	9	101	44	91
Preston North End	46	25	14	7	79	40	89
Swindon Town	46	23	10	13	76	57	79
Sheffield United	46	19	14	13	66	53	71
Chesterfield	46	19	12	15	68	55	69
Bradford City	46	17	14	15	55	55	65
Rochdale	46	19	6	21	72	66	63
Peterborough United	46	18	9	19	53	56	63
Fleetwood Town	46	17	12	17	49	52	63
Barnsley	46	17	11	18	62	61	62
Gillingham	46	16	14	16	65	66	62
Doncaster Rovers	46	16	13	17	57	62	61
Walsall	46	14	17	15	50	54	59
Oldham Athletic	46	14	15	17	54	67	57
Scunthorpe United	46	14	14	18	62	75	56
Coventry City	46	13	16	17	49	60	55
Port Vale	46	15	9	22	55	64	54
Colchester United	46	14	10	22	58	77	52
Crewe Alexandra	46	14	10	22	43	75	52
Notts County	*46*	*12*	*14*	*20*	*45*	*62*	*50*
Crawley Town	*46*	*13*	*11*	*22*	*53*	*79*	*50*
Leyton Orient	*46*	*12*	*13*	*21*	*59*	*69*	*49*
Yeovil Town	*46*	*10*	*10*	*26*	*36*	*75*	*40*

LEAGUE TWO 2014-2015

Burton Albion	46	28	10	8	69	39	94
Shrewsbury Town	46	27	8	11	67	31	89
Bury	46	26	7	13	60	40	85
Wycombe Wanderers	46	23	15	8	67	45	84
Southend United	46	24	12	10	54	38	84
Stevenage	46	20	12	14	62	54	72
Plymouth Argyle	46	20	11	15	55	37	71
Luton Town	46	19	11	16	54	44	68
Newport County	46	18	11	17	51	54	65
Exeter City	46	17	13	16	61	65	64
Morecambe	46	17	12	17	53	52	63
Northampton Town	46	18	7	21	67	62	61
Oxford United	46	15	16	15	50	49	61
Dagenham & Redbridge	46	17	8	21	58	59	59
AFC Wimbledon	46	14	16	16	54	60	58
Portsmouth	46	14	15	17	52	54	57
Accrington Stanley	46	15	11	20	58	77	56
York City	46	11	19	16	46	51	52
Cambridge United	46	13	12	21	61	66	51
Carlisle United	46	14	8	24	56	74	50
Mansfield Town	46	13	9	24	38	62	48
Hartlepool United	46	12	9	25	39	70	45
Cheltenham Town	*46*	*9*	*14*	*23*	*40*	*67*	*41*
Tranmere Rovers	*46*	*9*	*12*	*25*	*45*	*67*	*39*

League Two Play-offs

Plymouth Argyle vs Wycombe Wanderers	2-3, 1-2
Stevenage vs Southend United	1-1, 1-3
Southend United vs Wycombe Wanderers	1-1 (aet)

Southend United won 7-6 on penalties.

2015 F.A. Cup

Semi-finals

Reading vs Arsenal	1-2 (aet)
Aston Villa vs Liverpool	2-1

Final

Wembley, 30th May 2015

Arsenal 4 (Walcott, Sanchez, Mertesacker, Giroud)
Aston Villa 0

Attendance 89,283

2015 Football League Cup

Semi-finals

Liverpool vs Chelsea (1-1, 0-1 (aet))	1-2
Tottenham Hotspur vs Sheffield United (1-0, 2-2)	3-2

Final

Wembley, 1st March 2015

Chelsea 2 (Terry, Costa)
Tottenham Hotspur 0

Attendance 89,294

F.A. PREMIER LEAGUE 2015-2016

LEICESTER CITY	38	23	12	3	68	36	81
Arsenal	38	20	11	7	65	36	71
Tottenham Hotspur	38	19	13	6	69	35	70
Manchester City	38	19	9	10	71	41	66
Manchester United	38	19	9	10	49	35	66
Southampton	38	18	9	11	59	41	63
West Ham United	38	16	14	8	65	51	62
Liverpool	38	16	12	10	63	50	60
Stoke City	38	14	9	15	41	55	51
Chelsea	38	12	14	12	59	53	50
Everton	38	11	14	13	59	55	47
Swansea City	38	12	11	15	42	52	47
Watford	38	12	9	17	40	50	45
West Bromwich Albion	38	10	13	15	34	48	43
Crystal Palace	38	11	9	18	39	51	42
AFC Bournemouth	38	11	9	18	45	67	42
Sunderland	38	9	12	17	48	62	39
Newcastle United	*38*	*9*	*10*	*19*	*44*	*65*	*37*
Norwich City	*38*	*9*	*7*	*22*	*39*	*67*	*34*
Aston Villa	*38*	*3*	*8*	*27*	*27*	*76*	*17*

The Championship Play-offs

Brighton & Hove Albion vs Sheffield Wednesday	0-2, 1-1
Hull City vs Derby County	3-0, 0-2
Hull City vs Sheffield Wednesday	1-0

THE CHAMPIONSHIP 2015-2016

Burnley	46	26	15	5	72	35	93
Middlesbrough	46	26	11	9	63	31	89
Brighton & Hove Albion	46	24	17	5	72	42	89
Hull City	46	24	11	11	69	35	83
Derby County	46	21	15	10	66	43	78
Sheffield Wednesday	46	19	17	10	66	45	74
Ipswich Town	46	18	15	13	53	51	69
Cardiff City	46	17	17	12	56	51	68
Brentford	46	19	8	19	72	67	65
Birmingham City	46	16	15	15	53	49	63
Preston North End	46	15	17	14	45	45	62
Queens Park Rangers	46	14	18	14	54	54	60
Leeds United	46	14	17	15	50	59	59
Wolverhampton Wanderers	46	14	16	16	53	58	58
Blackburn Rovers	46	13	16	17	46	46	55
Nottingham Forest	46	13	16	17	43	47	55
Reading	46	13	13	20	52	59	52
Bristol City	46	13	13	20	54	71	52
Huddersfield Town	46	13	12	21	59	70	51
Fulham	46	12	15	19	66	79	51
Rotherham United	46	13	10	23	53	71	49
Charlton Athletic	*46*	*9*	*13*	*24*	*40*	*80*	*40*
Milton Keynes Dons	*46*	*9*	*12*	*25*	*39*	*69*	*39*
Bolton Wanderers	*46*	*5*	*15*	*26*	*41*	*81*	*30*

League One Play-offs

Walsall vs Barnsley	0-3, 1-3
Millwall vs Bradford City	3-1, 1-1
Barnsley vs Millwall	3-1

LEAGUE ONE 2015-2016

Wigan Athletic	46	24	15	7	82	45	87
Burton Albion	46	25	10	11	57	37	85
Walsall	46	24	12	10	71	49	84
Millwall	46	24	9	13	73	49	81
Bradford City	46	23	11	12	55	40	80
Barnsley	46	22	8	16	70	54	74
Scunthorpe United	46	21	11	14	60	47	74
Coventry City	46	19	12	15	67	49	69
Gillingham	46	19	12	15	71	56	69
Rochdale	46	19	12	15	68	61	69
Sheffield United	46	18	12	16	64	59	66
Port Vale	46	18	11	17	56	58	65
Peterborough United	46	19	6	21	82	73	63
Bury	46	16	12	18	56	73	60
Southend United	46	16	11	19	58	64	59
Swindon Town	46	16	11	19	64	71	59
Oldham Athletic	46	12	18	16	44	58	54
Chesterfield	46	15	8	23	58	70	53
Fleetwood Town	46	12	15	19	52	56	51
Shrewsbury Town	46	13	11	22	58	79	50
Doncaster Rovers	*46*	*11*	*13*	*22*	*48*	*64*	*46*
Blackpool	*46*	*12*	*10*	*24*	*40*	*63*	*46*
Colchester United	*46*	*9*	*13*	*24*	*57*	*99*	*40*
Crewe Alexandra	*46*	*7*	*13*	*26*	*46*	*83*	*34*

LEAGUE TWO 2015-2016

Northampton Town	46	29	12	5	82	46	99
Oxford United	46	24	14	8	84	41	86
Bristol Rovers	46	26	7	13	77	46	85
Accrington Stanley	46	24	13	9	74	48	85
Plymouth Argyle	46	24	9	13	72	46	81
Portsmouth	46	21	15	10	75	44	78
AFC Wimbledon	46	21	12	13	64	50	75
Leyton Orient	46	19	12	15	60	61	69
Cambridge United	46	18	14	14	66	55	68
Carlisle United	46	17	16	13	67	62	67
Luton Town	46	19	9	18	63	61	66
Mansfield Town	46	17	13	16	61	53	64
Wycombe Wanderers	46	17	13	16	45	44	64
Exeter City	46	17	13	16	63	65	64
Barnet	46	17	11	18	67	68	62
Hartlepool United	46	15	6	25	49	72	51
Notts County	46	14	9	23	54	83	51
Stevenage	46	11	15	20	52	67	48
Yeovil Town	46	11	15	20	43	59	48
Crawley Town	46	13	8	25	45	78	47
Morecambe	46	12	10	24	69	91	46
Newport County	46	10	13	23	43	64	43
Dagenham & Redbridge	*46*	*8*	*10*	*28*	*46*	*81*	*34*
York City	*46*	*7*	*13*	*26*	*51*	*87*	*34*

League Two Play-offs

Accrington Stanley vs AFC Wimbledon	0-1, 2-2
Plymouth Argyle vs Portsmouth	2-2, 1-0
AFC Wimbledon vs Plymouth Argyle	2-0

2016 F.A. Cup

Semi-finals

Crystal Palace vs Watford	2-1
Manchester United vs Everton	2-1

Final

Wembley, 21st May 2016

Crystal Palace 1   (Puncheon)
Manchester United 2 (aet)   (Mata, Lingard)

Attendance 88,619

2016 Football League Cup

Semi-finals

Stoke City vs Liverpool (0-1, 1-0 (aet))	1-1
Liverpool won 6-5 on penalties	
Everton vs Manchester City (2-1, 1-3)	3-4

Final

Wembley, 28th February 2016

Liverpool 1   (Coutinho)
Manchester City 1 (aet)   (Fernandinho)

Attendance 86,206

Manchester City won 3-1 on penalties